The
FULL ©™
Tilt
POKER
STRATEGY GUIDE

D0176676

ALSO BY MICHAEL CRAIG

The Professor, the Banker, and the Suicide King:
Inside the Richest Poker Game of All Time

The FULL Tilt ©™ POKER STRATEGY GUIDE

TOURNAMENT EDITION

EDITED BY MICHAEL CRAIG

GRAND CENTRAL
PUBLISHING

NEW YORK   BOSTON

Copyright © 2007 by Michael Craig
All rights reserved. Except as permitted under the U.S. Copyright Act of 1976, no part of this publication may be reproduced, distributed, or transmitted in any form or by any means, or stored in a database or retrieval system, without the prior written permission of the publisher.

Grand Central Publishing
Hachette Book Group
237 Park Avenue
New York, NY 10017

Visit our Web site at www.HachetteBookGroup.com.

Printed in the United States of America

First Edition: June 2007
10 9 8 7 6

Grand Central Publishing is a division of Hachette Book Group, Inc.
The Grand Central Publishing name and logo is a trademark of Hachette Book Group, Inc.

Library of Congress Cataloging-in-Publication Data

The full tilt poker strategy guide : tournament edition / edited by Michael Craig.—1st ed.
    p.   cm.
    Summary: "The best and most famous poker players on the planet gather to offer the most valuable and comprehensive strategy guide ever assembled."—Provided by the publisher.
    ISBN 978-0-446-69860-3
    1. Poker—Tournaments.   I. Craig, Michael, 1958–
GV1254.F86 2007
795.412—dc22

                                                        2006038992

Book design and text composition by Stratford Publishing Services, Inc.
Cover design by Andy Newman

CONTENTS

PART I

WELCOME TO THE TOURNAMENT EDITION

CHAPTER 1

Player Introduction: The Passion to Be the Best

by Phil Gordon

What does it take to be a champion at poker? What are the players at the final table of the World Series of Poker doing that is so special? How can I take my game to the next level? What are the fundamentals of winning online and in live games, in tournaments and cash games? If you're like me, these are the questions you ask yourself over and over in an effort to improve and gain insight into the fascinating game of poker.

I am very fortunate. I've been able to use my early success at the tables to infiltrate a unique fraternity of kindred souls—my fellow professional poker players. Very often, when we're standing around before a tournament (or, more commonly, drinking a beer or two after we've busted out), I get a chance to ask questions and learn from the best players in the game. Less desirably, I very often get firsthand lessons as pros like Chris Ferguson, Howard Lederer, and Ted Forrest stack my chips and count my cash.

I take every single opportunity to learn from these players. My combined experiences at and away from the table with the folks who wrote this book are my driving influence to improve, my guiding influences in my game, and my shaping influences for my ideas. In short, without their help, insight, and frequent theft of my blinds and bets, I wouldn't be the player I am today. In fact, I might not be a professional poker player at all.

See, if you're like me, you don't want to be good at poker—you want to be truly great. I want my name uttered in the same sentence with Doyle Brunson, Johnny Chan, Howard Lederer, and Erik Seidel. I want to be the greatest player in the world. And, perhaps egotistically, I think with continued hard work, practice, and tests, I can get there. I know it won't happen overnight, and I know that it won't happen easily. But that's okay. Just the thought that it could happen is all I need to continue working hard at the game.

The players who wrote this book, me included, want to help you become a better poker player. We want you to experience the same joy that we do when we make a great play, take a great read, cash a million-dollar check, and slide that bracelet onto the wrist.

Some players complain about the introduction of books that help other players improve. "Hey, why do you want to educate the fish? The games will be much tougher if you keep this up!" To those critics, I say, "Bring it on! I want tougher competition. I want my opponents to play better so that I have to play better. I want them to push me. I want them to force me to take my game to the next level." There is no Nicklaus without Palmer. There is no Jordan without Barkley. To be the best we can be, we need competition—fierce, tough, unwavering competition.

The strategies and plays you'll find in this book will absolutely help your game. There is no doubt in my mind about that. But it's up to you how aggressively you pursue improvement. It's up to you how patient you'll be with your improvement. It's up to you how courageous you'll be in trying out these techniques. It's up to you how resilient you'll be when you face the inevitable setbacks.

Aggression. Patience. Courage. Resiliency. These are the qualities of a champion poker player. These qualities and an intense desire to improve are why you see the authors of this book winning on television and cashing the million-dollar checks. Will you join us at the final table, push us, and give us a battle for the bracelet? We sincerely hope so.

See you at the final table.

CHAPTER 2

Editor's Introduction: The Role of Books in Poker

by Michael Craig

A Book Made Me Want to Play Poker

I didn't start playing poker until I was thirty-two years old, and I started playing because of a book. My dad loaned me his copy of A. Alvarez's *The Biggest Game in Town*. I had never been interested in playing poker, but I became fascinated by the stories of the lives and games of the competitors at the 1981 World Series of Poker. (I'm pretty sure I still have that copy; sorry, Dad.)

Not long after, almost by accident, I picked up and read Anthony Holden's *Big Deal*. Having read just one poker narrative, I approached this book warily and, like a gambler, asked myself, *What are the odds this is going to be as good as Alvarez?* After devouring thirty pages, I looked at the dedication and acknowledgments and found out Holden and Alvarez were good friends and had played in a weekly game together for decades. (I later learned that another poker writer, the late David Spanier, had gotten kicked out of the game for playing too tight, and WPT/WSOP winner Mel Judah, then a London hairdresser, had played in it.)

I could not have imagined that I would become close friends with Tony Holden, appear as a character in the sequel, *Bigger Deal*, and, through Tony, become pen pals with Al Alvarez. (I even wrote a column about one of my experiences with Tony for *Card Player*, titled "Thank Mel Judah." When I used the upcoming issue to introduce myself to Mel and ask him about his experiences in the Tuesday Night Game, he said, "Yeah, they kicked me out for winning too much. Terrible players.")

As I slowly overcame my fear of being the least experienced player in the crowded Mirage poker room, I started playing $3-$6 hold 'em whenever I was in Las Vegas. Soon I was finding excuses to "stop by" this poker room eighteen hundred miles from my home. I had moved up to $10-$20 and $20-$40 games and also played in some of the cardrooms outside Los Angeles and San Diego while on business in Southern California.

And I read.

It wouldn't be until the release of James McManus's *Positively Fifth Street* that I would find another poker narrative to fuel my imagination, but I found no shortage of challenging manuals on how to improve at the game. Like everyone else, I desperately wanted to get better.

Two Guns: David Sklansky and Mason Malmuth

I got lucky. The first book of poker strategy I ever owned was David Sklansky's *Hold 'Em Poker.* Originally published in 1976, this skinny book had a goofy cover, a typeface like a ransom note—and most of the concepts I have learned from the fifty to one hundred books I have read since (and the one you are reading now). With so many players learning poker and taking it seriously in the last few years, it may be difficult for a lot of people to understand how slow the learning curve was for a beginning player in the early nineties. With no poker rooms for almost two thousand miles, I probably played the same number of hands my first year as a new player today would in a week or two.

Semi-bluffing? Free cards? Pot odds? Imagine playing poker and being completely ignorant of those things. Just the idea that you played different cards based on your position at the table was a revelation.

Mike Matusow and Phil Ivey separately told me that that book was the only poker book they ever read. Howard Lederer told me, and he explains it in chapter 12, that Sklansky's book was responsible for his becoming a professional poker player. David and his collaborator/publisher Mason Malmuth deserve credit for permanently raising the quality of poker. I think I own a majority of the books they have written or published, have bought numerous copies for friends, and own multiple editions of a few.

The Book of Tells

Another book I picked up in the early nineties was Mike Caro's *The Body Language of Poker.* (It is better known by its current title, *Caro's Book of Poker Tells.*) I am not engaging in hyperbole when I say this book is as valuable to students of poker as Sigmund Freud's *The Interpretation of Dreams* is to students of psychology. Frankly, Mike's book would be pretty valuable to students of psychology too.

I read through Caro but didn't study it until years later. Several players dismissed the book, saying, "It was huge back then, but so many players are familiar with it that they correct for those tells, or incorporate them as false signals." I'm glad I finally rediscovered *Caro's Book of Poker Tells* a few years ago. First, even if not a word of it is true anymore, I owed it to myself as a writer to read any book that was actually responsible for changing human behavior on such a large scale.

Second, things haven't changed that much. Sure, Howard Lederer knows which players are likely to have that level of knowledge and how to fake some tells to exploit it, but I'm already handing over my chips to Lederer if he's at my table, unless I get lucky with the cards. I haven't played a tournament yet where I drew the same table as Howard, Annie Duke, Chris Ferguson, Chip Reese, Mike Matusow, Phil Hellmuth, Ted Forrest, Jennifer Harman, and Barry Greenstein. I have played with far, far more players who haven't mastered and exploited Mike Caro's revelations than I have played with those who have.

Third, and most important, when someone offers you something to help you at poker (or any activity involving skill), you can look at it in two ways—as a magic box or as a tool. Most criticism of learning tools is that they have flaws. They aren't a magic box.

Mike Caro's book is an incredibly useful tool, but not one to be used indiscriminately. I think close to 100 percent of the people who read it benefit from it, but that is far different from saying every word in it is correct or that for it to be worthwhile you have to automatically win every time you see a behavior described in the book and act on it.

Dolly Llama

I found the Rosetta Stone at the Gambler's Book Shop in 1992. I had just discovered the funky store on Eleventh Street in Las Vegas. A lot of the books that sell big at GBS can be found at your local bookstore—now. In 1992, the selection of poker books at bookstores was almost nonexistent. There were always a few titles, but they always managed to be years out of date and/or concerned games that I never saw spread at the Mirage or the Bicycle Club. David Sklansky? Maybe one title. Doyle Brunson? Never heard of him, and neither had the store's computers.

I can barely describe my excitement when I saw *Super/System* for the first time: shiny silver cover, silly caricature of a roly-poly man dribbling a basketball, 660 pages, $50 price tag. The book was practically an urban legend. I had read several things *about* it, but this was one of the few places on earth where I could see it and, better still, buy it. It didn't matter at all that I had never seen no-limit hold 'em (other than grainy VHS tapes of the final table of the World Series of Poker), or seven stud hi-lo split, or ace-to-five lowball, or that limit hold 'em as described by Bobby Baldwin was played with a single blind and antes.

Super/System described a way to think about poker. It didn't even matter what form the authors were writing about or what form you played. The best players in the world were discussing poker, and if you couldn't learn something by listening, then you weren't trying. I have described the book you are now holding as *Super/System* for tournaments, with better grammar and punctuation. Duplicating the concept of gathering great players (and great thinkers) and collecting their ideas was at the core of *Super/System*, and it is at the core of this book. *The Full Tilt Poker Strategy Guide: Tournament Edition* focuses on tournaments; *Super/System* and its sequel focused on cash games. This book has gathered a different but at least equally able group of gaming minds to share their insights.

Dan Harrington Detonates Poker

The current poker boom caught the strategists unprepared. Every-one wanted to play no-limit hold 'em, initially in tournaments. There were few books about tournament poker, though David Sklansky's *Tournament Poker for Advanced Players* introduced many important concepts, including the "gap concept" (referring to the gap in quality between the hand someone needs to bet and the hand needed to enter a pot after them).

But it was not the equivalent of the other *Advanced Player* guides. It was not a comprehensive examination of no-limit hold 'em tourna-ment poker. Dan Harrington and Bill Robertie became the first to fill that need with a product good enough that, like several of Sklansky's and Malmuth's books, it permanently increased the quality of play. Between late 2004 and early 2006, they released three volumes of *Harrington on Hold 'Em.*

Within a week of purchasing the first volume, I recognized that tournaments would soon consist of two groups of players: those who understood the concepts in *Harrington on Hold 'Em,* and those who didn't. The books are a thoughtful, comprehensive, carefully rea-soned approach to playing no-limit hold 'em hands and the strategic risks and opportunities created by how tournaments operate.

If I learned anything from conducting consecutive interviews with Chris Ferguson and Ted Forrest on no-limit hold 'em tourna-ment strategy, it is that many different approaches can succeed. Although the pros tend to act indifferent to poker strategy books, the following opinions were generally held by the players I asked about Dan's book: (1) Harrington was an extremely skilled player (and you would be surprised how few players other pros will say that about); (2) his book contains a lot of good advice in nearly every area of tournament no-limit hold 'em; and (3) approaches different from his can work just as well and sometimes a lot better.

This is not a criticism of *Harrington on Hold 'Em*. Those books improved my own game, probably benefited all of the hundreds of thousands of people who bought them (if they read them), and, as I said, permanently lifted the level of tournament poker. You won't find anyplace in this book where a contributor describes something out of *Harrington* and then attacks it or explains how a different approach is better. You will, however, read advice that contradicts Dan Harrington's.

But guess what? Dan Harrington has done pretty well with his advice and so have people who followed it. And Chris Ferguson has done pretty well with his advice, and when he has given it, the people who followed it were glad they did. For that matter, you will read essays in this book that conflict with other essays here. One of my favorites is chapter 5, "(Don't) Play Like Ted Forrest," by Ted Forrest. I encouraged contributors to contradict each other, and specifically asked Ted if he wanted to say something about the common pre-flop strategy of raise-or-fold, which has been explained in this book by Howard Lederer, Chris Ferguson, and Andy Bloch.

Why Full Tilt?

I approached Howard Lederer about this project in November 2005, making the following points:

- Although there were a few good books about tournament poker, there would always be room for a comprehensive tournament guide—all the games, advanced strategy on both the play of hands and tournament tactics.
- Full Tilt Poker had a brilliant and diverse group of poker strategists among its pros and their insights would be valuable and desired.
- A *Full Tilt Poker Strategy Guide* would be consistent with FullTiltPoker.com's identification with helping players improve and the site's connection with professional poker (e.g., the site's weekly "Tips from the Pros" and Fox Sports Net's *FullTiltPoker.net's Learn from the Pros* television series).

I must have been persuasive, because Howard convinced the site's software company and helped me get other players to contribute.

Although I am friends with several Full Tilt pros, play on the site, and have thoroughly enjoyed this collaboration, I was not, during production of this book, an employee, consultant, or in any way affiliated with Full Tilt Poker. I am not saying that to avoid an association during this period of legal uncertainty about the status of online poker; during post-production, I began writing The Full Tilt Poker Blog partly to promote the ideas of this book.

I am telling you this because I want you to know that this book will not ram FullTiltPoker.com (or .net) down your throat.

Full Tilt provided a unifying purpose to round up and motivate the contributors. But nobody will hector you to play poker online or to play on their site. There are few references to Full Tilt in this book that could conceivably be considered "persuasive" for the site. Even chapter 10, "Online Tournament Strategy," by Richard Brodie, mentions the site several times only because it was necessary to describe how the limits and levels of online tournaments compared to casino tournaments. It would have been pretty silly for Richard to pick a tournament structure from some *other* site.

The Structure of This Book

No-limit hold 'em dominates tournament poker. Therefore, especially considering the accomplishments of the contributors, it is covered in a comprehensive fashion in this book. Chapters 3 through 10 are all about no-limit hold 'em tournaments. Chapters 3 through 5 are essays by Chris Ferguson, Howard Lederer, and Ted Forrest. Chapters 6 and 7, by Andy Bloch and Chris Ferguson, respectively, are about pre-flop and post-flop play. Chapters 8 and 9 concern how to play a big stack (by Gavin Smith) and how to play a short stack (by Phil Gordon). Richard Brodie wraps up the no-limit hold 'em chapters by applying all these concepts to online tournaments.

Chapters 11 and 12 concern other forms of tournament hold 'em. Chapter 11 explains how to adapt no-limit strategy to pot-limit hold 'em tournaments, by Rafe Furst and Andy Bloch. Chapter 12, the longest of the book, is Howard Lederer's strategy for playing limit hold 'em tournaments.

Chapters 13 and 14 cover Omaha. Mike Matusow was responsible for chapter 13 on tournament Omaha eight-or-better. Chris Ferguson wrote chapter 14 on pot-limit Omaha tournaments.

The next section of the book consists of four chapters on forms of stud poker. Chapter 15, by Keith Sexton, describes the play of stud hands in tournaments. Chapter 16, by David Grey, explains strategic concepts in seven-card stud tournaments. Chapter 17, by Ted Forrest, describes his strategy for playing stud eight-or-better tournaments. Chapter 18 was actually written by me, as a witness to a remarkable conversation between Forrest and Huckleberry Seed in the form of a razz lesson they gave me the night before that event at the 2006 World Series of Poker.

The concluding materials include an unusual and innovative examination of the mental game of poker. Chapter 19, "Roshambo and the Mental Game of Poker," by Rafe Furst, explains how this children's game (or, more accurately, a game now played for money by adults who behave like children) can teach valuable lessons on the mental game of poker.

When I wrote *The Professor, the Banker, and the Suicide King*, I had an ambitious, egotistical goal, which I was smart enough to keep to myself. I wanted to write a book that would stand the test of time. My idols were Holden and Alvarez, and I placed McManus on that pedestal. I wanted to reveal a story, a world, and a group of people, all of which were too unusual to be real, but too compelling to be imagined.

But I have no need for false modesty with *The Full Tilt Poker Strategy Guide: Tournament Edition*. You will judge this book by the quality of its advice, the questions it leads you to ask, the answers it leads you to find, and, ultimately, the role it plays in your tournament poker experiences. I claim credit for gathering this remarkable team of contributors, keeping them on task, editing their work, and delivering it in completed form. The claim I am staking with the *Tournament Edition* is a bet on the quality and presentation of poker strategy by Andy Bloch, Richard Brodie, Chris Ferguson, Ted Forrest, Rafe Furst, Phil Gordon, David Grey, Howard Lederer, Mike Matusow, Huckleberry Seed, Keith Sexton, and Gavin Smith.

The twelve contributors to this book have won over *$30 million in tournament poker,* including the following:

- Two World Series of Poker Championships (and four more final table appearances)
- Twenty-one World Series of Poker bracelets (including multiple bracelets by six contributors)
- Four Hall of Fame watches
- Five World Poker Tour victories (and seven more final table appearances)
- Two World Poker Tour players of the year
- Two World Series of Poker Circuit rings (and three more final table appearances)
- One World Series of Poker Tournament of Champions winner (and two more final table appearances)
- One Professional Poker Tour victory
- One National Heads-Up Championship (and two runner-up finishes)

I want the *Tournament Edition* to stand the test of time. With these horses, I like our chances.

Notes on Hand Representations

Many, many hands are described in this book, and several are graphically depicted. Most readers will be familiar with the shorthand notations, but here are the conventions followed:

- In the community-card games (see chapters 3 through 14), an X represents a random card. For example, A-X means an ace and a random card.
- In the stud-card games (see chapters 15 through 18), an X represents a hole card as it appears to other players. The hole cards, when their identity is known, are denoted by parentheses. For example, (T♣9♦)T♦ is a starting hand with the ten of diamonds exposed (or "in the door") and hole cards of the ten of clubs and the nine of diamonds.

- Where the suits are not included with the cards, like A-T, that means the suits (and whether the hand is suited) are not material to the example. When listing minimum hand requirements, A-Ts means the ace and ten are suited, A-To means they are not suited, and A-T includes both suited and unsuited combinations of those two cards.

PART II

TOURNAMENT HOLD 'EM

Editor's Opening Remarks

For several good reasons, this book has, from its conception, been designed to be a *comprehensive* manual of tournament poker strategy. First, the stud games, the Omaha games, and the limit and pot-limit hold 'em games are still part of tournament poker. Although no-limit events are crowding out the other forms of poker, entries in those other events are still regularly breaking records. And who knows what the future will bring? As I describe at the introduction to chapter 18, razz has survived every conceivable means of killing it off. Finding experts willing to share their insights is a valuable service, even if most people are focusing on no-limit hold 'em. Second, whatever game you play, learning from great players, great teachers, and great strategic minds will improve your overall game. Howard Lederer points out at the beginning of chapter 12 that some central limit hold 'em skills may not have the same importance in other games but learning them at limit gives you an advantage when you can use them at those other games.

But the explosion of interest in tournament poker is due to no-limit hold 'em. The contributors to this book have won two World Championships and two other no-limit hold 'em World Series bracelets. They have also won two World Series of Poker Circuit Championships and three World Poker Tour events. I count at least eight other no-limit hold 'em wins, in other big buy-in events or major televised events. They have made dozens of final tables in no-limit hold 'em at the World Series of Poker, on the World Poker Tour, and elsewhere.

These pros have the pedigree to teach you a lot about no-limit hold 'em, even if one of the goals of this book was to teach all the games. This section of the book delivers.

Chapters 3 through 5 are essays by three of the most astute gaming minds alive: Chris Ferguson, Howard Lederer, and Ted Forrest. I asked Chris and Howard to pick something central to their no-limit tournament strategy that was either not well known or not well explained. Both chose aspects of betting strategy—Ferguson on how the best way to mix up your play is to play many different hands the same way, and Lederer on leverage, the process of making small bets that have the impact of big bets. I asked Ted to explain why he did things different from most other pros (especially some of the advice given by Chris and Howard, as well as Andy Bloch's advice about pre-flop play in chapter 6) and why it worked for him.

Chapters 6 and 7 are advanced guides to the fundamentals of no-limit play. Andy Bloch explains a comprehensive approach to play before the flop. Chris Ferguson, by explaining how fourteen sample hands play after a variety of flops, in different positions, following different pre-flop action, against different numbers of opponents, provides a comprehensive approach to how to play after the flop.

Chapters 8 and 9 concern two important modifications of poker strategy: how to play when you have a big stack and how you play when you have a short stack. Gavin Smith was the World Poker Tour player of the year for the 2005–2006 season on the strength of his ability to punish opponents with a big stack, winning one event and making two other final tables. Phil Gordon, whose *Little Black Book* (originally *Poker: The Real Deal*), *Little Green Book*, and *Little Blue Book* have introduced hundreds of thousands of people to poker and taught them both basic and advanced strategy, explains how to play a short stack.

The no-limit hold 'em chapters conclude with chapter 10, Richard Brodie's analysis tying all these concepts to online poker tournaments. Brodie has unique qualifications for writing the chapter. A brilliant software programmer (as an early employee of Microsoft, he wrote and then headed the project team for the original version of Microsoft Word) and game player, he didn't start playing hold 'em until 2003. He was drawn to poker by his friend Andy Bloch's success in the early days of the World Poker Tour and used online tournaments as a proving ground, then to sharpen his skills, and then because he made money playing online tournaments. He also used that experience to go from neophyte to professional. He would bristle at the designation, but the results speak for themselves: he immediately began making final tables of tournaments, seven of them since 2003.

In the no-limit craze, do not overlook the last two chapters of this section. Chapter 11, by Rafe Furst and Andy Bloch, explains how to adapt no-limit strategy to pot-limit hold 'em. Chapter 12, "Limit Hold 'Em" by Howard Lederer, describes how to play that game by a player long considered one of the world's best. Howard's concepts will help you even if you never play a limit hold 'em tournament.

CHAPTER 3

No-Limit Hold 'Em: How to Bet

by Chris Ferguson

Entering the Pot, Play All Your Hands the Same

One of the most important principles in no-limit hold 'em is to conceal the strength of your hand. To do this, experienced players agree you need to mix up your play. Most people believe this means playing the same hand in different ways, for example, sometimes limping with A-A and sometimes making a big raise with A-A.

This is wrong! To conceal the strength of your hand, you need to play *different hands the same way.* Once you decide you are going to play a hand, make the same bet whether it is the strongest hand you would play in that situation, like A-A, or the weakest, like 7-6. Playing the same hand in different ways may confuse some opponents but can still give away a lot of information about your hand. For example, if you sometimes limp with A-A and never limp with any other hand, and you sometimes make a huge raise with A-A but not with any other hand, observant opponents will be able to deduce exactly what you have whenever you limp or make a huge raise.

Raise, Don't Call

At all times, you should try to avoid calling and you should never be the first caller before the flop. Apart from the information you give away about your hand, raising puts pressure on the blinds and other players at the table. Chances are that by raising, you'll force marginal hands to fold before the flop, limiting the number of players you have to beat through the rest of the hand. You may even limit that number to *zero* and pick up the blinds and antes.

If you have A-A or A-K, you want strong hands to call you. A lot of strong hands that will call a raise, such as A-J, have a worse chance of beating you than weak hands that will fold to a raise, such as 7-6s. If everyone folds to the small blind (who calls) and you have A-K in the big blind, would you rather be up against A-7 or J-7? By raising, you will probably get the J-7 to fold and the A-7 will likely call, which is exactly what you want. If I told you I had a magical way to make opponents fold hands that do well against you and call with hands that do poorly, you'd think I was nuts.

Well, here it is: raising with your strongest hands frequently accomplishes this.

When you have no money invested in a pot, you never do worse with larger blinds. By making a small raise instead of limping, you are either picking up the pot, if the blinds fold, or effectively making the blinds larger if they don't. This means making a small raise is a win-win over limping. The fact is, any hand worth a call is automatically worth a raise. That is the *real* reason why you should always raise if you are the first player entering a pot.

Obviously, I don't agree that you should make the first call with hands that play better against a large field. The idea behind this reasoning is that your call is supposed to induce others to call and create a multiway pot. But because you are signaling that you have this kind of hand, what if this induces players behind you to *raise*? Even if they do call behind you, they too will have hands that do well multiway, but they have position, giving them the best of it. If you limp with a strong hand, you are encouraging a multiway pot with opponents whose hands don't play too badly against you. The only possible circumstance for limping, therefore, would be in a pot in which there are already limpers, you have a hand that plays well multiway, and *you* have position.

So I say, raise or fold. If your hand is worth playing, it is worth a raise. If not, you should fold.

If you raise or fold every hand, you are giving away the minimum amount of information. All your opponents know is that you don't have a folding hand. So you probably don't have 7-4o or T-6o. But you are equally likely to have 4-4 as A-A, and equally likely to have A-Ko as J-To.

Three Versions of Raise-or-Fold

There are three versions of the "never limp" rule: *strong, medium,* and *weak*. When I won the World Series in 2000, I played the *strong* version. I never called before the flop, except in the big blind or in a limped pot in the small blind. Never. If I was the first in, I raised or folded. If someone limped in before me, I raised or folded. If someone raised before me, I reraised or folded. That's the style I played back then. It was extremely effective against weaker players who played too many hands. If they limped in front of me, they had to give up their chips or play a weak hand for a bigger pot. It was also effective against stronger players who didn't want to gamble and gave too much respect to my raising hands, thinking, "If he raised instead of calling, he must be very strong."

I don't play such a strong version of "never limp" anymore, so I'm not saying it can't be improved on. But it is extremely difficult to defend against. This is the style I recommend for all beginners, intermediate players, and anyone playing against experts. This will give them the best chance to win.

I play the *weak* version now. I still never make the first call. With the weak version of the rule, you can limp after someone else limps first. They are making a strategic error by limping. They have to act before you for the rest of the hand, so suited connectors (which I generally don't like playing) and small pairs, where your goal is to win a big pot with a set or fold to a bet after the flop if you miss, become playable. You should have reservations about doing this, though. You are defining your hand more than the earlier limpers, who are more likely to be slow-playing. You have position over them, but you lose some of that advantage if someone limps behind you, and all of it if someone raises behind you. If you have to limp, do it where there are already limpers and when you don't expect players behind you to raise.

The difference between the weak and the medium version is that in the *medium* version you have to reraise or fold if someone enters before you with a raise. The difference between the medium and the strong version is that in the medium version you can call if someone limps in front of you. (In limit hold 'em, I still play the medium version of never-limp.)

2
2½
3

The Amount of Your Raise

The amount of your raise should not give away the strength of your hand. I think it is fine to vary your raises but, before the flop, vary them based on your position, not on your hand. In general, if there are no antes, raise in early position to twice the big blind. In middle position, raise two and a half times the big blind. In late position, raise three times the big blind. X

Here is the reasoning: I want to make my opponents' decisions as difficult as possible. If you make a big raise, you make your opponents' decisions easy: they can simply fold most of their hands, only playing their very biggest hands. Now, if you bluff with a big bet, you win very little most of the time, but when you get reraised, you lose big.

But I mostly want to make things difficult for the big blind. In big tournaments, especially against good players, there is very little limping. There aren't a lot of multiway hands. When I enter the pot, I'm thinking about what the big blind is going to do. It is easy to make his decision difficult, and a smaller raise from up front does that. By raising in early position, I am advertising a hand strong enough to beat seven or eight players who haven't acted yet. Because I am representing such a strong hand, the big blind needs great odds to call. Thus, I can bet small and still give him a tough decision with a marginal hand.

I don't mind if the big blind calls. I've got position. I expect, if I am playing in a game with experts, that everyone will fold around to the big blind a lot of the time. If someone wakes up with a monster behind me after I make that early-position raise, I'll be glad that I raised only two times the big blind. If I am holding A-J or possibly

A-Q and a player comes over the top, I can lay it down without having risked much. That's the main reason I raise small up front.

You might wish you had raised more if you make a small raise with A-A and get reraised. But if you had, you might not have been reraised. I'm not willing to telegraph that I make larger raises with some hands than others. Also, if you bet small, you will get your A-A reraised more often, because the players behind you are going to want to put a stop to you stealing blinds and antes with such a small raise. You are betting two units to win one and a half; someone may want to keep you from being successful with such a bet.

That small, uniform raise from early position accomplishes three things. First, it makes the big blind's decision as difficult as possible when he has a marginal hand. Second, it is cheaper to get away from the hand if someone reraises. Third, when you *want* someone to reraise you, you have made it easier for them to make that mistake.

If I am on the button and I am the first one in, I need to beat only the two remaining hands in the blinds, so I'm going to raise with nearly half my hands. If I make that same, small raise that I would make from early position, it is too easy for the big blind to call with a marginal hand. Since I am not representing as strong a hand from late position, I need to make a larger raise to give the big blind a difficult decision with his marginal hands. Of equal importance, I am less worried about getting reraised by a monster when I open the pot in late position since there are only two players behind me.

The amounts of these raises are not set in stone. I will take into account the players to act behind me including the big blind. For instance, if I think the big blind will call with weak hands, I will put in a larger raise to build a bigger pot. The idea here is that you are likely to get action. Your semi-bluffing hands, which are your weaker hands, lose value. That kind of opponent, however, will pay you off more on your stronger hands. Your weaker hands have gone down in value and your stronger hands have gone up in value. In fact, your weaker hands might even have a negative value, so these should be folded. By putting in larger raises, you make even more off your strongest hands.

If your table is particularly loose and you can't steal the blinds with a normal raise, tighten up your starting-hand requirements slightly and make larger raises. If your opponents are playing too loose, take advantage of it by building bigger pots when you think you are getting the best of it.

The raise should also be a little larger if there are antes. Add about half the total of the antes to your raise.

Betting When You Are Short-Stacked *less Than 10*

If you have less than ten times the big blind, your only real options are to move in all your chips or fold. The only exception occurs when you are in the big blind. If you have ten times the big blind, you can call a raise where you are getting good pot odds and still get away from the hand if you miss the flop.

Once you are under ten big blinds, when you bet, you are committed to calling just about any reraise, or at least having a very difficult decision when faced with a reraise. Likewise, you will have a tough decision on the flop if you are called. Try to stay away from difficult decisions and instead give your opponent as many difficult decisions as possible. By moving all-in in this situation, you are giving your opponents the tough decision and eliminating the chance that you have to fold or make a crying call.

After the flop, if you have less than about one and a half times the pot, you should move all-in or fold. If you are betting three-quarters of the pot, you are pot-committed so you might as well bet it all. By betting three-quarters of the pot instead of moving all-in, you are giving your opponent the decision of whether to fold, play for a three-quarter-pot-sized bet, or raise to make you put in all your chips. Why give your opponent that decision? By moving all-in, you eliminate one of those options.

Betting After the Flop

One of the biggest mistakes beginners make is sizing their bets to match the strength of their hand, making a small bet with a vulnerable hand and a huge bet with a huge hand. This does little more than telegraph the strength of their hand to their opponents. It is also easy and natural for opponents to defend against, frequently calling or raising small bets and usually folding to huge ones.

Just like before the flop, I don't want to size my bet in a way that reveals the strength of my hand. I do want the size of my bet to give my opponent a difficult decision with a marginal hand against my betting hands. After the flop, I ignore my actual holding and decide how much I'm going to bet *if* I bet. Once I decide the amount, I choose whether I'm going to bet that amount or check. This latter decision, whether to bet, takes into account my actual holding as well as several other factors. This gives away the minimum information about the strength of my hand. My opponent is getting information only on whether I bet, not the size of my bet.

The size of my bet depends on how my opponent is likely to think the flop hit my hand, as well as how likely it is to have hit my opponent's. If my hand looks very strong to my opponent, or if my opponent is likely to have few outs if he is beat, I will bet small, about half the pot. If it looks like my opponent has many outs against my betting hands, I will make a larger bet, somewhere between three quarters of the pot and the size of the pot.

For example, assume I made a minimum raise from first position and was called by the big blind and the flop came with an ace. From my opponent's perspective, even if I don't have an ace, I am very likely to have a pocket pair, so even if my opponent has a small pair, he has no more than five outs against my likely holdings. I don't need to bet more than half the pot to convince him to fold.

If the flop is

the player in the lead now is probably the player who will be in the lead on later streets. The player with the ace and the biggest kicker isn't giving anyone more than five outs (two outs if they have a pocket pair, three if they have an ace with a lower kicker, four if they have

an inside straight draw, and five if they have a middle or bottom pair).
You don't have to bet much to give your opponent a difficult decision, or at least a wrong decision to call if you have an ace. If you bet
half the pot, there is a good chance your opponent will fold, even if
he knows you could be bluffing. If you raised and an ace comes and
your opponent does not fold to your bet, you found out where you are
cheap. If you missed the flop, you know you are done with the hand.

Most flops are heads-up and the most aggressive player wins the
pot. Without a pocket pair, your opponent has only about a 1-in-3
chance of making a pair on the flop. Of course, those are your chances
too, but if you are the bettor, the other player doesn't have much choice
but to fold if the flop didn't hit him, and an A♣T♦5♥ flop doesn't
leave him with many hands he feels good about continuing to play if
you raised before the flop and bet after the flop, even if he knows you
are betting most of the time.

When my betting hands don't look as strong to my opponent,
I need to bet more to give him a difficult decision with a marginal
hand. Say I raised from middle position and was called from the big
blind and the flop came jack-high. Because the range of my betting
hands was a lot weaker in this situation, I need to bet more to give
him a difficult decision with a marginal hand like a small pair.

In addition, with a flop that creates a lot of potential draws, I am
going to have to bet more to give my opponent a difficult decision. On
a flop such as J♥T♦5♥, my hands and my opponent's are more likely
to be close in value. I could easily just have overcards in this case,
so my opponent is more likely to think his low pair could be good.
Because of the number of draws available, the next card could also
significantly change the percentages each player has to win the hand.
You have to bet more to give your opponent a tough decision with a
draw, in this case between three quarters of the pot and the pot.

One more factor influencing the size of my bet is the position
from which I raised. If I raised from early position, I am representing
a much stronger hand. Therefore, I don't have to bet as much to give
the big blind a difficult decision. For instance, if I raised from early
position and was called by the big blind, I might bet as little as one
third of the pot after a flop like A♣T♦5♥. With a flop like J♥T♦5♥,
I might bet two-thirds of the pot after my early position raise.

These are just guidelines. If I know something about a particular opponent, I might make a different bet even if that means varying my bet according to the strength of my hand. If he thinks a big bet looks like I'm trying to buy the pot, I will make a big bet when I have a big hand. If he thinks a small bet will look strong, I will make a small bet with a bluffing hand. This can turn into a guessing game, especially after my opponent sees I have tricked him. I try to stay away from guessing games. I let my opponents play guessing games and look for opportunities to pounce when I am confident they will guess wrong.

Whether to Bet

You can't completely avoid giving away information about your hand when you act after the flop. When I act first or it is checked to me, I have to decide whether to check or bet. I have to put my hands into at least two categories based on my action on the flop—those I'll bet and those I'll check.

To avoid giving away more information, I will end up playing similar hands differently. The later we are in the hand, the less I mind giving out information and the more straightforwardly I play. That's because there are fewer streets for my opponent to take advantage of the information. There are hands I will check and very similar hands that I will bet.

Using the same example from the last section, let's say the flop is A-T-5. If I have A-K, I like betting. With something like A-J, checking may not be bad. I might be up against A-K, A-Q, A-T, A-5, or even a set. With A-2, if I'm in the lead, I'm giving up, at most, five outs by checking, but I'm saving a lot of chips if my opponent has me beat. If I am behind, I am the one who has, at most, five outs (and probably just three). If it's checked to the river, then I'll bet.

Also, it is important to establish that your check is not a sure sign of weakness. You have to let your opponents know that you can have an ace and check, or have a set and check.

There are still many situations where I will play the same hand in exactly one way, especially if I showed strength before the flop. If I raised from *early position*, I am almost certainly going to bet the flop, especially if the big blind called my raise and has checked to me. Because the size of that bet is based on the flop and on my position and because I am betting with so many hands, he still has little information about what I have. All he knows is that I had a raising hand and I bet out.

When I raise from an early position, I'm giving pretty good pot odds to the big blind. For everyone else, when they play, they are saying they have value in the hand. Their call says they have as good a hand as mine, because we are putting in the same amount of money. What is the big blind saying when he calls? He is not saying that his hand is anywhere near as strong as someone raising with nine players acting after him. He is saying only that he is getting the right odds to call with his hand, and with a small raise I am giving him those odds.

If I raise before the flop and a player with position calls behind me, I like to bet the flop. I am out of position, but that is actually one reason I like to bet. Betting out of position takes away some of my opponent's advantage. If I check, my opponent can see the next card for free. This is a very powerful option I take away by betting. Now, if he wants to see the next card, he has to pay for it.

When I have position, there are many reasons why I may want to check after the flop if it is checked to me. If I bet, I am reopening the betting and can get check-raised. True, my opponent has shown weakness by checking, but I can't assume he isn't also trying to mix up his play. If I thought my opponent only bet his strong hands, I would definitely bet. Otherwise, I can check. I have position for the rest of the hand, so it is not as important for me to get the hand over with.

I particularly like to check with my weak draws such as inside straight draws. If I bet and get check-raised, I have to throw my hand away and miss out on the opportunity of hitting my draw and winning a monster pot.

Some Examples of Whether to Bet After the Flop

Some of the principles regarding whether to bet are easier to understand if you see them applied. I have started with two sample flops,

A♣T♥5♠ and J♠T♥5♠. In each example, my starting hand is in parentheses.

Example 1—I raise three times the big blind from late position and only the big blind calls. The flop comes A♣T♥5♠. The big blind checks to me. If I bet here, I will bet about half the pot. The ace scares my opponent more than it scares me so I can afford to bet small.

Example 1a (A-K)—I like my hand here. I am hoping my opponent has an ace too. I will probably bet.

Example 1b (A-J)—I will bet here too. I don't like this hand nearly as much as A-K because my opponent has more ways to beat me. But because I raised from late position, the player in the big blind probably doesn't have much strength anyway. If I feel like slow-playing some hands, this hand might be one of them.

Example 1c (A-2)—This is a hand I really want to check. I think I'm ahead, but if my opponent has an ace, I am hopelessly behind. On the other hand, if I am ahead, my opponent has few outs so I don't lose too much by giving a free card. I more than make up for giving free cards by inducing my opponent to bluff. I will probably check the flop and the turn and bet the river if my opponent has not bet. I will call any moderate-sized bet made by my opponent.

Example 1d (K-K)—I will play this exactly like A-2, and for the same reasons. Note that, since I don't have an ace myself, my opponent is about 50 percent more likely to have an ace than if I had A-2.

Example 1e (7-6)—I will bluff at the pot on this flop. I am betting so many powerful hands that I can afford to throw in some bluffs and still get my opponent to fold.

Example 1f (3-3)—This is a tough hand. The problem with checking this hand down is that you are giving your opponent a number of outs with overcards. Consequently, I am much more likely to bet this on the flop than K-K. I generally don't think you should bet with middle-strength hands, but this is an exception because I am making a continuation bet. I can get a lot of hands that have outs against me to fold. A hand with six outs, like Q-8, will probably fold. I might even get hands that beat me to fold. Would an opponent with 4-4 call?

Example 1g (9-9)—This is another middle-strength hand. It lies between K-K and 3-3. I would probably check this on the flop, but if I raised from early position I would bet.

Example 1h (A-A)—I would play this hand different ways. I might want to slow-play because I have the deck crippled, making it unlikely my opponent has an ace. By slow-playing, I am hoping to induce a bluff. But there is nothing wrong with betting. It may be hard to find an opponent to give you action on this flop. If you get the hand over with now, at least you avoid the disaster of letting your opponent make an inside straight draw.

Example 1i (A-T)—This is a very strong hand, and one I will probably bet. I have shown strength before the flop, so I am going to bet most of the time in this situation. I am looking to get three bets in with this hand—flop, turn, and river.

Example 1j (K-Q)—I will probably check this hand. I don't want to get raised and lose my inside straight draw. If my opponent has a pair but does not have an ace, I potentially have ten outs, making a straight or the best pair with a king, queen, or jack.

Example 1k (T-9)—Similar to 9-9, I will usually check this hand. Note that with a middle pair, I probably have five outs if my opponent has an ace. With a pocket pair, I have only two.

Example 2—In this example, I have again raised to three times the big blind in late position and been called by the big blind. The flop this time, however, is J♠T♥5♠.

Example 2a (A-K)—If I have A♠K♠, I will definitely bet. With two overcards, a flush draw, and an inside straight draw, this hand is a monster on this flop. If I don't have the flush draw, I will check. I don't want to give up my inside straight draw plus the likelihood that an ace or king could put me ahead. I don't want to have to give up this hand or make a weak call if I get check-raised.

Example 2b (A-J)—I will bet this hand to protect it.

Example 2c (A-2)—With A♠2♠, I would definitely bet. Without the flush draw, it is a close decision. I will likely check this hand down and hope ace-high is good.

Example 2d (K-K)—I like my hand and will usually bet to try to protect it.

Example 2e (7-6)—If I have 7♠6♠, I will likely bet this hand. Even if I don't have a flush draw, I will probably bet as a complete bluff.

Example 2f (3-3)—I will usually check this hand down and hope it is good.

Example 2g (9-9)—I am even more likely to check this hand than 3-3 because I am giving my opponent a lot fewer outs to beat me if I am ahead.

Example 2h (A-A)—I am equally likely to bet this hand to protect it as I am to slow-play and try to induce a bluff out of my opponent.

Example 2i (A-T)—With A♠T♠, I will definitely bet. A pair and the nut flush draw is a monster hand and I don't mind getting a lot of chips in on the flop. Without the flush draw, I am as likely to bet as to check.

Example 2j (K-Q)—With K♠Q♠, I have a monster hand, with a flush draw, an open-ended straight draw, and two overcards. I want to get as many chips in as possible on this flop. Even without the flush draw, I am likely to bet with the straight draw and two overcards.

Example 2k (T-9)—I would bet this hand if I also have the flush draw, but usually check it if I don't.

As you can see from these examples, I am frequently checking strong hands and betting weak ones. It is important that checking is not a sign of weakness and equally important to occasionally throw in bluffs when you are betting. The tough part is knowing which strong hands to check and which weak ones to bet. Hopefully, the examples I have set out will guide you to make better decisions when choosing how much to bet and which hands to bet with.

Conclusion

One of the most important principles guiding how I play is keep-ing opponents from knowing my cards. Therefore, I base as many decisions as I can during a hand on things other than my cards. If I never call before the flop, opponents can't group my playable hands into "calling hands" and "raising hands." Likewise, if the size of my pre-flop raise varies only based on my position, they gain no informa-tion about my hand from the size of my raise. After the flop, it gets much more complicated, but when I can, I will decide how much to bet based on factors other than the strength of my hand, such as the flop and the pre-flop action. That way, even if my opponents know exactly how I play, they can't use that knowledge to beat me because they still can't figure out my cards.

2
2½   x   big blind
3

CHAPTER 4

No-Limit Hold 'Em: The Theory of Leverage

by Howard Lederer

The Concept of Leverage

There is a concept in no-limit hold 'em that nearly all successful tournament players understand and use, which I call leverage. It has never really been written about and few players outside the top pros are aware of it. It should be every player's main strategic thought whenever they sit down at a no-limit hold 'em tournament.

Leverage is the ability in no-limit hold 'em to make a small bet (relative to the size of the pot) but implied with that bet is the potential and threat of more bets on later streets. You give someone a tough decision on *this* card, but when they start adding up how many chips they are risking to look you up all the way to the end, it becomes a very poor proposition. A leveraged bet allows you to limit the amount you lose if you lose that bet, while still leaving open the possibility of winning much more in future betting rounds. The less you bet relative to your stack, while still being appropriate for the situation, the more leverage you have in that hand.

Here is a simple way to look at leverage. If there is 100 in the pot and I bet 75 on the flop and you think there's a fifty-fifty chance you have the best hand, I have given you a tough decision. Calling 75 to win 175 on a coin flip should be easy, but if your hand is unlikely to improve, what additional bets will you have to call? If I keep betting slightly more than half the pot, that means you may have to call

32

175 on the turn and 400 on the river. What if my hand has a better chance to improve? What if you aren't really fifty-fifty? All of a sudden, it is not 75 to you after the flop. It is really 650 to you.

Employing leverage is the best way to play aggressive poker. You put opponents on the defensive because they constantly have to deal with the threat of your future bets. The only way you can create leverage is by underbetting the pot, by betting less than the size of the pot. By knowing the best situations to use leverage—the kinds of flops where leverage is particularly useful and powerful—you can build your tournament no-limit hold 'em game around leverage.

Success in tournament poker is about putting your opponents to as many difficult decisions as possible, and making your decisions as easy as possible. By betting small amounts relative to the pot, especially when you bet the same way regardless of the strength of your hand—leveraged bets are the same whether you miss the flop and bluff or flop the nuts—your opponents have to keep making difficult decisions. If they fold, those chips go in your stack. If they call, they have ensured that they will have another difficult decision on the next street, because they have given you information about the strength of their hand, while gaining no information about your hand.

If they make a stand and move all-in on you, you usually have an easy decision. You can fold your bluffs and medium-strength hands, conceding the small pots (and encouraging opponents to continue doing this). But when you have a big hand you can call and be a big favorite when you play big pots. Your ability to take control of the hand—with a bluff or with the nuts, with your opponents knowing you could have either—is the key to leverage. You can bluff and lose small pots—though you will also win a lot of small pots—and when you have a good hand, you win big pots.

With this style of play, you are constantly entering into leveraged propositions. Even though more than half of them don't work out, it doesn't matter. Your stack grows.

You need to be aggressive to employ leverage. You need to bluff some. You need to get caught bluffing. If you are betting often, but betting small, you can be very active. Leveraged bets allow you to bet without having the best hand. You put people back on their heels. They then have to play into your leverage to find out if this is the hand where you are bluffing. Your risk is limited to the small bets you have already made. Their risk, potentially, is their whole stack.

You don't have to be a maniac and play every hand. I think my table image has morphed from tight and aggressive to solid but capable of anything and aggressive. Phil Hellmuth is never betting a lot into the pot. He constantly fires small bets. On the other hand, Daniel Negreanu has a reputation of playing any two cards but he, likewise, accomplishes it by leading with small bets. The master of leverage among today's most successful tournament players is Gus Hansen. He may have 6-3 or he may have A-A, but he's attacking with small bets. It can work with a solid style like mine—if "solid" means you don't need a great hand every time you bet—and it works for the best loose, aggressive players in the world.

Leverage Early, Leverage Late

Early in a tournament, even though the blinds may not seem worth contesting, you should still be employing leverage. Many opponents are playing tighter than they should because they don't want to go broke early. This is the time when you should be active, winning small pots, giving up your bluffs, and establishing yourself as a player who will fire exactly the same bet at the pot with the nuts or with a bluff.

Opponents will usually get out of your way when you boss them around with small bets. What choice do they have? If you are bullying the table with small bets early in the tournament, look at what happens when an opponent wants to take a stand. If he wants to make a big bet at you, he has to think, "All my chips may be at risk here, and even if I'm right I'm going to win just a small pot." It is very hard for them to catch you for a lot of your chips and *they* have to put up a lot of *their* chips to try.

You're going to win plenty of small pots. You're out there, you're probing, and you're using all your poker skills to decide which pots you should be probing after. But you're putting pressure on people in these small pots, using the leverage of the larger bets later on, making them very uncomfortable. Of course, you will lose some small pots too.

Late in tournaments, there are no small pots. Almost everyone is on a relatively short stack as you get in or near the money, and your opponents will be playing too tight. They want to avoid risks while other players bust, so they can make it into the money or move up in the money. Your opponents will usually let you steal, or they will be nice enough to cost you only your initial bet when they try to end the hand early with a giant raise.

2003 WSOP Main Event: Phil Ivey Leverages Me into a Difficult Decision

A perfect illustration of the power of leverage was a particular hand I played with Phil Ivey in the Main Event of the 2003 World Series of Poker. The hand played out in a very simple way, so it was unremarkable from a TV perspective—even if it had taken place at the final table, they might not have shown it—but it put the entire tournament on the line for me, because I was on the short end of the leverage equation.

We were down to fewer than forty players. I was in the big blind, with approximately 150,000 in chips. Blinds were 3,000-6,000, with a 1,000 ante. Phil Ivey, with 300,000 in chips, made it 18,000 to go. It was a standard opening raise of three times the big blind, and Phil plays a lot of pots, entering with this size raise, so he could have almost any hand.

I looked down at J-J. In figuring out how to play it, I suddenly realized I was in a negative leverage situation. If I called the additional 12,000 and then reraised, I would have to put more than 60,000 in the pot. If I was going to commit more than 60,000 of my chips to playing this pot, it would be hard to fold for the last 85,000. Plus I would be giving Ivey all the advantage of being able to see what I do with my last 85,000 after the flop.

Phil got the leverage by betting, and by betting just 18,000. That bet was all he was risking, yet my only responses were giving up the hand or committing all my chips.

I remember moving all-in and hating it. "If he has aces, kings, or queens," I thought, "he's got me." I realized that he was the one who had all the leverage. Look what he got by seizing the leverage and taking it away from me:

- He gave away nothing about the strength of his hand. I had to give away everything about the strength of mine.
- All he could lose was 18,000 but he could win over 150,000. I had to bet my whole stack to win 30,000.

My decision was very difficult. I was putting my tournament at risk against a raiser who could have had A-A or 7-6. After I moved all-in, Phil Ivey's decision was very simple. With A-A, K-K, or A-K, it would be an easy decision for him to call. With Q-Q, it might be a little harder to call. And he might have a tough decision with T-T or the other two jacks. But he wouldn't have trouble laying down any other hand, including most of the hands he could have opened the pot with. He folded. But, as you can see, the hand left a lasting impression on me.

Leverage versus Moving All-In

So many new players think "aggressive" means "move all-in." That is actually the worst way to play aggressive poker. If you play a lot of pots, you have to expect people to look you up. And when your leverage is gone, you have committed all your chips to win a small pot. When you get caught bluffing, you lose all your chips. When they fold to you, all you win is a small pot. The best you can hope for is 1-to-1: committing all your chips to win an equal amount.

That doesn't mean I don't move all-in a lot, particularly when I'm on short chips. That's one of the disadvantages of being short-chipped: you don't have leverage anymore. Your only weapon is pressure. By moving all-in you can exert pressure with your entire stack. You can steal a few pots to keep your stack alive. Of course the worst scenario is when your stack is so small that you can't even use pressure. If I survive being short-chipped and build a decent stack again, I can go back to making leveraged bets, picking up pots with small bets and disguising my strong hands with identical bets.

If you are moving all-in frequently simply to bully the table, you can prey on people's natural risk aversion and pick up some chips. But you better have a lot of other poker talents to go along with it. You better have the skills for reading people and hands to identify the players who won't call you.

Once you've identified that a player doesn't have a good enough hand to call you, you can apply pressure and make them fold. But it is an awfully risky strategy. You could apply those same skills using leverage and get the same players to lay down those same hands, without the cost of making the wrong play at the wrong time.

If I look at a player and think, "He just doesn't have a good enough hand," or "He's just not ready to go broke," I don't need to move all-in to get him off the hand. I can apply plenty of pressure by betting a little more than half the pot, with the implication of bigger bets on later streets. Imagine blinds of 50 and 100, with a raise to 300 and call before the flop. My opponent has J-J and the flop comes K-8-2, three suits. With 750 in the pot, I would bet 400. If he calls, my next bet into the 1,500 pot will be 900. If he calls that, he has to assume I will bet 1,800 into the pot of 3,300 on the river.

If my read is correct, maybe I have to bet 400 and then 900 to convince him. Maybe I have to go all the way and bet 1,800 on the end. But why bet the entire 3,400 in one shot? If my read is wrong, I can give up the bluff and lose less than the 3,400. Or I can use leverage and fire all three barrels. But at least I can back out at any point. If I bet the whole 3,400 on the hand immediately, all I can do is win a small pot if my read is correct or lose it all if I'm wrong.

Leverage Before the Flop

So what do you need to employ leverage before the flop? You need to be aggressive, you need to bluff occasionally, and you need chips. But how many?

Obviously, you can destroy people with leverage if you have a big stack. You are opening a lot of pots for small raises, but your activity and your stack make if clear that anyone who wants to look you up has to be prepared to commit all their chips. (You, in contrast, have to commit only a few chips out of your big stack, which is why it simply isn't worth it for them to play back at you unless they have a monster hand. And against most opponents, their sudden willingness to challenge you gives away the strength of their hand.)

But you don't need to have a huge stack, or even more than your opponents, to use leverage before the flop. The critical ratios are *3-10-30*. That is, to open for *three* times the big blind, you need a stack of more than *ten* times the big blind. If someone else has opened for a raise, to make a leveraged reraise, you need more than *thirty* times the big blind.

Three—If my opponents are playing passively and they will allow it, I will use leverage before the flop. I like to open the pot small. The better player you become and the better you get at no-limit hold 'em, the more you should be using leverage before the flop. The way you do that is by opening for less.

I think three times the big blind is a nice leverage point. You should always raise if you are the first to enter the pot, and the amount of your raise should give away nothing about the strength of your hand. (In chapter 3, Chris Ferguson advocated raises of approximately the same size, but varied slightly based on position. I believe in raising three times the big blind regardless of position, but his reasoning is sound, because those raises don't give away anything about the strength of his hand.)

Ten—Before the flop if no one's opened, ten times the big blind is the cutoff for leverage. Even if you are on a relatively short stack and other players at the table have more chips, you can still have leverage over them with a small raise if you get to the pot first and have more than ten times the big blind.

Let's say we are playing with blinds of 1,000-2,000 and I have 25,000 in front of me. Now I can open for 6,000 with A-A and I can open for 6,000 with J-Ts. If I think the position is right and it's appropriate to do it, I will open with either hand because I *can* fold for the other 19,000. As long as I'm not pot-committed for my opening bet, I'm going to raise three times the big blind regardless of the strength of my hand. I'm going to open for an amount that will leave me folding money. Now I have some leverage—even if I'm short-stacked. Even if my opponents are experienced pros and they have 100,000 in chips to my 25,000, I'm still going to open for 6,000 because I still have the leverage of my remaining chips in that position.

Despite their bigger stacks, they still have to decide whether I've got it. If they decide to put me all-in, they have to bet 25,000 to win 9,000 plus antes (if I fold), and I get to make an intelligent decision for my last 19,000. I can double up if I have a big hand, and pick up the blinds and antes if an opponent doesn't want to risk a quarter of his stack for such a small return. Even though I am outchipped, they can't leverage me. By getting my 6,000 in first, I have leveraged them.

But if I was down to 15,000, I'm not going to open for 6,000. I'm just going to put maximum pressure on my opponents by moving all-in. I might do it with A-5o and I might do it with Q-Q. But I'll make them make a tough, uncomfortable decision to call me. Even if the big blind has 100,000 in chips and I've raised his 2,000 to 15,000, that's a tough decision for him. But my leverage is gone. All I have is the pressure of moving all-in, and that's how I survive when I'm short-stacked.

Ten times the big blind is not enough to use leverage if someone opens to my right. If, in this hypothetical, someone makes it 6,000 to me, I need to have a darned good hand to play because I have to go in for all my chips. I might fold A-J in that situation and, if it is folded to me on the next hand, move all-in with A-5. I would rather move in with A-5 than reraise all-in with A-J if it looks like I will get called.

Thirty—Thirty times the big blind is what you need to make a leveraged reraise before the flop. Look back at my hand against Phil Ivey. I had about twenty-five times the big blind. Even though that should be enough to use leverage, reraising the opener requires a bet of approximately ten times the big blind. If I had reraised Phil Ivey from 18,000 to 60,000, I was pot-committed. With fewer than thirty times the big blind, you can't make a leveraged reraise. If someone has opened, you have to fold or move all-in.

If, in the hand against Phil, I had 200,000 instead of 150,000 at the start of that hand, I could have reraised to 60,000 and reclaimed the leverage. Even if you gave him more chips in the hypothetical, say 500,000, he has to view my reraise as a leveraged bet. I can potentially win 200,000, 40 percent of his stack, but if he plays back at me, I can make an intelligent decision and fold for my last 140,000 and all he can win is my 60,000 plus what is already in the pot. I can make a big laydown and still have enough chips to continue using leverage in future hands.

Leverage After the Flop

Leverage rears its lovely head the most after the flop. Post-flop play is also where most new tournament players have the most difficulty. If you gain your experience from online tournaments or TV final tables, you are playing or watching situations where everyone is relatively short-stacked. This is not the usual situation in a big buy-in tournament or even a smaller buy-in event or online tournament after you acquire some chips.

There are fewer hard-and-fast rules after the flop, which intimidates players with less experience and less knowledge about what is happening. These are the muddy waters of post-flop play.

I mean, poker is messy. Players who are totally committed to pre-flop play sometimes feel like it doesn't have to be. If you devote all your attention to pre-flop play, maybe that is true. Pre-flop, it is just two cards against two cards. The odds of every hand against every other hand are pretty straightforward. There are more clear decisions. After the flop, it gets messy, and if you and your opponents have deep stacks, you have to know how to play after the flop.

It's beautiful stuff.

The Texture of the Flop—Untextured Flops

The starting point is the texture of the flop. You need to recognize what is a "leverage flop" and what isn't. This is one area where you can start with some specific guidelines. Your action after the flop, if you have leverage and you led the betting before the flop, has almost nothing to do with the strength of your hand, and almost everything to do with the texture of the flop.

Texture is about draws. Are there a lot of draws out there or not?

A highly textured flop is T-8-7, two suits. A nontextured flop is something like K-8-2, three suits.

K-8-2 is a leverage flop. It is relatively unlikely the best hand will change on the turn or the river. If I have A-K, my opponent either has me beat already with a set or is drawing to two outs (trying to make trips with a pocket pair) or three outs (hitting his lower kicker). This is not a flop where they can put one of those cards on the board that just makes you moan and groan and think, "Oh my God, now what?"

A nontextured flop with few draws is one where you can make maximum use of leverage. Let's say our opponent called the pre-flop raise with J-J.

On a leverage flop, I want to bet about half the pot and maybe a little more. And I will do that on a K-8-2 flop whether I had A-K, A-Q, or T-T. (The strength of my hand has no impact at this point.)

What does the poor guy with J-J do? With only two outs, he can't count on improving. He has to decide, "Am I prepared to call on this street and the next street and the next street?"

If there is 650 in the pot (50 and 100 blinds, my raise to 300, his call from the big blind) and I bet 400, we can go through the math. He calls, so now the pot has 1,450. If I bet 800 on the turn and he calls, the pot will have 3,050. My bet on the river would be 1,800.

This guy is calling 400 on the flop to win 1,050. He is getting better than 3.5-to-1 by calling and has to beat only 28 percent of my hands to show a profit. On the flop, it looks like a good price. But he is potentially risking another 2,600 on the next two streets. If you imagine all the hands I could have raised with pre-flop, J-J would probably beat a lot more than 28 percent of them following this kind of flop. But it's not that simple. If he wants to go all the way, he has to call 3,000 to win 3,650. That's just a little better than even money, which means he needs to win half the time to show a small profit.

And it gets even worse for my opponent. If we assume that I am going to stop bluffing most of the time after I get called on the flop, but continue betting when I have a real hand, my opponent might then be faced with a truly impossible situation. He might only win my 400 bluff plus the 650 already in the pot for a 1,050 win when I bluff, but lose 3,000 when I have him beat. All of a sudden, he better be right almost 75 percent of the time just to break even! This is a far cry from the 28 percent needed to pass break-even on the initial flop bet.

On a flop where the best hand is unlikely to change, that's when you can maximize this kind of leverage. Since you are going to bet most of the time on the flop, even when you miss, the hand actually starts when the guy calls you on the flop.

If you have nothing and your opponent is the type who will call you down to the end, you have to identify that guy. Using your poker skills and the tools we describe throughout the book, maybe you pick him out early and don't have to bet into him very much. But if you bet 400 on the leverage flop and he calls, he is not calling with nothing. He probably has top pair or a pocket pair a little below the high card on the board.

Of course, if you have a hand, this guy will pay you off. If you have strong starting cards and didn't hit the flop, you can still pass him. It's not like you automatically lose with A-Q when he calls you on the flop. But maybe you have to check the turn and fold if he bets.

So you lost 400. And he saw that you were bluffing. Maybe you even show it. I'm not big on showing. But if you think he needs reinforcement, let him know. "You got me."

What does this guy (and the rest of the table) think next time when you bet 400, get called, and bet 800 on the turn—which you have to do sometimes, even without a hand?

All you have to do is keep planting the seed that you'll make this bet on a bluff every once in a while. You don't have to do it that often.

Leverage works only if you are willing to bluff. If you have no bluff, there is no leverage. No one ever has to worry, "Does he have it or not?" They know to fold when you bet and bet when you check.

Against a calling station, you will pick up the pot when he doesn't hit a flop and get paid off when he keeps calling bets when you have a strong hand and his hand is less strong. Against better players, you will pick up more pots from your bet on the flop. Since you are betting 400 to win 650, you profit if this works only 40 percent of the time. Against good players, that is what will end up happening. The leverage part—profiting from escalating bets when you have a strong hand—is gravy. You can get caught 60 percent of the time while still profiting. You win while the players at the table think you are a maniac. "God, he's bluffing all the time."

Textured Flops

You have to be much more careful using leverage on a flop that is attractive to drawing hands. Because you are making small bets, you are unlikely to get opponents to abandon their draws after the flop. The most you can do is make them pay to draw out.

If I have opened before the flop, I will bet 80–100 percent of the pot on a nonleverage flop. The reason to bet more than on leverage flops is to take away the leverage from the draws. Just by virtue of having a draw, they have acquired leverage: they pay a limited amount to draw but can potentially win a lot more if they hit their draw. Your bet makes the ratio between cost-to-hit and payoff-after-hitting less attractive.

It doesn't matter what hand you have. It is very important that your decision whether to bet or how much to bet doesn't give away the strength of your hand. On a flop of J♥T♥6♣, your bet should be the same whether you have K♦Q♠, A♥6♥, K-K, 8-8, or J-J.

If you led the betting before the flop, even if you are on a draw, it is important to bet here. Nothing gives away the nature of your hand more clearly than giving up the betting lead. You might check with draws in position occasionally in multiway pots, just to mix it up. But you should want to end the pot right away. You don't have to hit your draw. Chips in the middle are better in your stack.

When you bet on this flop, it is a lot easier to go broke. If you are careful, however, you most likely won't lose more than your bet on the flop. Your main problem is that his call of your bet on the flop gives you very little information. He could have J-T, A-J, A-T, K-Q, 9-8, 6-6, a nut flush draw, or a non-nut flush draw. Depending on the suits on the flop, he could have some combination, like Q-J and a flush draw.

Not that it is necessarily a bad thing for you to continue to bluff on the turn, if you don't have a good hand or a good draw, but you could go broke very easily if he is trapping with a big hand or makes his draw, because you don't know what he has.

Once you get to the turn, your hand starts to matter, but your opponent's taste for running you down matters even more. If you don't have a big hand or a draw to the nuts by now, you probably usually give it up here. You need very, very convincing evidence to keep betting at an opponent who just called on the flop with all those draws available.

The point of leverage is that usually you'll give it up if they stick around. And that plays into the whole strategy. Now they think you have something if you bet the turn. And if they catch you here, you still haven't sustained a huge loss, and look at what you have gained for the next play: they know that you will fire a second bullet without having it.

An occasional bet on the turn can pay great dividends. You give up your leverage if it becomes clear that you will bet the flop regardless of the situation but will only bet the turn if you have something.

Of course, we are playing poker here. You have to continue on the second street *just often enough*, and continue on the river *just often enough* without the hand.

Sometimes you need to bet the turn and sometimes you need to check. If you are on a draw, in position, and your opponent called you once and you think he will call again, take the free card.

Ironically, even if your hand can't beat a straight or a flush, it is important to bet the turn if the turn card appears to have hit a draw. You do this for several reasons (in addition to the possibility that *you* were the one who hit the draw). First, what if your opponent wasn't on a draw and didn't have the courage to check-raise you before? You could have nothing, represent you hit the draw, and make him fold. Second, as much as you are worried that someone just hit a draw, it is much more likely that *now* they have a draw. They have Q♠J♥ and the flop is K♠J♦6♠. They called your bet on the flop with second pair but picked up a flush draw when the turn is the eight of spades. If you have A♦A♥, you had your opponent down to five outs on the flop. Now he has fourteen outs. You are still a nice favorite, so it is important for you to cash another bet against a pair and a flush draw.

You have to take your read. Did it seem like he hit his draw? You can't know for sure, but the danger is if you check and a blank comes on the river and he bets, you're probably going to call the bet anyway. It's so important to punish what is now a newfound draw.

Post-flop play is a swamp. There aren't rules for most of the situations that come up and this section isn't intended to tell you all there is to consider. The goal here was to get you thinking about how leverage can help you after the flop—situations where it helps you roll over opponents as well as situations where you can get yourself in trouble. As you become more experienced in tournaments and more familiar with leverage, along with the principles described for post-flop play in chapter 7, you will start to figure it out.

Defending Against Leverage

One of the virtues of leveraged bets is that they give away almost nothing about the strength of your hand. Therefore, the defense against leverage can't give away anything about the strength of your hand.

The way you defend against leverage is by raising or calling with nothing on the flop. If you are willing to occasionally raise with nothing on the flop, you put the decision back on the aggressor.

If you will play only a strong hand—where you hit the flop or have a strong draw or had a strong starting hand which still might be in the lead—you are not defeating leverage. To the contrary, you are telegraphing the strength of your hand in response to the aggressor's leverage, which is exactly what you want when you are the aggressor.

You have to make a stand with nothing. You need enough chips to be able to fold if this fails, but it never *really* fails. Unless you make some unleveraged reraise bluff—by moving all-in—you are controlling your downside if you get caught. But in getting caught, you send the message that you don't need a hand to call or raise. That way, in the future, when you play back, your aggressive opponent can't regard your plays as automatic signals that you have the best hand.

This is how you get the respect of the best players in the world, and how you can bust them. One of the distinguishing characteristics of the top players is their ability to get away from good hands when their opponents have better hands. This is because very few players can disguise a monster hand against a professional. How can they play back without revealing the strength of their hand?

So when you play back at the aggressor, you can't limit yourself to situations when you have a big hand. Because few players beyond the top pros are familiar with leverage, an experienced pro has a slightly easier time believing his amateur opponent is telegraphing a bigger hand. It is still hard to lay down a big hand, but great tournament players have to do that, and understanding leverage (and how their opponents are ignorant of the concept) helps.

Phil Hellmuth made a big laydown early in the Main Event of the 2005 World Series; it was one of the best-remembered hands of the Main Event broadcasts on ESPN. With blinds of 250-500, he raised to 1,500 with A-K. A player behind him reraised to 3,000. Phil called and checked blind. (The pot was now 6,750.) The flop came A-4-4 and his opponent also checked. A queen came on the turn. Phil checked and his opponent bet 10,000. After a lot of thinking and posturing, Phil laid down his A-K, and his opponent showed A-A.

Hellmuth no doubt employed all his skills in reading his opponent. But one of the reasons he was able to get away from the hand was that he probably didn't believe his opponent could make such a large bet with a worse hand than ace-king. Unless this opponent had either K-K or J-J, he had to have Phil beat. A-A, Q-Q, and A-Q had Phil crushed. But what if the same opponent had bet 4,000, less than two-thirds the pot? And what if the same opponent had been active enough with that kind of play that Phil couldn't take for granted that it represented a giant hand?

Phil Hellmuth prides himself on being the world's best reader of his opponents, and it was difficult for him to get away from that hand. It would have been much more difficult, and maybe impossible, for Phil or any other top pro, to get away from that hand against an opponent betting smaller amounts who displayed a history of playing back on a bluff.

Generally, you are playing solid cards, being aggressive with small bets, and not taking your bluffs too far. But you sometimes have to take your bluffs to the next level and you need to defend against leverage with bluffs. Between players who know how to use leverage, you are playing chicken. You and your expert opponent are driving toward each other, and the loser may be the one to turn away first. But you have to do it at low speed.

Concluding Thoughts About Leverage

Leverage should be your fundamental principle in no-limit hold 'em tournaments. These guidelines are enough to get you started, but you have to take it to the tables and try it out. How often should you bluff? How long do you maintain the bluff if you get called? How often should you bluff-raise in response to an opponent's leverage? How do you handle multiway pots after the flop? How do you handle drawing hands, opponents' draws, and the consequences of you and opponents making and missing draws?

The rest of the no-limit hold 'em chapters will help you answer these questions. Ultimately, you have to experience it. You will make mistakes but you will be pleasantly surprised, both by how the game reveals itself to you when you understand leverage and by how much you learn from both your successes and your mistakes.

No-Limit Hold 'Em: (Don't) Play Like Ted Forrest

by Ted Forrest

Editor's Note by Michael Craig

I was lucky enough, several years ago, to attend a speech given by Saul Bellow, the late Nobel Prize–winning author. The audience submitted questions and he happened to read mine first.

"I want to be an author. How do you write a great book?"

He paused for a moment and said, "That's the dumbest question I've ever been asked. If you have to ask it, you have no chance."

Poker is like writing that way. Anyone wanting to give it a try wants a formula, a checklist, some rules. Consequently, we all search for anything that will help us improve, sometimes mistakenly believing that book knowledge is a substitute for experience, instinct, trial and error, and hard thinking. Book knowledge is a supplement, not a substitute. No matter how many rules, charts, and concise explanations the authors provide, they all recognize, as Howard Lederer has told me several times, "You have to work it out at the table."

The main contributors to the hold 'em chapters (Howard Lederer, Chris Ferguson, and Andy Bloch) use their instincts, experience, and ability to adapt to great advantage. But because the foundation of their success has been based on understanding certain principles better than their opponents, they have shared that information to help you improve.

Ted Forrest plays poker without rules and charts. Although his ideas are theoretically very advanced—see his chapters on stud eight-or-better (chapter 17) and razz (chapter 18)—he eschews the idea that "rules" should govern your play, especially in no-limit hold 'em. This essay is not so much a rebuttal to the methodical framework provided by the other authors of the no-limit hold 'em chapters as a reminder: learn as much as you can from this book, but test it out and find what works best for you.

Ted makes this point himself far better than I possibly can, so I leave the balance of the chapter to his words. His ability to buck "conventional wisdom" and achieve great success has earned him, from friends, the nickname of Professor Backwards.

Rarely Say "Never" in Poker

I don't believe you should use the words "never" or "always" in discussing how to play poker. Michael Craig told me, for example, that Howard Lederer, Chris Ferguson, and Andy Bloch argue against being the first limper in a pot. I know they don't say "never," but they are generally against it in principle. I disagree.

Never be the first limper?—A lot of times, I'm the first limper in. I'm not afraid to look at a flop and mix it up and try to play after the flop. A lot of times in no-limit hold 'em, you want to get your opponents into certain habits, because when they get into certain habits they are easy to read and easy to deal with. If your type of game is one where you like to see a lot of flops and have some play after the flop, limping in early position can encourage others to do the same.

Say you have K-Qs. Why not limp with that hand so that even if somebody makes a normal raise, you can still see the flop? If you raise with that hand and get reraised, you are probably going to have to fold. Also, by limping with K-Qs, it encourages other players to limp with hands you have dominated, like K-J, K-T, and Q-J. If you raise, these players are probably going to fold these hands—the ones you want to stay in.

Another spot to limp is if you have a tight image or you have folded every hand for a couple rounds and you pick up A-A. If you believe your raise will cause everybody to fold and all you'll do is pick up the blinds, you might want to just call the big blind.

Any pair might be a good limping hand. You really don't want to price yourself out of seeing a flop, having a chance to make a set and bust somebody for their whole stack. With a pair, you can call a normal raise, but if you raise and someone reraises, you may be forced to fold.

Another time to limp is when you are on the button. One off the button with a playable hand, I am more likely to raise because I want to be able to act last throughout the hand. On the button, there is no reason to raise to gain position. With a hand like T-9s, I may just limp on the button. Another thing: if you raise on the button (especially if you are wearing a Ted Forrest mask), people will put you on a steal and play back at you. But if you limp, they may say, "What the heck is going on here? I'm a little nervous." A more conservative player can get away with raising on the button with T-9s. If you play fewer hands, other players are less likely to assume you are stealing.

In other words, you need to be aware of what the table thinks about you when deciding whether to raise or not. Other pros will tell you the same thing, but if they don't limp, their decision with a medium-to-speculative hand in late position is (a) raise because it is a playable hand and you raise with playable hands, or (b) fold because your table image has opponents ready to play back at you.

If you are wearing the Ted Forrest mask, you can add (c): limp and see the flop cheap.

If the table is really respecting your raises as signifying a big hand, then go ahead and raise on the button with whatever you have. Don't limp. But the last time someone respected one of my raises on the button seems like it was 1993. If the table is likely to think you are stealing their blinds with trash, mix it up and confuse them a little bit by calling. If the table thinks you are playing a lot of trash hands and you *do* have a trash hand, feel free to fold your button.

Conversely, if you have a big hand and they're likely to suspect you of stealing, go ahead and raise it on the button. Maybe they'll play back at you. In other words, disappoint them. Whatever they expect you to do, confuse them.

A lot of people tend to look at the button as a license to steal and a license to raise. I'm happy to have position for the hand, but I don't want to be in there with the kind of hand that people expect me to be playing the button with, which is a lousy hand. So I tend to fold lousy hands, because I don't want to be in there playing the hand they expect me to have.

By limping, you put yourself at some risk that somebody will raise behind you. If they raise an amount that is just too expensive to call, well, go ahead and forfeit that single bet that you limped into the pot with. If they do this a little too much, you can limp with a hand you are going to smash them with.

At the same time, you may find yourself at a table where they will follow your lead. This is the benefit, I suppose, of the Ted Forrest mask. Some players want to follow what the better players at the table are doing. But even if players aren't trying to compliment you by imitating your play, they may use your limping as an excuse to do the same themselves.

Always raise the same amount?—If you think the table may do what you're doing, don't limit it to the decision to limp. If you feel it's to your advantage that people make small raises, start raising the minimum and see if they follow. So many times, an active player will raise a certain amount and the rest of the table just follows it.

What if you are at a table where an active or well-known player has raised four times the big blind? Soon that's the standard raise for the table. It's too expensive for you to see many flops for that much. Maybe you need to do something about this. Limp a little bit. Make some small, awkward-looking raises. Get the table away from the idea that four times the big blind has somehow become the law.

I believe you need to vary, rather than standardize, the size of your bets. Sometimes you need to vary them according to the strength of your hand and sometimes you need to reverse that and make the size of the bets such that it will totally confuse people as to the strength of your hand. If you keep zigging and zagging, they're really going to have a tough time nailing you down. If you are always raising three times the big blind, it doesn't necessarily give away the strength of your hand, but the percentage of flops that you're seeing will give a good player a pretty good indication of the types of hands that you're playing.)

And let's not forget, a reason to vary the size of your bets is to try to manipulate the other players at the table into making a mistake against you. You want them to jump on a weak-looking raise or shy away from a strong one, when you are betting opposite the strength of your hand. That's overly simple, but you get the opportunity to throw people off their game by varying the size of your raises. You don't give away anything if you raise the same amount (though the hand percentages will still give opponents some information on you), but you don't *get* anything either. You get more information if you vary the size of your raises, and you give up the opportunity to give out misinformation if you always raise the same amount.

One of the skills that separates the great players from the good ones is the ability to induce your opponents to make mistakes. I feel my style allows me the best opportunity to do that. You'd be surprised at how often players get on a mission to keep me from limping or making small raises. (It would probably happen even more if I didn't wear the Ted Forrest mask.)

For example, say you've kind of been limping around, making a lot of weak-looking raises, playing a lot of hands, and having to fold sometimes when people come over the top of you and now you happen to get A-A or K-K. If you make that weak-looking raise and you get someone to jump on you with A-T or better, that's a huge mistake you've induced.

Sometimes it's as simple as you see a player three spaces to your left and he's itching to raise. He's almost unaware that you've limped in and he's just waiting for his turn to raise. That's part of being aware. If you weren't aware and you had A-A and you raised three times the big blind in early position, now he may just call or may not even play the hand. Now you've lost that opportunity. On the other hand, you may see that same player and you realize he has strength. Then go ahead and raise three times the big blind and maybe he will come over the top for a ten-times-the-big-blind raise.

Your game should be constantly changing. You don't want people to get a handle on what you're doing. A lot of the time you can let the cards dictate the style that you're going to play. If you are seeing a few more playable starting hands than would be normal, set up that maniac image. But you're going to have to have the goods a lot more often than is normal, just because you're getting the cards.

If you are a little bit card dead, let that play into your image. You are folding a lot of hands, so people have pegged you as "tight." Now put in a big raise up front with the 7-6s and people are probably going to give you respect and you're going to win the blinds.

My goal is not only to win the blinds and antes in that situation. I am trying to make it easier for my opponents to make a huge, costly mistake against me. If I get action with my 7-6s, I'm not likely to get outplayed after the flop. On a flop like T-6-6, when I bet, I'm going to get action from relatively weak hands and players who think I missed and am stealing.

This kind of flexibility—sometimes calling, sometimes raising small, sometimes raising big, all without a pattern—gives me the potential to lose less on my losing hands too. That might even be more important. When I limp in with a hand like Q-Js and get bet out of the pot, all I lose is the minimum. And I can call a modest-sized raise from an active player. But if I raise three times the big blind, I have tripled my losses when I get reraised and have to fold. A player who feels he has to raise with all his starting hands won't get to see as many flops as I get to see with hands like 8-8, K-Qs, and J-Ts. These are hands that you really don't want to shut yourself out of seeing a reasonably priced flop with. With these kinds of hands, you could flop a big hand and take another player's entire stack.

Playing my way, especially with the Ted Forrest mask, frequently takes me in the opposite direction of the crowd. If you ask Andy Bloch or Chris Ferguson what percentage of hands to play on the button, they will tell you about 50 percent, and they have some reasonable data and explanations for their numbers. With my loose image, ironically, I probably play a lot fewer hands than that on the button. Opponents think I'll play any two cards in that situation, so when I raise with one of the weaker hands they would play, they come over the top of me with reraises. I have to fold hands those guys can get away with playing. On the other hand, I'm happy when I play quality hands in those situations and find someone who wants to "teach me a lesson" and finds out I'm holding A-A or K-K.

Play After the Flop: The "Feel" Game

The real success in no-limit hold 'em tournaments (assuming a reasonable tournament structure) comes from playing well after the flop.
That's why I place a premium on being able to see more flops. I am
not an advocate of shutout poker. In other words, someone with A-A
moves all-in to shut out their competition and just wins the blinds and
antes. I really don't think that's maximizing your chances of winning
the tournament or your chances of creating a big stack. I think you
need to see some flops and be willing to take some chances. Have
the confidence in yourself that you'll be okay to play after the flop,
that you will make the right decisions often enough to warrant seeing some flops and taking a chance on getting a good situation where
you can be a big favorite to win a big pot from somebody or take
somebody's stack.

A lot of post-flop play is about feel, concentrating at the table, and
picking up on strength and weakness in your opponents. A lot of it is
experience and allowing yourself to see a lot of flops and play a lot
of flops and get comfortable with the different types of situations that
you're going to find yourself in. If all you do is shove in all your chips
before the flop to win the blinds or hope to win a race, you really miss
out on the learning experience of how to play after the flop.

My game relies on being able to understand my opponents. A lot
of reading opponents and feeling strength and weakness does come
naturally, but it can be improved upon too, to a certain point. The
ability to read people can be improved, simply by focusing and concentrating and being in the moment at the table.

When you're not in the hand, look at what the players are doing
around you. Concentrate. See what types of hands players turn over
and remember the betting patterns that preceded them. By the way
players conduct themselves during the hand you should try to get a
general sense of strength or a general sense of weakness and see if
this corresponds to what they turn over. You can hone your sense of
feel at the table by concentrating, focusing, and being in the moment.

Here's what you can say to yourself. Watch a player in a hand. See
the amount that he bets when he's leading in the hand. Ask yourself,

"What was this player trying to accomplish with this size of a bet and this action on the flop, this size of a bet on the turn, this action on the turn, and this bet on the river? What is the feeling that this player is trying to convey? What does he want his opponent to do?" Does that feeling correspond with what you see when he turns over his hand? When you are correct, you can start to trust your judgment with this player when he takes similar actions. When he does something different, ask yourself, "What is he trying to accomplish with this different action?"

I know there are certain physical signs that correlate to strength or weakness, but even that only takes you so far. You're not looking for particular signals or going through a checklist. You want to give yourself a chance to develop an overall feeling based on the whole picture.

It's not always easy to articulate this. It's just a feeling you get at the table. Ask yourself, "How is this player trying to manipulate his opponent or me in this case? What is he hoping that I will do, based on the strength of his hand?" And then disappoint him.

It's a combination of betting patterns and a general feeling. "Is this guy lying? Is this guy comfortable and he's telling the truth? Is this guy legitimately uncomfortable? Does this guy want me to think he's uncomfortable because he has it and he wants me to call a big bet? What is it that he wants me to do? What is it that he truly wants me to do? Does he truly want me to call because he has the best hand? Does he truly want me to fold because he doesn't think he has the best hand?" When you can confidently answer these questions, you can take the appropriate action.

If you look hard enough, if you feel the truth of the situation, the truth will come out and you'll know what to do. This might be a little too Zen, but just because it is difficult to describe and not objective doesn't mean you can't try to use it at the table to improve your game. You probably have some kind of an innate genetic potential for how much truth you are capable of seeing. But how much truth at the table you are capable of seeing can be improved upon by relaxing, concentrating, focusing, feeling, and learning. And if you do this—stay in the moment, concentrate, focus, and pay attention—you should be able to approach your innate potential for seeing the truth.

This kind of focus isn't easy. I joke that I can play for a hundred hours straight, but it's hard to be completely focused for more than forty. In a tournament, especially at the World Series where there is a different tournament every day (or, if you do well, you are playing on from a previous day's tournament), it is hard to maintain that super level of concentration and focus for a full tournament. But what you can do is try to maintain that focus and concentration when it's important. *When it's really important is when you have accrued a big stack.* That's when you really want to maintain your focus and concentration level.

It's much harder keeping a big stack than getting one. You want to take chances to get that big stack, but once you have it, protect it. Focus and concentrate, because now you have put yourself in a situation where you could be looking at a huge payday.

Two Examples

The editor of this book, Michael Craig, wrote an article about me for *Card Player* magazine in which we described two hands I played at the final table of the 2005 Mirage World Poker Showdown that illustrate my ideas about how no-limit hold 'em is part art and part science.

At this final table, it seemed like I was going to be able to see some flops. This isn't always the case at no-limit hold 'em final tables, especially on the World Poker Tour. But based on the players and the stack sizes, it seemed like there was a chance to play. It was still early and we were four-handed when I picked up a 4-4 in the big blind. The only caller was Thang "Kiddo" Pham, the chip leader, in the small blind. There was 72,000 in the pot.

I thought if I could flop a set, I might win a big pot. Otherwise, I would risk a small bet if it was checked to me and I thought my pair was still good. I checked.

The flop was

I got my set but it was a dangerous flop. Pham checked to me and I bet the pot. He raised it to 220,000. I thought he was bluffing, or semi-bluffing, and I didn't want him to stop, so I just called. There was now over 500,000 in the pot.

The third spade, a king, came on the turn. Pham checked and I bet 300,000. (I started the hand with about 1.3 million, so I had 800,000 left after the bet.) He immediately raised all-in. Kiddo then started playing to the camera and the crowd. He got up and walked around, going into the audience. He stood behind me and massaged my shoulders. He looked at me through the camera.

Obviously, when I bet the 300,000, I didn't think he had spades. I bet an amount that would make it unprofitable for him to call with one spade but that he might call with hands I could beat, like two pair or a king.

The first thing I do in this situation is ask myself, "Does it feel like the guy's got it?" As I thought back through the hand, his betting was completely consistent with spades: checking the flop, check-raising as a semi-bluff, checking when he made the flush to get me to bet, then moving all-in. His antics were consistent with the flush (or if he flopped a straight).

Usually, when someone is bluffing, they try to be as inconspicuous as possible. He sure wasn't doing that. He looked pretty confident.

Then I thought about the tournament situation. If I folded, I would still have 800,000 in chips left. That was enough even at 20,000-40,000 blinds for a fair amount of play. I could still finish in the top three, instead of fourth if I called and was wrong.

My first impression was that he had the flush. He had so many chips that he didn't need to take this kind of risk for almost all his chips. I had played with him the day before and he played very solid.

Then I weighed the reasons not to fold. Pham could have been raising with several nonbluffing hands I could beat, like kings, kings up, or any two pair. Then I added in the ten outs I had on the river to beat a straight or flush if my call turned out to be a crying call.

I thought for about two minutes, which seems like a long time in a poker game when nothing else is happening. I wasn't assigning percentages, but I decided that I had the following in my favor: the likelihood he was bluffing, the likelihood he wasn't bluffing but had a hand I could beat, and the likelihood I could outdraw him if he had a flush or straight.

I finally called.

Kiddo turned over 9-5o, no spades. He was drawing dead on the river. After eliminating Pham a few hands later, I had 3 million in chips. Chris Bell had 1.8 million. Gavin Smith had 1.5 million.

The second hand took place about thirty hands later. Chris Bell had shifted gears and started playing very aggressively, making big bets in every pot he played. He took over the chip lead, 2.6 million to my 2.3 million. With blinds of 25,000-50,000 and a 5,000 ante, there was 90,000 in the pot, and I picked up A♣-J♣ on the button. I raised to 140,000. Chris called in the small blind and Gavin folded. There was 370,000 in the pot. The flop was

I bet 170,000, and Chris called, which was good. I wanted him to call.

The deuce of spades came on the turn. There was now over 800,000 in the pot. I bet 250,000. Chris check-raised to 700,000. I thought about it for a while. I felt my A-J was the best hand, so I asked myself, "What's the best way to play it?" Chris had 1.4 million left; I had 1.2 million. If I reraised, he might throw away his hand, so I just called. I wanted him to try to bluff on the river.

The river card was another seven, the seven of clubs. Bell pushed all-in. I went into the tank on this one. He went into the audience and talked with some people who had come to watch. Based on his actions, I thought he wanted me to call. He looked very natural, not like any of this was forced. Even though I thought he would bluff at the river, I didn't think he would move all-in. If he had bluffed off 750,000, that would have crippled him but he would still have nearly 1 million left, enough to fight with Gavin Smith for second.

I had a feeling that he could beat top pair, because of that seven on the river, so I folded. Chris had 7-6. I'd like to think that with any other card, he would have bluffed at the pot but I'd have gotten a different vibe.

I hope these hands illustrate that there isn't some magic signal I follow. I try to use everything: mannerisms, betting patterns, the odds, the tournament situation. Even after all that, there may not be a clear answer. The important thing to get out of these examples is that you should focus on all the information available and make the best decision you can. You can't avoid having to make some difficult decisions. No matter how much you know, you are going to be wrong sometimes, or be right and still lose. But your best results are from always being open to learning and trying new things at the poker table.

Conclusion

There are a lot of ways to play tournament poker successfully. *Teaching* successful poker requires focusing on the fundamentals. I am the son of teachers and you can see from the chapters I have contributed on stud eight-or-better and razz that I consider the fundamentals to be very important. But the fundamentals aren't absolutes. There are ways to succeed where you contradict the fundamentally correct approach. Because so much of poker involves adjusting to your opponents and how they adjust to you, your best bet is sometimes doing the opposite of everybody else. In fact, it is highly likely that I will do the opposite, at least until the other players adjust and start trying to outguess me by playing fundamentally wrong themselves.

CHAPTER 6

No-Limit Hold 'Em: Play Before the Flop

by Andy Bloch

Introduction—A Single Framework

Play before the flop in no-limit hold 'em can be studied like chess openings, even though no one looks at it that way. Every decent chess player has studied chess openings. But very few poker players have studied poker "openings" other than generally knowing that you should "tighten up" in early position and play more hands in late position and categorize hands in groups like "big pairs" and "suited connectors."

Of course, poker differs from chess in the key way that it is a game of incomplete information. You can obtain an advantage in poker that you can't in chess by observing how your opponents play. There is no disadvantage, however, to starting from the chess analogy and studying opening play. You *should* vary your pre-flop play in certain situations (though not as often as most players think), but mostly you should follow a single framework. Even when you vary from it, your different play should be based on that framework. I admit that I do not play this precisely before the flop, though I should. Preparing this section of the book has made me rethink and sharpen my approach.

The single framework is the ranking of the hands, along with the percentage of how often you will be dealt those hands (or better

60

hands). When you have the exact ranking, instead of having general groups or categories, you can make better decisions before the flop.

There are many ways your game can benefit from starting with precise information. For one thing, knowing these percentages prevents you from getting taken advantage of. If you raise in late position and get reraised, you may suspect your opponent is restealing. If you aren't really sure, you want to play in a way that makes it unprofitable for an opponent to resteal indiscriminately. Knowing where your hand falls in the range of hands you are playing—and what your opponent could reraise with and not be restealing—will help you decide whether to call. Many players correctly raise with a lot of hands in late position but then too frequently fold to a reraise.

Ranking Starting Hands

I am going to give you a ranking I developed for starting hands and explain where it came from. (At the end of the chapter in tables 6.7 through 6.10, I will provide some additional hand rankings, based on how hands do against certain classes of hands—random hands, top-half hands, top-quarter hands, and top 10 percent hands.) But ranking the hands is an objective exercise only if you make certain subjective assumptions. Many things can change the value of the hands, including if there will be further betting, stack sizes, and whether you are betting or calling. Therefore, you should modify the rankings as you see fit, or replace them if you find or develop something you like more.

There are several ways of ranking starting hands. You can see how each hand does against a random hand. Or you can gather data on how opponents play and rank the hands to take advantage of those findings. Or you could track your online tournament play and see which hands win the most chips and which lose the most. The important thing is to have *some* ranking system that you are willing to trust.

These methods require enormous amounts of data and work, but at least you have tools today to assist you if you want to go the route of developing your own rankings: online poker and hand-simulating

Web sites and software. When I started playing tournament poker in the mid-nineties, those tools weren't around or were not sufficiently advanced. I wanted to generate a hand ranking, so I created a simple poker-game simulation on my computer and spent months running hands on it. (I didn't learn until later that Chris Ferguson, at the exact same time, was doing the exact same thing.)

The game we simulated was a heads-up game where the small blind had to move all-in or fold. Even though these rankings don't specifically account for post-flop play, the data organized the hands very well, placing the premium hands at the top and the lesser playable hands below them, with a reasonable mix of hands that play well *against* those premium hands.

I have made some modifications based on obvious differences between tournaments and a jam-or-fold game. In jam-or-fold, A-K comes out ahead of K-K, which makes sense for that game. If you have a huge stack and you're going to push all-in or fold, A-K reduces the likelihood that you are facing A-A or K-K, the only two hands that really cripple A-K. Whether A-K is higher than K-K or vice versa doesn't matter much in tournament play. Both are at the very top of the rankings and you are going to play both very strong. I moved K-K above A-Ks and A-Ko, however, because it could make a tiny difference when you decide what to do when you are reraised. I put both A-K hands ahead of Q-Q, though that is questionable. At least with A-Ko, you could rank it below Q-Q if you want.

You should consider modifying the rankings based on your post-flop play. It might be difficult to take records at casino tournaments, but you can when you play online. Go back over your hands and see which hands you play well and which you don't. If you think you play suited connectors really well, you can move them up slightly in the rankings. If you don't feel comfortable playing ace-rag, then move those hands down.

There are 1,326 possible two-card combinations in a fifty-two-card deck. If we ignore the suits of the cards (except for whether they are suited or unsuited), the number of possible combinations is 169. You will not receive these hands with equal frequency. For each pair (e.g., 7-7), there are six possible combinations. For each suited hand (e.g., 8-7s), there are four. For unsuited hands (e.g., 8-7o), there are twelve.

The percentages refer to the frequency with which you will be dealt a particular hand or a better one.

In the simulation I developed, these were the rankings (with modifications) based on what I would raise with from the small blind. In a calling situation—like where someone raised and you are in the blind—you should consider moving up the suited connectors and lowering ace-rag. Ace-rag is a difficult hand to play after the flop if you call a raise with it out of position. Unless it is suited, you will rarely get a flop where you are happy getting action. Suited connectors will hit (or clearly miss) a lot more flops. (The jam-or-fold table, both for raising in the small blind and for calling in the big blind, is table 6.6, included later in this chapter.)

Pre-flop, every hand you bet is a semi-bluff or a value bet. If you have aces, you are making a value bet. If you have T-9s, you are making a semi-bluff. There are two types of semi-bluffing hands: hands that are less likely to get called but have little equity when they are called, and hands that run into more premium hands but have more equity against them. For example, A-5o has little equity against A-A but is only half as likely as 7-6s to run into A-A. The ace in your hand means there are only three A-A combinations left in the deck, instead of six.

If you do get called, however, hands like A-5o and K-Q don't have much equity against premium hands like A-A and A-K. Therefore, A-5o is better for raising than 7-6s, but 7-6s is better than A-5o for calling a raise. You should keep that in mind when using or adapting these rankings.

Let me explain why A-5s appears so high in the rankings. A-5s is a very interesting hand. It is a good semi-bluffing hand because it cuts in half the chance you will get called by A-A or by A-X and run into an ace on the board. You can make straights and flushes with it. In addition, if your opponents catch you raising with A-5s, they are likely to misconstrue how you actually play. You should consider including a hand like this toward the top of your rankings. You could instead put a hand like 9-8s in the top 10 percent. If you pick up the blinds and antes, it doesn't matter what you had. If you get action and hit your hand, you might get paid extra if you raised in early position because they couldn't put you on this kind of hand.

TABLE 6.1 ◆ RANKINGS OF 169 TWO-CARD COMBINATIONS

Rank	Hand	Frequency	Rank	Hand	Frequency	Rank	Hand	Frequency	Rank	Hand	Frequency
1	A-A	0.5%	43	A-6s	18.6%	85	J-6s	41.5%	127	T-6o	69.8%
2	K-K	0.9%	44	Q-8s	18.9%	86	K-8o	42.4%	128	J-3o	70.7%
3	A-Ks	1.2%	45	Q-Jo	19.8%	87	T-8o	43.3%	129	9-6o	71.6%
4	A-Ko	2.1%	46	J-8s	20.1%	88	6-4s	43.6%	130	J-2o	72.5%
5	Q-Q	2.6%	47	K-7s	20.4%	89	K-7o	44.5%	131	9-3s	72.9%
6	A-Qs	2.9%	48	A-2s	20.7%	90	K-6o	45.4%	132	T-5o	73.8%
7	J-J	3.3%	49	A-9o	21.6%	91	J-5s	45.7%	133	T-4o	74.7%
8	T-T	3.8%	50	A-8o	22.5%	92	Q-4s	46.0%	134	9-5o	75.6%
9	A-Js	4.1%	51	8-7s	22.8%	93	9-5s	46.3%	135	9-2s	75.9%
10	A-5s	4.4%	52	Q-To	23.7%	94	K-5o	47.2%	136	T-3o	76.8%
11	K-Qs	4.7%	53	A-7o	24.6%	95	8-7o	48.1%	137	T-2o	77.7%
12	A-Ts	5.0%	54	J-To	25.5%	96	J-4s	48.4%	138	8-5o	78.6%
13	A-Qo	5.9%	55	K-To	26.4%	97	Q-3s	48.7%	139	8-3s	78.9%
14	K-Js	6.2%	56	A-5o	27.3%	98	Q-8o	49.6%	140	9-4o	79.8%
15	Q-Js	6.5%	57	9-7s	27.6%	99	K-4o	50.5%	141	7-5o	80.7%
16	K-Ts	6.8%	58	K-6s	27.9%	100	Q-2s	50.8%	142	8-2s	81.0%
17	9-9	7.2%	59	T-7s	28.2%	101	K-3o	51.7%	143	9-3o	81.9%
18	A-Jo	8.1%	60	7-6s	28.5%	102	J-8o	52.6%	144	7-3s	82.2%
19	Q-Ts	8.4%	61	A-4o	29.4%	103	7-4s	52.9%	145	6-5o	83.1%
20	8-8	8.9%	62	A-6o	30.3%	104	K-2o	53.8%	146	5-3s	83.4%
21	J-Ts	9.2%	63	J-7s	30.6%	105	T-5s	54.1%	147	6-3s	83.7%

Rank	Hand	Frequency	Rank	Hand	Frequency	Rank	Hand	Frequency	Rank	Hand	Frequency
22	7-7	9.7%	64	K-5s	30.9%	106	9-7o	55.1%	148	8-4o	84.6%
23	6-6	10.1%	65	8-6s	31.2%	107	J-3s	55.4%	149	9-2o	85.5%
24	5-5	10.6%	66	A-3o	32.1%	108	T-4s	55.7%	150	4-3s	85.8%
25	A-9s	10.9%	67	6-5s	32.4%	109	Q-7o	56.6%	151	7-4o	86.7%
26	K-Qo	11.8%	68	A-2o	33.3%	110	7-6o	57.5%	152	5-4o	87.6%
27	K-9s	12.1%	69	Q-7s	33.6%	111	Q-6o	58.4%	153	7-2s	87.9%
28	4-4	12.5%	70	T-9o	34.5%	112	T-7o	59.3%	154	6-4o	88.8%
29	T-9s	12.8%	71	9-6s	34.8%	113	Q-5o	60.2%	155	5-2s	89.1%
30	J-9s	13.1%	72	Q-6s	35.1%	114	J-7o	61.1%	156	6-2s	89.4%
31	A-8s	13.4%	73	K-4s	35.4%	115	J-2s	61.4%	157	8-3o	90.3%
32	Q-9s	13.7%	74	K-9o	36.3%	116	Q-4o	62.3%	158	8-2o	91.3%
33	K-Jo	14.6%	75	7-5s	36.7%	117	8-4s	62.6%	159	4-2s	91.6%
34	3-3	15.1%	76	J-9o	37.6%	118	Q-3o	63.5%	160	7-3o	92.5%
35	A-To	16.0%	77	5-4s	37.9%	119	T-3s	63.8%	161	5-3o	93.4%
36	A-7s	16.3%	78	Q-9o	38.8%	120	Q-2o	64.7%	162	6-3o	94.3%
37	K-8s	16.6%	79	T-6s	39.1%	121	8-6o	65.6%	163	3-2s	94.6%
38	9-8s	16.9%	80	9-8o	40.0%	122	J-6o	66.5%	164	4-3o	95.5%
39	A-4s	17.2%	81	Q-5s	40.3%	123	J-5o	67.4%	165	7-2o	96.4%
40	A-3s	17.5%	82	K-3s	40.6%	124	T-2s	67.7%	166	5-2o	97.3%
41	T-8s	17.8%	83	K-2s	40.9%	125	9-4s	68.0%	167	6-2o	98.2%
42	2-2	18.3%	84	8-5s	41.2%	126	J-4o	68.9%	168	4-2o	99.1%
									169	3-2o	

Getting "caught" playing a hand like A-5s or 9-8s as a premium hand confuses your opponents. If they see you raise with A-5s, they may assume you will similarly value any ace-rag suited. If they think you play that way, if you raise and bet out after a flop of 8-3-3, they can't automatically say, "He can't have a three." Likewise, if they find you raising in early position with 9-8s, they are going to have trouble convincing themselves you missed a flop like 8-7-6 on your *next* early-position raise.

You can pick some hands for out-of-character raises based on situations. If they are letting you steal, you can raise with a few more hands. If you are card dead, you can risk raising with a weaker than usual hand because the table may have you pegged as too tight. If you succeed in stealing in those situations, fine. If you have to play the hand and the table sees it, you gain the benefit from deception. But choose your situations carefully. With the whole table to act behind you, you can easily get into trouble if you play a lot of hands like 9-8s and A-5s in early position.

Deception is also a reason to keep low pairs among your premium hands. Without small pairs, your top 10 percent doesn't include any hands with cards lower than ten. If you don't raise with the small pairs, you will be giving your opponents too much information when you raise.

Hands to Play by Position as the First Raiser

If you open with a raise—and I think you should always enter first with a raise of about three times the big blind—your raises should succeed in picking up the blinds and antes approximately 50 percent of the time. Your opponents should be playing about half of your raising hands. After you open, smart opponents will be calling or reraising with about half the hands you are going to open with.

Why should they call a raise with only half the hands? Put yourself in their position and simplify it by using numbers instead of cards. Instead of being dealt cards, everybody at the table is given a two-digit number with the highest number winning. Each person decides to play or not play in turn. If you follow someone who decides to play their number and you know they play only numbers 80 and higher, you are going to win exactly half the time if you play 90 and more than half the time when you play higher numbers. Why would you play any more numbers than that? You don't want to bet money if you are going to win less than half the time.

There are other variables in a poker game that influence these calculations slightly in one direction or the other, but they tend to even out. If there is dead money in the pot, you might play a little more than half the hands of the player before you. If you have players after you, you have to worry about their having superior hands, so that would encourage you to play fewer hands.

If you are in the big blind, the equation is different. You have money in the pot so you don't have to call the entire bet. That encourages calling more. Also, if you have to call an all-in bet, you don't have to worry about playing out of position. Therefore, you aren't worried about whether you have a better hand. You just want to make sure you get the right odds to call.

If someone raises in early position with eight players to act and you are two players to their left, you have to worry about the six players to act after you. You want a hand that is better than the raiser's average hand. If you are just calling, you might also play if you have a hand that plays well after the flop and/or in multiway pots. If you have control over your opponent, you might call with hands outside the range to play following an early-position raise, like Q-Js, J-Ts, or 5-5. (To do this, you need to conclude that the players behind you are tight and will fold around to the raise and call, or are passive and will call rather than reraise following the raise and your call.)

Say an opponent raises under the gun. You think they are playing reasonably, so they have a top 11 percent hand or better (in a tournament without antes)—A-9s, 5-5, or better. If you are the player to their immediate left, you have to eliminate a lot of hands. You can't play the *worst* hands they would play, so you shouldn't be playing 6-6, 5-5, or A-9s. (Later in this section, in my explanation of playing after a raise, I will describe circumstances in which you deviate from playing the top-half hands your opponent is playing.) You should be playing a top 6 percent hand. Even that might be stretching it because you've got the rest of the table to act after you. Even if your opponent doesn't have a big hand, someone else at the table might.

To win the blinds 50 percent of the time in a game with antes, you should play the following percentage of hands in each position (column 2). In a game without antes, you have to play tighter. In column 3 is the percentage of hands with which you should make an opening raise when there are no antes.

TABLE 6.2 ◆ PLAYABLE HANDS BY POSITION*

Players to act	Percent to play (with antes)	Percent to play (without antes)
9 (under the gun)	15%	11%
8	16%	12%
7	18%	14%
6	22%	16%
5	26%	19%
4	32%	24%
3 (cutoff)	41%	31%
2 (button)	59%	45%

Methodology—I developed these percentages of playable hands in each position with the starting assumption that opponents are going to call or reraise with half the hands that you're playing with. Basically, opponents are going to call when they think they can beat your average hand.

The assumption that opponents will call or reraise with 50 percent of your raising hands isn't exact, but it is a good approximation. When you are in early position, the players to your immediate left have to worry about all the other players still to act and they'll probably play even tighter than that. The button (based on position) and the blinds (based on not having to call the entire raise) will play more than half your raising hands. I think overall, especially when you are in early position, those two things are going to counteract.

If you raise under the gun, the player to your left is probably going to muck A-Jo. In my ranking system, A-Jo is in the top 8 percent of the hands. You should raise with 15 percent of the hands and they should play about 7.5 percent of the hands. Even without these percentages, A-Jo *seems* like a borderline hand. In fact, A-Qo is probably a borderline hand for the player on your left if you raise under the gun and have not been raising a lot. Opponents are not going to play unless they have A-Qo or better. They might call with A-Js, but that is a tough call because A-Js does not play very well after the flop. The first few opponents to your left will probably play tighter. In the blinds, some players will play looser, though the under-the-gun raise usually gets a lot of respect.

These 50 percent estimates tend to be self-correcting. If you played in the manner I've described, then shift gears and start playing a lot more hands, your opponents will adjust. If, instead of playing 15 percent of your hands under the gun, you play 30 percent, the players to your left will no longer be afraid to play A-Jo against you. Therefore, it will no longer be profitable for you to raise with that many hands.

Likewise, if you advertised that you were going to play A-A, K-K, and nothing else, how do you think your opponents would adjust? They would play against you only with the 50 percent best hands you are playing: A-A.

To make raising worthwhile, you need to pick up the blinds and antes about 50 percent of the time. You are putting in three units with your raise, to win two and a half units (with antes). If you pick up the blinds and antes much more than 50 percent of the time, then you are breaking even on the blinds and antes, and freerolling on the flop. Usually, opponents will reraise rather than call and you will have to throw away your marginal hands. But when they call, your marginal hand still has equity. Therefore, if they play more than half your raising hands but a lot of those are calls—especially in the blinds—you will often pick up the pot after the flop. You may even hit your hand and get paid off.

Without antes, you are betting three units to win just one and a half. That's why you play tighter when there are no antes and stealing isn't as important. Getting everybody to fold 50 percent of the time is not enough of a profit if you lose a lot of your hands when they don't fold, especially because you will probably be betting at least once more, increasing the cost of raising without very strong cards.

So how did I get from these 50 percent assumptions to percentages of playable hands? Say you are playing a tournament hand and everybody folds to you on the button. To win the pot 50 percent of the time, you want the big and small blinds to each fold 70 percent of the time ($.7 \times .7 = .49$, or approximately 50 percent). That means they are, on average, each calling about 30 percent of the time. If they are calling with your average hand or better, then you should raise twice as often as their 30 percent average, or approximately 60 percent of the time. (I have rounded the numbers for this illustration.)

Having these numbers gives you a starting point for all your pre-flop decisions. Your instincts and ability to read the table are important, but now you don't have to make decisions in a vacuum. Everyone knows to "play tight up front" and "respect an early-position raise." The rankings and percentages of playable hands give you exact answers when you don't have any opponent-specific information.

TABLE 6.3   ◆   HANDS BY POSITION—ANTE TOURNAMENT*

Hands to Play with Nine Players to Act—15%	
Pairs	A-A, K-K, Q-Q, J-J, T-T, 9-9, 8-8, 7-7, 6-6, 5-5, 4-4
A-Xs	A-Ks, A-Qs, A-Js, A-5s, A-Ts, A-9s, A-8s
A-Xo	A-Ko, A-Qo, A-Jo
K-Xs	K-Qs, K-Js, K-Ts, K-9s
K-Xo	K-Qo, K-Jo
Q-Xs	Q-Js, Q-Ts, Q-9s
J-Xs	J-Ts, J-9s
T-Xs	T-9s

Hands to Play with Eight Players to Act—16%	
Pairs	A-A, K-K, Q-Q, J-J, T-T, 9-9, 8-8, 7-7, 6-6, 5-5, 4-4, **3-3**
A-Xs	A-Ks, A-Qs, A-Js, A-5s, A-Ts, A-9s, A-8s
A-Xo	A-Ko, A-Qo, A-Jo, **A-To**
K-Xs	K-Qs, K-Js, K-Ts, K-9s
K-Xo	K-Qo, K-Jo
Q-Xs	Q-Js, Q-Ts, Q-9s
J-Xs	J-Ts, J-9s
T-Xs	T-9s

---

*Hands in bold are those added in that position.

TABLE 6.3 ◆ **(Continued)**

Hands to Play with Seven Players to Act—18%

Pairs	A-A, K-K, Q-Q, J-J, T-T, 9-9, 8-8, 7-7, 6-6, 5-5, 4-4, 3-3
A-Xs	A-Ks, A-Qs, A-Js, A-5s, A-Ts, A-9s, A-8s, **A-7s, A-4s, A-3s**
A-Xo	A-Ko, A-Qo, A-Jo, A-To
K-Xs	K-Qs, K-Js, K-Ts, K-9s, **K-8s**
K-Xo	K-Qo, K-Jo
Q-Xs	Q-Js, Q-Ts, Q-9s
J-Xs	J-Ts, J-9s
T-Xs	T-9s **T-8s**
9-Xs	**9-8s**

Hands to Play with Six Players to Act—22%

Pairs	All (adding **2-2**)
A-Xs	All (adding **A-6s, A-2s**)
A-Xo	A-Ko, A-Qo, A-Jo, A-To, **A-9o**
K-Xs	K-Qs, K-Js, K-Ts, K-9s, K-8s, **K-7s**
K-Xo	K-Qo, K-Jo
Q-Xs	Q-Js, Q-Ts, Q-9s, **Q-8s**
Q-Xo	**Q-Jo**
J-Xs	J-Ts, J-9s, **J-8s**
T-Xs	T-9s T-8s
9-Xs	9-8s

Hands to Play with Five Players to Act—26%

Pairs	All
A-Xs	All
A-Xo	A-Ko, A-Qo, A-Jo, A-To, A-9o, **A-8o, A-7o**
K-Xs	K-Qs, K-Js, K-Ts, K-9s, K-8s, K-7s
K-Xo	K-Qo, K-Jo
Q-Xs	Q-Js, Q-Ts, Q-9s, Q-8s
Q-Xo	Q-Jo, **Q-To**
J-Xs	J-Ts, J-9s, J-8s
J-Xo	**J-To**
T-Xs	T-9s T-8s
9-Xs	9-8s
8-Xs	**8-7s**

(continued)

TABLE 6.3 ◆ *(Continued)*

	Hands to Play with Four Players to Act—32%
Pairs	All
A-Xs	All
A-Xo	A-Ko, A-Qo, A-Jo, A-To, A-9o, A-8o, A-7o, **A-6o, A-5o, A-4o**
K-Xs	K-Qs, K-Js, K-Ts, K-9s, K-8s, K-7s, **K-6s, K-5s**
K-Xo	K-Qo, K-Jo, **K-To**
Q-Xs	Q-Js, Q-Ts, Q-9s, Q-8s
Q-Xo	Q-Jo, Q-To
J-Xs	J-Ts, J-9s, J-8s, **J-7s**
J-Xo	J-To
T-Xs	T-9s, T-8s, **T-7s**
9-Xs	9-8s, **9-7s**
8-Xs	8-7s, **8-6s**
7-Xs	**7-6s**

	Hands to Play with Three Players to Act—41%
Pairs	All
A-Xs	All
A-Xo	All (adding **A-3o, A-2o**)
K-Xs	All (adding **K-4s, K-3s, K-2s**)
K-Xo	K-Qo, K-Jo, K-To, **K-9o**
Q-Xs	Q-Js, Q-Ts, Q-9s, Q-8s, **Q-7s, Q-6s, Q-5s**
Q-Xo	Q-Jo, Q-To, **Q-9o**
J-Xs	J-Ts, J-9s, J-8s, J-7s
J-Xo	J-To, **J-9o**
T-Xs	T-9s, T-8s, T-7s, **T-6s**
T-Xo	**T-9o**
9-Xs	9-8s, 9-7s, **9-6s**
9-Xo	**9-8o**
8-Xs	8-7s, 8-6s
7-Xs	7-6s, **7-5s**
6-Xs	**6-5s**
5-Xs	**5-4s**

	Hands to Play with Two Players to Act—59%
Pairs	All
A-Xs	All

TABLE 6.3 ◆ *(Continued)*

A-Xo	All
K-Xs	All
K-Xo	All (adding **K-8o, K-7o, K-6o, K-5o, K-4o, K-3o, K-2o**)
Q-Xs	All (adding **Q-4s, Q-3s, Q-2s**)
Q-Xo	Q-Jo, Q-To, Q-9o, **Q-8o, Q-7o, Q-6o**
J-Xs	J-Ts, J-9s, J-8s, J-7s, **J-6s, J-5s, J-4s, J-3s**
J-Xo	J-To, J-9o, **J-8o**
T-Xs	T-9s, T-8s, T-7s, T-6s, **T-5s, T-4s**
T-Xo	T-9o, **T-8o**
9-Xs	9-8s, 9-7s, 9-6s, **9-5s**
9-Xo	9-8o, **9-7o**
8-Xs	8-7s, 8-6s, **8-5s**
8-Xo	**8-7o**
7-Xs	7-6s, 7-5s, **7-4s**
7-Xo	**7-6o**
6-Xs	6-5s, **6-4s**
5-Xs	5-4s

Without antes, you need to play tighter. You are not gaining as much by raising, so you need to succeed more often. These percentages adjust for that, though you could roughly approximate these charts by using the ante-tournament charts and adding two players when you are in early position and one player when you are in late position.

TABLE 6.4 ◆ **HANDS BY POSITION—NO-ANTE TOURNAMENT***

	Hands to Play with Nine Players to Act—11%
Pairs	A-A, K-K, Q-Q, J-J, T-T, 9-9, 8-8, 7-7, 6-6, 5-5
A-Xs	A-Ks, A-Qs, A-Js, A-5s, A-Ts, A-9s
A-Xo	A-Ko, A-Qo, A-Jo
K-Xs	K-Qs, K-Js, K-Ts
Q-Xs	Q-Js, Q-Ts
J-Xs	J-Ts

(continued)

---

*Hands in bold are those added in that position.

TABLE 6.4 ◆ *(Continued)*

	Hands to Play with Eight Players to Act—12%
Pairs	A-A, K-K, Q-Q, J-J, T-T, 9-9, 8-8, 7-7, 6-6, 5-5
A-Xs	A-Ks, A-Qs, A-Js, A-5s, A-Ts, A-9s
A-Xo	A-Ko, A-Qo, A-Jo
K-Xs	K-Qs, K-Js, K-Ts
K-Xo	**K-Qo**
Q-Xs	Q-Js, Q-Ts
J-Xs	J-Ts

	Hands to Play with Seven Players to Act—14%
Pairs	A-A, K-K, Q-Q, J-J, T-T, 9-9, 8-8, 7-7, 6-6, 5-5, **4-4**
A-Xs	A-Ks, A-Qs, A-Js, A-5s, A-Ts, A-9s, **A-8s**
A-Xo	A-Ko, A-Qo, A-Jo
K-Xs	K-Qs, K-Js, K-Ts, **K-9s**
K-Xo	K-Qo
Q-Xs	Q-Js, Q-Ts, **Q-9s**
J-Xs	J-Ts, **J-9s**
T-Xs	**T-9s**

	Hands to Play with Six Players to Act—16%
Pairs	A-A, K-K, Q-Q, J-J, T-T, 9-9, 8-8, 7-7, 6-6, 5-5, 4-4, **3-3**
A-Xs	A-Ks, A-Qs, A-Js, A-5s, A-Ts, A-9s, A-8s
A-Xo	A-Ko, A-Qo, A-Jo, **A-To**
K-Xs	K-Qs, K-Js, K-Ts, K-9s
K-Xo	K-Qo, **K-Jo**
Q-Xs	Q-Js, Q-Ts, Q-9s
J-Xs	J-Ts, J-9s
T-Xs	T-9s

	Hands to Play with Five Players to Act—19%
Pairs	All (adding **2-2**)
A-Xs	A-Ks, A-Qs, A-Js, A-5s, A-Ts, A-9s, A-8s, **A-7s, A-6s, A-4s, A-3s**
A-Xo	A-Ko, A-Qo, A-Jo, A-To
K-Xs	K-Qs, K-Js, K-Ts, K-9s, **K-8s**
K-Xo	K-Qo, K-Jo
Q-Xs	Q-Js, Q-Ts, Q-9s, **Q-8s**

TABLE 6.4 ◆ *(Continued)*

J-Xs	J-Ts, J-9s
T-Xs	T-9s, **T-8s**
9-X s	**9-8s**

Hands to Play with Four Players to Act—24%

Pairs	All
A-Xs	All (adding **A-2s**)
A-Xo	A-Ko, A-Qo, A-Jo, A-To, **A-9o, A-8o**
K-Xs	K-Qs, K-Js, K-Ts, K-9s, K-8s, **K-7s**
K-Xo	K-Qo, K-Jo
Q-Xs	Q-Js, Q-T s, Q-9s, Q-8s
Q-Xo	**Q-Jo, Q-To**
J-Xs	J-Ts, J-9s, **J-8s**
T-Xs	T-9s T-8s
9-Xs	9-8s
8-Xs	**8-7s**

Hands to Play with Three Players to Act—31%

Pairs	All
A-Xs	All
A-Xo	A-Ko, A-Qo, A-Jo, A-To, A-9o, A-8o, **A-7o, A-6o, A-5o, A-4o**
K-Xs	K-Qs, K-Js, K-Ts, K-9s, K-8s, K-7s, **K-6s, K-5s**
K-Xo	K-Qo, K-Jo, **K-To**
Q-Xs	Q-Js, Q-Ts, Q-9s, Q-8s
Q-Xo	Q-Jo, Q-To
J-Xs	J-Ts, J-9s, J-8s, **J-7s**
J-Xo	**J-To**
T-Xs	T-9s, T-8s, **T-7s**
9-Xs	9-8s, **9-7s**
8-Xs	8-7s
7-Xs	**7-6s**

Hands to Play with Two Players to Act—45%

Pairs	All
A-Xs	All
A-Xo	All (adding **A-3o, A-2o**)

(continued)

TABLE 6.4	◆ (*Continued*)
K-Xs	All (adding **K-4s**, **K-3s**, **K-2s**)
K-Xo	K-Qo, K-Jo, K-To, **K-9o**, **K-8o**, **K-7o**
Q-Xs	Q-Js, Q-Ts, Q-9s, Q-8s, **Q-7s**, **Q-6s**, **Q-5s**
Q-Xo	Q-Jo, Q-To, **Q-9o**
J-Xs	J-Ts, J-9s, J-8s, J-7s, **J-6s**
J-Xo	J-To, **J-9o**
T-Xs	T-9s, T-8s, T-7s, **T-6s**
T-Xo	**T-9o**, **T-8o**
9-Xs	9-8s, 9-7s, **9-6s**
9-Xo	**9-8o**
8-Xs	8-7s, **8-6s**, **8-5s**
7-Xs	7-6s, **7-5s**
6-Xs	**6-5s**, **6-4s**
5-Xs	**5-4s**

Hands to Play When Someone Limps in Front

First limpers are giving away information and giving up value when they limp. If someone comes to your table and you know nothing about them, their limp could indicate a playing flaw, or they could be someone who limps only with a big hand. Not knowing, I would follow my regular strategy, except add two players to act behind you. If someone limps with four players to act and you are next, it is almost like there are six players to act. And if you raise, this person actually does act behind you, at least before the flop.

Also, I am more likely to limp after a limper with a lot of hands myself. If I am in middle position, I might be able to induce a multiway pot, which I'll do if I have the right kind of hand. Or, if I am in late position, I can play almost anything for one bet and try to flop two pair or better. If someone limps with a strong hand (like aces or A-Q or A-J), the way to punish them is to limp after them.

Try to understand what your opponent thinks is being accomplished by limping, especially an early-position limper. Very often, you will find if someone limps under the gun, they have A-T or A-J, a hand they want to play but are afraid to raise with. You will often see a lot of limpers with small or medium pairs. Then, of course, you have players who limp with a big hand.

Whatever they have, they are unlikely to fold for a small raise. You won't get them out of the pot or get much information by raising. You have position on them and you should use it to your advantage. The best way to punish them is to limp yourself.

If someone limps in late position, it's a different story. They just want to play a lot of hands. Either the 60 percent I recommend they raise with is not enough, or they want to play the bottom half of those hands but are afraid to raise with them. Or maybe they are trying to be tricky and get action with aces or kings by slow-playing. There are a lot of possibilities and you have to take them into account when executing your strategy.

The only time I advocate limping is in the small blind or following other limpers. If you are the type of player who likes to limp a lot, here is my advice: don't. Consider, at least, raising the minimum. This will give you some information on the strength of the hands of the big blind, the small blind, and the button.

Here is my advice to players who are confounded by limpers: don't try to change them. You want to encourage them to keep limping, because you'd much rather have that compared with having them raise and force you to fold a marginal hand that could bust a superior hand by hitting the flop just right. Limp right along, liberally playing hands like 7-6s and 7-5s, and maybe folding off-suit ace-rag.

Some players seem to be on a mission to stop others from limping, trying to pick up multiple-limper pots by making large raises in the blinds. You want to tighten up when you are sandwiched in one of those situations. If you see it coming, this might be the rare instance in which I'd recommend limping with a monster.

But realize that you don't have to be the traffic cop in that situation. Those indiscriminate raisers are not doing themselves (or you) a favor by raising. All they will "succeed" in doing is getting the limpers to play properly, either folding or raising. Between limping on my blind and raising it, I'd much rather have opponents limp. If I can flop two pair or better, I can get someone who limped with kings to double me up.

Obviously, if the limper has been at the table a while and doesn't play many hands, it could be that he is just very, very tight and passive, or he is trying to slow-play aces. You might want to limp behind this player, unless you are worried about getting sandwiched. It is a great position to be in, knowing you are facing a monster hand but getting to see the flop cheap. You can lose a small pot—just the one call before the flop—or win all your opponent's chips. But with a lot of players behind you, you have to be careful about someone in late position making a move because of all the limpers.

It's easy to get into trouble with a strong hand when someone limps in early position. Once, with two tables to go in a tournament, I was in the small blind with Q-Q. After an early-position limper, there was a late-position raise. It is hard to follow a hunch that someone is slow-playing a better hand than Q-Q and throw it away, so I called. The limper reraised all-in and the original raiser folded.

Did this player limp with A-A? I have seen people make this play with J-Ts. I've made that play myself. The early limper hadn't been limping, so the raiser could have limped with A-Js. Getting three to two to call, I doubled up the limper, who had K-K. Be prepared, if there is an early limp followed by a raise, for the limp reraise. Think carefully before raising a limper.

Hands to Play When Someone Has Raised

When someone has raised in front of you, when you are either acting after them or are in the small or big blind, you have to make two decisions: whether to play and, if you play, whether to call or reraise.

The decision whether to play is pretty simple. You want to play half the hands the raiser is playing. Start with the hands they *should* be playing, adjusting for what you have learned about them at the table.

If the game has antes, you should play the percentage of hands, based on the position of the raiser, indicated in table 6.5, column 2. If there are no antes and your opponents are playing tighter, you too will play tighter following a raise (column 3).

Also consider your position in the hand. How many more players are there to act behind you? If you are both still in early position,

TABLE 6.5 ◆ **PLAYABLE HANDS BY POSITION AFTER A RERAISE**

Players to act	Percent to play (with antes)	Percent to play (without antes)
8	8%	6%
7	9%	7%
6	11%	8%
5	13%	9%
4	16%	12%
3 (cutoff)	20%	15%
2 (button)	30%	22%

you want to play tighter. If you are on the button, you can call a lot of raises and try to outplay the raiser after the flop.

If you are in the big blind, you can call more raises because you don't have to call the full amount of the bet. You can also close the betting by calling. After the flop, you benefit, at least for one betting round, by having quasi-position on the raiser. If you call the raise and check the flop, most players who raised before the flop will bet. Your check reveals very little information and you will probably get to act after the raiser on the flop.

The top 5 percent hands are almost always playable after a raise: A-A, K-K, Q-Q, J-J, T-T, A-K, A-Q, A-Js, K-Qs, and A-Ts. A-5s is also in the top 5 percent but that hand is there for deception. You have to be more careful playing this hand following a raise than most of the others. Just outside the top 5 percent are hands like K-Js and Q-Js, which probably play better after more flops, or at least make for easier decision-making after the flop.

If you conclude your hand is playable after a raise, do you call or reraise? You will make that judgment based on several factors: avoiding being predictable, stack sizes, position, and how your hand will play after the flop.

If there was an "always" rule, it would be that you call with the very strongest and most speculative hands and reraise with the medium-strength hands and those that have the most problems playing after the flop. But there are few, if any, "always" plays in no-limit hold 'em tournaments. If you play certain hands in a specific way, your opponents will pick up on it and outplay you. Therefore, even the general guidelines I give you require you to consider specific circumstances for making the best play. Those circumstances usually make one play better than another and also have the benefit of encouraging you to mix up your play, playing the same hands in different ways and playing different hands in the same way.

You will never be deciding in a vacuum, but if you did, you would call with hands like A-A, K-K, and suited connectors. You can afford to see a flop with aces; you *need* to see it with suited connectors. You would reraise with hands like Q-Q, J-J, and T-T. Pocket pairs, unless you make a set, force you to make difficult decisions after the flop.

Just as what you have observed about the raiser affects whether to play, that same information affects whether you call or reraise. Against tight opponents, you will tend to call more. You have to give them credit for having a very strong hand. If you are starting with the better hand, they could go broke overvaluing their hand after the flop. If you are starting out behind, you can see the flop and try to break them if the board hits you just right.

Position and stack size will frequently influence your decision whether to call or reraise. If you are out of position and your stack is small enough to reasonably get all-in before the flop, you should reraise with pocket pairs like Q-Q, J-J, and T-T. Not only can you benefit from picking up the pot right away, but just calling with those hands can lead to a lot of difficult decisions on the flop.

Reraising makes sense for a lot of reasons in this situation. First, you aren't getting the right odds to call for the purpose of hitting a set. Say you have 10,000 in chips, blinds are 300-600, antes are 75, and a raiser in front of you makes it 1,800. Your maximum payoff for calling and flopping the set is roughly 12,000—on average it will be much less—not enough to justify risking 1,800 for all the times you don't make the set and have to fold. Unless you hit a set, T-T doesn't play very well after the flop, especially when you are out of position.

Second, unless you limped and are now facing a raise from behind, you are in the big or small blind. Particularly if the raise came from a player in late position, you are pretty likely to have the best hand and you want to take the opportunity to keep that player, especially if they are an aggressive player, from thinking they can run over you.

If you are going to raise and can reasonably get all-in, then you should do it. A three-times reraise in this situation would cost you more than half your stack. You would be pot-committed, so if you raise at all, you should move all-in. This also keeps you from having to make decisions about your hand after the flop, and takes away the raiser's positional advantage.

If you have position on the raiser with one of those hands and you have a fairly short stack, you probably want to reraise as well. There will still be players to act behind you and your call of the raise could encourage them to call. Those pocket pairs play even worse post-flop multiway than heads-up (unless you make a set). If you have a fairly big stack, you can reraise a late-position raiser, though you are more likely to call an early-position raiser.

There are players who will just call with pairs and push all-in on the flop unless there is an ace or king on the board. Those people are probably going to get outplayed. What if the late-position raiser had K-J and would have folded to your reraise? In late position, the raiser could have had K-5s or Q-9s. If you don't reraise, you are finished against those opponents. They can win all your chips, but you usually can't do much better than picking up the pre-flop chips with this strategy.

When you have position on the raiser and a big enough stack where you can't reasonably get all-in before the flop, you want to just call with those pairs. If you have 20,000 in the previous example, the outcome is much different. I would usually call with J-J or T-T, especially against an early-position raiser. If they are aggressive, I might reraise them with Q-Q.

An important ratio to consider is the amount in your stack compared with the size of the raise. Just like raising with ten times or less the big blind commits you to the pot, a stack of ten times or less the size of the raise commits you if you reraise. With 20,000, you are right on the borderline. A reasonable reraise would be to 6,000, about one-third of your stack. What are you going to do if the original raiser moves all-in? What if the original raiser calls your reraise and moves in after the flop? If you think T-T is the best hand before the flop, why not push in? And if you think you're behind and need to hit your set, why raise?

If you want to just call, you are getting the right odds to call with a pocket pair and hit a set. You have a 12 percent chance of flopping a set (or better). Therefore, to break even on your call of 1,800, you would need to make about 15,000 or more when you hit. If you have 20,000 at the start of the hand, the chances you'll get paid off are pretty good. Occasionally, your opponent could make a bigger set or some other bigger hand, but you'll still be getting the right odds if you've got a stack of approximately ten times the size of the raise.

If you have less than ten times the big blind, you aren't getting the right odds to call and flop a set. Therefore, you shouldn't try this with low or medium pairs. You will usually push in or fold 5-5. If you reraise all-in with a hand like 5-5, assuming you are not facing an under-the-gun raise from a tight player, you can get a lot of players to fold and pick up the blinds, antes, and the money from the raise. And you may get action from overcards where you are a favorite.

With ten times their bet or less, you're thinking about getting all the chips in right away with pocket pairs, as well as hands like A-K or A-Q. But not with A-A, maybe K-K, K-Q, and the suited connectors. You should usually call with those and try to get paid off after the flop. You want to balance your calls among different kinds of hands. You don't want your opponents to put you on A-A when you call their raise. You have to play those other hands the same way and just call. There will be some hands you just call with. But not too many.

If your stack is above these threshold amounts—ten times the size of the big blind, ten times the size of the raise—you are not as likely to push it. With a big stack, you are not likely to get outplayed too badly if your goal is to call to flop a set. You are getting the right odds to do that and you can get away from your hand if you miss.

Although I have been referring to the size of *your* stack when considering these things, your decisions should be similar if your stack is bigger but *your opponent's* stack is less than one of the threshold amounts. Therefore, if the blinds are 300-600 and you have 100,000 and your opponent has 20,000, you should play the hand the same way as if the stack sizes were reversed. For example, it doesn't make sense, just because you have a big stack, to put in a raise that pot-commits one of you—in this case, your opponent—without betting enough to put him all-in. Otherwise, if your opponent understands the game, if he is going to call your raise and play the hand, he will push in. You'll end up making the same decision for the same amount of chips, except you will be calling someone's all-in bet, rather than putting them to the decision. You lose whatever value your bigger raise would have had to make him fold.

If you both have deep stacks and your opponent plays back at you, you should take into consideration position and playing styles. If my opponent has raised on the button, I will reraise from the blinds with hands like T-T. My hand is probably good, plus it gives me a chance to make the button stop stealing my blind.

But what if you reraise that late-position raiser with T-T and he pushes in? Then you have a difficult decision to make. It depends on the opponent. There are a lot of players who assume that if someone reraises on the button, they must be stealing. Of course, they will have a real hand sometimes. *3-3*   *T-T*

I saw a hand where Dan Harrington, on the button, raised Erik Seidel's big blind. Erik reraised and Dan pushed in. Erik called. Dan turned over 3-3. Erik had T-T. Some other players were amazed, but it made perfect sense. Dan knows Erik likes to reraise when people raise on the button and Erik's in the blind. Because of that, Dan's going to reraise a lot. So Erik's going to call when Dan reraises. Then they get it all-in and you see 3-3 called by T-T.

This was similar to a key hand between me and Jim Bechtel at the final table of the $50,000 H.O.R.S.E. at the 2006 World Series of Poker. We were four-handed. I had about 1.6 million in chips and Jim had 1.2 million. Blinds were 12,000-24,000 and there was a 4,000 ante. Jim raised to 80,000 from the button on my big blind. I looked down and saw T-T. (I had eliminated T. J. Cloutier with T-T against 7-7 just a few minutes earlier.) I reraised to 280,000. Bechtel pushed all-in.

It was about 770,000 more to me and I called. Jim had 7-7 and my hand held up. I had to call with T-T because I know Jim Bechtel is an aggressive player. I also know that he knows I'm an aggressive player, capable of reraising with a lot worse hands than T-T to keep him from stealing.

Keep in mind that in both of these examples, the hands involved experienced players who knew each other's play. I didn't describe these hands to illustrate how you throw around chips. These hands show you the importance of thinking these things through ahead of time. When you are in either position—the late-position raiser or the big blind reraiser—it is important to think ahead. When putting in the initial raise, think about whether the big blind is the kind of player who will assume you are stealing and raise with any two cards, or whether the big blind won't do that without a hand. If you are in the big blind and you decide to reraise, think in advance about how the raiser will react. Not only will thinking of these things make it easier to decide what to do after your opponent plays back, but it might make you reconsider your initial move. If you think the big blind is going to reraise your late-position raise with anything, do you have a hand that's comfortable against "anything"? If not, don't even put in the first raise. On the other hand, if you know the big blind plays tight, you may still raise with just about anything, but you have to respect the occasions he reraises you.

If you are in position and have hands like Q-Q, J-J, or T-T and someone has raised in front of you, you have the luxury of calling the raise and trying to hit your set, but there is often a reason to not just call but to reraise. There are players to act after you—the blinds, at least—and calling may encourage them to do the same. Especially if you or the raiser has a short stack, you want to isolate the raiser and play heads-up. You don't want the blinds calling with suited connectors or ace-anything.

It's possible, if you have A-A, that an early-position raiser has a strong enough hand (or one of you has a short enough stack) where you can get all the chips in before the flop by reraising. If that's likely, you should reraise. However, sometimes with A-A and other very strong hands, you should just call so you can call in the same situation later with suited connectors without giving away too much information.

Also, by calling, you may encourage someone to put on what's come to be called the "squeeze play" or "sandwich play." Your call looks weak and a player on the button or in one of the blinds, if he thinks the raiser isn't necessarily strong, will put in a big reraise. When he reads the situation right, he is able to steal from the initial raiser, either because that player wasn't very strong or because he is worried about your flat-call. If your flat-call was an attempt to draw with a low pair or suited connections, you would fold too. And if one of you calls, the reraiser has that dead money in the pot to compensate him for trying the play with an inferior hand to the player who called the reraise.

This time, however, the play would backfire because you would be a strong favorite to win a big pot.

Finally, if you call with A-A, your opponent may push in on the flop no matter what happens. Your opponent could also not have that in mind but catches enough of the flop to decide to push in.

When deciding whether to reraise or call, think about it from your opponent's perspective. Remember, as I explained at the beginning of this section, you raise before the flop to pick up the blinds and antes 50 percent of the time. If opponents call you instead of reraising, you still have equity because you will win sometimes after the flop. The raise doesn't have to succeed as often if opponents call and give the raiser a chance to see the flop for no additional chips.

If your opponent is raising too often, you can loosen up a little, but don't take this too far and act like the cop for the entire table. If one player is raising too much and the other players in their blinds aren't calling or reraising enough, you shouldn't alter your play too much. You can loosen up a little, but only a little. Although you are losing out because you can't steal as much with this player doing it, you should be well compensated because you are getting paid off more on your big hands.

Getting Reraised

Against a good opponent, you want to make sure you don't fold too often to a reraise. Whatever hands you are starting with, you want to be calling or playing back often enough that it won't be profitable for them to try pushing you out by reraising with nothing. Make it so it is not worth their trouble to come over the top unless they have a very strong hand.

Say you are in a situation where you are going to enter with a raise with 15 percent of your hands. There are thirty-three hands you would play. K-Jo is worst and 9-9 is the median hand. If someone reraises you, you want them doing it with a hand in the top 7.5 percent, 9-9 or better. To keep from being pushed around, you have to call or reraise with more than half the hands you would play in that situation. Knowing where your hand lies in the range of playable hands is also why it is important to rank all the hands, rather than settle for groupings.

You need to know your threshold ahead of time, before you look at your cards. If you are raising with one of the hands at the bottom of the range—like A-9s under the gun, where, without antes, you should raise with 11 percent of your hands—you know in advance that you are going to muck it if you are facing a big reraise. This is the worst hand you could have raised with in this spot with pre-flop and you got reraised. Throw it away.

Thinking ahead is also how you start taking account of the table conditions. By telling yourself that you are going to raise with a hand that you will throw away if you get reraised, you might get the feeling a reraise is coming. Maybe you've been playing a lot of hands and you sense they want an excuse to play back. Or the table is so aggressive that early-position raisers are getting reraised a lot. Measure your instincts *before* you put in that raise.

You need to call or put in a third raise with at least half of your raising hands. That way, your opponents won't be able to take advantage of you by reraising at will. It's great if they play too tight when you are raising with a borderline hand. You want everyone to fold when you raise with A-9s and 9 players to act after you. And if they play back at you much too often, you know that your hand, if it is in the top half of your raising hands in that situation, is at least as good (on average) as the hand your opponent reraised with.

Let me give you an example from a made-for-TV tournament in which I played in early 2006. This was a team event, so the other pros on my team were watching the hand from another room. In a six-handed game, I raised three times the big blind on the button with K-5s. The small blind reraised to three times my raise, betting about 30 percent of his remaining chips. How often do I need to call (or play back) to keep my opponent from doing this with any two cards?

I thought my opponent looked weak, but I didn't feel I had a reliable enough read to base my decision on that alone. So I went to the math. On the button, I should raise about 60 percent of the time.

If I don't call at least half the time when I get reraised, my opponents can reraise me with almost anything.

Is K-5s in the stronger half of my raising hands or the weaker half? I hadn't committed the exact percentages of my hand rankings to memory, but I knew it was very close to the middle of my best 60 percent hands. (It is actually 30.9 percent.)

Therefore, I could have gone either way. I seriously thought about pushing all-in—my opponent left himself enough chips to fold—or calling and seeing the flop. But I also recognized that calling wouldn't give me any information about his hand, and he could have chosen the size of his bet to give me the false impression that he left himself folding chips. Finally, I decided to fold for another important reason: I had been able to steal pretty regularly. I didn't need to risk a lot of my chips on one hand.

It turned out my opponent had 5-4. Not knowing his hand at the time, of course, I was pleased with how I resolved this close decision. Several of my teammates told me they were surprised I took so long thinking about possibly calling with K-5s.

That should tell you a lot. Even accomplished tournament players don't always understand how often you need to defend your raise against a reraiser. Just about all decent tournament players know you raise in late position with a lot of hands, but many don't understand that you can't fold all but premium hands when someone plays back at you. (Of course, if an opponent who has let you steal a lot suddenly moves in on you, that's a different story. I'm talking about situations with opponents who may or may not be restealing and you aren't sure.)

If you raise on the button with K-5s and get reraised, it is not an automatic muck, especially if your opponent is the kind of player who may put a move on you. You have to watch your opponents, both to see which ones are capable of restealing and to see whether they are somehow telegraphing different signals when they reraise from strength than when they reraise to steal. Make a list of all the hands with which you will raise in late position. Against an opponent capable of restealing, will you throw away K-5s? J-To? Q-To? A-2s? If you are also raising with Q-5o and 7-6o, hands you will automatically fold to a reraise, then throwing away all those other hands means you could be throwing away two-thirds of your raising hands to reraises. Your opponents should—and the observant ones *will*—reraise your late-position raises every time.

If the small blind reraises you all-in and you're not getting 2-to-1 on your money, then you muck K-5s. But if the small blind makes a small enough raise so you can call and see the flop, you may be able to get value from the hand. Or maybe you can push in as a semi-bluff pre-flop. You have to be willing to make those plays occasionally or you have to tighten up when there is an aggressive player to your left. An aggressive player will abuse you when you raise his blind but are quick to give up when he plays back at you.

On the other hand, don't go crazy trying to prove how aggressive you can be. I've had opponents who raised in late position with 8-5s and put their entire tournament on the line after I reraised them from one of the blinds. Playing back at the late-position raiser from the blinds has become so common that some players raising in late position automatically assume you are making a play at them if you reraise from the blinds. (The resteal play probably became more common because so many players in the cutoff and on the button were raising every time. Then, because so many of those late-position raisers failed to grasp the importance of defending at least half those raises, the resteal play became widespread.)

The amount of the reraise will help determine how often you need to call or play back. To make it unprofitable for another player to reraise the minimum with any two cards, I am going to call a minimum reraise every time. (If my hand was good enough to bet in the first place, it is good enough to call a small reraise.) For example, with blinds at 100-200, you raise to 600. The big blind makes a small raise, to 1,100, risking an additional 900 to win 900. If he gets you to fold just half the time, he is freerolling on the hands where you call.

Besides, look at the odds you are getting to call. After the big blind reraises, there is 1,800 in the pot. You have to call only 500 to see the flop. Hardly any hand is more than a 3.6-to-1 underdog to another hand. 3-2o is just a 2-to-1 underdog against a random hand. If the reraiser had a top 10 percent hand (7-7 or better, A-8s or better, A-To or better, or K-Qs), you are getting the right odds with any suited cards (including 7-2s), any ace, any king, any queen (except Q-3 and Q-2), J-7 or better, and any other unsuited cards that can make more than one straight except for the very lowest cards. Even 7-2o has a 24 percent chance against a top 10 percent hand, and you are putting up 27.8 percent of the pot to call a minimum reraise.

If there are antes, the case for calling the minimum reraise is even stronger. If you add a 25 ante to this pot at a nine-handed table, the reraiser is betting 900 to get 1,125 if you fold. If you call, it costs you 500 to try to win 2,025. You can never fold to that reraise.

If, on the other hand, the reraise is the size of the pot, you can't call with any two cards. Modify this example so the reraiser in the big blind makes it 2,100. Now he is risking 1,900 to win 900 (without antes). You don't have to worry as much about being taken advantage of. You also aren't getting nearly as favorable pot odds as when he makes a minimum reraise. You have to call 1,500 to win a pot worth 2,800. If he has a top 10 percent hand, you are a favorite only with pairs above 9-9, A-K, and A-Qs. If he has a top-quarter hand, you are a favorite with a few more hands: pairs 6-6 and higher, A-9s or better, A-To or better.

You are, however, usually going to call as an underdog when the pot is laying you the right odds. If you call the reraise of 1,500, you will be contributing 35 percent (34.88 percent to be exact) of the pot. If there is no further betting, you should call with any hand that is more than 35 percent likely to win. Against a top-quarter hand, you are getting the right odds with the following hands: any pair, any ace, K-3s or better, K-9o or better, Q-3s or better, Q-9o or better, J-5s or better, J-8o or better, T-6s or better, T-8o or better, 9-5s or better, 9-8o, 8-5s or better, 8-7o, and 7-5s or better. If you put your opponent on a top 10 percent hand, you have a 35 percent or better chance to win with the following hands: all pairs, A-9s or better, A-To or better, K-9s or better, K-Qo, Q-Ts or better, J-Ts, and T-9s. (Q-9s has exactly a 34.88 percent chance of beating a top 10 percent hand.)

I hope you don't look at this and think, "I have to call with 9-5s?" Of course, you don't *have* to. But you are getting the right odds if you put your opponent on a top-quarter hand. If you can't bring yourself to do it, then maybe there is a problem with your read. If you simply can't commit the chips after getting into this situation, then you are learning a valuable lesson about what kind of playing style suits you: don't raise with 9-5s if you find yourself unwilling to ever call a reraise when you are getting the odds to do so.

There are many variables that affect these decisions. First, if this is not an all-in situation, you have to play after the flop. You might have to put in more chips. You may not be able to see all five cards. This opponent may be a player you especially fear in post-flop play. You might not be getting very good implied odds if you hit your underdog hand. When there is the possibility of more betting, the percentages are just general guidelines.

Second, you may need to call with some rough hands if there is any chance you are being taken advantage of. Good players will notice if you are folding too often to reraises.

Third, you need to consider tournament-specific information that may be more important than pot odds, especially when it is a close decision. If you are freely stealing from this table, especially if calling and losing will impair your ability to steal later, you may need to fold even though the odds suggest calling. That convinced me to fold in the example I described with K-5s. I knew it was a close decision either way, but I thought I would have easier ways of picking up chips than making that borderline call (or reraising).

Finally, your play can't be as precise as the numbers in the tables. For example, against a top 10 percent hand, A-9s is 35 percent to win, J-9s is 34.97 percent, and Q-9s is 34.88 percent. It's hard enough to put your opponent just on a *range* of hands pre-flop, much less to distinguish between hundredths of a percentage point whether you are getting the right odds.

The reason for learning about these percentages isn't to make all your decisions in advance; it is to understand the guidelines for making those decisions in the heat of battle. When you raise to 600 with J-9s and the big blind moves all-in for 2,100, now you know you are getting approximately the right odds against a top 10 percent hand. Maybe calling will be a mistake because this player is so tight that he wouldn't push unless he had a top 5 percent hand. But it would be a mistake to fold without thinking it through because you just assumed J-9s couldn't stand up against a decent hand. A lot of experienced players make that mistake; now you know better.

Just because you know these numbers doesn't mean you don't have to guess or gamble. Knowing them, however, keeps you from making some very big mistakes, and points you in the right direction to use your best judgment.

Modifying the Framework

You should modify the basic opening strategy, but only when there are clear reasons for doing so. One reason for modifying the framework is based on your opponents' image of you. Sometimes, you can get a sense that your opponents—especially when you notice how tight they are compared to you—are just waiting for a hand to reraise you with. Their standards are going to keep dropping the more you raise. In that situation, you might want to tighten up a little bit so that when they do reraise, you have a big hand.

But even then you shouldn't overdo it. If you have raised three hands in a row, you might think that you should play tighter. Your opponents could think you were running over them and will want to put a stop to it. But some opponents will assume the opposite: that you are going to tighten up after making all those raises, so that you will have a big hand the next time you represent one. Unless you are really comfortable with the depth of their reasoning, pretty much stick to your same strategy. (In chapter 19, Rafe Furst talks about the successive levels of thinking and counterthinking that go into making these decisions.)

It is reasonable to assume that opponents will call (or reraise) half of your raises, but you can adjust it based on your opponents' style of play. If you are playing an online tournament, you might find it hard to steal with half your raises. Of course, players that loose may be bringing weaker hands against you, which you don't mind. Usually, though, reasonable opponents, especially in big buy-in tournaments where you start with 10,000 to 50,000 chips and the blinds start at 25-50, are not going to play back at you with the lower half of the hands.

But these things tend to counteract. Say your opponents are playing tight, encouraging you to raise more. Or you are playing in a tournament without antes, so winning the blinds is not worth as much. This is where you can refine your play, making adjustments based on the players at the table, the stage of the tournament, or even whether you've raised the last few hands.

You might consider how well you play after the flop. Some experienced players call a lot of raises in position with weaker than expected hands because of their ability to outplay opponents after the flop. If you think you are more likely the victim than the perpetrator of this kind of play, you will want to tighten up against those opponents. Winning 50 percent of the blinds after you raise with a marginal hand may not be enough if you can't compete with these players after the flop. You need to play a little tighter, raising with stronger hands so you will be in better position after the flop. By ranking the hands, you get this framework where you can ratchet it up a little bit if you're not comfortable at this table.

Pre-Flop Play in the Blinds Against a Raise

The ranking system and percentages of playable hands by position will give you an idea of what hands players should be raising with on your blinds. Modify it based on your observations of how they actually play.

If you are in the big blind, assuming your opponents are raising by reasonable amounts, you should be playing a lot of hands. First, you already have one bet in the pot, so you don't have to call the full raise. Second, unless there have been limpers or it has been reraised, your call will close the betting round. Third, you want it to be unprofitable for late-position players to steal your big blind with any two cards.

So forget about playing *half* the hands your opponent would raise with. You should play *every* hand that the raiser could have in that position and maybe a few more. Say you have 8-7s. In the worst case, you are way behind an early-position raiser. But your implied odds are great: there are about six big blinds already in the pot (with antes). The raiser will almost always, if you check, bet 50–100 percent of the pot, which would be another four to eight big blinds. If you check-raise the times after you catch flops like two pair, a straight, a flush, top pair and a flush draw, and straight and flush draws, you will win enough to pay the two big blinds you spend on the times when you check-fold. Many times, when you hit your hand, you can bust the raiser.

The same is true with a small pair. If you call for the 12 percent chance to make your set, you will probably get paid off for even more bets.

When you are in the small blind, you should play tighter against a raise. You have only a half bet in the pot, plus you have the big blind to play after you. Now you should play according to the principles I have already described: call with half the hands you think the raiser would play.

Unless you or the raiser is short-stacked, there is something to be said for rarely reraising in the big blind. You are going to want to play a lot of hands by just calling. If you reraise with only your strongest hands, you are giving away a lot of information. If you camouflage your reraises with A-A and K-K by reraising with other hands, then you are playing a lot of bigger pots out of position, against an opponent who has already shown strength.

Of course, like everything else, it depends on your opponents. How will they play after the flop? Will they lay down a hand to a pre-flop reraise? Some players like to reraise in the blinds to "resteal" from a late-position raiser. Players who do this will reraise with as many as half their hands. It seems like reraising that often would not be profitable, but a lot of players will not call enough of those reraises.

Another common play from the blinds is to make a big raise if there are several limpers. The time to consider this is when you are short-stacked, with ten times the big blind or less. Even if the other players suspect you are on a steal, you have a good chance of succeeding with the play. The player you are worried about is the first limper. That is the player most likely to have limped with a big hand, hoping for a chance to reraise. The other limpers, if they had big hands, likely would not have limped. But to use plays like this, you need to understand how your opponents play.

When you have a medium-strong reraising hand, like T-T, you don't want to just call in a multiway pot (unless it's a situation where you are looking to play based on flopping a set or folding). Granted, some of the hands your opponents lay down will be hands you want to be against, like 7-7 or A-5. But you don't want to be against all of them at once. Besides, it is difficult to get paid off with T-T even if it is the best hand after the flop.

Blind versus Blind

There is a lot of opportunity in blind versus blind play; most players really don't know how to play in this situation. To start, you should hardly ever be folding. If the big blind is aggressive and raises a lot when you limp, fold hands like 7-2o and the others at the bottom of the hand rankings.

In the small blind, you want to play 75 percent or more of your hands. If you can, limp a lot because you are out of position. Even if the big blind raises you a lot, you want to play any two suited cards, any face card, and any connecting or nearly connecting cards.

Tighten up a little if the big blind is always raising, but not a lot. Once the big blind sees you fold (before the raise) a few times, your limping calls are going to get more respect. Once you tighten up a little, the big blind will suspect you are limping to try to trap with big hands like A-A. And maybe you are.

Assuming you have a big stack, you are going to play a lot of hands. If your opponent raises, you don't have to call every time, but you have to call a lot. If you don't call with at least half your hands, your opponent can raise you with any two cards and make that a profitable play.

If you play 75–80 percent of your hands in the small blind, you probably have to call raises with the top 40 percent hands. Against a tighter, passive opponent, you can muck the borderline hands.

You should think about pushing in with your raising hands from the small blind when your stack (or the big blind's stack) gets to be fifteen to twenty times the big blind or less. By pushing in, you eliminate the positional disadvantage. You don't want to see a lot of flops when you are on a short stack in the small blind.

In the big blind, if the small blind limps, you should be willing to check a lot and see the flop because you have position. If the player in the small blind is predictable, you can fold a lot of hands on the flop when they bet and pick up the pot by betting after they check.

If the player in the small blind bluffs a lot after the flop, you should generally be calling, not raising pre-flop with your strong hands. You'll make them pay when they bluff on the flop. It's like they raised before the flop but you get to see the flop before you decide whether to call the reraise.

You generally don't want to limp in the small blind when you are short-stacked (i.e., ten to twenty times the big blind or less). You are out of position and you want to get the chips in pre-flop and not have to play the flop. With all pocket pairs, A-K, A-Q, K-Qs, even hands like Q-9s, with ten big blinds or less, push in. You'd like to trap by limping with A-A and K-K, but you can't always be raising in that situation except with A-A or K-K. You should also pick some hands that are among the weaker, more speculative holdings to play the same way, hands like 7-6o and 5-4o. Other than those few hands, you want to fold or raise, pushing all-in on a short stack.

Most hands where you are going to limp and call an all-in raise, you are obviously better off being the one to push all-in. When you have a short stack, especially with antes, you are doing well enough to pick up the blinds and antes. The hands people tend to limp with and then call raises, like Q-9o, are rarely a big favorite (55 percent to win) over a random hand. Your edge with that kind of hand is picking up the pot before the flop and still being in fair to good shape against most of the hands that call you.

I see players limp in the blinds with 4-4 or 6-6 when they or the other blind is short-stacked. Then they call an all-in raise. The call of the raise is fine, but the limp is wrong. With 4-4, if you push in from the blind, you'll get a lot of mediocre hands with two overcards (like 8-6 or T-5) to fold. But by "trapping" the big blind into moving all-in with hands like 8-6 and T-5, you have a much lower expected profit out of the hand. You are just a small favorite. On the other hand, if you go all-in with 4-4 or 6-6 when someone is short-stacked, you'll get called by some hands you want to see, like A-2.

The Data for All-In Decisions

Jam-or-fold—The blind versus blind game brings up a situation where knowing the math can give you a huge advantage. Once you or the other blind gets very short-stacked, especially when there are antes, you have to understand that the hand values are much different than you are used to playing. In the small blind, you are going to either push or fold. In the big blind, therefore, your options are to call or fold.

This is the game that Chris Ferguson and I separately figured out when we started playing no-limit hold 'em tournaments. Between the two random hands in the blinds, there are times when it is appropriate to raise all-in, as well as to call all-in, with any two cards, including 3-2o. 3-2o is about a 2-to-1 underdog (ironically, 3-2o is about 32 percent to win) against a random hand. If you play in enough tournaments you will be in a situation where you can get better than 3-to-1 on your money with 3-2o with either you or your opponent all-in. Nevertheless, at TV final tables, you frequently see players in the blinds in situations like that folding hands much better than 3-2o.

A lot of players have no idea how their hands do against a random hand, let alone against a top 10 percent or top-quarter or top-half hand. Because they don't know that, they don't realize how to play in most of these situations. When you have this information, you can make better decisions. Because some of the information is surprising or conflicts with what a lot of people assume, just being aware of it will cause you to think differently (and more accurately) about the game.

The jam-or-fold game is a simplified form of poker. The small blind, with the button, acts first, but can only fold or move all-in. The big blind, therefore, wins when the small blind folds, or has to decide whether to call or fold when the small blind pushes.

Table 6.6 shows the optimal way to play jam-or-fold. If either player has a stack smaller, in number of big blinds, than the number in the table, you should go all-in from the small blind. If you are in the big blind, the ratios and ranking of the hands are different. But you call if either stack is smaller than the number of big blinds indicated next to that hand. (Technically, this table contains modified results from my original jam-or-fold game.)

Chris and I each used a branch of mathematics called game theory to figure out how to play the jam-or-fold game and how to rank two-card poker hands, for both betting and calling. It has occasional but very important applications in real tournaments. The jam-or-fold information becomes relevant a lot at the end of a tournament, which is where the real "money" decisions in tournament poker are made.

In David Sklansky and Ed Miller's *No Limit Hold 'Em: Theory and Practice*, they include a version of the jam-or-fold game, from which the "Sklansky-Chubukov rankings" were derived. The Sklansky-Chubukov rankings are based on a game where the small blind moves in and turns his hand face up. Because the big blind is assumed to be a perfect player who calls only when his hand has the proper odds against the already known hand of the small blind, the first player has to play accordingly. This is a less realistic game than Chris and I developed. The first player to act in the Sklansky game will play too tight because he has to assume the big blind knows his hand. The other flaw as a result of this is that the hands are ranked in the wrong order. Some hands (like suited connectors) have more semi-bluff value than others. His system gives no value to that, therefore causing those hands to be ranked too low. (Those hands are also the hands that do best after the flop and include the hands that play best against A-A.)

I saw a version of Sklansky's rankings online and want you to understand the similarities and differences between his numbers and mine, and the reasons. For many hands in the middle of our tables, our numbers are significantly different. My version of the game is more advanced. Although there are differences between both our games and a real poker game, I have tried to make the simulation reflect poker in ways David didn't. First, in his game, the small blind reveals his cards, so the big blind will only call when getting the right price. It is easier to do the math if you assume the other player knows your hand, but it makes the numbers unrepresentative of the value of raising all-in. Second, in that kind of game, you don't get any guidance about how to play from the big blind, after someone has moved all-in.

His ranking system also does not give any value to semi-bluffing. In his jam-or-fold game, the small blind has to turn over his cards before the big blind acts. If you play based on his guidelines blind versus blind or heads-up, you will be playing too tight and will undervalue suited and connecting cards.

If you see the Sklansky-Chubukov numbers online or in Sklansky and Miller and compare them to table 6.6, you need to double my number and subtract 1 so it equates to Sklansky's. (My jam-or-fold numbers are expressed in multiples of the big blind; his are multiples of the small blind, minus a big blind. If you double my number or halve his, you'll get an idea of our equivalent rankings.) For K-K, in the small blind, you push in if either player has 478 big blinds or less. If you multiply that number by 2 and subtract 1 (ignoring the decimal

TABLE 6.6 ◆ JAM-OR-FOLD

(Jam from SB, call from BB if either stack has fewer BBs than the number in this table.)

Hand	SB	BB	Hand	SB	BB	Hand	SB	BB	Hand	SB	BB
A-A	inf.	inf.	K-9s	78	23	J-7s	32	9	8-7s	42	6.7
K-K	478	572	K-9o	24	17	J-7o	8.5	6.5	8-7o	14	4.8
Q-Q	266	221	K-8s	56	18	J-6s	19	7	8-6s	31	5.7
J-J	182	156	K-8o	18	14	J-6o	6.5	5.5	8-6o	6.6	4.1
T-T	179	119	K-7s	49	15	J-5s	15	7	8-5s	19	4.8
9-9	105	96	K-7o	16	13	J-5o	6	5	8-5o	3	3.6
8-8	102	80	K-6s	36	14	J-4s	14	6	8-4s	7.9	4.2
7-7	90	66	K-6o	15	11	J-4o	5.5	5	8-4o	2.4	3.2
6-6	97	56	K-5s	32	13	J-3s	11	8	8-3s	2.8	3.7
5-5	90	42	K-5o	14	10	J-3o	5	4.5	8-3o	2	2.9
4-4	74	31	K-4s	25	12	J-2s	8.5	5.5	8-2s	2.6	3.6
3-3	64	23	K-4o	13	9	J-2o	4.5	4	8-2o	1.9	2.9
2-2	52	15	K-3s	20	12	T-9s	73	12	7-6s	35	5.5
A-Ks	808	372	K-3o	12	9	T-9o	27	8.5	7-6o	9.8	4.1
A-Ko	583	194	K-2s	19	11	T-8s	54	9.5	7-5s	24	4.8
A-Qs	195	119	K-2o	12	8	T-8o	16	6.5	7-5o	2.6	3.6
A-Qo	141	90	Q-Js	122	28	T-7s	36	7.5	7-4s	12	4.2
A-Js	176	76	Q-Jo	50	20	T-7o	9	5.5	7-4o	2.2	3.2
A-Jo	102	63	Q-Ts	103	22	T-6s	21	6.5	7-3s	2.5	3.7
A-Ts	136	63	Q-To	40	15	T-6o	5.5	4.5	7-3o	1.9	2.9
A-To	58	50	Q-9s	71	16	T-5s	11	5.5	7-2s	2.1	3.3

	SB	BB
A-9s	89	47
A-9o	45	38
A-8s	72	42
A-8o	43	34
A-7s	57	35
A-7o	40	29
A-6s	51	31
A-6o	32	21
A-5s	272	30
A-5o	37	21
A-4s	429	27
A-4o	33	18
A-3s	54	25
A-3o	30	17
A-2s	48	24
A-2o	29	16
K-Qs	150	55
K-Qo	79	41
K-Js	126	45
K-Jo	68	26
K-Ts	108	31
K-To	37	23

	SB	BB
Q-9o	21	12
Q-8s	51	13
Q-8o	13	10
Q-7s	26	11
Q-7o	10	8
Q-6s	27	10
Q-6o	10	7.5
Q-5s	20	9
Q-5o	9	7
Q-4s	15	8.5
Q-4o	8	6.5
Q-3s	14	8
Q-3o	7.5	6
Q-2s	12	7.5
Q-2o	7.3	5.5
J-Ts	98	18
J-To	39	13
J-9s	72	13
J-9o	24	9.5
J-8s	50	11
J-8o	12	7.5

	SB	BB
T-5o	4	4
T-4s	11	5
T-4o	4	4
T-3s	7	5
T-3o	3.5	3.5
T-2s	6	4.5
T-2o	3	3.5
9-8s	54	8.5
9-8o	20	6
9-7s	36	7
9-7o	11	5
9-6s	27	6
9-6o	5	4.3
9-5s	14	5
9-5o	3.5	4
9-4s	6	4.5
9-4o	2.5	3.5
9-3s	4.5	4
9-3o	2.5	3
9-2s	3.5	4
9-2o	2	3

	SB	BB
7-2o	1.6	2.7
6-5s	29	5
6-5o	2.5	3.7
6-4s	16	4.3
6-4o	2.1	3.3
6-3s	2.4	3.8
6-3o	1.8	3
6-2s	2	3.4
6-2o	1.6	2.7
5-4s	24	4.7
5-4o	2.1	3.5
5-3s	2.4	4.1
5-3o	1.8	3.2
5-2s	2.1	3.6
5-2o	1.6	2.9
4-3s	2.2	3.9
4-3o	1.7	3.1
4-2s	1.9	3.5
4-2o	1.5	2.8
3-2s	1.8	3.3
3-2o	1.4	2.7

rounding), you get Sklansky's 954. For the very best and worst hands, the numbers should be the same. With K-K, the only hand your opponent would call with would be A-A. Likewise, with hands like 3-2o, your opponent will call with every hand.

For the hands in the middle, where you benefit much more from having more accurate information than the top and bottom hands (though, as I will explain, people even misplay some of those), I rated and ranked many hands significantly differently than Sklansky. For example, he rated T-8s at 17.5, which would be the equivalent in my rankings of 9.2 big blinds. T-8o rates as 12.2, which equates to 6.6 big blinds. He has just sixteen hands separating T-8s and T-8o. According to my rankings, both are much higher. You would jam in the small blind with T-8s with 54 or fewer big blinds. You would jam with T-8o with 18 or fewer, and I have 45 hands separating the two.

You can learn some things by looking at his rankings, but you can't learn anything about *calling* all-in. You also won't be factoring in the fold equity you get when you raise with any two cards, because in Sklansky's game the opponent knows your hand. By doing the higher-level math (i.e., game theory), the jam-or-fold table in this chapter better reflects the value of semi-bluffing and ranks the calling hands.

The jam-or-fold game was the beginning of my developing hand rankings. Another way of ranking hands, which has more applications in actual tournament situations, is measuring how each hand does against random hands and certain groups of hands (like top-half hands, top-quarter hands, and top 10 percent hands).

Playing against random hands—Suppose you are in the big blind. Everyone folds to the small blind, who pushes all-in without looking at his cards. What hands can you call with? You'll actually see this sometimes, though more often you will see a certain player being so aggressive that it's clear he is pushing in because he is the first one in the pot and thinks the players after him (or, in this case, the one player after him) will fold unless they have a strong hand. For this example, the blinds are 50-100 and he moves in for 2,000.

The jam-or-fold numbers have only limited applicability. They apply to how people *should* play. Looking at the jam-or-fold table, if either of you has twenty times the big blind or less, you would call with pocket pairs (except 2-2), any two cards ten or higher (except J-T and Q-To), and any ace (except A-4o, A-3o, and A-2o).

But this guy didn't even look at his cards! Against two random cards, you need to call with any hand that beats a random hand 50 percent of the time, or a little less to take into consideration that you are calling 1,900 to win 2,000. The worst hands you would call with would be T-6s, J-4s, 9-7s, and Q-4o. You can extrapolate almost all the rest of the calling hands from there: 9-7s or better, T-6s or better (and T-8o or better), J-4s or better (and J-7o or better), Q-4o or better (and any suited queen), and any king, any ace, and any pair.

3-2o is not only sometimes playable but it can be a *raising* hand if the stacks are small enough. Suppose everyone folds to you in the small blind. Blinds are 1,000-2,000 with 300 antes, so there are 6,000 chips in the pot if the table is ten-handed. The big blind has 1,000 more. You look down and see you have 3-2o. It costs you 2,000 to put him all-in, and you pick up 7,000 if you win the hand. You are putting up 22 percent of the final pot (2,000 of 9,000) and 3-2o has a 32 percent chance to beat a random hand. You would always raise.

How big a bet would you call all-in if you were in the big blind with 3-2o? If you were convinced that the small blind was moving in with any two cards, a raise of 6,000 by the small blind, in this example, would require you to call 6,000 to win 13,000. Converted to percentages, your call would constitute 31.6 percent of the final pot, and you have a 32 percent chance of winning against two random cards; you are getting the right price to call all-in. (Incidentally, if you thought the small blind was moving in with the top 50 percent of his hands, you should call a raise up to 5,000. You would be putting in just under 30 percent of the final pot and 3-2o wins about 30 percent of the time against the top 50 percent of hands. Against a top-quarter hand, 3-2o wins 29 percent of the time, so you would call a similar raise. Even against a top 10 percent hand, you would call all-in a raise of 3,500, putting in 25 percent of the final pot with a 26 percent chance to win.)

In a situation without antes, you have to play a little tighter. For this example, blinds are 100-200. You are in the small blind and the big blind has 400 before the hand, exactly two big blinds. Raising him all-in costs you 300. The final pot will have 800 chips, and you are putting in 37.5 percent with your raise. What hands beat a random hand more than 37.5 percent of the time?

You would raise with any two cards where the smaller card is four or greater. 5-4o and 6-4o win 38 percent against a random hand. You also raise with any two cards when the bigger card is nine or greater. 9-2o beats a random hand more than 39 percent of the time. 8-3o is right on the borderline, winning against a random hand just under 37.5 percent of the time. You would also raise with any pair and any suited cards except for 4-2s and 3-2s. You will be raising with nearly 90 percent of your hands.

If you have a very short stack in this kind of situation, unless you are close to the money, you should be thinking solely about your chip equity. If you are one player from the money, you will probably fold all the borderline hands, and maybe a lot more. Otherwise, your only consideration is whether you have the right percentage chance to win the hand compared with the percentage you have to put into the pot.

The range of how hands perform against random hands is narrower than most people expect. A-A wins 85 percent of the time, 3-2o 32 percent. After A-A, the winning percentages drop pretty quickly. Fewer than 3 percent of hands win 70 percent of the time or more—9-9, T-T, J-J, Q-Q, K-K, and A-A. Once you drop out pairs, the range narrows even more. A-Ks wins 67 percent of the time, so it is just barely twice as good against a random hand as 3-2o.

You don't need to know all the percentages in table 6.7 but the better you understand it than your opponents, the bigger advantage you will have. You will definitely face tournament situations where knowing this is relevant and where a lot of people get it wrong.

For fun, test yourself (before you commit this table to memory). Pick some random hands and see how well you guess the win percentages. Ask some other players. For example, most poker players would probably not guess that T-6s beats a random hand 49 percent of the time. A lot of people would guess a much lower number, and the consequences of getting that number wrong can be significant. Especially later in a tournament, where one of the players in the hand or the blinds yet to act is severely short-stacked, the usual ideas about hand values and percentages of playable hands have little meaning. Given the presence of the dead money from blinds and antes, and sometimes your own chips if you have raised and are considering calling an all-in reraise, you don't need anywhere near a 50 percent chance to win the pot to call.

In most situations, if the pot is laying you 2-to-1 odds and there is no further betting, you will be calling because almost all hands have a greater than 33 percent chance of winning. (Of course, there are exceptions. A very tight opponent will usually have a much better than random hand. The tables that follow will show the win percentages against top 10 percent hands, top-quarter hands, and top-half hands. Even against better than random hands, however, you will usually have a better than 1-in-3 chance of winning.) You automatically call if you are getting 3-to-1 odds; you are almost never under 25 percent to win, and certainly not often enough to presume the other player has A-A. If you are getting 3-to-2 odds to call, you are going to call whenever you have a chance to win greater than 40 percent. If the other player has a random hand—he is severely short-stacked, making this move from the blind, or you are in the small blind and have only the random hand of the big blind behind you—you are going to commit your chips with all but your worst hands.

Top-half hands—At the beginning of this chapter, I explained how you should be raising on the button if it is folded to you 45 percent of the time without antes and 59 percent of the time with antes. If you have an opponent on the button who generally plays that way, betting about half his hands on your big blind, what do you need to call all-in or make a bet that will put him all-in?

The "top-half hands" consist of 49 percent of all hands, including the following: any pair, any hand with an ace or king, Q-Xs, Q-7o or better, J-6s or better, J-9o or better, T-9, T-8s, T-7s, 9-6s or better, 8-7s, 8-6s, 7-6s, 7-5s, 6-5s, and 5-4s.

Assume for this next example that you are in the big blind with a short stack. You have 8,300 in the big blind. Blinds are 1,000-2,000 with 300 antes, so you have 6,000 left after posting your blind. Everybody folds to the player on the button, who has a big stack and seems to be playing about half his hands in this situation. He raises to 8,000, which seems calculated to get the small blind to fold and put you all-in if you want to see the flop. To call, you will be putting 6,000 into a pot with a final value of 20,000, or 30 percent of the pot.

You almost don't even need to look at your cards. If you read the situation right and the raiser is playing half his hands, you are getting the odds to call with just about any two cards. The only hand you should fold is 7-2o, which is 29.97 percent to win. If you are close to the money and survival matters, you might fold a few hands at the very bottom of table 6.8.

If you have 20,300 chips before the start of the hand and get raised all-in, you will obviously have a lot more folding hands. For this example, this same player on the button has raised to 20,000. You have K-8s. Hopefully, the circumstances make it easier for you to conclude the raiser has a top-half hand: aggressive player, big stack, usually plays top-half hands on the button, oversized raise to scare out small blind and force you to commit all your chips. (There is no substitute for watching how your opponents play. After the first few levels, you may not see many showdowns and will have few opportunities to correlate how the other players play with particular hands. But you should always be keeping track of how often they play. If the player on the button has folded on your blind just once in eight opportunities, you can probably put him on just a little better than a random hand. If he has raised your blind for the first time in eight opportunities, it is likely he has a hand much better than a top-half hand.)

K-8s wins over 49 percent against a top-half hand, so you should call. The pot has 26,000 when the action comes to you. If you call with your last 18,000, you will be putting 41 percent of the chips into a pot with a final value of 44,000.

A lot of players are uncomfortable calling all-in with K-8s or Q-To or some of the even weaker hands that win 41 percent or more against top-half hands. That's one of the reasons why aggressive play works: other players don't realize how weak an aggressive player's cards are when he is playing a lot of hands.

Top-quarter and top 10 percent hands—You can imagine several situations where you can put your opponent on a top 10 percent or top-quarter hand.

- A tight opponent raises all-in under the gun.
- You raise in middle position and the big blind reraises an amount that puts you all-in if you call.

- You are on the button and a player in middle position raises. It would cost 80 percent of your stack to call, and you feel the blinds will fold.

You might conclude in the first two examples that your opponent has a top 10 percent hand. In the third example, you could decide the raiser has a top-quarter hand.

You can rarely put your opponent on an exact hand before the flop. But if you can put them on a range of hands based on how they play and what you think their motivation is for playing this particular pot, you can pick hands that do well against that range of hands. When you do this at tournaments, you don't have to be exact. Even playing online with these numbers in front of you, you don't know your opponent's exact hand so knowing every one of these percentages isn't necessary.

I recommend you pick several hands and remember their percentages for each table. If you generally understand how different kinds of hands perform, you can extrapolate. Here are some examples:

- *T-T*—I have found in discussions with other players that they are quick to assume that T-T is no good if they get reraised late in a tournament. Apart from the possibility their opponent may *think* they think that, hardly any hands are better than T-T. Against a top-quarter hand, T-T wins 63 percent of the time. Only six hands do better. T-T even beats top 10 percent hands 54 percent of the time.
- *4-4*—Against a top-quarter hand, 4-4 wins 47 percent of the time. Against a top 10 percent hand, it still wins 40 percent of the time. With dead money in the pot—blinds, antes, your initial raise if you are contemplating calling a reraise—you are usually getting the odds to call. Against a top 10 percent hand, 2-2 wins 38 percent of the time. The reason people tend to underestimate the strength of low pairs is because they are big underdogs to any higher pair. They are just a small favorite to premium unpaired cards, but your opponent is much more likely to have unpaired cards, even when he is playing just the top 10 percent hands. Of the 124 two-card combinations making up the top 10 percent hands, more than 61 percent (76) are unpaired high cards. Just under 39 percent (48) are pairs.

- *A-Ts*—Against a top-quarter hand, A-Ts wins 56 percent of the time. Against a top 10 percent hand, the win percentage drops to 39 percent. With A-X, compared with a pocket pair, you have to worry about being dominated by better aces.
- *K-Jo*—K-Jo wins 42 percent against a top-quarter hand and 34 percent against a top 10 percent hand. Against top 10 percent hands, hands like K-Jo are clustered in a narrow range: K-Qo is 35 percent, Q-Jo is 34 percent, K-To and J-To are 33 percent. Against top-quarter hands, the gap is a little larger. K-Qo wins 45 percent of the time, K-To wins 40 percent, and Q-Jo and J-To both win 38 percent.
- *T-9s*—This hand is a good proxy for the upper end of how suited connectors perform. T-9s wins 40 percent against the top-quarter hands and 35 percent against the top 10 percent hands. Hands like 9-8s, 8-7s, and T-8s win 1–2 percent less against these ranges of hands.
- *8-6o*—Against top-quarter hands, 8-6o wins 34 percent of the time. Against top 10 percent hands, it wins 29 percent of the time.

You should pick out some hands of your own and see how they do against each range of hands. For example, T-8o is pretty close to a random hand. It wins almost 50 percent of the time against a random hand. Against a top-half hand, it wins 39 percent. It wins 36 percent against a top-quarter hand and 30 percent against a top 10 percent hand.

If you raise with 2-2 and get reraised in an all-in situation, do you have the right odds to call? Against a random hand, you are barely a favorite, ahead just a fraction more than 50 percent of the time. But the win percentage of 2-2 drops much more slowly than T-8o as the quality of the raiser's hand rises. 2-2 wins 47 percent against a top-half hand, 44 percent against a top-quarter hand, and 38 percent against a top 10 percent hand.

You are going to call a lot more all-in reraises with 2-2 than T-8o. If you put your opponent on a premium hand, it is going to take a huge reraise for you to be putting less than 39 percent of the chips in the pot by calling—in addition to the reraise, the pot already contains the blinds, antes, and the chips from your original raise. For example, with blinds of 1,000-2,000 and 300 antes, you pick up 2-2 in the cutoff. It is folded to you and you raise to 6,000. The button reraises all-in for a total of 25,000. The blinds fold. If you call the 19,000, you are putting 33.9 percent into a final pot of 56,000. If you put the reraiser on a top 10 percent hand, you would call because you expect to win 38 percent of your confrontations against those hands. With the same betting, you would not be getting the right price to call with T-8o.

The "top-quarter hands" consist of 24 percent of all hands, including the following: any pair but 2-2, any hand with an ace except A-3o and A-2, K-9 or better, and K-8o.

The "top 10 percent hands" consist of pairs 7-7 or better, A-T or better, A-8s, A-9s, and K-Qs. (To be exact, these are 9.4 percent of the hands you will be dealt.)

One of the things you can see from these charts is that certain hands are not particularly good trapping hands. A-K, for example, doesn't do much better, relatively, against a random hand than against a premium hand.

Trapping with a hand like this is a mistake. You don't really benefit much luring weak hands to play you compared with strong hands. And the benefit of raising out weak hands is that many of the strong hands that will call you are big underdogs. If you have A-K, you would much rather be against A-Q, which will probably call a raise, than 5-4o, which probably won't.

Conclusion

Some of the information in this chapter will surprise people. There are a lot of marginal situations in no-limit hold 'em tournaments, especially after the first few levels. No one wants to commit all their chips on less than a premium hand, so players tend to assume opponents have (or will have) good cards. Unless you want to give up control of the tournament to the aggressive players, however, you have to realistically evaluate the quality of the hand your opponent has and look him up (or make a bet he may call), even with an ugly-looking hand, if you have the right odds.

TABLE 6.7 ◆ EVERY HAND AGAINST A RANDOM HAND*

Hand	Win %	Hand	Win %	Hand	Win %	Hand	Win %	Hand	Win %
A-A	85.20%	A-4s	59.03%	K-5o	53.31%	9-6s	47.42%	8-5o	41.43%
K-K	82.40%	A-7o	58.84%	J-9o	53.25%	J-2s	47.38%	6-4s	41.33%
Q-Q	79.93%	K-8s	58.31%	K-2s	53.21%	Q-2o	47.30%	8-3s	40.87%
J-J	77.47%	A-3s	58.22%	Q-5s	52.77%	T-5s	47.22%	9-4o	40.67%
T-T	75.01%	Q-Jo	58.13%	T-8s	52.33%	J-5o	47.18%	7-5o	40.51%
9-9	72.06%	K-9o	57.81%	K-4o	52.33%	T-4s	46.53%	8-2s	40.27%
8-8	69.16%	A-5o	57.70%	J-7s	52.32%	9-7o	46.30%	9-3o	40.02%
A-Ks	67.04%	A-6o	57.68%	Q-4s	51.86%	8-6s	46.24%	7-3s	40.00%
7-7	66.24%	Q-9s	57.66%	Q-7o	51.77%	J-4o	46.19%	6-5o	39.94%
A-Qs	66.21%	K-7s	57.54%	T-9o	51.53%	T-6o	46.09%	5-3s	39.69%
A-Js	65.39%	J-Ts	57.53%	J-8o	51.49%	9-5s	45.72%	6-3s	39.53%
A-Ko	65.32%	A-2s	57.38%	K-3o	51.43%	T-3s	45.69%	8-4o	39.45%
A-Ts	64.60%	Q-To	57.29%	Q-6o	51.02%	7-6s	45.37%	9-2o	39.10%
A-Qo	64.43%	4-4	57.02%	Q-3s	51.02%	J-3o	45.28%	4-3s	38.64%
A-Jo	63.56%	A-4o	56.73%	9-8s	50.80%	8-7o	45.05%	7-4o	38.55%
K-Qs	63.40%	K-6s	56.64%	T-7s	50.64%	T-2s	44.89%	7-2s	38.16%
6-6	63.28%	K-8o	56.02%	J-6s	50.61%	9-6o	44.49%	5-4o	38.16%
A-9s	62.78%	Q-8s	56.02%	K-2o	50.51%	8-5s	44.44%	6-4o	38.01%

108

Hand	Win %	Hand	Win %	Hand	Win %	Hand	Win %	Hand	Win %
A-To	62.72%	A-3o	55.84%	2-2	50.33%	J-2o	44.35%	5-2s	37.85%
K-Js	62.57%	K-5s	55.79%	Q-2s	50.17%	T-5o	44.25%	6-2s	37.67%
A-8s	61.94%	J-9s	55.66%	Q-5o	50.12%	9-4s	43.86%	8-3o	37.48%
K-Ts	61.79%	Q-9o	55.36%	J-5s	49.99%	7-5s	43.68%	4-2s	36.83%
K-Qo	61.46%	J-To	55.25%	T-8o	49.72%	T-4o	43.50%	8-2o	36.83%
A-7s	60.98%	K-7o	55.19%	J-7o	49.68%	9-3s	43.26%	7-3o	36.60%
A-9o	60.77%	A-2o	54.93%	Q-4o	49.13%	8-6o	43.24%	5-3o	36.26%
K-Jo	60.57%	K-4s	54.88%	9-7s	49.12%	6-5s	43.13%	6-3o	36.08%
5-5	60.32%	Q-7s	54.30%	J-4s	49.07%	8-4s	42.70%	3-2s	35.98%
Q-Js	60.26%	K-6o	54.22%	T-6s	48.94%	9-5o	42.67%	4-3o	35.15%
K-9s	59.99%	K-3s	54.05%	J-3s	48.23%	T-3o	42.59%	7-2o	34.58%
A-5s	59.92%	T-9s	54.03%	Q-3o	48.22%	9-2s	42.42%	5-2o	34.28%
A-6s	59.91%	J-8s	54.02%	9-8o	48.10%	7-6o	42.32%	6-2o	34.08%
A-8o	59.87%	3-3	53.69%	8-7s	47.94%	7-4s	41.85%	4-2o	33.20%
K-To	59.74%	Q-6s	53.61%	T-7o	47.91%	T-2o	41.67%	3-2o	32.30%
Q-Ts	59.47%	Q-8o	53.60%	J-6o	47.84%	5-4s	41.45%		

*Note about the win percentages: my references to the likelihood of winning are a generally accurate shorthand for your pot equity, which includes both the likelihood you will win and the likelihood you will get half the pot in a tie.

TABLE 6.8 ◆ EVERY HAND AGAINST TOP-HALF HANDS

Hand	Win %	Hand	Win %	Hand	Win %	Hand	Win %	Hand	Win %
A-A	85.15%	A-3s	52.08%	Q-7s	42.28%	9-5s	37.79%	5-4o	35.12%
K-K	77.14%	4-4	51.76%	T-8s	42.01%	J-3s	37.79%	8-3s	35.00%
Q-Q	73.85%	A-2s	51.47%	9-8s	41.98%	6-4s	37.72%	J-4o	34.87%
J-J	70.36%	A-6o	51.21%	Q-6s	41.74%	T-5s	37.70%	8-5o	34.82%
T-T	67.68%	A-5o	50.98%	K-4o	41.72%	Q-5o	37.60%	4-2s	34.70%
A-Ks	66.98%	Q-Js	50.47%	Q-8o	41.15%	8-7o	37.57%	8-2s	34.64%
A-Ko	65.30%	A-4o	50.00%	J-9o	41.09%	J-7o	37.34%	6-2s	34.43%
A-Qs	64.46%	3-3	49.60%	Q-5s	41.02%	T-4s	37.33%	9-5o	34.27%
9-9	64.30%	K-8s	49.53%	K-3o	41.00%	9-7o	37.17%	6-4o	34.24%
A-Js	62.66%	K-9o	49.45%	8-7s	40.89%	J-2s	37.16%	J-3o	34.19%
A-Qo	62.59%	A-3o	49.30%	J-7s	40.72%	T-7o	37.07%	T-5o	34.16%
8-8	61.29%	Q-Ts	49.25%	T-9o	40.53%	7-4s	37.04%	3-2s	34.06%
A-Ts	61.17%	A-2o	48.66%	9-7s	40.52%	5-3s	36.96%	T-4o	33.75%
A-Jo	60.53%	K-7s	48.28%	T-7s	40.44%	Q-4o	36.83%	7-2s	33.74%
A-To	59.05%	Q-Jo	47.73%	K-2o	40.33%	T-3s	36.71%	J-2o	33.51%
7-7	58.64%	2-2	47.44%	Q-4s	40.31%	7-6o	36.70%	7-4o	33.50%
A-9s	58.56%	K-6s	46.96%	7-6s	40.06%	8-4s	36.64%	5-3o	33.47%
K-Qs	57.86%	J-Ts	46.76%	8-6s	39.72%	8-6o	36.32%	T-3o	33.07%

Hand	Win %	Hand	Win %	Hand	Win %	Hand	Win %	Hand	Win %
A-8s	56.80%	Q-9s	46.68%	Q-3s	39.68%	4-3s	36.31%	8-4o	33.06%
A-9o	56.26%	K-8o	46.67%	J-6s	39.40%	9-4s	36.16%	4-3o	32.78%
6-6	56.21%	Q-To	46.42%	9-6s	39.29%	Q-3o	36.14%	9-4o	32.52%
K-Js	56.12%	K-5s	45.82%	6-5s	39.26%	6-3s	36.09%	6-3o	32.50%
K-Qo	55.61%	K-7o	45.34%	T-6s	39.18%	T-2s	36.07%	T-2o	32.39%
A-7s	55.40%	K-4s	44.92%	Q-2s	39.06%	J-6o	35.91%	9-3o	32.13%
K-Ts	54.77%	Q-8s	44.31%	J-5s	39.05%	6-5o	35.87%	7-3o	31.74%
A-8o	54.37%	K-3s	44.26%	J-8o	39.02%	9-6o	35.85%	5-2o	31.69%
5-5	54.01%	J-9s	44.22%	Q-7o	38.98%	9-3s	35.80%	9-2o	31.44%
A-6s	53.84%	K-6o	43.92%	T-8o	38.73%	T-6o	35.74%	8-3o	31.30%
K-Jo	53.72%	J-To	43.81%	9-8o	38.71%	J-5o	35.56%	4-2o	31.05%
A-5s	53.29%	Q-9o	43.67%	7-5s	38.66%	Q-2o	35.47%	8-2o	30.91%
A-7o	52.88%	T-9s	43.66%	5-4s	38.53%	7-3s	35.40%	6-2o	30.73%
A-4s	52.73%	K-2s	43.64%	J-4s	38.41%	5-2s	35.31%	3-2o	30.38%
K-To	52.27%	K-5o	42.69%	Q-6o	38.38%	7-5o	35.23%	7-2o	29.97%
K-9s	52.13%	J-8s	42.30%	8-5s	38.27%	9-2s	35.16%		

TABLE 6.9 ◆ **EVERY HAND AGAINST TOP-QUARTER HANDS**

Hand	Win %	Hand	Win %	Hand	Win %	Hand	Win %	Hand	Win %
A-A	86.17%	A-3s	42.71%	Q-7s	36.63%	T-7o	34.31%	J-6o	32.12%
K-K	74.05%	A-2s	42.26%	7-5s	36.61%	T-4s	34.25%	6-4o	31.98%
Q-Q	69.28%	K-Jo	42.12%	Q-6s	36.52%	6-3s	34.24%	J-5o	31.76%
J-J	66.28%	Q-Js	41.77%	K-6s	36.50%	8-4s	34.23%	Q-4o	31.49%
A-Ks	65.19%	J-Ts	41.61%	T-6s	36.36%	4-3s	34.17%	9-5o	31.48%
A-Ko	63.55%	A-6o	41.45%	5-4s	36.24%	8-6o	34.14%	5-3o	31.38%
T-T	63.28%	A-5o	41.24%	J-9o	36.23%	J-2s	34.08%	K-4o	31.37%
A-Qs	61.07%	Q-Ts	41.11%	8-5s	35.99%	T-3s	34.02%	7-4o	31.23%
9-9	59.65%	T-9s	40.21%	K-9o	35.98%	6-5o	33.83%	Q-3o	31.21%
A-Qo	59.08%	A-4o	40.07%	9-8o	35.98%	T-2s	33.67%	K-3o	31.08%
A-Js	58.33%	K-To	39.70%	Q-5s	35.91%	K-8o	33.65%	T-5o	31.05%
8-8	56.81%	J-9s	39.60%	K-5s	35.85%	J-7o	33.62%	J-4o	30.98%
A-Jo	56.16%	K-9s	39.42%	J-6s	35.75%	5-2s	33.58%	Q-2o	30.83%
A-Ts	55.50%	A-3o	39.38%	T-8o	35.71%	7-3s	33.56%	J-3o	30.71%
7-7	54.45%	9-8s	39.35%	Q-9o	35.65%	9-3s	33.38%	K-2o	30.69%
A-To	53.14%	T-8s	39.09%	8-7o	35.55%	9-4s	33.34%	6-3o	30.56%
6-6	52.19%	Q-9s	39.08%	6-4s	35.55%	9-6o	33.27%	T-4o	30.56%
A-9s	51.72%	8-7s	38.93%	J-5s	35.41%	K-7o	33.27%	8-4o	30.54%
5-5	49.90%	A-2o	38.91%	Q-4s	35.18%	7-5o	33.11%	4-3o	30.52%

112

Hand	Win %	Hand	Win %	Hand	Win %	Hand	Win %	Hand	Win %
A-9o	49.09%	Q-Jo	38.49%	9-5s	35.11%	Q-7o	33.03%	J-2o	30.33%
A-8s	48.88%	J-8s	38.48%	K-4s	35.11%	9-2s	33.03%	T-3o	30.29%
K-Qs	47.46%	J-To	38.38%	J-8o	35.02%	8-3s	32.95%	T-2o	29.92%
4-4	47.26%	7-6s	38.19%	5-3s	34.99%	Q-6o	32.92%	5-2o	29.88%
A-7s	46.61%	9-7s	38.15%	Q-3s	34.94%	8-2s	32.89%	7-3o	29.84%
A-8o	46.04%	Q-8s	37.95%	K-3s	34.85%	K-6o	32.85%	9-3o	29.61%
K-Js	45.14%	Q-To	37.82%	7-4s	34.85%	6-2s	32.84%	9-4o	29.58%
3-3	45.12%	T-7s	37.78%	7-6o	34.79%	T-6o	32.81%	4-2o	29.48%
A-6s	44.60%	8-6s	37.61%	9-7o	34.71%	4-2s	32.79%	9-2o	29.24%
K-Qo	44.59%	K-8s	37.30%	T-5s	34.71%	5-4o	32.73%	8-3o	29.16%
A-5s	44.39%	6-5s	37.28%	J-4s	34.68%	8-5o	32.42%	8-2o	29.10%
2-2	43.74%	J-7s	37.15%	Q-2s	34.57%	3-2s	32.39%	6-2o	29.08%
A-7o	43.60%	T-9o	36.92%	K-2s	34.49%	Q-5o	32.28%	3-2o	28.62%
A-4s	43.31%	K-7s	36.89%	J-3s	34.44%	7-2s	32.19%	7-2o	28.38%
K-Ts	42.88%	9-6s	36.76%	Q-8o	34.43%	K-5o	32.17%		

TABLE 6.10 ◆ EVERY HAND AGAINST TOP 10 PERCENT HANDS

Hand	Win %	Hand	Win %	Hand	Win %	Hand	Win %	Hand	Win %
A-A	85.02%	K-Jo	33.77%	Q-7s	31.94%	A-5o	29.67%	6-4o	28.11%
K-K	70.92%	Q-Jo	33.61%	Q-4s	31.88%	9-3s	29.66%	Q-4o	28.10%
Q-Q	65.02%	K-6s	33.48%	6-4s	31.73%	K-7o	29.64%	5-3o	28.06%
J-J	59.20%	K-8s	33.46%	5-3s	31.62%	K-5o	29.64%	7-2s	27.87%
A-Ks	58.29%	A-5s	33.45%	Q-3s	31.52%	3-2s	29.63%	Q-3o	27.71%
A-Ko	56.24%	T-8s	33.45%	T-9o	31.50%	T-3s	29.59%	4-3o	27.71%
T-T	53.81%	A-8s	33.40%	J-9o	31.40%	Q-8o	29.54%	8-5o	27.71%
A-Qs	51.74%	J-8s	33.39%	8-5s	31.40%	7-6o	29.47%	J-5o	27.50%
A-Qo	49.25%	K-7s	33.38%	K-9o	31.39%	5-4o	29.46%	T-6o	27.40%
9-9	48.79%	8-7s	33.37%	4-3s	31.36%	9-7o	29.42%	J-6o	27.36%
A-Js	45.07%	K-5s	33.36%	J-5s	31.25%	6-5o	29.41%	Q-2o	27.31%
8-8	45.04%	Q-8s	33.27%	Q-9o	31.25%	A-8o	29.38%	9-5o	27.31%
A-Jo	42.10%	A-4s	33.14%	Q-2s	31.16%	A-4o	29.33%	J-4o	27.17%
7-7	41.51%	K-4s	33.06%	T-6s	31.13%	K-4o	29.32%	7-4o	26.97%
6-6	40.25%	9-7s	33.05%	J-6s	31.12%	9-2s	29.30%	J-3o	26.78%
5-5	40.01%	7-6s	33.03%	A-9o	31.11%	7-3s	29.30%	6-3o	26.69%
4-4	39.53%	5-4s	32.99%	9-5s	31.05%	T-2s	29.23%	5-2o	26.58%
A-Ts	39.12%	6-5s	32.94%	J-4s	30.95%	6-2s	29.01%	J-2o	26.39%

114

Hand	Win %	Hand	Win %	Hand	Win %	Hand	Win %	Hand	Win %
3-3	38.99%	A-3s	32.77%	7-4s	30.68%	K-3o	28.93%	8-4o	26.28%
K-Qs	38.97%	K-3s	32.71%	9-8o	30.67%	A-3o	28.93%	4-2o	26.26%
2-2	38.41%	J-To	32.70%	J-3s	30.59%	8-6o	28.88%	T-5o	26.20%
K-Js	37.27%	K-To	32.69%	6-3s	30.40%	8-3s	28.68%	T-4o	26.14%
Q-Js	37.08%	Q-To	32.54%	5-2s	30.30%	8-2s	28.63%	9-4o	25.88%
K-Ts	36.24%	8-6s	32.51%	J-2s	30.23%	Q-6o	28.55%	3-2o	25.86%
J-Ts	36.15%	A-2s	32.40%	8-4s	30.06%	K-2o	28.54%	9-3o	25.82%
Q-Ts	36.06%	K-2s	32.35%	T-5s	30.00%	A-2o	28.51%	T-3o	25.75%
A-To	35.73%	Q-6s	32.30%	4-2s	30.00%	9-6o	28.49%	7-3o	25.49%
K-Qo	35.47%	A-7s	32.28%	T-4s	29.95%	Q-5o	28.43%	9-2o	25.43%
K-9s	35.06%	Q-5s	32.18%	T-8o	29.83%	7-5o	28.38%	T-2o	25.36%
T-9s	35.03%	9-6s	32.17%	8-7o	29.79%	A-7o	28.37%	6-2o	25.21%
A-9s	35.00%	A-6s	32.10%	K-6o	29.77%	T-7o	28.36%	8-3o	24.79%
J-9s	34.97%	T-7s	32.05%	J-8o	29.72%	J-7o	28.28%	8-2o	24.73%
Q-9s	34.88%	J-7s	32.00%	9-4s	29.72%	A-6o	28.21%	7-2o	23.97%
9-8s	34.25%	7-5s	31.99%	K-8o	29.70%	Q-7o	28.15%		

TABLE 6.11 ◆ **ACE-KING**

	v. Random	v. Top half	v. Top quarter	v. Top 10%
A-Ks	67.04%	66.98%	65.19%	58.29%
A-Ko	65.32%	65.30%	63.55%	56.24%

A person noticing the number of tables in this chapter may assume the approach is "too mathematical." The analysis in this chapter takes advantage of certain calculations, but my own game also depends a lot on feel and tells, and you need some of that to use this information. Granted, if you can put your opponent on one particular hand, then you don't need most of this information (though even then, if you are making decisions with several players still to act, you need it). But who can actually do that?

With very few exceptions, the way you play your opponents is by watching how they play and what hands they show. That kind of observation is essential to benefiting from this chapter. My advice on how to play before the flop when there will be further decisions on the hand assumes a certain type of play from opponents. You should loosen or tighten up based on how the players at the table actually play. When you get into all-in situations later in a tournament, you almost always have to put your opponents on a range of hands to use the tables properly.

You should use the advice of this chapter as a tool. Improve it based on your own experience with different hands and situations. Develop your skill in understanding how opponents play to modify the rankings and the percentages of hands to play by position at the beginning of the chapter. Use those same skills to put an opponent on a range of hands when using the tables concerning all-in decisions at the end of the chapter.

Even though I have been working on these concepts for more than a decade, my pre-flop game has improved since I started writing this chapter. The key to playing your best isn't knowing everything precisely or having all the answers; it is about having all the questions. Once you know how to figure out whether you should raise, reraise, call, fold, or check, you can use the data available and your poker skills to find the best answer for that decision.

CHAPTER 7

No-Limit Hold 'Em: Play After the Flop

by Chris Ferguson

Why Bet After the Flop?

For people who generally understand how I play, that might be an unusual question to start an essay about how to play no-limit hold 'em tournaments after the flop. Every successful no-limit hold 'em player is aggressive, and I was known, when I won the World Championship in 2000, for never calling before the flop (except in the blinds) for the entire tournament. You can't get much more aggressive than that, right?

My game has evolved since then, but I am still known for my advice about never calling. I have introduced a few exceptions, but my style is still very aggressive. Everyone knows that you have to be aggressive to succeed at no-limit hold 'em. They also know that when you raise before the flop, you are expected to make a continuation bet after the flop.

But no-limit hold 'em becomes much trickier after the flop. There are relatively few situations in which being aggressive before the flop hurts you. After the flop, aggressiveness can get you into trouble. More important, you may not *need* to be aggressive to accomplish your goals for the hand, which are to give yourself the best chance to win the pot, win the most chips when you win it, or lose the fewest chips if you lose it.

What do you expect to accomplish by betting? Just one of three things: *(1) you can get a better hand to fold; (2) you can get a worse hand to call (or raise); or (3) you can protect the best hand*. If you can't accomplish any of these things, you should not be betting.

How do you get a better hand to fold or a worse hand to call? I would really be a genius if I could tell you that. There isn't one answer. It usually is not a matter of the size of your bet, though it occasionally is—I will try to point out those situations. You mostly have to recognize, based on your hand, the board, and the hands your opponent is likely to have, what kinds of hands will call (or raise) if you bet and what kinds of hands will fold.

The editor of this book, Michael Craig, told me about the first hand he played in the first event of the 2006 World Series of Poker. He got into trouble because he made the kind of mistake a lot of players make. He made an "automatic" continuation bet without considering why he was betting and what was likely to happen if he bet or if he checked. I think his mistake was a common one.

He was an alternate in the $1,500 no-limit hold 'em event, so he started playing during the second level, when blinds were 25-50. In middle position, his first hand was 8♦8♥. No one bet in front of him, so he raised to 150. A player in late position called and the blinds folded. The flop was K♠T♠9♦. With 375 in the pot, Craig bet 250. His opponent called. After an off-suit three came on the turn, he checked, his opponent bet, and he folded.

His instinct was to bet the flop because he was expected to make a continuation bet. I agree with the instinct, but it was wrong in this situation. If there was any time to not make a continuation bet, it was here. He was out of position and the nature of the flop made it unlikely he would get value from a bet.

After a flop of K♠T♠9♦, a hand worse than 8♦8♥ isn't going to call, so it doesn't work as a value bet. All the hands he dominates would fold. Getting a smaller pocket pair to fold wouldn't really help him. Getting a worse hand to fold is great if that player had a lot of outs or if that player had just a few outs but could win all your chips if he hit one of them. But getting 7-7 to fold doesn't really help him. A player with 7-7 is getting only two outs if he gets a free card, and Michael is unlikely to pay him off if he hits a seven. The player with

7-7 is unlikely to try to bluff with that board for the reasons Michael shouldn't bluff.

Michael's pocket pair is too weak to bet for value but it's also too strong to bet as a bluff. If he were making this play with 5-4, he would have a chance to make a player with a better hand (bottom pair or a pocket pair below 9-9) fold. But very few hands better than 8-8 would fold to a bet after that flop. A player with 9-8 or 9-7 might fold (if he didn't have spades), but what's the chance he has one of those exact hands? This was his first hand at the table so he didn't know anything about how that person plays, but nearly all the hands someone in late position could flat-call with are either ahead and would call, or are behind and would fold.

True, if he checks, he is inviting the other player to bet. If he checks with 8-8, he had to be willing to check sometimes with A-K, K-Q, or K-J. You can't always bet when you are strong and check when you are weak. But this hand goes into the checking category because he couldn't get a better hand to fold or a worse hand to call.

I'm in favor of aggression after the flop, but as a means to get better hands to fold or worse hands to call. I will usually make a continuation bet. But I don't *have* to make that bet if it doesn't accomplish anything.

Let's say you have either 8-8 or 7-6 and the flop is Q-9-2. Do you bet 8-8? Do you bet 7-6? A lot of players would bet 8-8 and check 7-6. Just because 8-8 is stronger than 7-6 doesn't mean you should bet 8-8 and check 7-6.

If you bet 8-8 because you want to get an opponent with overcards such as A-J to fold and deprive him of the chance of drawing to six outs, you gain so much more by betting 7-6 against that opponent. If he is going to fold to your bet, you kept *yourself* from having to draw to six outs.

Circumstances That Influence Post-Flop Play

You will play the same hands after the same flops in different ways based on many circumstances. You should be familiar with some of the most important factors that influence your decisions after the flop; they will come up several times in the examples provided in this chapter.

Number of players in the hand—This will frequently be a deciding factor in how to play a hand after the flop. If I am against five opponents, I have to beat the best of five hands. Let's say I have K-K against five opponents and the flop is A♠7♠7♥. Any player with an ace or a seven is ahead of me. If they have random cards, there is about a 70 percent chance I am beat. Heads-up, on the other hand, if my opponent bets, there is about an 80 percent chance I have the best hand.

How about if I have A-K with that flop against five opponents? I am going to beat anybody with an ace, but lose to anybody with a seven. Five opponents with random hands have better than a one-third chance of having a seven. If I bet and get raised, I'm not sure if I can call. But if I call and that player bets the turn, I am going to fold.

This might be a situation where I induce a bluff. If I had any two spades, I might semi-bluff and represent that I have A-A or a hand with a seven.

Position of the original raiser (yours or one of your opponents)—The position of the initial raiser usually provides information on the strength of that player's hand. If I am flat-calling a raise in position or calling from one of the blinds, I will try to make assumptions about the likelihood of my opponent having certain hands based on his position. For example, if the flop is T♣6♥6♦, it is pretty unlikely my opponent has a six in his hand if he raised from early position. Even if he is raising with 20 percent of his hands from that position, the only legitimate hands he would have with a six would be 6-6 and possibly A-6s. On the other hand, if he raised on the button and I think he's playing about half his hands from there, there is nearly a 10 percent chance he has a six.

When you raise before the flop, opponents are going to make assumptions about the strength of your hand based on your position. If you raised before the flop from early position and the flop is A-T-5, your opponent will fold most of the time if he doesn't have an ace. If he thinks you are playing about 10 percent of your hands, he has to put you on a 40–50 percent chance of having an ace.

Your prior action—This comes up many times in the examples. The way I play, I am usually the raiser. When I see a flop where I didn't raise, I either called from one of the blinds or I flat-called with position.

The most frequent instance where my pre-flop action affects my decisions after the flop is the continuation bet. (If I raised before the flop, I am expected to bet after the flop, and usually will. Likewise, if I called in the blind and another player is expected to bet, I will usually check to that player. Why should I bet when I am reasonably certain my opponent will do the betting for me?)

The concept of the continuation bet does not really apply in a multiway pot. Even if I raised and showed strength before the flop, if I am facing multiple opponents I do not play as though I am expected to bet because with multiple opponents the flop is much more likely to hit someone. That doesn't mean I am going to bet only my strongest hands. It just means that I am going to find some reason other than my showing strength before the flop to determine whether or not I should bet. Whatever that reason is, it has to accommodate checking some strong hands. Even though multiway pots require you to play *more* straightforward, you can't make your bets, checks, and calls correlate directly to the strength of your hand.

Stack size—When you or an opponent is short-stacked, the likelihood that one of you will be all-in or pot-committed can affect your strategy. Although "pot-committed" is a term frequently used in poker, I want to make sure you understand it. Say you have 4,000 chips. You are at the level of the tournament where blinds are 300-600, with an ante of 100. It is your turn to act and you have a playable hand.

If you raise to 1,500 and someone moves in behind you and everyone including the blinds folds, you are pot-committed. He has reraised 2,500 into a 4,800 pot. It costs you 2,500 to call. If you win, the total pot will be 9,800, so the chance you need to win to make the call correct is 2,500/9,800, or 25.5 percent. What kind of hand could you have that you don't expect to have a 25.5 percent chance to win?

By making it 1,500 instead of moving all-in, you give your opponent two options if he wants to play: he can play for 1,500 or he can play for 4,000. Why should you give your opponent that choice? In game theory, it is never bad to give your opponent fewer choices.

Therefore, it is generally a mistake to pot-commit yourself. That gives your opponent the choice of how much to play the hand for.

Reduce your opponent's options to calling all-in or folding by moving all-in yourself.

Not all decisions that depend on stack size involve short stacks. In very deep-stack situations, you have to be aware of how certain hands, though very strong, can cost you so many chips if you lose that you have to alter how you play them. This is demonstrated in several examples, describing how to get away from good hands as well as why you should play certain hands that are big underdogs because of their potential to win large pots in deep-stack situations.

Nature of the flop—You are going to play "action flops" differently than other flops. What is an action flop? Obviously, it is a flop where you expect to see a lot of action. Certain flops stimulate action when they cause the hands to be close in value. Action flops create the possibility that someone is drawing to a straight or a flush. J♣T♦8♣ would be an example of an action flop. A classic no-action flop is A♦A♥K♠. The best hand after that flop is almost always going to hold up.

Calling when all you can beat is a bluff—I hear people say, "I couldn't beat anything but a bluff so, of course, I folded." The fact is, more than half the time I call a pot-sized bet on the river, I can beat only a bluff. Suppose you always fold when you could beat only a bluff. You'd sure be getting bluffed a lot! It wouldn't take long for opponents to figure this out and start bluffing a lot and checking the worst hands they would normally bet for value.

Straightforward play, tricky play, and "mixing it up"—It is important not to play straightforward all the time, and not to play tricky all the time. If you are going to check some flops, you need to do it with both weak hands and big hands. If you are going to bet some flops, you need to do it with both weak hands and big hands. (Your weaker hands could be draws that are worthless if you miss but could turn into very strong hands.) If you always bet your big hands, you are giving your opponents way too much information. They can take pots away from you with mediocre hands and get away from some pretty good hands themselves.

The question is, when do you play it tricky? Here are some situations to look for.

First, you should slow-play when you have a good hand, but your opponent might have an even stronger hand.

Second, you should slow-play when you are letting your opponent improve to a hand that still doesn't beat you.

Third, you should slow-play when your opponent is likely to bet, especially as a bluff. You shouldn't slow-play when it's suspicious, such as when you showed a lot of strength earlier in the hand.

You don't want to slow-play when your opponent can improve to a hand that beats yours. That's why I am more likely to slow-play A-A and bet Q-Q, because I don't want to give an opponent with an ace or a king a free card to beat me.

I won't slow-play a low flush for the same reason. If I have 8♦7♦ and the flop is all diamonds, I will bet because I want to make a hand like A♠T♦ fold. I won't be able to get the ace of diamonds to fold because he is drawing to the nut flush, but someone with one diamond that is higher than mine could fold. After all, they have to worry about hitting their draw and losing to a higher flush.

When do you play tricky? Hopefully, the examples in this chapter will help answer that question.

The balance of this chapter will consist of fourteen sample hands, with explanations of decisions I would make about how to play them after a variety of flops (and some turns and rivers). I have tried to add, among the examples, the circumstances that affect those decisions.

Example 1:

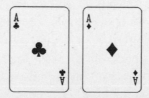

The action before the flop—The action before the flop will affect what you do on the flop. If I am the first one in the pot with A-A, I will raise. If someone has raised in front of me, however, I will frequently call instead of raising. If multiple players enter the pot in front of me, I will almost never flat call. Against multiple opponents, the chances of pocket aces holding up go down dramatically, so you would like to both limit the field and increase the size of the pot.

If one opponent raises in front of you, base the decision whether to call or reraise on your opponent. If your opponent likes to call reraises, reraise. If he is skittish about calling reraises, just call and hope he makes the continuation bet. That way, you are much more likely to get an extra bet out of him.

Another factor affecting whether I call a pre-flop raise or reraise with A-A concerns stack sizes. Ideally, when I have A-A, I want to get all-in. If I can reraise less than 3 times the pot to get one of us all-in, I will do that. You should always want to get your money in when you are a big favorite.

Monster flop—You flop

If I raised with A-A and was called by the big blind and it was checked to me, I would bet it. There are a limited number of hands that will give you action here, so you have to be careful about the size of your bets. You want to try to get an opponent to call or raise you with a flush draw. Don't bet so much that he is going to fold that draw. It's hard to teach the right amount to bet to keep an opponent drawing dead to a flush (or, better still, raising you on the draw). You have to be aware of what your opponents are willing to do, or you have to take a guess.

The problem with checking is that it looks too suspicious. If it looks suspicious, your opponent probably will not try to bluff. If you check, what is your opponent going to catch if he doesn't have enough to call a bet on the flop? If he has K-Q or K-J and catches a king, you might get one more bet out of him. If he has a big ace, a seven, or a flush draw, you do better by not slow-playing. The only real upside to slow-playing is if your opponent has a pocket pair and catches a set, and that won't happen nearly often enough to make that worthwhile.

Same flop with K-K—If you had K-K, you would be happy to check it down. If your opponent checks the flop, you check. Do the same on the turn. If your opponent bets, he is betting into a very suspicious check. I would tend to call one bet, but not more.

Same flop with A-K—I might or might not slow-play this flop with A-K. I am more likely to bet, but if I check and the other player bets the turn, I would call. Then I would do the same on the river. In a multiway pot, as I explained in the first section of this chapter, there is a decent chance you are up against a set, so you need to be willing to get rid of this hand. The advantage of slow-playing is you can avoid the decision of being bet off your A-K.

Multiway with A-A and the monster flop—If I raised before the flop and picked up a flat-call behind me and a call from one of the blinds, slow-playing becomes an option. If I am in early position and have someone acting behind me, I am still giving them a chance to bet. In addition, my check won't look so suspicious in a multiway pot. Multiway, I don't think a continuation bet is automatic. I frequently make a continuation bet if I raised and the pot is multiway, but I am much more likely to check, and it no longer looks suspicious.

Overpair flop, unthreatening board—If the flop is

I will bet. Heads-up, I am expected to make a continuation bet whether or not I hit the flop. I think my hand is good and I don't mind getting raised. Also, my opponent is much more likely to have a hand because I don't have the deck "crippled." By crippled, I mean having a lot of the cards an opponent needs to make a hand. With A-A and a flop of A-A-7, only five cards hit that flop and the player with A-A has two of them. With the Q-8-4 flop, there are nine cards that hit that flop and the player with A-A has none of them.

The issue of laying down aces—If I get raised when I bet after a flop of Q♥8♠4♦, I'm not going to lay down my aces, though there is an amount of pressure that could make me lay them down later. If I bet and my opponent raises, I will call. If he bets the next street, I'll call again. If he bets the river, at this point, I don't think I can beat anything but a bluff. On the turn, I can still beat A-Q and K-K, but not 4-4, 8-8, Q-Q, or unlikely hands like Q-8 or Q-4. By the turn, I don't really like calling but I think aces still have some value because he could have A-Q or K-K. But if he bets the river, I can beat only a bluff. Would I call or fold? I'd take my read and probably fold.

If you are short-stacked, you don't have to worry. You can go all-in with your aces, and if you get beat, you get beat. But if you are playing deep stacks like in the first round of the World Series Main Event, you have to be careful. How to play in a deep-stack tournament is not a commonly recognized skill. In most tournaments, you don't even start with an especially large stack. You are willing to gamble to double up early, so getting all your chips in with aces is fine. Both you and your opponents need to have very deep stacks to consider laying down aces with this flop.

Multiway, it is easier to lay down A-A. Suppose you have five opponents and the flop is Q♠Q♣9♣. There is almost a 40 percent chance that one of them has a queen. You have to slow down with aces against five opponents. You are worried about giving straight and flush draws a free card, but how are you going to get rid of all those draws, especially when you may already be behind? I would call one bet with A-A, but not a bet and a raise. That would be an easy laydown. I would even fold to a bet and a call. Suppose it is checked to me and I check but a player behind me bets the pot and the big blind calls. If the original bettor doesn't have a queen, the big blind almost certainly does. Checking and folding can save me a huge amount of chips.

Straight or flush draw—With A-A, a flop that gives you a straight draw or flush draw generally gives your opponent the possibility of a made straight or flush. Consider a flop of K♥Q♣J♠.

This flop makes me nervous. K-K, Q-Q, and J-J beat me, and so do K-Q, K-J, Q-J, A-T, and T-9. Those are a lot of winning hands that my opponent could have when he called my raise in the big blind. The problem with checking is that my opponent likely has a lot of draws to beat me. I'm generally going to bet small on the flop and call if I get raised because my opponent could have A-K, A-Q, A-J, or Q-T. I'm not going to like calling a bet on the turn and I will certainly fold if he bets the river as well.

Another kind of drawing flop would be a flop of

I like to semi-bluff if I have a big draw, as I do here with the nut flush draw with A♣A♦. I try to think about what those hands can turn into by the river. Suppose I had the ace of diamonds but my hand was A♦2♠. I generally bet as a semi-bluff. If I don't catch another diamond, the only hand I can beat is no pair/no ace. But if a diamond comes, I can beat every single hand out there. A♦2♠ does almost as well against my opponent's calling hands as his folding hands since I always have at least seven outs to the nut flush. A♦2♠ isn't better than K-Q but it is pretty close. It is also pretty close to 4-3, and I can get that hand to fold. I am going to get J-7 to fold by betting. These hands that fold do pretty well against me, and I do pretty well against the hands that will call me. That's why I like to semi-bluff.

Even though A♦A♣ is better, of course, I am more likely to check. Slow-playing keeps me from getting trapped if my opponent already has two diamonds. The reason I sometimes check this hand is that it does well against the hands that will fold.

If I have A-A but not the ace of diamonds, my preference is to check the flop. If a diamond comes on the turn, I am done putting more chips in the pot. If a diamond does not come on the turn, I will bet. A player with a diamond and a pair is a favorite against me on the flop, and I probably won't be able to get him to fold by betting. But if a diamond doesn't come on the turn, I'm now a favorite.

Example 2:

Monster flop—After a flop of Q♦8♥4♣, I am likely to slow-play my top set. On that flop, what could my opponent have? The only hands I could get a lot of action from would be A-Q, K-Q, 8-8, or 4-4. (An opponent with A-A or K-K is more likely to have reraised before the flop.) Even if I miss the bet on the flop against one of these hands, no card can come that could scare them from giving me action on the turn.

If I was the aggressor before the flop, I will occasionally make the continuation bet heads-up, since a check would look suspicious.

Queens as an overpair—If my queens are an overpair to the flop but there are straight and flush draws, as in a flop like

I am going to bet. With queens, I don't want to give a free card to the straight and flush draws, or to opponents with an ace or a king. Queens are very likely the best hand right now; the only hands that beat them are A-A, K-K, T-T, 9-9, 4-4, T-9, 9-4, and T-4. 8♥7♥ or A♥4♥ are slight favorites.

Getting raised with the overpair—If I bet my queens and get raised, I will call. The raiser could be on a big draw; that's not a bad way to play a big draw. He could have A-T or J-T and think his hand is leading. Or he has one of those hands where I am already beat. I will call unless a pot-sized reraise by me puts one of us all-in, in which case I will reraise.

Trouble flops with overcards and draws—If the flop is K♥J♣T♠, I will bet but I'm not going to like it if I get raised. The raiser could already have a straight with A-Q or Q-9, and I could be behind if he has A-K, K-Q, K-J, K-T, or J-T. I might call the raise, but more on the basis of my straight draw than on my pair of queens.

If the flop is three spades, like J♠8♠5♠, I am likely to bet, more likely if I have the queen of spades. This kind of flop is more troublesome with Q-Q than A-A. If an opponent has an ace or king of spades, they have at least eleven outs, depending on whether I have the queen of spades. I want to bet, but you can see how aces are so much better than queens because of the nut flush draw and the lack of a possibility of losing if an overcard hits.

Ace on the flop—After a flop of A-T-7, Q-Q is a good hand to slow down with. Either your opponent has you beat, or you aren't giving too many outs with a free card. A player with a king has three outs. You are giving five outs to a player with T-9. 9-8 is the only hand you are giving as many as eight outs. Let the other player bluff his money off. Every so often, you let him get there. If it is checked on the flop and turn, you could check if you are first to act on the river. If you are last to act, you should bet the river.

Example 3:

Hitting a monster flop—If I hit a perfect flop, like Q♠J♥T♦, I will play it fast. Not only am I expected to make a continuation bet if I bet before the flop, but there are a lot of hands my opponent might get tricky with (like K-K, K-J, K-T, Q-Q, J-T), so let's get the chips in there now. If I slow-play, I could lose action if a card like a nine comes on the turn, or lose half the pot if a straight card comes like an eight, nine, king, or ace.

If I had decided to get sneaky and just call from the blind with A-K before the flop, I will check and raise when the pre-flop raiser makes a continuation bet.

Top two pair—If you catch a flop like A♥K♦5♣, you can play it any way you want. You want to get a couple bets in, but that doesn't mean you have to play it fast. The only thing you are worried about is your opponent hitting a gut-shot draw or a set. If there were two suited cards on the flop, you would bet to avoid giving a free card to make your opponent a flush.

Three undercards flop—If the flop is

I will make a continuation bet. Heads-up, I will almost always make a continuation bet if I raised before the flop and I have position. When I make this bet with A-K, I don't know if I'm bluffing or making a value bet. I could easily have the best hand and I can get even get better hands to fold. I want to get my opponent off undercards or gut-shot draws. Maybe I can even get him to lay down a small pair.

If the flop is all the same suit and I have one of that suit, like J♠8♠5♠, I will make a continuation bet as a semi-bluff, maybe even with three or more opponents. If someone raises me, I have a tough decision whether to fold, call, or reraise.

If I have A♠K♣ with that flop, I know I have between seven and nine outs to the nuts, and five more outs to beat a pair below kings. (If my opponent already has a flush, at least two of the remaining spades are false outs. If my opponent has T♠9♠, a flop of J♠8♠5♠ gives him an open-ended straight flush draw, leaving me with only five outs—the king, six, four, three, and two of spades.)

If I have A♣K♠ and I get raised after betting that flop, it's probably time to lay that hand down. My opponent may have the ace of spades. I'm much more likely to keep playing if I have the ace of spades myself.

Continuation bets in a multiway pot—If someone limped into the pot and the limper and the big blind both called my raise, I would still bet on a flop of J♦8♣5♥; it's a semi-bluff. Against more than two opponents, however, the continuation bet doesn't apply. The presumption that I had the strongest hand before the flop and the flop probably missed my opponent is no longer true. I will check A-K against three or more opponents with nothing but overcards on the flop. If someone makes a very small bet, I might call.

Example 4:

The problem with A-Q is that you can lose a lot when you hit an ace against A-K. The same is true with K-Q—you can hit your hand on the flop and be outkicked. At least with A-Q, you know your kicker is good if you hit your queen.

Monster flop—The monster flop example for this hand would be J♥8♥7♥, making me the nut flush. If I raised, I will make a continuation bet. What I'm thinking when I bet this flop is the following: "If I give him a free card, what am I hoping he catches?" The best he could have is a king of hearts. Maybe he has Ax-Kh.

The player with the king of hearts in this situation has to worry about the ace of hearts and can't go too wild with the second nut flush draw, but I expect him to at least call my bet on the flop. I don't expect him to call a similar bet on the turn.

By the way, he might semi-bluff by raising with his flush draw on the flop. I might make more from his flush draw if I bet now. He might take a stab at the pot with K♥J♦. It is very likely he would raise if he had K♥K♣. If he is inclined to do that, I can get a bunch of chips in the pot when both those hands are in very bad shape.

If my opponent has a set, he can't afford to slow-play and let an opponent with one heart draw out. The only way a free card can improve him is to give him a full house or quads. I want to get my chips in when I am a favorite for sure.

Monster drawing hands—If I flopped 8♥7♥3♣, I would play it fast. I am very likely to have the best hand now. It is, at worst, a very small dog against any hand except a set or two-pair. I want to get a lot of chips in the pot after the flop.

If I get raised, I will reraise. I'm not a huge favorite over many hands but I still don't mind getting more chips in the pot; what I really want to do is get my opponent to fold.

These monster draws are big hands—nut flush draws with overcards, straight flush draws, flush draws with a pair. Play these very fast. A♥3♥ with this flop would be a monster draw. I would be a favorite against any flush draw. Even if I have 5♥3♥, I have a monster draw. I am a favorite over anyone with a flush draw, even A♥Q♥. I am going to raise and reraise with 5♥3♥ and get a lot of chips in with that hand for the same reasons.

Monster draws in multiway pots—Say I have A♥Q♥ and raise. Two people behind me flat-call and the big blind calls. The flop is

The strong hands on that flop aren't very far apart. For this example, the other players have T♥9♥, 6♣5♣, and 8♠8♣. After the flop, 8-8 is the favorite, but it will win just 44 percent of the time. It is vulnerable to flush and straight (and straight flush) draws, so that player will want to play fast. With A♥Q♥, I won't mind getting a lot of chips in there. I'm in bad shape against a set, but I still have nine outs and I can't assume I am up against a set. I am 17 percent likely to win. T♥9♥ is going to get as many chips in the pot as possible. He is more worried about A♥Q♥ than he is about a set.

If I had A♥3♥ on the button and two people limped in front of me, I might limp on the button. I wouldn't raise and there is a good chance I wouldn't even call. I am not a big fan of limping, especially with this hand. What am I hoping for on the flop? If an ace hits, I am winning a small pot or losing a bigger one. The only hand I am trying to hit is a flush and that happens less than 1 percent of the time on the flop. The only other flop I like is a monster draw like this one. The reason I don't like these hands is I don't like drawing to a draw.

Middle pair—If I have A♥Q♥ and the flop is K♦Q♣8♠, I will call one bet if I was in the blind and called a raise before the flop. If I was the original bettor, this is a flop where, even if I am expected to bet, I might slow down. An opponent who called me from the blinds with K-T might be suspicious of my check and think I was trying to slow-play A-K or Q-Q or 8-8. Against a king, I can save money by checking.

Another question to ask myself before checking a hand like this is whether an opponent who is behind has a lot of outs to beat me if I give a free card. In this case, I am not giving my opponent more than seven outs and probably a lot fewer. Also, by checking, I am giving those players a chance to bluff. That's why I will call if the player in the blind leads out after I check the flop. I will win more chips if he is bluffing or has a pocket pair (other than A-A), a queen, or an eight. If he has a king, a set, or two pair, I will probably lose just that one bet.

The only reason to bet this flop is to keep the player with J-T and seven outs from getting a free card. But if I bet, he's probably going to at least call anyway. I prefer to wait for the turn to bet where I can now get this player to fold.

Overcards—If I raised with A♥Q♥ and the flop is 9♥9♦8♦, I will make a continuation bet against one opponent but not against three or four. I'll fold if I am check-raised.

Example 5:

This is a sexy hand, but not one I like very much. The problem is that when you make a non-nut flush you need to consider the possibility that you are up against the nut flush. Even if your opponent doesn't have a higher flush, your hand could be vulnerable to a higher flush draw. Furthermore, anytime you hit top pair, you need to worry about your opponent having you dominated with a higher kicker. Q-Js is a lot better than 5-4s, but with more people playing high cards, there is still a decent chance the nut flush (or a nut flush draw) is out there.

Monster flop—If the flop is A♦9♦8♦, I am not too worried about being up against the nut flush because he would have to have K♦T♦, K♦7♦, K♦6♦, K♦5♦, K♦4♦, K♦3♦, or K♦2♦, and these are not hands my opponent is likely to play. Still if I have a big stack, something like twenty times the size of the pot or more after the flop, I'll try to avoid going broke when I'm up against the nut flush. I am not going to make an extravagant bet on this flop. I want to get a player who just paired his ace to call a bet. That's what I'm thinking when I make a flush with that board. It will depend on the opponent. You should get one call from an ace, and maybe more. If I call from the big blind with this hand I would assume the aggressor is going to bet and I would go for the check-raise, though slow-playing with a check-call is also a possibility.

If I check-call the flop and the fourth diamond doesn't get there on the turn, I will lead with a bet on the turn. My opponent may read my bet as representing an ace, and I was scared of a diamond and don't want to give him another shot at a fourth diamond. This is a better flush to slow-play than 5♦4♦, because with the 5♦4♦ I don't want my opponent drawing to a winning flush with a lone small diamond in his hand.

If the ace of diamonds wasn't on the board, I would be more worried about my queen-high flush. If the flop was K♦9♦6♦, I have to worry about A♦X♦, because a lot more players will play hands like A-3s or A-4s than K-3s or K-4s. There is a greater chance I am up against the nut flush on the king-high board. This supports playing the queen-high flush fast with the ace-high board. You want to punish the other single-diamond flush draws. Be more inclined to play it faster after a flop of A♦9♦6♦ than K♦9♦6♦ or 9♦6♦2♦.

Two pair—If the flop is Q♥J♠4♠, I will play fast. Only five exact hands have me beat at the moment: Q♣Q♠, J♣J♥, 4♣4♦, 4♣4♥, and 4♦4♥. If the other player has a random hand, that's a 215-to-1 shot. More realistically it is not nearly that unlikely because these are hands my opponent will probably play. I am still willing to lose money to those hands, because I can't let the flush and straight draws get there for free.

Top pair—If the flop is Q♥7♠5♦, I will bet if I was the pre-flop raiser. If I get raised, I will call, but I'm not going to put more money in on later streets. The other player could have a straight draw or a pocket pair like 8-8, 9-9, or T-T, or he could have me beat. If I called from the big blind before the flop, I would probably go for a check-raise. I will want to win it right there. Just check-calling with Q-J would also be a reasonable way to play it, especially against players who think check-calling is a show of weakness.

Nothing—Assume the flop is A♠6♦3♥. If I called a raise from the big blind and I miss the flop completely, I'm going to check and fold if it's bet to me. However, if I was the aggressor before the flop, I'm going to take at least one stab at the pot with a small bet, the same bet I would make if I bet with an ace in my hand. The big blind has to suspect I hit the ace. A small bet here should be enough to pick up the pot if my opponent doesn't have an ace. If my bluff gets called, sometimes I'll give up the pot and sometimes I'll take another stab at it on the turn.

Example 6:

Playing quads—If I flop Q♠9♣9♠ with my 9♥9♦, I will slow-play even if I am expected to bet. I'm not worried my opponent will slow down with Q-Q and save a bet because there is no card that can come that will slow him down and allow him to save chips. The money is going into the pot anyway. By slowing down on the flop I am more likely to get an opponent who hits a flush or a straight or a full house to give me their chips.

If there is no betting on the flop, I will probably check the turn as well. I'm hoping someone will hit a monster hand or already has one. I'll have to bet the river of course. Even if no one makes a big hand, playing this way can induce an opponent to bluff or make a weak call on the river thinking I might be bluffing.

Ace on the flop—If the flop is something like A♦7♥4♣, I'll make my continuation bet if I raised before the flop because that board should worry my opponent more than it worries me. I don't want to give him outs with hands like K-J or K-T; those are easy folds for him when I bet. I might even get a player with J-J to fold. If I get raised, I'm done with the hand.

If I get called, I'll slow down on the turn. If he has a lower pair, I'm not giving him very many outs. If he has an ace I'll lose fewer chips by checking. He may even check it down if he has a bad kicker and give me two chances to hit my nine.

If I'm in the big blind and I called an early-position pre-flop raiser, I will just check and fold. The decision isn't nearly as easy if I called a late-position raise from the big blind. My hand could easily be good here, but this is a decision I won't have to make often because I would have generally reraised a late-position raiser with pocket nines. The main reason to reraise pre-flop is to avoid this type of decision on the flop. Always plan ahead and try to steer clear of tough decisions when you can.

High pair on the board—With a flop of

I'll play the hand differently than on the previous flop. It's true that if my opponent has a jack I have the same two outs as I did if he has an ace on the previous flop. The difference is that my opponent is much more likely to have an ace in the previous example for two reasons. First, there are three remaining aces in the ace-high flop and only two jacks he could have on this flop. Furthermore, my opponent is much more likely to be playing a hand with an ace than a jack. If my opponent raised before the flop, I will probably attempt a check-raise. If he keeps giving me action, I'm done with putting money in the pot.

Overpair to the board—With 9-9, a board of low cards like 8♣4♣3♠ gives me an overpair. I have to worry about a lot of overcards that can make someone a higher pair. In addition, for my medium pair to be an overpair to the board, the flop must have some connecting cards or a low pair. Even though this flop is safer than the last one, it's not a lot safer. If I raised before the flop and one of the blinds called, I would make my continuation bet. If I called a raise in the blind, one way to play is to go for a check-raise to find out where I am. If my hand is good I'll probably win it right there. If I get called or raised, I'll be pretty sure my hand is no good.

The problem with check-raising is that I'm not likely to get worse hands than mine to call, or better hands to fold. Because of this I don't mind checking and calling with this hand. I prefer making a check-raise with something as weak as an inside straight draw. Think about it. It's going to be hard for me to win a huge pot with 9-9. I'm more likely to hit an inside straight (with 7-6) than a set (with 9-9) and I will make as much or more with a straight. Furthermore, when I check-raise with an inside straight draw I will get the same hands to fold, but this hand might do better against the hands that will call. If I'm reraised I'll fold in both cases, so both hands have the same value there and 9-9 has more equity when I call because it could be good.

Scare card on the turn—If I have 9-9 and the flop is 8♣4♣3♠ there are a number of scary cards that can come on the turn if my opponent calls my bet on the flop. What could the other player have if he called my bet after this flop? Most hands that are ahead of me would raise my bet on the flop. A set or a higher pair is vulnerable to a flush. I think a player with overcards would fold, but maybe not. If I am ahead, the hands I am most worried about are A-2, A-3, A-4, or A-5, an eight, or a club draw. An ace, deuce, three, five, eight, or any club on the turn puts one of those hands ahead of me.

If a scare card comes and my opponent bets into me on the turn, I have a tough decision to make. If the third club comes and I have the nine of clubs, I would check and call assuming I bet the flop and was called. If I don't have the nine of clubs, I will check and fold. My check will potentially encourage some weaker hands to try to take the pot away. A player with 9-8 may think his hand is good. A player with a low pair or a straight draw that hasn't gotten there may represent that the card that scared me made his hand. Between the hands that already beat me and those that beat me based on the turn card, I have to run the risk of folding to a worse hand. The exceptions are if I have the nine of clubs, or if a non-club deuce comes on the turn. I am not going to put my opponent on A-5 or 5–6, and I'll bet. If I get raised, I will fold.

On an 8-7-6 flop, I have a big hand and a big draw. Even if the other player has a high pair like A-A, I have nearly a 40 percent chance to win. I can win with a nine, ten, or five. I have approximately a 49 percent chance to beat two pair because I can now hit a pair on board or a running pair to make a higher two pair than my opponent. Because of this I want to put on the pressure. If I called an early-position raiser with 9-9 in the big blind, and the flop is 8-7-6, I will check with the intention of raising. If he calls, I'm ahead if he has a similar hand to mine like 9-8 or 9-7, but I'm pretty sure he has at least T-T, J-J, Q-Q, K-K, or A-A. There is a good chance he will fold anything else to my reraise. If he moves all-in on me, I am going to have to do a little math to figure out if I should call. First, I have to figure out what chance I think I have of winning. He could have a straight where I'm nearly drawing dead, or a high pair where I have about a 38 percent chance to win, or he could be bluffing on a draw. If he has a draw, I'm a decent favorite. I think he's more likely to have a draw than a straight, so I'll guess my chance of winning is a little over 38 percent—say about 40 percent. If my opponent's final raise is any more than twice the size of the pot I won't be getting the correct odds to call, so I'll have to fold. I'll call any bet smaller than twice the size of the pot.

Multiway pots—On most of the flops described here, I am not going to like my nines against more than one opponent. A pair of nines is still a good hand multiway after a flop of 8-4-3. I want to bet out the draws or make them pay. I feel the same way if the flop is 8-7-6. I could give a free card here but I would rather make a pair or a draw pay. If I get called, I would bet the turn for the same reasons. I probably would not bet on the end, especially because anybody calling bets on the flop and turn either has me beat or is drawing to a lot of outs. Unless my opponent had A-8, he would probably fold every hand I could beat if I bet. Other than possibly calling one bet or raise on the flop, I am going to fold if anyone else shows real strength.

Example 7:

A pair of sevens will frequently play similarly to a pair of nines.

Flopping a set—If the flop is K♦J♥7♣, I will play the hand fast. If I raised before the flop and am expected to bet, I will. If I called someone else's raise before the flop, I will check-raise. If the other player has a straight draw, I want to make him pay to draw. If he has A-K or K-J, I want to get him to call some big bets or even reraise me.

Pair and a flush draw—If the flop is

and I bet before the flop, I will continue to bet. If I get raised, that tells me that my sevens aren't good, or my seven of diamonds won't be good if a fourth diamond gets there, or both. I'll fold, but it is important to bet the flop to protect the sevens if they are good. I have some potential extra outs with the seven of diamonds, but those have value only if the hand gets checked down after the fourth diamond appears. My opponent may not bet a low diamond, whether he has my seven beat, and he won't bet if he doesn't have a diamond. I am betting to get all the worse hands with draws to fold. If that fails, my best hope is to check it down.

Mixing up your play—This brings up the need to mix up your play on the turn. I bet the flop almost all the time when I raised before the flop. If someone else raised pre-flop and I called from the big blind, I will invariably check to the raiser. In many of those situations, I am betting or raising on the flop with drawing hands or hands that could be behind or hands that are vulnerable to draws that might not fold. As a result, I frequently bet the flop and slow down on the turn.

You can't let opponents stereotype your play. "He's always betting the flop but he checks the turn if he is weak." You have to find situations where you play very strong hands the same way, betting the flop and slowing down on the turn. This is not about slow-playing to induce a bet or slow-playing so someone makes a good enough hand to pay you off. I don't recommend the former very much and I have told you about some of the specific situations where you want to consider the latter.

This is a different reason for slow-playing. You have to slow-play some strong hands so your opponents can't take the pot away each time you slow down on the turn. Suppose with the flop of J♦6♦4♦, you had A♦Q♦. I had described in example 4 how you generally play this fast, at least on the flop. If you have a player with a lower flush or with the king of diamonds and he catches another diamond on the turn, you will get called if you bet.

But sometimes you should slow-play it on the turn. It works better if you are out of position, so your check (following a check-raise on the flop) looks like a clearer sign of weakness. In addition, if you are out of position and show weakness, your opponent may bet and you won't lose a bet. If you have position and check, you lose a bet that might have gotten called and made the pot larger, which would have made it possible to get a larger bet called on the river.

In general, find some situations where you can demonstrate that slowing down on the turn does not automatically mean you are weak. Do it just often enough so opponents can't punish you for showing strength then weakness. In no-limit hold 'em, you are giving up way too much information if you play straightforward all the time. Betting the flop and slowing down on the turn is an appropriate strategy for a lot of marginal situations; it works best if you can discourage other players from testing you after you slow down.

Ace on the board—If I have 7-7 and the flop is

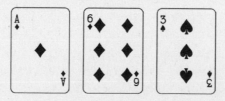

I don't like that flop at all. If I called with 7-7, I might check and fold, especially if the raise before the flop did not come from late position. (If the button raised before the flop, I would probably reraise with 7-7

in the big blind.) The only time I might call a bet on the flop is if it's a small enough bet or it comes from the button or cutoff position. However, I prefer reraising before the flop to prevent being in this situation.

If the raise didn't come from the button, the ace is a very scary card. In addition, even if he doesn't have an ace, he can have a higher pair or overcards to my pair, like K-Q. I also have to be concerned that he has two diamonds and could make a flush on the turn.

I am more likely to call a bet after that flop with a hand like 6-5 than with 7-7. The two hands have about the same chance of being the best hand, but I have just two outs to beat an ace with 7-7. I have five outs with 6-5 and I can potentially win a big pot if I catch one. If a five comes on the turn, that's not a scary card for my opponent. Is he going to put me on 7-4? Unlikely. I could get a bunch of chips from a player with A-K. Therefore, I would call a bet after that flop with a pair of sixes (with 6-5) but fold with a pair of sevens.

If I raised with 7-7 and the big blind called, I will make a continuation bet after a flop of A♦6♦3♣. The time to skip the continuation bet is with an ace-high flop when you have K-K. (This particular flop, because of the straight and flush draws, would not be a good time to give a free card.) It looks suspicious when you pass up a continuation bet, but that's fine. If he has an ace and thinks you have A-K or a set, you will lose less. Assuming there aren't any draws (such as a flop of A♦6♥3♣), you can do that with K-K but not 7-7 because you aren't giving many free cards with K-K. Any card higher than seven is potentially a card that beats you if you check with 7-7.

Example 8:

Small pairs are favorites over unpaired cards. I want everyone to fold, because a small pair isn't likely to hold up unless you make a set. When you call with a small pair, you are hoping to make a set. Unless you make a set, regardless of whether you raised or called, 5-5 doesn't have much value. Occasionally you will see flops where a small pair might be good, and you don't want to pass up the opportunity to take the pot, but don't go wild. Most likely, if you get called, you will lose the hand.

Flopping a set—If you have 5-5 and the board is J♣8♣5♦, you should play it fast. Bet if you were the raiser, and check-raise if someone else raised. In a multiway pot you want to raise if someone bets and check if you think someone else will bet; then you raise.

Overcard, underpair—If you get a flop like Q♦4♠4♣, you will bet if you raised pre-flop and fold if you get raised. If you called from one of the blinds with 5-5, this could be one of the situations where you might check and call one bet. If you check and your opponent bets, you have a difficult decision. Betting is also possible in this situation.

Straight draw—I don't like 5-5 with a flop of 7♥6♣4♦ nearly as much as I liked 9-9 with an 8-7-6 flop. I don't have an overpair anymore so I will slow down. I would check-call instead of check-raise. In position against one opponent, I will make a continuation bet and call a raise, but I won't put any more chips in the pot unless I make a straight. If you make a straight, there will be four cards to a straight on the board, so you are unlikely to get a huge payoff for making your straight.

Middle pair—After a flop like 7♦3♣2♣, I think my pair of fives is good but I'm not going to get too excited. I will make a continuation bet, but other than that, I am hoping to check it down. If my opponent had a hand like T♣8♣, he has fifteen outs and is the favorite. How much pressure can I take if he bets or raises after I bet?

Missing the flop—If three overcards flop, like A♣T♣9♦, I am going to fold at the first opportunity, unless I raised before the flop. If I raised and it is checked to me in position, I will make one bet to try to steal the pot right there.

Suited Connectors in General

I don't like suited connectors as much as most players. I play them occasionally but not enthusiastically. I like hands that can make the nuts. With a hand like 9-8s, you can't make the nut flush. You can, however, make a flush and lose to the nuts. If you aren't raising with this hand from steal position, you also need to have a lot of chips and a weak opponent who has a lot of chips to make the implied odds worth it, and then you need someone to make an inferior hand and be willing to pay you off. Finally, you have to fend off draws to better hands.

Example 9:

Flopping a straight—If you have suited connectors like J♣9♣ and the flop is

you play it fast. If you and your opponent have very deep stacks, at some point you might want to slow down because he could have A-J. If he has a random hand, there is about a 1.5 percent chance he has A-J. But if he raised from early position and you think he raises about 15 percent of the time, then it is about 10 percent likely he has A-J! You definitely don't want to go too wild here. You don't want to go broke if you both have deep stacks.

If you bet and get raised, you aren't even going to assume he has A-J. He could have A-K and you don't want to give him a free or inexpensive shot at the jack. He could have J-J or K-J or Q-J and you don't want to give him a free or inexpensive shot at the ace (or nine to split). He could have two pair or a set. You can get a lot of chips in after this flop. But if you have 10,000 and blinds are 50-100, you might want to slow down before you get it all in there. How many hands below the nuts would your opponent be willing to go broke with?

You should be more worried about A-J on a flop of K-Q-T than T-9 on a flop of 8-7-6. It should be in the back of your mind, but T-9 is part of a large group of hands your opponent could have that he would play and bet on that flop. If he called in the blind, T-9 is just a little more likely than a random hand. He won't call your raise with 6-2o or 8-3o, but he will call you with a lot of hands. If he raised in early position and you called with 9-9, it's very unlikely he has T-9. And if he raised in late position or called from the blinds, he could be doing that with half his hands. If you are worried about him having A-J, chances are a lot more than random if he raised in early or middle position. Just about everybody raises with a lot more hands in late position and calls raises in the big blinds with a lot of hands, so it is not as big a concern there.

Flopping top pair and the art and science of putting opponents on hands—If the flop is J♠3♦3♥, I don't like the jack I just flopped. If my opponent has a jack, he probably has J-T, J-Q, J-K, or J-A. It is unlikely I have him beat if he has a jack. If he has a three, I'm beaten. What's the likelihood he has a jack or a three?

This is how I make that kind of estimate during a hand. There are four cards that beat me and he has two shots to hit them—his two hole cards. If he is playing a random hand, he might have a 20 percent chance to beat me. If he raised, it is pretty unlikely he has a hand with a three, though it might be a little more likely he has a hand with a jack. Maybe he has a 12 percent chance of having a three or a jack. You also have to add in the chance he has A-A, K-K, or Q-Q. If he raised in early position and you think he is raising about 15 percent of the time, 10 percent of his raises are with those three hands. Boost the 12 percent to 14 percent.

If the flop was A-3-3 and I had a pocket pair, I have to worry about three aces and two threes. Now he has two shots at five cards (instead of four) and if he raised, the chances of him having an ace are much greater than random. I might put the chances of him having me beat at 33 percent. These are very rough approximations but I don't need any better than that.

There is an old saying that goes something like, "Measure with a micrometer, mark with chalk, and cut with an axe." After all, even if I knew exactly the likelihood of him having each of those cards, I'm still not sure how to play my hand. I'm going to be swinging an axe no matter how precisely I measure, but I'll feel a lot more confident swinging that axe if I feel comfortable with my measurements. I *wish* I had a micrometer to measure which hands other players had but I don't really need one. These percentages can't be exact and since I have to modify them based on how my opponents play, I can still use them. If I know the raiser is a really tight player, his chances of having a jack aren't much higher, but I am going to be against A-A, K-K, or Q-Q more often.

Flopping top pair, less scary board—When I flop top pair with J-9, I feel a lot better hitting the nine than the jack. If the flop comes 9♦6♠4♥, the only hands I'm worried about are A-A, K-K, Q-Q, J-J, T-T, 9-9, 6-6, and 4-4. I'm not too worried about him having two pair because these are hands he is unlikely to play. I am not at risk as much against another nine because my kicker is pretty good. If my opponent has a nine, he is likely to have T-9 or 9-8, which I can beat. The problem with hitting the jack is that my kicker isn't very good.

If I called with J-9 in the big blind, I will check-raise. On the J-3-3 flop, I like the check-raise because I don't want him drawing with something like A-Q. With the 9-6-4 flop, I am less worried about being behind but still worried about him drawing with overcards or 8-7.

If I raised in late position and one of the blinds called, I would make a continuation bet if it is checked to me. I would make the same bet if I completely miss, so my opponents can't know that I'm strong.

There is only a small chance I'm behind with J-9 after the flop, but I want to win the pot right there because I don't want him drawing to overcards.

Missing the flop—If the flop is T-6-5, I am more likely to check with A-K than I am with my J-9. With A-K, better hands will usually call and worse hands will fold. If I check, I have a chance to hit one of my outs to beat my opponent if he is ahead. If I am ahead, he may not have many outs. If he has A-9 or K-Q, he has only three outs.

I am usually against the big blind in these hands, and he called because of the pot odds. If I raised to two and a half times the big blind in middle position or three times the big blind in late position, most players will call a lot of hands to see if they can hit a pair. He could miss the flop with a hand like A-6 and, even though he has the better hand, lay it down to a bet. Even if we both miss and I am ahead because he called with 6-5, I want to win the pot right there. He has six outs to beat me and I don't want to give him two more cards to hit one of them.

Being able to get good hands—better hands than mine, hands that can draw out—to fold to a continuation bet is one of the reasons for always opening with a raise before the flop. If I call with position, I might sometimes get credit for a hand, but not as much as if I raised. True, they will check any hand to me and maybe check-raise, but if they do it when I have J-9 and completely miss, they can have it.

Flopping a straight draw—If I flop a straight draw like A♥T♣8♦, the ace creates an interesting situation. If I raised, I would make a continuation bet, though a small one because of the ace on the board. I don't have to bet very much to convince someone without an ace to lay down a hand. This is a hand that can get me in trouble. I may give my opponent a lot of action with this hand. I have a very weak hand with a lot of outs—at least eight. That makes this a good spot for a semi-bluff.

Flopping middle pair—If the flop is K♠J♥6♣, I don't like my J-9 very much, especially in a multiway pot. With multiple opponents, the chance of someone's having a king or a better jack are significant. If they have Q-T, I probably won't be able to get them to fold.

If the pot is heads-up, of course I will make a continuation bet. If I get raised, I have to be very careful about folding. A lot of players will routinely fold in that situation to a check-raise. I will probably call in situations like this. From my opponent's perspective, I could have a lot of different hands after raising in late position. If I fold a hand as good as middle pair (which my opponents won't know

I have if I fold, though they will figure it out because I am usually folding to check-raises if I need something better than middle pair to call), I am giving my opponents a chance to profit by check-raising me no matter what comes on the flop.

Look at the other hands in this category. If I had 9-8 and completely missed, I would have to fold to a check-raise. 7-6? I have bottom pair, though I would have to fold to a raise if I am willing to fold middle pair. 5-4? I have to fold that. There are a lot of hands where I will have less than middle pair and I have to throw those away.

If I fold significantly more than half my hands to a check-raise, he could check-raise me all the time and win chips. The specific percentage depends on the size of his raise. For example, if there is 300 in the pot, I bet 200 to win 300. A normal raise would be 500 more, so he is risking 700 to win 500. If I don't call more than five-twelfths of his check-raises, he is winning chips by check-raising me with any cards. Even if it is close, he is freerolling on the situations where he has a real hand or draws to a better hand than mine on the next card. If all the cards are out and the bet and pot size are the same, calling five-twelfths of the time keeps him from making money by bluffing every time.

Limping in a multiway pot—If two people limped in front of me and I have J♣9♣, I might limp after them. I will sometimes fold. The small blind will almost always call and if the big blind checks, five players will see the flop. They say suited connectors play better in multiway pots but that's not always true. If you can't make the nuts, you want to be up against a big pair and a big pair is very unlikely to limp or, if he can help it, play the hand in a raised pot multiway.

If the flop is J-6-6, I don't like my top pair very much. Suppose my four opponents have random hands. There are four cards they could have to beat me, though if they have random cards they could have a jack with a lower kicker. About half the time they have a jack, they will have lower kicker. Each jack has half a chance of beating me, so count the two jacks as one card. That's about twenty-four chances, or about half the deck. I don't even like making a crying call unless it was a small bet and there wasn't anyone to act behind me.

If low cards flop, like 6-4-3 or T-6-5, and the pot is multiway, I am done with J-9. Even if I raised and all these people called, I am not expected to make a continuation bet. I might, on rare occasions, try to steal but my opponents have to show a lot of weakness.

Example 10:

Flopping bottom two pair—If I flop

with this hand, I am in a conflict between playing fast and playing slow. My hand is very vulnerable to draws. Hands like T-T, J-J, Q-J, Q-T, J-9, and T-9 have nine or ten outs. All but J-9 and T-9 pick up another three outs on the turn because a running pair (like a deuce on the turn and another deuce on the river) gives those other hands a higher two pair. Against those hands, my instinct is to make them pay to draw or chase them out. But I'm not that big a favorite over those hands and they are unlikely to fold.

Although there are many hands that will pay me off, there are several hands that already have me beat. I'm hoping if I bet and get called or raised that my opponent has A-Q, A-A, or K-K. But he could have Q-Q, 9-9, 8-8, J-T, or Q-9, leaving me drawing dead or at best to four outs.

If I'm not that deep, I may try to get all my chips in the pot, though if I get check-raised, I am more likely facing J-T than A-Q.

Whenever there is a possible straight on the board, you want to consider slowing down. Not only do you have to worry about the straight, but there are multiple straight draws that combine with players having connecting cards for two pair, or combination hands like a pair with a straight draw. Those are powerful hands with a lot of outs.

In these situations, I think about slowing down on the flop and speeding up on the turn if a scary card doesn't come.

I know that sounds like the opposite of what you want to do when your hand is vulnerable and a free card (or a missed opportunity to make the turn card more expensive) can beat you. Suppose I check and a scare card comes on the turn, like a ten. If that makes my opponent a straight, a set, or a higher two pair, then I missed an opportunity to get him off the hand. But maybe I wouldn't have been able to get him off his hand anyway. If he had a set or a straight, I was already beat. If he had a pair and a straight draw, he might not have folded to one bet.

There are flops like this where the player drawing is actually the favorite. A flush draw with two overcards is a favorite over a pair. Even without a flush draw, if the flop had been T-9-8, a player with J-T has thirteen outs (any seven, ten, jack, or queen) against 9-8, and he picks up three outs on the turn because he can make a higher two pair with a running pair on the board. J-9 has eleven outs and J-J has ten. I am already beat by Q-J, 7-6, T-T, 9-9, 8-8, T-9, and T-8.

If the turn card is a blank, I can play the last two streets without going broke if I'm beat. And if I bet the pot on the turn, those draws aren't getting the right odds to call with just one card to come.

If a scare card comes, it is going to scare the other player a lot of the time too. A-Q isn't going to take this pot away from me with a bet on a board of Q-8-9-T. Even some of the hands that had me beat, like 8-8 or Q-9, have to slow down.

Here is an important point about scare cards: if I don't have the nuts, a scare card costs me less when I win than it costs my opponent when I lose. Why? If I have 9-8, the flop is Q-9-8, and the turn is a ten, I am probably winning less than if the turn was a blank. The hands I am beating, like A-Q or K-K, aren't going to be happy putting any more chips in the pot after a ten turns. But how much am I giving up? I have to worry about the hands that already beat me, plus the draws I let get there. But if I am behind, I am saving a lot. I could potentially lose a lot of chips with 9-8 to a player with 8-8 or J-T. Now the ten on the turn slows me down and maybe slows us both down. Letting the scare card on the board saves me chips if I was already losing, and it could save me a lot of chips.

Playing the big draws fast—9♠8♠ becomes a monster drawing hand after a flop like

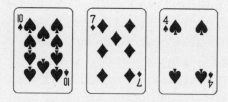

I have fifteen outs to a straight or a flush. I think of thirteen outs as being a coin flip, so if I am the one drawing and I have that many outs or more, I want to take control of the betting. I can get some hands that are ahead to fold so I don't actually have to hit my draw, and I also can go for a free card on the turn. If I have a straight draw and flush draw, that is a monster hand for me on the flop. I love those kinds of hands because I can put pressure on my opponent. If I run into a set, I won't be happy but I'm not that big an underdog to a set. I am a favorite against an overpair, so I want to get that money in. I might scare the overpair out of betting the turn and get to see two free cards, or I can bluff on the river if I miss, or get paid off on the river if I hit. I can even continue the semi-bluff on the turn. If I slow-play, I am less likely to get a free card on the turn if a blank comes.

Playing a weak draw in position—With certain draws, you may not be getting the right odds to continue, but the potential payoff is so big that you want to maneuver, if you can, to see another card. An example of this might be flopping T♥6♦3♣. If you raised before the flop, you would generally make a continuation bet. This might, however, be a place where you can make a suspicious check. If you hit your gut-shot draw, you can win a lot of chips.

So wouldn't you want to get more money in on the flop if that happens? No, and it's not because of the cost of that bet on the flop if you don't hit a seven. The kinds of hands you will win a huge pot from with a straight are the hands that would check-raise you on the flop. You have a weak draw with four outs, but the payoff potential for that draw is huge. You would hate to fold it to a check-raise but you would probably have to fold. The player who would check-raise you off that hand isn't going to consider a seven to be a scare card. He would check-raise with hands like A-T, J-J, T-T, 6-6, and 3-3, and he will probably pay you off if you hit your seven. If you don't hit the seven on the turn, fold if your opponent bets.

The problem is if you bet the flop and get raised, you are giving up a lot more value than people realize by folding 9-8. If you check when your opponent intended a check-raise, you could win a monster pot because he is still likely to give you a lot of action on the turn. Making that suspicious check instead of a continuation bet keeps me from having to make a painful fold, and I still have a chance to steal the pot on the turn or river.

If I have a double-gutter, my draw is even more powerful. Two inside straight draws—an example would be if I had 9-7 and the flop was J-8-5—gives me eight outs and also the same kind of deception as the previous example. The board isn't screaming "STRAIGHT!" like it would if the flop was Q-9-8 and a ten turned. The player who likes his hand after a J-8-5 flop is probably still going to like it after a six comes on the turn.

When you are looking at your outs, you are also trying to figure out how much you can get paid if you hit your hand. Some ugly-looking draws make up for not having many outs because of the big payoff when you hit. But not all inside straight draws are like that. If you have A-5 and the board is K-Q-T, you probably aren't going to get paid off if you make your straight. When a jack hits, there is a good chance you are splitting the pot or your opponents are going to fold. The best you can hope for is a crying call from someone who flopped a set, though that doesn't happen very often. Most players would reraise before the flop with K-K or Q-Q. If a jack does come, make a small bet. No one is calling a big bet without an ace.

Example 11:

Flopping a flush—If I have 8♥7♥ and the flop is

I am going to play that pretty fast. I don't want a naked ten of hearts to call me. If I get raised, I'm not going to like it too much, though if I can get all-in, I will. Otherwise, I will slow down. If he is raising me with the ace of hearts and I can't bet enough to make him fold, I'm going to let him hit it. If I am out of position (calling a raise from the big blind) and I flop the flush, I will check-raise.

If another heart comes on the board, can you throw away your low flush? You want to play your hands so you don't have to fold a monster, but you can't always do it. That's why I say if you can get all-in while a higher card is trying to draw, you won't have to fold and you won't have to make a tough decision. But with deep stacks, getting too aggressive may not scare out the ace of hearts, and if you make a giant bet, then you are dead if your opponent already has a larger flush. Keep the pot small compared with the size of the stacks when you have a vulnerable hand.

If I raised with a hand like 8♥7♥ and I flop three hearts, I'll bet. If a fourth heart turns, I'll check. If my opponent is capable of bluffing and bets the river, I'll probably call, though it's a coin flip. I can only beat a bluff.

If you keep the pot smaller, then you can afford to call that bet on the end. Maybe you can even beat some nonbluffs because the other player may think the reason you stopped betting is because you don't have a flush. He could bluff or think a low heart is good.

In this example, there are five hearts higher than my eight that aren't on the board. It is not too likely that someone flopped a higher flush, but there will be four or five hearts higher than mine out if another heart comes on the turn or river. I ask myself two things when deciding how fast to play a strong hand that isn't the nuts: (1) How likely am I to be beaten? (2) How deep am I?

If I am one card short of the nuts, I still have to worry about the nuts, especially here, where the ace is out. But with my highest card being an eight and only one overcard heart on the board, there is a good chance the other player has a higher heart. If I had J♠8♠ and flopped K♠T♠4♠, I have to concern myself with only two higher spades in my opponent's hand, the ace or the queen.

Whether I slow down also is a function of the size of my stack. If I have ten times the size of the pot—for example, the pot is 500 and I have 5,000 in chips—I will lose all my chips on this one, so I can play it very fast. If there is 100 in the pot and I have 10,000 in front of me, I really don't want to go broke on my flush or on a non-nut straight. Even if I have fifteen times the pot, there is nothing I can do if I flop the second nut straight and my opponent flops the nut straight. It is worth it for me to protect my hand against draws to straights or flushes that beat me. I can't do that and avoid losing all my chips if I'm beat or I fail to chase out the draws and they get there.

If I have 50 or 100 times the pot, I need to worry about losing all my chips when I might be able to avoid it. Think about what the other player needs to have and the likelihood they have it. If I have K-K and the board is A-A-K-K, the only hand I have to worry about is A-A. That's a 1,000-to-1 shot. If I have 100 times the pot in my stack, I'm willing to lose all my chips.

If you have thirteen times the size of the pot, all your chips will be in the pot by the end of the hand if you call pot-sized bets on the flop, turn, and river. There are circumstances where you make a straight or flush and can get away without putting even that much in. If the board is K-Q-J-T-2, how big a bet would you call with a nine? The answer should be, not very big. If your opponent bets five times the pot on the river, it should be an easy laydown. He is risking five to win one, betting that you don't have an ace. If he has an ace, he should get called only by an ace and have to split the pot. He has made a mistake by betting five times the pot, regardless of what his cards are. So give him the pot. You will more than make up for it by punishing him when you do have an ace. For two times the pot, you probably have to call. It depends on how likely it looks to your opponent that you have an ace.

Flush draw—If I flop something like K♥T♥2♣, I will check-raise. If I get reraised, I will call. If I am not all-in or pot-committed, I will fold if I don't catch a heart and my opponent bets the turn.

If I check-raise and the bettor just calls, I will bet the turn and probably the river whether I make my flush or not. I will bet it the same way if the third heart comes on the turn. I have to guard against an opponent with a single heart that's higher than mine beating me with a fourth heart on the board on the river.

Straight draw—If the flop is Q♦9♣6♦, I would play it the same way. I don't like suited connectors as much as a lot of other players, and these situations are the reasons why:

- You have to play them aggressively, but you can be forced to call a reraise from a player with a made hand.
- You are exposed on the turn if you don't make your draw.
- You can make a straight but someone else can make a flush.
- You can make a flush but someone has a higher flush.
- Even if you make the winning flush, you might not get paid off.
- While you are trying to "protect your hand," if your opponent already has a higher flush, you are drawing dead and could lose the maximum.

I still play suited connectors, but they force you into some difficult decisions. With a hand like 8♥7♥, you are better off making a straight than a flush, because it is possible to make the nut straight with 8♥7♥, but not the nut flush.

There is also the question with suited connectors of how deep a stack you or your opponent has. To get the right implied odds, you need to be able to win a lot of chips. But if you have 8-7s and flop a flush, how comfortable are you getting a lot of action? By the third pot-sized bet, you can beat only a bluff.

Example 12:

You are most likely to play this hand from one of the blinds, calling a late-position raise, though you might open a pot with this hand with a raise in late position yourself. The problem with this hand is that it's hard to hit a great flop. If you hit an ace, you have to worry about being outkicked by someone having an ace with a kicker higher than four. If you hit a four, you've improved but you still can't like your hand. In either case, even if your hand is good, you aren't going to win a big pot with it.

Flopping a straight—I will play a low straight fast after a flop of 2♣3♣5♥. This is a case where an opponent, if he raised before the flop, might think he has more outs than he does. If he has A♦Q♥, he could put you on a hand like 7-7. Counting his outs, he thinks, "Three aces, three queens, four fours. Ten outs? That's juicy! I have a 40 percent chance of winning. I can put some pressure on a pair of sevens."

If you check-raise someone like that, he could move in on you. By the way, you will lose a lot of chips to 6-4, but that's the way it goes; that's poker. It's more likely if you raised his blind, but even then that's a 100-to-1 shot.

He might have a flush draw, so you don't mind getting a lot of chips in on the flop. If another club comes on the turn, slow down.

Two pair—If the flop is A♣T♠4♦, I like that flop a lot. I will make a continuation bet or check-raise from the blind. I want to play fast because I want to win a big pot from A-K and keep K-Q or K-J from making an inside-straight draw.

Top pair—I obviously don't like my kicker after a flop of A♣T♦7♠. The good thing about this flop is that if you are ahead, you will be ahead on the turn. K-Q has four outs. 9-8 has eight outs. An opponent with a ten has five outs. If he has an ace, though, you are probably going to lose, though you could get lucky and split the pot if he has something like A-9 and a seven comes on the board.

This is one of those situations where you may want to give the draws a chance to beat you on the turn. You will give up the pot once in a while but you will save chips against all the players playing bigger aces. I prefer checking the flop if possible.

Missing and check-raise bluffing—If the flop is 9-3-2, you have an inside straight draw, though it doesn't even make you the nuts. You should usually check and fold, but this is the kind of situation where a check-raise bluff could be appropriate.

You need to check-raise bluff occasionally, to keep your opponents guessing. Why not do it when your hand has some value, like an inside straight draw? My bluffing hands should be very weak but have a chance to beat an opponent whose hand is strong enough to call. An inside straight draw is just the hand.

When I check-raise bluff, I like to have a little bit of a hand. I want to check-raise bluff after flops that don't connect with the kinds of hands my opponent would raise with, and those that seem like they might particularly fit my random hand. I would rather check-raise bluff this flop with A-4 than Q-J. A raise with any two cards should have the same chance of getting him to fold. If he calls, I have four outs to make a straight, which could win me a big pot if he likes his hand. If he has a big pair, the aces are good, which gives me three more outs.

This is not a value bet; it's a bluff. I know I'm behind. But I like being able to bluff with a hand that has some value if I get called. This is one of those situations.

Example 13:

This is one of the garbage hands I would hardly ever play, even to call a raise in the big blind. I would probably play this hand only if it's limped to me in one of the blinds or if it's folded to me on the button.

Flopping a set—If the flop is 8♠3♠3♥, slow-playing is probably not a good idea. If he has A-9, bets, and I just call, that will look suspicious. How much can I make from this player? I am worried about the flush, but I am more worried that it will slow him down. If he has T-T, he will be willing to get a lot of chips in the pot on the flop but a third spade on the turn is going to slow him down. He might check-fold after that.

Making other hands—In most situations, this hand will play like A-4o. If I flop two-pair after a flop like K♥T♠3♦, it should play like the example where I make top pair/bottom pair with A-4. Likewise, if I make top pair after a flop of K♥T♣8♠, I worry enough about being beat that I might let the drawing hands have their free card.

Example 14:

This is a big-blind-only hand. If I flop a straight (after a flop of 9♣8♠7♥), I will check-raise, even though this is not the nut straight.

If I flop two pair (after a flop of K♦T♣6♣), I will also check-raise to protect the hand against straight and flush draws (as well as someone who could make a better two pair). I also want to win a big pot from A-K. If I make top pair after a flop like T♥8♥5♣, my hand is a lot rougher. I am beat by any ten, though check-calling gives my opponent a bunch of outs.

Conclusion

There is no single "correct" way to play after the flop. You have to understand all the circumstances that can affect your decisions, and you have to understand that you don't have any business betting unless you protect your hand, get a worse hand to call, or get a better hand to fold. After that, there are only two things you can do: think and play.

CHAPTER 8

No-Limit Hold 'Em: Big-Stack Play

by Gavin Smith

Steal Early, Steal Often

Stealing is more important after the antes start, but I like to use the levels preceding the antes as an image-builder, and as a chance to get chips. The traditional strategy in tournaments has been to play ultra-tight until you get to the antes. My philosophy is that if everyone else is playing that way, those blinds are out there every hand and no one wants to fight for them. I want to build up chips *before* the antes.

That way, I am the guy with the power at the table and I can steal the blinds and antes more liberally than everyone else. I generally raise the first hand of every tournament I play.

It will probably sound from the advice that I'm giving you that I steal every single hand. That's an exaggeration. I *want* to steal every single hand. All I'm proposing is that you steal more than your share. If you can steal two or three pots per round, that's fantastic. If you are in there taking shots a few times a round and you know what you're doing, your successes will pay for the times you have to give it up, keep pace with the rising blinds and antes, and add to your stack. You will also get tons of action when you pick up a big hand or a big flop. That's how you get a monster stack.

The steal plays I am always looking to use are the *first-in steal* and the *flat-call steal*.

The First-In Steal

This is the common stealing situation. If the hand is folded to me and I have any two cards I want to play, I am going to bring it in for a raise. If you look at the sections of this book talking about what hands to play in what positions—ignore that! I don't care what position I'm in, and I don't need very good cards. I care only about being the first in, and having cards that I have some desire to play.

Bet-sizing—To play this way, I always make my raises a little smaller than most players. If we are playing 200-400 with a 25 ante, I will probably bring it in for 900–950. My style is to make lots of small raises and lots of small bets throughout the hand. If that makes it easy for the blinds to call, that's fine. I can pick up even more chips if they call. No-limit hold 'em is so contingent on position. If people want to call me out of position, they are counting on outplaying me while giving me the huge advantage of acting last on every street.

The continuation bet—If I get called by one of the blinds, I'll bet the flop if it is checked to me 80–85 percent of the time. Most of the time when I don't make the continuation bet, I'm looking to check it down and either make something on the turn or act like I'm slow-playing a monster flop. That means I occasionally check when I do make a great hand on the flop. I don't want my check to mean they can fire at me on the turn, plus I want to be able to steal on the turn as well.

Starting hands and position—I am going to do this with a lot of hands, regardless of position. I will play my strong hands exactly the same. You will never see me limping (or making extra-large raises) with A-A, K-K, or A-K. If I am raising with everything, and raising by the same amount, my opponents have to guess what I have and I haven't given them any clues. One of the secrets to no-limit hold 'em is removing the guesswork. Whoever guesses the least is probably the person who is going to win. A key to how I handle just about every stealing situation is that I want to make my opponents guess, and I want to make them play straightforward, so *I* don't have to guess.

An important part of no-limit hold 'em is interpreting the bets. Everyone's goal is to make their bets impossible to interpret, and to make their opponents bet in a way where you know exactly what they are trying to do. If I can get an opponent to make his bets scream out that he has a monster hand, I'll get out of his way. But if my bets are always mumbling something he can't understand, then he'll get out of my way when he doesn't have a hand (and neither do I), and he may not be able to get out of my way when I have a monster hand.

It is easy to play against the A-B-C guy who you know doesn't raise in early position unless he has tens or better. But it is difficult playing against the guy who could have 7-6s, 6-4o, or K-K if he plays them all and he plays them the same way.

When they flat-call behind you—I will explain my favorite stealing play, the flat-call steal, in the next section. This is what you have to think about when someone flat-calls *you*.

Most of the time, people flat-calling behind you aren't doing it with big pairs, so I'll start by assuming they have big cards or small pairs. If the flop is nondescript, like Q-7-5, I am going to bet at it most of the time. If an ace or king flops, I'll make a judgment based on my opponent. I might just check-fold it; you can't be afraid to do that sometimes. Continuation bets are great and will pick up some pots, but they aren't mandatory.

You need to mix up your play on the flop. You are in so many pots with so many different kinds of hands (and you are going to hit some of them) that you sometimes have to check-raise. If you have established that you will check-raise sometimes, you have two ways of getting away cheap: reading correctly that your opponent picked up something good on the flop, and discouraging other players from trying to steal when you check.

If the flop is A-Q-4, I might check-fold my 8-6o. If they flat-called you with an ace, you want to lose as little as possible. If you have passed up some continuation bets and then check-raised and feel they probably won't bet with nothing, you aren't losing much. Reading your opponent is what is most important, but you make your job easier if he knows your check doesn't mean *Take it*.

I am still going to steal a good amount of the time with my 8-6o and a flop of A-Q-4. If they don't have an ace and they are afraid I'm setting up a check-raise, they will probably check. Now the pot is up for grabs on the turn and I'll fire out a small bet. They will fold, happy that they didn't get check-raised, and I'll grumble about how I can never win a big pot with A-K.

If I check the flop with nothing, I will nearly always fold if the other player bets. With a few flops, however, I might check-raise with nothing. You have to feel very attuned to the table to even try it. I'm thinking of a flop like K-5-2. If I check and my opponent bets, I think he has to have A-A, A-K, or a set to keep going with it. I will sometimes check-raise. If there was 600 in the pot pre-flop—remember, I'm making small raises, so at the 50-100 level, I might raise to 200 or 225—and I check, the other player may make it 350. I would raise to 900–1,100. My bets are usually small, but my raises will be of more standard sizes. (An exception would be a bigger raise when I have a made hand on a drawing board. I'm not even doing it to protect against the draws as much as because people always put you on a draw when you make a big raise in that situation.)

Getting reraised—I think it's important to get away from your steals when they don't work, and for the smallest possible loss. But that doesn't mean you can fold whenever someone reraises. If you are going to raise as many pots as I do, people have to know that you won't always give them up. That leads to me defending my raises *more* than someone who doesn't steal as much as me. Unless someone reraises by a huge amount and calling won't affect my chips that seriously, I want to defend my raise. I want my opponents to know that you have to have a hand to reraise me. If you are going to play a style where you are in a lot of pots, you have to be confident in your post-flop play. If I flop some kind of hand or draw, I am coming at them after the flop. (I might even come after them with nothing, if the board looks scary enough.) I want to play a lot of pots, steal a lot of pots, and get resistance only when my opponents have big hands. Defending my raise and being aggressive when I catch something on the flop is how I do it.

At a WPT event at the Borgata, I had a tight player to my left. It was folded around to me and I raised with J-6o. The player to my left reraised me. I felt he wasn't reraising me with a big ace. He had a big pair. I thought there might be an opportunity here so I called. The flop came A-little-little. I led out with a bet, and pretty quickly he showed me Q-Q and folded.

I know it seems ridiculous to be calling a reraise with J-6o, but I am always looking for opportunities to build my stack and put myself in a position to outplay people. I felt if an ace hit the board, I could make him lay down a much better hand than mine, and I was right.

Bet versus check-raise—In that situation where I tried to steal and called a reraise, I think it is important to lead out if I want to steal on the flop and not check-raise. It costs less if you are wrong, but that's not the main reason. I think people don't like getting check-raised. It gets their back up a little bit, it feels like you are challenging them when you check-raise, and you don't want someone to feel they have to "prove themselves" by staying with their hand.

Leading out with a bet, especially when they have a big pair and an ace flops, seems friendlier. That's how it feels to me, and it's been my experience that people are more likely to call your check-raise with an underpair than if you bet out. It's almost like they think you are showing them respect with your bet: "I want you to know that you had the better hand before the flop but I got lucky and paired my ace."

The Flat-Call Steal

Flat-call a lot, rarely reraise—One of the prime stealing opportunities is flat-calling people who raise when you are in late position. If you flat-call with everything—I almost never reraise pre-flop—the raiser doesn't have any idea whether I am flat-calling with A-A, K-K, Q-Q, A-K, 7-5, 6-4, or 9-3. This puts them in a precarious situation, because they are going to miss the flop most of the time. I can take these pots away from them without really investing much money. If they miss the flop and check, I will usually fire a bet of half the pot and pick it up a large amount of the time.

Targeting opponents—The key to the flat-call steal, and every kind of stealing play, is that you have to assess your table. You need to decide who at the table is looking to gamble and who is waiting on big hands. You can attack the people who are weaker, and stay away from those who are stronger.

Basically, though, everybody misses flops in hold 'em almost all the time. The ideal player to target is someone who raises but won't bet the flop out of position without hitting something. I will flat-call that player with any two cards. But as the continuation bet becomes more common, you may not find players who make it that easy to steal.

Which players at the table won't fire a second bullet? A lot of conservative players will bet the flop if they raised, but not too many players will bet the flop and the turn with nothing. Target those players; stay away from the people who will bet twice without anything. Look for players who are timid and need to hit their hand to put chips in the pot, at least by the turn. There will usually be a lot of players in any tournament like this, and you have to identify them as soon as you can.

If you expect to make two flat-calls (before the flop and after the flop), you need more chips to flat-call steal than if you think you can take the pot away on the flop. You don't want to invest more than about 10 percent of your stack on both bullets, so you need to have a good-sized stack to do this.

I usually give myself two chances to pick up the pot with the flat-call steal: if they check the flop, and if they check the turn. Most of the time, if a person is willing to fire a second shell, I am going to give it up.

Sometimes, they hit—Of course, there are also the times when the other player hits the flop. You spot the timid player, flat-call, and then he fires on the flop. If you felt comfortable when you called that he was the kind of player who didn't make continuation bets, give it up. Live to fight another day.

About two-thirds of the time, the raiser isn't going to make anything on the flop. If you find the players who will check-fold in that situation, you are going to pick up a ton of chips without much risk. The other one-third of the time, they are going to hit something and bet. Even then, you won't lose every one of these hands. You are going to play this way with your strongest hands and your steals, and you are going to hit some of these flops too.

But sometimes, you hit—When you play this way, flat-calling in position with the idea of stealing, a lot of good things can happen. If you understand your table, you will pick up a lot of chips without investing very much. You can also pick up a gigantic amount of chips when you have a hand or get lucky and your "steal" turns out to be the best hand. At a WPT event in Tunica in January 2006, I was the chip leader when play was ten-handed. Blinds were 8,000-16,000, with a 2,000 ante.

The player on my right, Gary Gibbs, raised in the cutoff to 48,000. I flat-called him with T♠8♠. The flop came up K♠Q♣5♥. He bet 65,000, which I expected. I called, thinking I would steal the pot on the turn. The turn brought a seven of spades, giving me a flush draw. Gary bet 150,000 but I felt he was weak—it was just a feeling. Because I now had a draw, I didn't want to get myself into a precarious situation, so I just called. The river brought the nine of spades, making me a flush. He checked, so I bet 400,000. He moved all-in for 650,000. I called and he turned over 8-6, having made a runner-runner straight while I was making a runner-runner flush.

The interesting thing about this pot was that there was never a time when I wasn't going to win it. If I had raised him on the flop, I was going to win the pot. If I had raised him on the turn, I would have won the pot. If he hadn't hit the up-and-down straight draw, he would have check-folded the turn. If he had missed the straight, he would have check-folded on the river.

Part of the moral of this story is about being able to sense weakness. That is something you can develop, but it's not easy to teach. The other part, though, is that if you play this style, good things can happen to you. If you play your strong hands the same as your steals, you will get some action. And when you are stealing, sometimes you will get lucky and have the best hand, or get lucky and make the best hand. If you sit back and fold until you pick up a big hand, that never happens.

Check-bet-call on the flop—Sometimes, the player who raised checks to me on the flop but calls when I bet. I am going to get a feel whether they are calling me with a made hand or chasing. That's something I think most people can get a get a pretty good idea of. If I think they are chasing—like they had A-K and flop was three low cards—I am going to bet again on the turn.

The situation would be something like this. I call a pre-flop raise with J-7o. The flop is 9-6-3. The raiser checks, I bet, and he calls. What if an ace comes on the turn? If the other player bets out, I'll give it up. If he checks, the ace is actually a very interesting card. I will check behind him. I'm reserving my right to still steal this pot on the river. The other player has represented an ace, but that doesn't mean he has it. He could have K-Q or K-J or something like that. I can still steal the pot on the river from that player. If he doesn't have an ace, he has to be worried I have one.

You can wait and steal at different stages of the hand. You don't always have to do it on the turn. When you bet that flop, they think, "He's probably got a nine," and they put you on top pair. If an ace comes off and no one bets the turn, they will usually be afraid to bet the river because they didn't show strength on the turn. They figure you will probably call with your pair of nines. If they check to you, your bet on the river says, "My nines are good now." You are going to get that pot from a player with two high cards or a low pair.

The other player might even think I checked the turn with an ace to see if I could get him to bluff at the pot on the river. Someone thinking that way sees my bet as saying, "Okay, you didn't fall for it so now I'm betting my ace."

This kind of hand comes up a lot and I think it points out two things. First, betting is like a language during a poker hand. Everyone is trying to figure out what those bets are saying. Second, to certain players, bets are always screaming at them: "He flopped top pair! He bet with overcards and caught an ace on the turn! He's had a set of threes all along!" When I tell you to target tight, timid, predictable players, I'm talking about all the people who think that way—players who are afraid to gamble and will look for excuses to get out of a hand. There are plenty of them out there and they make your job of stealing a lot easier.

Most players just don't like to bluff, especially on the river. They don't like to fire empty bluffs. Those chips are out there all the time, and you have to get some of them.

If a timid player doesn't make his hand in by the turn, he is going to give up the hand. If he had an ace and calls me at the end, he'll get some of my chips. But if he doesn't have an ace, he is going to be afraid I have it. Unless someone knows you are the kind of player who tries to flat-call steal, they assume you have a big hand—a big ace or a pocket pair—if you flat-call a raise.

To keep those opponents timid and playing straightforward, it is important when you actually have a big hand and someone has raised that you flat-call and not reraise. People think you don't want to play A-Q in a multiway pot and you should reraise to isolate a player with a worse ace. I think it is important to flat-call raises with big aces in late position to make it easier to get away with flat-calling with 7-5, T-4, or any other two cards.

You need to send the message that you can have a big hand when you flat-call their raise. It doesn't take long to condition a table. Flat-call with A-K one time and show it. It will be in the back of their minds whenever you flat-call that you are trying to trap them with a big hand. This gives you more license to steal.

Bet-sizing—I typically bet between one-half and two-thirds of the pot on the flop, if the raiser checks to me. If I have to make another bet to win the pot, the size is going to depend on the opponent. If I am bluffing, I want to bet the least amount that will get him to fold. There's no formula. If I think this kind of player will give me a courtesy call on a small bet, I will have to bet a substantial amount. If I think this guy will think a small bet is suspicious and I'm asking for a call, I'll bet smaller and let him think he is smart to fold and save that small bet.

It's a matter of feel and a matter of degree. If this happened at the 50-100 level of a tournament, the pot would probably have about 750 before the flop (the blinds, his raise to 300, my call). If he checks, I will bet 350–400. If he calls, the pot will have about 1,500. If no one bets the turn and he checks the river, a standard bet might be 800–1,000. (I usually favor smaller bets throughout the hand.) If I want the other player to think I'm screaming for a call, I'll bet 500. But if it feels like he has something and could call one more bet if he can "afford" it, I'll bet the pot or even more, if I think he is evaluating how much he can lose on his hand if he is wrong.

Attack Weakness, Avoid Strength

You have to watch the players at your table every hand. Even if you don't have the ability to sense when someone is weak, you can pick up a lot that you can use when you play the stealing game. I look at how people put their chips in the pot. When a player puts chips in the pot with extra force, that often means they are weak. When people verbalize a bet when they usually just put in the chips, they rarely have a hand. When a player is confrontational and staring you down, it seems like they are usually full of crap.

These are examples, not rules. I expect some people reading this will do those things when they are strong, especially if I'm at their table. For some players, sometimes, these signals mean the opposite. The only way to figure it out is to watch them when they bet. Were they strong or weak? Try to put people on hands when you aren't in the hand. If you keep doing that, you will become more accurate.

But you can't be afraid of being wrong. That's going to happen a lot, even after you get good at it. Take your loss, try to learn something from it, and go on to the next hand. If you bust, go on to the next tournament. The two important things are: (1) learn from every mistake, and (2) get back in there and see flops, play pots, and pick up all those chips that your opponents don't seem to want to fight for.

Escaping

Playing this way obviously isn't a no-lose proposition. When it works, it seems like the easiest thing in the world to bet all the time and everybody just lays down to you. More often, you are going to succeed enough for it to be profitable, especially if you get action when you actually pick up a big hand. Your return for this style of play, however, is thrown seriously out of whack if you can't get away cheap when the steal doesn't work. I've tried to explain situations where you should check-fold, or even fold after getting raised. If you succeeded in getting players to play straightforward, that is going to happen sometimes. If you steal and steal and steal, you have to expect they will sometimes have a hand. Be glad if they were nice enough to let you know by playing straightforward and making a big bet.

Just because you put chips in the pot doesn't mean you are married to it. There is no shame in getting caught stealing. Depending on the size of the blinds and antes, you are picking them up hand after hand, round after round; even if someone bets back at you and you have to fold, you are still way ahead.

As you get deeper in a tournament, you have to be very aware of stack sizes. Knowing the stack sizes and how players manage their stacks is your early warning system against what I call the "courtesy double-up." There comes a point in a tournament where your stack can become so large that you should actually shift gears and put on a little less pressure. If I raise with J♦4♦ and a player on a short stack moves all-in, I may have such a big stack that it costs me just 5 percent to call. Or I know I'm an underdog but based on the size of my raise and his stack I priced myself into calling as a 2-to-1 dog. If you do that a few times, the next thing you notice is that your big stack has become a medium stack.

You have to be willing to give up some hands later in the tournament. If people play back at you, hopefully you have conditioned them to do it only with a big hand. You got caught. Big deal—give it up and go on to the next hand.

Even better, you should pick the right players to steal from. In addition to looking for passive, straightforward players, you should target medium stacks. A short stack is looking for a reason to gamble. Unless it's clear a short stack is folding every hand to make the money, be careful about giving him an excuse to go all-in with the first playable hand.

Of course, you have to be careful against the other big stacks because they can hurt you. But you can hurt them too. You don't want to encourage confrontations with other big stacks, unless you know those players really well. If a really tight player has picked up a big stack by doubling up with monster cards, he might be protecting his stack and either folding his way to the final table or convinced he can keep getting paid off with big hands and wait for those.

Big stack or not, I want to steal from a player who thinks that way. Because he has a big stack, I want to make sure I have position on him.

I'm not afraid to get into confrontations with another big stack, but I'm not necessarily right to think that way. I win a lot of those confrontations and build up a huge stack when it happens. But I go broke a lot from losing those confrontations too.

More often, you want to go after the medium stacks. Even then, if they start playing back at you and you're losing chips, you can always tighten up a little. One of the beauties of a big stack is that it gives you all the options in the world. Shift gears.

Late in the Tournament

The bubble is a time, when you have a big stack, to be as aggressive as your table will let you be. I played a $5,000 buy-in tournament at the Bellagio, and as we approached the money, one guy at my table was actually folding every hand without looking at his cards, and counseling everyone else at the table to do it too, because he wanted to make sure he got in the money. I raised every hand at that table. I finally got in a situation where a small stack moved in on me when I raised with T♦6♦, but I didn't want to call him. I wanted to stay on the bubble.

Make sure you know your table. At that table at the Bellagio, if we had stayed on the bubble long enough, I could have stolen from those guys until they were all-in on their blinds. Other times, you get a table of players who are looking to steal in those situations, not fold. They want to gamble with a short stack and double up so they have a chance to make the serious money. They are willing to risk the relatively small payout for bottom money if they miss.

After the bubble pops, you want to tighten up. There is usually a mass exodus of people as soon as you get into the money. Once that settles, you can get back to stealing.

In fact, you can steal more as you get deeper into the money. Especially if it is a high buy-in tournament or a tournament with a TV final table, people are going to want to get on TV. Hardly anybody wants to gamble and miss out on that. Doing some good stealing now can make you The Man at the final table. Again, you are looking at opportunities provided by medium stacks who seem to be waiting for the short stacks to bust or other medium stacks to gamble and lose.

The same thing is true at the final table. Most players don't want to do anything crazy and bust out. If it's on TV, they don't want to look foolish on TV. Whether or not it's on TV, there will usually be several players who are content to sit back and let some others bust, especially if they have a medium stack and see some very short stacks.

As I do once we start getting near the money, I go after the medium stacks and usually want more of a hand against the short stacks. There is also a benefit of keeping the short stacks at the table. All those players who want to move up are playing extra tight until the short stacks are gone. If there are several people worrying about getting $27,000 for seventh instead of $22,000 for eighth, I can keep stealing from those players, whittling down their chips while letting the short stack hang around.

There is no collusion in it. If I have a good hand, I'm playing no matter whose blind it is. If it's my blind and the short stack makes a move, I'm going to play if I think I have the best hand. But stealing from the shortest stack when I don't have anything doesn't make sense. First, when the short stack makes a stand, he will probably have a better hand but the pot odds will be too good to fold. Second, as long as he hangs around, it is easier to steal from the medium stacks.

Conclusion

A big stack puts pressure on other players. Just being in the hand is threatening to some people and they want to look for reasons to avoid playing a pot with you. By taking advantage of the opportunity the big stack provides you to play more hands and target certain players, you can intensify the pressure. If you really work on this part of your game—looking for opportunities, trying to understand the players at your table, figuring out when the best times are for stealing, how different bets and different boards affect your opponents—you can really take advantage of a big stack. This style of play isn't for everyone, but if you can develop it, you can steal your way to an even bigger stack and get a lot of action when you pick up a big hand or flop one. That's how I think you get deep in tournaments and give yourself the best chance of winning them.

CHAPTER 9

No-Limit Hold 'Em: Short-Stack Play

by Phil Gordon

This chapter contains several of the concepts I consider most important when you find yourself short-stacked in a no-limit hold 'em tournament. But none of them will work for you if you don't follow this first piece of advice: *Never give up!*

You see this all the time in online tournaments, and quite a bit even in big casino events: a player loses most of their chips on a bad beat and shoves in the rest of his chips on the next hand with something like Q-3. Or he limps into the next hand and moves all-in after the flop. You can call this frustration or hopelessness or irrational thinking. ("I lost with the best hand so it's my turn to get lucky and double up with garbage)."

But it all boils down to the same thing: going on tilt. Poker involves emotional swings that, combined with swings of luck, can put people in situations where they do reckless things. If you want to get better (and you must if you are reading this book), then you already know that you can't succumb to tilt temptation.

There have been many instances of tremendous comebacks in poker tournaments. One of the most famous stories in the history of the World Series of Poker involves Jack Straus in 1982. On the first day, Straus lost a big pot and thought he was eliminated from the tournament. As he got up from his chair, he discovered a single chip beneath a cocktail napkin. He went on to win the World Championship. That's where the expression "a chip and a chair" came from.

I had a similar experience the very first tournament I entered as a professional. I quit my job, decided I was a pro, and went to Atlantic City in February of 1997 to play poker for a couple weeks in the U.S. Poker Championships. In my first event, I made it to the final table, but took a bad beat and was down to 100. The average stack was about 13,000. Blinds were 400-800, so I would be all-in on both blinds. I got lucky on the next few hands, survived the blinds, and was back in action.

I won the tournament.

Obviously, there has to be a component of luck to rebound from that situation. But when I got a couple chips—really, it wasn't more than a couple chips—I made smart decisions with them. No matter what happens, you have to stay focused and continue to make winning decisions.

What Is "Short-Stacked"?

It is generally agreed that if your stack is ten big blinds or less, you have only two options: all-in or fold. Understand the reason why: if you bet one-third of your chips (the approximate size of a raise of three times the big blind when you have ten big blinds), you are *pot-committed*. Specifically, you will be getting odds of better than 2-to-1 to call a reraise, and even if you were attempting to steal the blinds with a pre-flop raise, you are usually not a 2-to-1 underdog. You have to call; you are committed to the pot. If you had 8♦5♦ and your opponent put you all-in with A♠K♠, you have to call; you are only a 62/38 dog and you'll be getting more than 2-to-1 on your call. Folding here would be a very bad, negative equity decision.

When you have ten times the big blind, why raise only three times the big blind when someone can easily put you all-in or call and force you to make a difficult decision if you miss the flop? You get several benefits being all-in. First, it is more difficult for opponents to call the larger bet. If you move in with 8♦5♦, you will get called by A♠K♠, but there is a chance you will get a lot of hands nearly that good (or hands that have you dominated and in way worse shape than A-K) to lay down—K-9, J-T, Q-8. Second, you eliminate any chance of getting outplayed after the flop. This is especially important if you are in the blinds and would have to play the hand out of position.

Even before your stack is that small, you need to modify your strategy based on your stack size. You are still vulnerable even if you have a little more than ten times the big blind. If you can't get away from a hand if one-third of your chips are in the pot, then it's at least *difficult* getting away if you had to bet one-quarter of your chips. Even if you can get away from a hand, you will be limited to folding or moving all-in *next time*. In addition, barely being able to get away from a hand is, in some ways, worse than being pot-committed.

Good players will know that you have just enough chips to fold. (You should be aware of this when other players are in this position and prepare to take advantage.) They will look for ways to put you to difficult decisions, like calling from the blind and moving you all-in on the flop.

That's why I think you have to consider yourself as short-stacked at thirteen to fifteen big blinds. You generally should not be looking to steal blinds or see flops. Stealing blinds is problematic at thirteen to fifteen big blinds. You are investing a significant portion of your stack. If you have to fold to a reraise, then you aren't just short-stacked—you are short-stacked and are in danger of losing one of the most profitable strategies you had, the all-in resteal. You are not in danger of being blinded or anted away. You can look for opportunities but your goal has to be getting enough chips to extricate yourself from this vulnerable position.

Once you get above fifteen to eighteen big blinds, you have all your weapons available. You have enough chips to scare people and enough chips to fold and not materially damage yourself. Around fifteen big blinds, however, you have to play a different game.

Thirteen to Fifteen Big Blinds (The All-In Reraise)

You have enough chips to make an all-in *reraise* and you should look for opportunities to do that. This is your ideal situation: someone who is playing too many hands raises three or four times the big blind. Everyone folds to their raise, and you are in the cutoff position, or the button, or one of the blinds. This is a good time to take a shot and move all-in.

This reraise can be even more effective if someone has called between the raiser and you. In Dan Harrington's books, he refers to this as the "sandwich effect." That caller in the middle sweetens the situation considerably. First, the pot is much larger. With 400-800 blinds and antes of 75, the pot starts at 1,875 nine-handed. If you have 10,400 chips (thirteen times the big blind), your stack would increase to 12,275, or fifteen-plus big blinds if you won the blinds and antes. By stealing over a player who raised three times the big blind, your stack would increase to 14,675, eighteen-plus big blinds. When you catch someone who cold-called the raise, your stack grows to 17,075, twenty-one-plus big blinds. You could win seven or eight big blinds without any confrontation. That is an extraordinarily profitable play.

Second, the caller is relatively unlikely to be much of a threat. After all, wouldn't that player have raised if his hand was worth fifteen bets?

Third, the original raiser, however, has to consider the likelihood of two players having a better hand than his, especially if he is a loose-aggressive player.

Fourth, even if you are wrong and one of them had a big hand, the dead money in the pot—over 4,000 chips if one opponent calls—helps compensate for having the worst of it.

The flat-caller is just a bonus; you don't need a raise and a call before making an all-in reraise. You want to target a loose-aggressive player, ideally one who has a medium-sized stack. If you try this against a player on a short stack like you, he may decide he is pot-committed or nearly pot-committed. If the raiser has a very large stack, he might make a loose call. You would prefer a player who is putting his tournament on the line if he calls.

If you do a reasonable job choosing your opponent, you don't even need a big hand. I recommend you *don't* try it with a hand that can easily be dominated by the kind of hand likely to call you, like A-5 or A-7 or K-J. Don't make this play with a weak or medium ace or even a king—and a queen is a death card in this spot. Obviously, you are not looking to get called, but if you do get called, you are probably better off with a pocket pair (even a low pair) or suited connectors.

If you made a "mistake" and the raiser calls you with A-K, you are not in terrible shape with 7-6s or 6-6. With the pocket pair, you are a favorite (55–45 percent if the A-K is unsuited, 53–47 percent against A-Ks). With 7-6s, you are a 60–40 percent underdog (even less if the A-K is unsuited). That's just about the odds you are getting if there was a flat-caller who folded. (If you started the hand with thirteen big blinds, you would win eighteen-plus, or fifteen-plus without that player in the middle.)

To summarize, these are the keys:

• Loose-aggressive raiser
• Raiser with an average stack
• A hand that is relatively unlikely to be dominated
• (Bonus) a flat-caller between the raiser and you

The player is more important than your cards.

Eight to Eleven Big Blinds (The All-In Steal Raise)

At eight to eleven big blinds, I am looking to go all-in from late or even middle position to steal the blinds. In early position, if you go all-in, you have to avoid completely dominated hands. You don't want to play a hand like A-5s all-in from early position. The hands likely to call you are going to have you crushed. If you have A-5s and you get called by A-T or above, even unsuited, you have only a 30–35 percent chance of winning.

At approximately ten big blinds, you have some time, so don't panic. The key is to use your entire stack to maximum efficiency, while you can still exert some force on your opponents. I think you should play tighter than you normally would from early position, and looser than you normally would from late position. If you are in the cutoff or on the button with ten big blinds and everyone has folded, you can move in with just about any hand to steal the blinds.

It is very important to profile the players in the blinds. Ideally, you are looking for average stacks. You want them to be able to fold. Their stack sizes and tendencies are as important as the cards you are dealt.

For example, say you are in the cutoff with nine times the big blind. The players in the blinds have average stacks and are tight, conservative players. It gets folded around to you. If you have 9-8s, don't hesitate to move all-in. With A-2, you should probably pass. Your opponents know you are forced to take risks. They are likely to call you with any ace and probably a decent king. You want to put pressure on the average stacks and your hand selection is secondary, but you can't afford to do it with a hand that is dominated.

This short-stacked, your goal is to get out of the critical range. Picking up two-plus big blinds helps but you don't mind a coin flip here. If you happen to pick up A-A or K-K, get called, and double up, it's great that you got lucky, but you can't expect that or wait for it. You have to be prepared to gamble.

If someone bets in front of you, you don't have enough chips to make anyone fold with a reraise. Only reraise with a hand you are comfortable showing down, because that's what will happen. A-K and maybe A-Q are the only unpaired hands you would feel comfortable reraising with. You definitely don't want to play a hand like A-T or K-J against a raiser. Against an active opponent, you could reraise with any pocket pair, but you should probably fold small pairs against tight opponents or when you can't decide how loose the raiser is playing. Against a tight opponent, if you have a hand like 4-4, a coin flip is the *best* you can hope for, and you could be facing a higher pair.

Stop-and-Go

This is the play where, out of position, you call a raise rather than reraising. (This means you are doing this from one of the blinds.) First to act after the flop, you take over the betting lead. Unless your opponent had a monster starting hand, like A-A (or a high pair and the flop is all undercards), or has the flop hit him just right, it is a very powerful move.

Should you use it as an all-in move when you are short-stacked? I think it is a good play in limited circumstances. First, you have to be capable of pulling the trigger, just closing your eyes and moving in no matter what comes on the flop. I see too many people intend to use this play and then not follow through because they miss the flop and they worry the flop hit the raiser. That's bad, because you ruined your chance of reraising all-in before the flop. Instead of potentially inducing an opponent to make a mistake before the flop, you called off a substantial portion of your short stack.

Second, you need to use it against a player with approximately the same size stack as you. If the raiser has a big stack, he is probably getting the odds to call you with just about any hand he would raise with, if he has any suspicion you are putting a move on him.

Third, this play is primarily useful for the eight-to-eleven blinds range. With fewer chips, you will definitely get called. With more, you are putting too many chips at risk on what is usually a naked bluff. You are in one of the blinds, so there is less dead money in the pot. With more than eleven big blinds, there are better ways to put pressure on opponents.

Fourth, you want to do this against an opponent in early to middle position. Against a late-position opponent, you should move in if you are going to play. There is a greater chance that (a) they will make a mathematical mistake and fold their steal attempt, or (b) your hand is a favorite if they call.

Fifth, you need to find an opponent willing to fold—a timid player or a loose-aggressive player. This is the same player you might target for an all-in resteal, except you are afraid you don't have enough chips to avoid getting called. (The all-in resteal is a better play, which is why stop-and-go is recommended only when you have too few chips to make an all-in resteal.) You are expecting an opponent to fold post-flop a hand with which he would have called the same bet before the flop.

Don't be afraid to use tells in this spot. This is one of those spots where reading your opponent after the flop can be extraordinarily useful. One of the key tells in this spot is when, as soon as the flop comes down, he looks at your chips or he looks at his own chips. That's a bad sign. If he continues to look directly at the flop, then you're probably safe to go ahead with the stop-and-go. Likewise, if your opponent is trying to count down your chips, that's a bad sign for you as well.

Four to Six Big Blinds (All-In Showdowns)

Anytime you put chips in the pot, you are going to show down your hand. You may have to call all-in, and you can expect to get called when you move in. Players will occasionally not think through the math, but if you have five times the big blind and raise, the pot would contain seven-plus big blinds. The big blind has to call just four times the big blind. That's pretty close to good enough odds for 7-4s to call A-Ko.

Because you are going to get called, this changes the hand selection criteria. Medium or small connecting cards go down in value. You want hands where you are *hoping* for a coin flip: pocket pairs, A-K, A-Q, A-J, A-T. In late position, K-Q and K-J are all-in hands.

You are desperate, but there are a few things to consider before you move in. First, if you decide to take a shot with a hand like 9-8s, either calling all-in or raising, do it from late position, not from the blinds. I know the impulse with a reasonable hand like 9-8s when you are in the big blind would be to call. But think about it: there's no *dead money* in the pot. If you call all-in from late position with that hand, you get the benefit of (a) one and a half big blinds' worth of chips when the blinds fold, or (b) a possible call from the blinds, which increases the payoff if you get lucky.

Second, look for a multiplayer pot. This is a variation of the sandwich play. If a player in middle position raises and another player calls, you get several advantages by reraising all-in. The original raiser is pretty likely to move in to isolate you. He is out of position and potentially facing pressure from the flat-caller after the flop. (The alternative is that the original raiser had nothing and fears the flat-caller, folding and leaving you heads-up against the player whose hand probably wasn't good enough to reraise.) In any event, that provides three big blinds of dead money, in addition to the blinds and antes. Now you are definitely getting the pot odds to put in all your chips with 9-8s against A-K. The other possibility is that they both call and, at least if you get lucky, you triple up and you go from the critical condition of having just five big blinds to having seventeen. Having opponents who are still active after the flop who can bet and raise each other out (thus limiting the number of hands you have to beat) is a great advantage as well.

One Hand to Live

What if you have just enough for the big blind and you are under the gun? How good a hand do you need to call all-in? Or, to put it another way, how bad does your hand have to be to throw it away and take your chances on the random hand you will get in the big blind? Hopefully, this doesn't happen too often to you, but it is useful to know what hands are above average and which aren't.

Here is a list of all the hands that beat a random hand over 50 percent of the time. (This information comes from PokerStove.com, a terrific program that runs hold 'em hands against each other, against random hands, or against specified percentages of hands in 8–25 billion hand trials. You can also find the same kind of information in chapter 6 from Andy Bloch.)

- Any pair
- Any ace
- Any king
- Any suited queen and any off-suit queen down to Q-5
- J-T, J-9, J-8, J-7s, J-6s
- T-9, T-8s, T-7s
- 9-8s

Technically, you should play more than 50 percent of your hands under the gun because of the likelihood the big blind and small blinds will be dead money if someone raises. Consequently, hands outside the 50 percent mark would be playable, like J-5s (which is better than 49.98 percent of random hands). In fact, if you put in your last chip under the gun, someone raises, everyone else folds, and you win the hand, your stack will rise from one big blind to four and a quarter big blinds (1 BB + 1 SB [½ BB] + antes [¾ BB] + raise [= 1 BB] + your bet). This means that you are getting incredible odds for this kind of play, betting one big blind to get four and a quarter. If you look at the end of chapter 6, Andy Bloch's analysis of the pre-flop game, the tables show that you are getting the odds to put that last big blind in with just about any hand.

If you beat one opponent with your last chip on your big blind, your stack will rise to just three and a quarter big blinds. Arguably, you should play quite a few more hands under the gun. As a practical matter, though, your position with three and a quarter or four and a quarter big blinds is still so serious that the extra chips are probably worth less than taking a better hand into this showdown.

You have a choice. Even if you win with a weak hand right before your big blind forces you all-in, you are still so short-stacked that you don't give up too much by waiting. The pot odds, though, suggest that your hand doesn't matter. The dead money from the blinds and antes give you such a big return on your last chips that any hand has the right odds to commit.

Short-Stacked in the Money

Once you are in the money, use these short-stack strategies aggressively until you make the top four. In most tournaments, the prize money goes disproportionately to the top three spots. It is important to give yourself a chance to win top-three money. I see a lot of people playing too tight to move up from eighth to seventh, not making correct plays for relatively little gain. Over the long run, you are better off taking your shot and making the best possible short-stack plays than trying to move up one spot (until you make the top four). If you are successful with these strategies, you are going to end up winning more than your fair share of tournaments.

In the top four, there may be situations where it might make more sense to pass up a good play. If someone is even more short-stacked, letting someone else bust is now meaningful, because the jump in prize money is usually fairly significant between fourth and third, and certainly between third and second.

Playing Defense with a Short Stack

When you are on a short stack, your blinds are frequently under attack by the bigger stacks. This happens all the time on the bubble. All pros will tell you that you shouldn't be worried about busting on the bubble: bottom money is barely more than your buy-in, building your stack at this time is how you *win* tournaments, etcetera. I agree with that, but I also recognize that everyone reading this isn't playing twenty events at the World Series, and that some people considering these strategies for the Main Event got in on a $200 satellite, so bottom money of $10,000–$15,000 is a gigantic return, not to mention worth bragging rights in your home game forever.

If that is your situation, put your head down and get into the money, and don't be ashamed about it. If you play tournaments on a more regular basis, however, and want to both improve and give yourself a chance to win, you have to take advantage of the bubble, even with a short stack. With fifteen times the big blind, opponents are going to assume that you won't be willing to go broke on the bubble. A late-position player with a decent stack will probably raise your blind with any two cards. This is exactly the type of situation where an aggressive reraise from you will work.

You will occasionally guess wrong and run into a big hand. Or you will be right, get called, and get unlucky. It hurts busting out on the bubble, especially if you are relatively new to tournament poker. But if you play a lot of tournaments, you will be more satisfied with your results if you use the bubble to increase your stack (even if, as here, you have to do it from a defensive short-stacked posture), compared with letting your stack dwindle in the hope that someone else goes out before you.

Conclusion

Being short-stacked isn't the end of the world. Stay focused. Play aggressively. Get your money in the pot in the best situation you can, based on your stack size and position, and try to preserve as much folding equity as possible. If you can help it, make your move before your situation becomes critical and realize that there is no shame in making the right move but getting the wrong result. With good timing and a little luck, you'll find yourself right back in the hunt for the bracelet and the big prize money.

CHAPTER 10

No-Limit Hold 'Em: Online Tournament Strategy

by Richard Brodie

My Introduction to Poker: Andy Bloch and the $11 SNG

I had never played no-limit Texas hold 'em when I received an e-mail from my friend Andy Bloch telling me that he would be appearing on two televised final tables as part of something called the "World Poker Tour." The broadcast dates and even the network weren't yet known, but I was intrigued.

I thought, if a math guy like Andy can succeed at poker, maybe I could challenge myself and see what I could learn. I started playing $11 sit-n-gos (SNGs). I was very quickly able to win in sit-n-gos, so I moved to multitable tournaments (MTTs, or "multis"). I actually won my first multi, which was lucky, and within a few months I was playing in live tournaments. I finished runner-up in my third-ever live tournament in July 2003, and have been playing live and online tournaments ever since.

A sit-n-go is a one-table tournament so named because it begins as soon as enough players sign up to fill a table. As a result, every on-line site runs SNGs around the clock with buy-ins as small as $1 and as big as four figures. The typical SNG starts with nine or ten play-ers, depending on the site, though they can be played short-handed or even heads-up. At a full-table SNG, the final three spots share the entry money (minus the juice). The split is usually 50 percent for first, 30 percent for second, and 20 percent for third.

SNGs are not entirely an online phenomenon. Eric Drache pioneered single-table satellites at the World Series of Poker in the early eighties. The popularity of these single-table satellites and, in the last few years, online SNGs has led to more poker rooms offering one-table freeze-outs for cash. The advice about online SNGs, with obvious adaptations, can apply to live SNGs. Some of the advice in this chapter can apply to satellite tournaments, both online and live, but there is one important difference. Satellite tournaments have a different payout structure from cash tournaments. Unlike the gradually increasing payouts for the top 10 percent of the field in a cash MTT, with the big money going to the top few finishers, in satellite tournaments everybody who wins gets the same payout, a tournament buy-in. Based on the satellite buy-in, the number of winners may be a lot smaller than 10 percent of the field.

Small buy-in sit-n-gos are a great way to learn no-limit hold 'em. First, you can't lose very much. I limited myself to $11 sit-n-gos, but you can play even lower. Second, you get experience at both a full table and a final table every time you enter. Short-handed play, especially late in a tournament, involves different skills from playing at a full table. Playing well short-handed, which is a necessity at the final *two* tables in a poker tournament, is extremely important to your return in tournament poker because first prize is typically much bigger than the other prizes and the top three spots receive a large portion of the total prize pool.

In a sit-n-go, you start at the final table. You have to finish in the top three to make any money. You will learn strategies for short-handed play fast.

Overview: The Two Games of Tournament Poker

No-limit hold 'em is a game that changes quite a bit based on the sizes of the stacks. When the stacks are big and there are no antes, no-limit hold 'em is a game of implied odds. What you are trying to do is make a hand that is so big that you will win all of your opponent's chips when your opponent makes the second-best hand. For example, you could make three of a kind and possibly get paid off with all your opponent's chips if he makes top pair with an ace kicker.

In the early stages of a deep-stack tournament, you are looking to pick up chips in large amounts. Ironically, you may be more likely to do this with 7-7 than with A-A. In fact, when you have 7-7, you *want* to be against A-A. If you flop a set, especially with a ragged board, your opponent with aces could lose all his chips to your set.

Imagine this situation: You are playing the third hand of a tournament where you have 3,000 in starting chips. Blinds are 25-50. The second player to act raises to 150. Everybody folds to you on the button. You have 8♣8♠ and call. The blinds fold. There is 375 in the pot. You and your opponent both have about 2,800 left. The flop comes 2♣7♦8♦. You hope the raiser has a big pocket pair. Your goal is to get that player to bet the rest of his chips. Unless he has A♦K♦ or a hand he'll fold to any show of strength, he will want to protect that big pocket pair against straight and flush draws. If he bets and you raise, he may even think you are making a semi-bluff on a draw and move all-in.

You will flop a set approximately once every eight and a half times you see a flop with a pocket pair. But the potential payoff when you are against a strong second-best hand can be enormous. That's why I say, when stacks are deep, no-limit hold 'em is a game of implied odds.

When the blinds and antes get big compared with the stacks, it is no longer a game of implied odds. You most likely can't afford to keep calling raises to try to outflop opponents. In fact, you will see fewer flops as players on short stacks are looking for starting cards on which to bet all their chips. At this stage in a tournament, no-limit hold 'em is a game of winning the blinds and getting the best of heads-up matchups. You have to steal a lot more in late position to pick up the blinds and antes and you have to make mental calculations about the strength of your opponents' hands. If there is a raise to your right, is this a time to come over the top, either because you have the best hand or because you think your opponent will fold?

This is the way you should approach all poker tournaments—live, online, SNGs, MTTs. In general, you get the most opportunities to play the implied-odds game during at the early stages of large buy-in live tournaments. At the Main Event of the World Series of Poker, for example, players start with 10,000 in chips, blinds are 25-50, and levels last two hours. You won't find nearly that much play in online tournaments. On the other hand, a well-structured online tournament could give you more play than a preliminary World Series of Poker event, at a much lower price.

Different sites have different tournament structures. The Full Tilt structures typically have ten- to fifteen-minute levels and blinds increase relatively gradually. For example, compare a $1,500 buy-in World Series event with the $500 buy-in Full Tilt Online Poker Series (FTOPS) championship. Playing 40 hands per hour in the World Series event, you will play 120 hands (three hours) before the big blind exceeds 10 percent of the starting stack (i.e., 100-200 blinds in an event with 1,500 in starting chips). In the FTOPS championship, you start with 3,000 in chips. Playing 60 hands per hour, after 120 hands, blinds are just 80-160. Antes kick in at $1,500 buy-in Series events at level 5, after you have played approximately 160 hands. In the FTOPS event, they start at level 10, after you have played approximately 135 hands.

In Full Tilt "double stack" tournaments, players also start with 3,000 in chips and blinds increase every ten or twelve minutes rather than every fifteen. In lower buy-in Full Tilt tournaments, players start with 1,500 in chips.

You have to adjust to each structure, evaluating when (and how) to play hands with great implied odds and when you have to steal blinds and antes and commit your chips based on the showdown value of your starting cards.

Distinguishing Online and Live Styles of Play, and Finding Your Style

It is a mistake to dismiss the mass of online players as "donkeys" or "unbluffable." Although you find a lot of rookie mistakes online, I don't think online players get enough credit for taking *correct* approaches to the game. In many instances, I think the live-tournament players who complain are the ones with the wrong idea. Besides, you have to take your opponents as you find them. Adjusting to your opponents is the most important skill you can develop in poker. Where is the benefit of figuring out a theoretical "correct" play, recognizing that it will fail because your opponents aren't sophisticated enough to get it, trying it anyway, and then complaining *your opponents* are dumb?

For me, the main difference between online and live tournaments is that players in live tournaments play weaker than online tournament players. It takes a pretty good-sized bet to get someone off a hand online, and there are more situations where an online player will refuse to give up on a hand for any amount of chips. More often than many people recognize, the live player is the one making the mistake. In live tournaments, people seem so scared to go bust that you practically breathe on the pot and they will fold.

There are many possible reasons for this. Live tournaments have higher buy-ins, are more anticipated and planned-for, and require a greater time commitment and, often, travel. Online tournaments generally cost less to enter, run all the time, and are wherever your computer is. Live-tournament players tend to put a higher value on survival and staying in action—I think, sometimes, too much value. Online, if you make a mistake, there's always another tournament about to start.

I have developed an online playing style that takes this into account. In general, I find that playing good starting hands, making good hands, and betting them seems to be the way to win. I've played over a thousand tournaments online and I have good results with this style.

It is true that, generally, online players are less likely than live players to fold if they have any kind of hand or even a draw. Adjust to that and exploit it. Stick with quality hands. Don't expect bluffs or even semi-bluffs to work. Play strong hands in a straightforward way and expect to get paid off if your opponent has anything at all. I find that I bluff less online and bet more when I make a hand.

Throwing around chips to get people to fold works much better in live tournaments. People are afraid of aggressive players in live tournaments. They are afraid to bluff, afraid to fire a second bullet, afraid to call a bluff, and afraid to show down a weak hand. The mistakes in online tournaments are of an opposite nature. Online players tend to pay you off too much.

An additional benefit I get from straightforward play in online tournaments occurs later. When it becomes necessary to steal blinds and antes, my raises get more respect from opponents who have seen me showing down nothing but premium hands. By the time they figure out I have been robbing them blind, I may have already stolen my way to a big advantage the rest of the way.

SNG Strategy

Early levels—What kind of a tournament is a sit-n-go? Is there room to see flops and play the implied-odds hands? What kind of table image works best?

In the Full Tilt sit-n-go structure, you start with 1,500 in chips. Blinds start at 15-30 and move up in small increments (20-40, 25-50, 30-60, 40-80, etc.) every six minutes. There aren't any antes. For the first level or two, you may have an opportunity to outplay opponents after the flop, but not later. Even in the early stages, you may find players who want to commit themselves to their starting hands. You don't have enough chips to call raises on several hands, see flops, and then fold if you miss.

Certainly, in every kind of tournament, you want to be playing pairs and flopping sets and winning your opponent's stack for the first couple levels. After that, you are more concerned with the showdown value of your starting hand.

To play sit-n-gos well, you have to develop a sense of what the starting hand values are, and what kind of hands your opponents are playing. Having a framework like Andy Bloch described in chapter 6 for valuing starting hands is essential. If you disagree with his rankings, adapt them or find something you like better. In sit-n-gos, you can almost work out a mathematical formula: how often you have to move in, how often you have to reraise all-in. In sit-n-gos, there is a lot of reraising all-in before the flop.

Most players can't tell you how often to move in or reraise all-in, or with which hands to do it (which is really the same thing). If you play hundreds or thousands of sit-n-gos, you may be able to intuit what works. But if you start with a framework, you are ahead from the beginning. And if that framework isn't right, then you can use trial and error to improve it.

You are not just evaluating hands (yours and your opponents'), you are also evaluating position. One mistake players starting out online make is thinking a hand like A-Jo is a playable hand in early position at a nine-handed table. It is not a very good hand. Any savvy player would expect an early-position raiser to have a very strong hand, so the raiser will get action only from hands that are better than A-Jo. And A-Jo is a very difficult hand to play after the flop. Unless you make two pair or better, you really don't know where you are.

This is the mantra of all forms of poker: position is very important because you get to act last every time, and if everyone has folded to you, the chances of someone after you picking up a bigger hand are much smaller. By the time it gets to the button, you can play a lot of hands. You can even play garbage hands to steal the blinds. (Andy's analysis concluded that, without antes, you should play 45 percent of your starting hands as the first bettor on the button.) In fact, against observant opponents, you have to play mediocre hands occasionally or else you'll never get action when you pick up a good hand.

Early in an online tournament, I will fold almost anything in the first couple positions. I want to play only really good hands until I get in the cutoff or the button. I am more conservative than many players against online opponents, but that is key to my success. If online players overcommit to their starting hands or stick with them longer than they should, I don't want to be out of position with an inferior hand.

Endgame—I don't think you should change your strategy of playing and showing down strong cards until the stacks become small relative to the blinds or the table becomes short-handed.

When that happens, the definition of quality starting cards changes. If opponents are pushing in more often, especially on your big blind, you have to adjust your starting hand selection. Likewise, acting under the gun five-handed is different from in a full-table game. You have just four players acting behind you, not eight. This is why the number of players still to act (rather than the number of players who have acted before you) determines what kind of hands you should play.

There is a special situation on the bubble in SNGs—when three places get paid but there are four players left. In this case, you have two conflicting goals: letting the other players bust themselves out so that you make the money, and robbing your scared opponents blind. This will take all your poker experience to decide whether to play very aggressively or very carefully depending on what the other players are doing.

In any case, once you are three-handed, you should shift gears. You will see the inexperience of online players in short-handed or heads-up situations. Especially in lower buy-in sit-n-gos, inexperienced players tend to fold too much short-handed.

Three-handed, you need to put pressure on the blinds. Every time you are on the button, you have the best position throughout the hand. If the blinds are going to fold a good percentage of the time, you should be betting all but your worst hands.

But you need to adjust to the other two players. If the blinds tend to shove all-in with a wide range of hands, then you may want to fold more hands or limp with a big hand to trap them when they jam.

If you have cultivated a tight, solid image, hopefully it will take the blinds several hands before they conclude you're not picking up aces every time. When your passive opponents pick up on what you are doing—if they do—and start playing back at you, be more selective. Likewise, you should not be afraid when an active opponent raises your blind to jam with a marginal hand and hope he folds all but his best hands.

Heads-up, the blinds are likely to be so high that it may come down to who gets the first big hand. In multitable tournaments, there tends to be more opportunity to feel out your opponent and adjust at the end of a tournament.

Assuming you spend more than one or two hands heads-up, the best advice I can give is to start aggressive but treat heads-up play like a dance. If you start aggressive and your opponent is mostly folding, stay aggressive. If your opponent tries to be more aggressive, then slow down (especially out of position) and look for opportunities to trap.

Multitable Tournaments (MTTs)

Initial considerations—You will see differences in how opponents play based on the size of the buy-in. At the lower buy-in tournaments, you will see a lot of inexperienced players. These events are a great, low-risk training ground, but you can't take the kinds of strategies that work at the World Series of Poker and expect them to work in a $5 tournament.

You learn two important skills from playing low buy-in events: (a) valuing your starting hands and position, and (b) understanding why your opponents are doing the things they do. If you play the right hands by position, bet them strongly, and continue betting when you hit them or they are still likely to be the best hand, and you develop a basic understanding of your opponents, you should succeed in these tournaments.

For example, say you have A-Ks under the gun. You raise three times the big blind. You get called by the button and the big blind. The flop comes A-Q-3, rainbow. If you bet and get a call from the button, what do you think he has? The turn is a five. You bet again and get called again. The pot is getting large by this time. If the blinds were 25-50, there could be more than 2,000 chips in this pot.

If you are playing in a live tournament with a substantial buy-in, you have to worry that A-K is no good. For the button to call the flop and the turn, you have reason to believe he has A-Q or 3-3 (A-3s is also a possibility). Top pair/top kicker is the kind of hand I want in a big pot . . . for my opponent.

That is much less likely in a small buy-in online tournament. Beginning players don't value their starting hands properly and don't give enough weight to position. They don't give much thought to what their opponents have. In a small buy-in tournament, you are much more likely to get someone calling your early-position raise with a hand like A-T and calling all the way down. Sometimes you'll run into A-Q or 3-3 or A-3s and you'll have to pay off. But you'll make a lot more in these tournaments than you'll lose in those situations because you'll run into players calling with hands like A-T or Q-T in the blind and unable to release the hand because they made something.

These are basic skills and good ones to learn if you are just starting out. A lot of your profit in small buy-in events will be from building your stack from players who haven't learned the basics. On the other hand, you aren't going to get far bluffing those players. So don't represent a flush and expect them to drop top pair (or even second pair).

When you get into higher buy-in events, more players will vary their play based on how they think you're playing. You will still see some rookie errors in higher buy-in online tournaments. Some new players may be willing to learn in more expensive tournaments, or players can satellite or even freeroll their way into bigger events. But as the buy-in goes up, you have to give your opponents credit for knowing at least the basics.

A more important consideration is the number of starting chips and how fast the blinds increase. On Full Tilt Poker, players start with 1,500 or 3,000 chips. The blinds start at 15-30 (though some start at 10-20) and increase every ten to fifteen minutes. The progression is relatively slow:

TABLE 10.1   ◆   FULL TILT ONLINE NO-LIMIT HOLD 'EM TOURNAMENT STRUCTURE

Level	Small blind	Big blind	Ante
1	15	30	
2	20	40	
3	25	50	
4	30	60	
5	40	80	
6	50	100	
7	60	120	
8	80	160	
9	100	200	
10	120	240	25
11	150	300	25
12	200	400	50
13	250	500	50
14	300	600	75
15	400	800	100

(*continued*)

TABLE 10.1 ◆ *(Continued)*

Level	Small blind	Big blind	Ante
16	500	1,000	125
17	600	1,200	150
18	800	1,600	200
19	1,000	2,000	250
20	1,200	2,400	300
21	1,500	3,000	400
22	2,000	4,000	500
23	2,500	5,000	600
24	3,000	6,000	750
25	4,000	8,000	1,000
26	5,000	10,000	1,000
27	6,000	12,000	1,500
28	8,000	16,000	2,000
29	10,000	20,000	2,500
30	12,000	24,000	3,000
31	15,000	30,000	4,000
32	20,000	40,000	5,000
33	25,000	50,000	6,000
34	30,000	60,000	7,500
35	40,000	80,000	10,000
36	50,000	100,000	10,000
37	60,000	120,000	15,000
38	80,000	160,000	20,000
39	100,000	200,000	25,000
40	120,000	240,000	30,000

This is a pretty good online tournament structure. Especially in the double-stack tournaments—and accounting for playing approximately 50 percent more hands per hour online—there isn't much less play in a $26–$215 buy-in double-stack tournament on Full Tilt than you get in a $1,500 buy-in World Series of Poker event.

So for how much of the tournament do you play implied-odds poker, and when do you start playing showdown poker?

The implied-odds phase—To play all the implied-odds hands, you'd like to have the stacks be at least twenty times what you're paying to see the flop, which means sixty times the big blind if raisers are making it three times the big blind. There are precious few online tournaments where you will have that much beyond the first few levels, and in some you don't even have that in the first level.

In the standard-stack Full Tilt tournaments, the first level is the only level in which you want to take shots at the implied-odds strategy. As your stack increases, you might be able to extend this part of the tournament, though you generally want to do this only if your opponents' stacks are rising as well. You may be able to afford calling more raises and folding with your big stack, but against a short-stacked opponent you aren't getting the implied odds to get paid when you hit your long-shot draw.

In the Full Tilt double-stack tournaments, you have at least three or four levels to play in the implied-odds game. (In a World Series of Poker $1,500 buy-in event, you barely get any deep-stack play. You start with 1,500 in chips, blinds of 25-25, and likely raises to 75–125 or more in the first level.)

That's why I say in online tournaments the implied-odds portion of the tournament is very short. In the Main Event of the World Series, the implied-odds portion lasts quite a long time.

Implied-odds poker still exists when the stacks are smaller, but only when you can pick your spots, such as limping in position in multiway pots or being the first raiser in late position with a hand that you would raise with anyway, such as 7-7 or T-9s. In late position you should play pretty much any pair, suited connector, or suited ace in this phase and win a big pot when you have the nuts. You are, however, going to need big stacks of treasure to aim at, or it will cost you too much to see all those flops.

In the implied-odds stage, you are looking to flop sets and make flushes and straights. You want to make a big hand, where you can win your opponent's stack. That's the benefit of no-limit hold 'em, where you can start with any two cards and make a big hand and win a huge amount. So the fact that you are paying to see the flop with those two cards even though you are likely behind isn't really so much of a factor if you think your opponent is going to give you his whole stack if you make your hand. When you play this way with suited aces, suited connectors, and pairs (my favorite), recognize the risks you are facing with each kind of starting hand.

The suited weak aces are hands you win money with but they are also hands you can lose money with. If you hit an ace, you may not even call the first bet. If you hit your ace and your kicker, you can win a big pot, but you also have to worry about losing to a higher two pair. You want to make a flush with this hand. Ideally, you want to make a flush better than someone else's flush and take their whole stack. Flushes are difficult to get paid on unless someone else has a worse flush.

With suited connectors, you would like to play in position because you might just be drawing on the flop, or you could hit your hand and not make the nuts. Position is important with big cards because you want to keep the pot small, and it is easier to do that in position. Position is not as important with a pair because sets can be played pretty easily out of position.

In general, therefore, I would rather make the big hand with a pocket pair than with suited connectors. I'll play any pair in any position in a deep-stack situation. Some people say, "Don't play deuces and threes because you can get set-over-set," but being scared of that unlikely scenario seems too conservative even for me. If that happens, you go broke and play another tournament.

Online, at the beginning of a tournament I might conceivably limp (or raise the minimum) in early position with a medium or small pocket pair. Say I have twenty times the big blind and I have 6-6. I might limp under the gun and hope the pot is unraised and that I can get a set and win some money if someone makes top pair or two pair.

The hand I really want to be up against, though, is A-A. If I raise under the gun with 6-6, the guy with A-A can reraise me out of the pot. The same is true if my opponent has other hands he may be unable to get away from (like A-K, K-K, or Q-Q) if we both get the flop we want. In late position, I can call their raise with my 6-6. But in early position, I can't call their reraise. If I limp, I can call one raise.

I am not generally in favor of strategies where you play a defined group of hands different from other hands. It may, however, be worthwhile out of position to limp with low pocket pairs early in online tournaments for the following reasons. First, you aren't giving away much about how you play. You don't face the same opponents very often in online tournaments. You won't get pocket pairs very often in the relatively short implied-odds portion of a tournament, and I don't think you should do this later in the tournament. With antes, you probably want to raise. Especially in early position, you get so much respect that you might just win the blinds and antes.

Second, you have a lot of cover in your favor online. Other players are limping, some are limping with any ace, any two suited cards, or any two connected cards. (I don't even think you should do this with suited connectors, because a likely scenario is that you have to play a draw out of position against the raiser.) Therefore, between all the other limpers and all the opponents who aren't paying as much attention as players in a live tournament, an occasional limp may not stand out. It will be pretty rare when they actually see your hand—mostly likely when you hit your set and bust your opponent.

These seem like reasonable risks in exchange for busting somebody and doubling up.

The role of observation online—In any poker game, you should spend the first few minutes observing how your opponents play so you can play properly against them. If certain players are raising every other pot, you are going to play against them a lot different than if they enter only one pot every three orbits.

You can't see that twitch in their left ear when they are bluffing, but you can see how many hands they play and what kind of hands they show down. So if you see a guy raise under the gun and show down A-3o, then you know he is not a very good player because that's a very poor hand to play from that position. With that information, you may be looking to play a wider variety of hands against him and trap him when he has to pay off with his weak ace. You may also fold when an ace flops, knowing that he seems to want to play any ace from any position. And if the flop comes A-4-3 and you're getting a lot of action, you may remember that he could have two pair, whereas most players may not at that point. (You run into some players in the early part of online tournaments who play every ace and every two suited cards. Spotting these players can potentially save you from losing your entire stack, or set up a chance to win their entire stack.)

I will look to see who is overbetting the pot. Those are people you can make a lot of money from when you hit your hand.

But by far, the most common observation is seeing how loose they are, how many hands they are playing. That gives you a range of hands you can put them on. Should you respect their raises?

You also want to look to see who folds to reraises and who calls reraises. If you have opponents who typically raise and then fold to reraises, you can win a lot of chips relatively safely by reraising them. And just when they get sick of it and decide to make a stand, you actually have A-A. (Unfortunately, I can't teach you how to *get* A-A.)

There is one particular online observation that you should always make. Sometimes people may not actually be at their computer even though they are registered for a tournament. This is very valuable information, especially in tournaments where you qualify in advance, like certain freerolls. I once saw a player limp in the small blind against a player who was not present and check down on every street and lose to the absent player because he didn't notice the other player time out on the first hand and instantly (automatically) fold every subsequent hand.

This brings up the general subject of online tells. Most online tells have to do with timing. I can't really quantify it, but if you are really paying attention to the table, you can almost detect a hesitation and figure out what it means. But you have to be careful. They could be typing in the chat box, playing four other tables, or paying for a pizza.

I have found that if people bet exactly the pot, they have a real hand. They just hit the "pot" button. It means they aren't fooling around. But in general, as I will explain in the next section, it generally takes bigger bets to get players to fold online.

I used to fool around with bets ending in 99. People tend to not take you seriously if your bet ends in 99. For some reason, when I want to get called and bet _99, opponents usually assume I'm making some kind of a play.

Post-flop betting—As I become more experienced at live tournaments, I have been making relatively smaller post-flop bets. Numerous pros have told me their experience has been the same, and Howard Lederer has suggested that no-limit hold 'em tournament history, since the time when Doyle Brunson wrote his original *Super/System* chapter, has mirrored this. In a live tournament, the modern experienced player may bet as little as one-third of the pot in a post-flop continuation bet. Rarely will an experienced player bet the pot.

That won't work online.

People don't seem to respect small bets online. I'm not sure exactly why, but if you don't bet at least the size of the pot, people don't believe you. You can work that to your advantage. If you can get away with it—an observant opponent should pick up on you betting strong hands different from weak ones—you may want to play a little backwards. If you don't want a call, bet the size of the pot. If you do want a call, bet less.

Online, your opponents are much more likely than in a live tournament to interpret a half-pot-sized continuation bet as weakness. Indeed, if you don't have anything and will fold if your opponent raises, then it is probably not a good bet. In a cash game, where you play with the same people until someone leaves, you can train your opponents. Once they see a half-pot-sized bet is your standard bet (or they get burned incorrectly assuming you have nothing when you are strong), you can continue betting the way you consider optimal.

You may not have that opportunity in an online tournament. You may play only one pot with someone at one table before the table breaks or somebody moves. Also, your online opponents are not as observant because they are doing laundry or playing four tables at the same time.

Manipulate the situation to your advantage. Make your small bet on the flop, expecting to get called. Then make a big bet on the turn. Then you get their extra chips from the bet on the flop. This also allows you to win a big pot from opponents who think they can take advantage of your "weakness" by playing back at you with nothing because they see your small bet as an invitation to take the pot away.

When the showdown game starts—Even before the antes kick in, the implied-odds phase of almost all online tournaments is definitely over. You are still looking for chances to bust someone who has a great starting hand, but you can't afford to take shots indiscriminately. You will also notice your opponents playing tighter. Because the blinds have gotten so high, it is not correct to call raises with speculative hands to see the flop.

This is the time when properly valuing your starting cards increases in significance. There are few limped pots, fewer multiway pots, and fewer flops seen. This is also the time when you start looking to steal.

I think when the stacks get down to twenty times the big blind, you can start stealing more. But it really depends on the table. There is no point stealing the blinds in the first few levels because it will not increase your stack by a significant amount. (Against decent opponents you should make a few position raises to avoid having an overly tight image, because otherwise you'll never get action on your big hands. If you have opponents who will call you down with anything, as is sometimes the case online, your image doesn't matter. But against better online players, there is a certain point at which being "tight" can cost you when you raise with a strong hand.)

Once you or your opponents are under twenty big blinds, every hand you play has a significant likelihood of ending with someone committing their stack. That means you have to play your hands more for their showdown value and less for the implied odds offered by hitting your hand.

When someone enters the pot before you, you need quality cards. But it's also easier to steal the blinds and antes when *you* are the first one in. For instance, at the 200-400 blind/50 ante level, there are 1,050 chips in every pot. If you have twenty times the big blind, you increase your stack by 12 percent with a successful steal. By raising to 1,000 or 1,200, your opponents with twenty times the big blind will be predisposed to folding if they don't have a promising starting hand.

Raise-sizing—In a deep-stack situation, if I have a hand I want to win a monster with, I'll raise to three and a half or four times the big blind, because I want to build a big pot. Of course, if I am stealing, I want to raise as small as I can to steal. To keep from defining your hand with your bet, you may need to make your raise the same size in both situations. (It is difficult to accomplish both goals, but if you can vary the size of your raises and make it appear random, you also get the benefit of scaring the hell out of people and getting them to fold, simply because they don't want to play a pot with someone so unpredictable.) For most players, raising by a standard amount works best. Ironically, even though small continuation bets don't work, small pre-flop bets may, once the blinds and antes start getting substantial.

In an online tournament, when the blinds get big, a pre-flop raise of two and a half times the big blind, even with antes, tends to work. If you are against a good opponent who will call and potentially outplay you, you may want to make it more. A lot of players just press the "pot" button, which is three and a half times the big blind or even more with antes, which is a huge bet. You probably don't have to bet that much if you are stealing, and it may be too much to get action if you want to get called.

Generally, you get a feel from the table for when a raise seems big enough to scare players out. There's a time when the jump in the blinds makes it seem like two and a half times is a lot of money. Somewhere between the 100-200 level and the 200-400 level, a two-and-a-half-times raise starts looking big and accomplishes what a three- or four-times raise accomplished earlier.

One pre-flop betting strategy that has become a weapon of many tournament players is the sandwich play. This bet is not likely to work as well online. Dan Harrington described this play in his books. There is a late-position raiser and a caller and you are in the big blind. You figure they are both weak and don't have premium hands, so you move all-in and they fold.

There are two problems with the sandwich play in online tournaments. First, because so many people have read Harrington's books, everybody knows about it and late-position raisers are either raising their standards for playable hands or lowering them for calling reraises because of it. Second, even if that play still works in live tournaments, it doesn't do so well online. It mathematically still makes sense because, even when you get called, there is so much dead money in the pot that you are usually getting the right odds even as an underdog. But you don't make the sandwich play to get called, and you have to expect to get called more online.

Bubble time—As you get near the bubble, people play more conservatively in both live and online tournaments. That should be your license to steal (though you have presumably been doing that already). The bubble provides some additional opportunities. You want to target the medium stacks just as you would in live tournaments. The short stacks may have the odds to call you and the big stacks may want to swat you down so they can steal more themselves. But if you have enough chips that a confrontation can cripple or eliminate a medium stack short of the money, you are in position to go after the blinds of the medium-stack players.

But beware. Online players tend to be more aggressive and more reckless, and less afraid. It is not as easy to take advantage of people's fear and steal online. Players are also increasingly aware of what you are trying to do and are more willing to play back at you online than in a live tournament.

In the money—One benefit to playing an online tournament is that you have ready access to the payout structure, the average stack size, and where you are in relation to the field. That is valuable information and you should take advantage of it. For instance, if I see I am last or second to last in chips, then I know I have to make a move soon. But if I am above average in chips, I may sit back and wait for a good hand. You can generally get this information in a live tournament, but it is more specific and updated right in front of you online.

This information is even more important in an online supersatellite. If you see that your position in the field is one of the positions getting paid (i.e., winning entry to the main tournament or whatever is at stake), you are much safer just sitting pretty and waiting for the short stacks to bust out. If you are below that threshold, you have to start looking to make a move. It is important not to use this information to make a rash decision. It is possible that other people will bust themselves out and you will move up that way. But where you stand in relation to the field is a good marking point for deciding whether you have to make a move.

Once I get into the money, my goal is always to win the tournament. The payouts are so heavily weighted toward the top few spots that it is worth being active and taking risks to put yourself into position to win. I do not advocate sitting back and hoping a rush hits you. You have to get lucky to win a tournament. There is no strategy for winning that will succeed without luck. But being aggressive—especially when other players are sitting back with small stacks to fold themselves a few places higher or with medium stacks to fold their way to the final table—improves your chances of winning. You have to pick up every chip to win and it doesn't matter in what order you get them. Besides, if you are active, you are more likely to get action when your rush comes.

I am looking for players who will fold to a reraise and come over the top of them and win a lot of chips that way. I am looking for big hands and winning with them. But playing your way to the final table is about stealing until you get a big hand. At some point, you may have to gamble.

The safest way to win chips is to get your opponent to fold, so raising and reraising before the flop with a wide variety of hands against scared opponents is a good strategy, especially when you usually aren't that big an underdog to most hands, unless you have one of these weird super-dominated hands like K-2 and you run into K-K. Otherwise, the worst you are likely to be is a 4-to-1 dog. More likely, you are a 3-to-2 dog and maybe even a favorite. Even if you have to pay off when your opponent is pot-committed and you lose, given all the times they have been folding to your raises, you are still way ahead.

When you put pressure on opponents, they are eventually going to play back at you, either because they are smart and are adjusting to the hands you must be playing, or because they finally picked up a big hand. You have to get away from failed steal attempts, especially when the action comes from a player acting behind you instead of one of the blinds *and* you know this to be a conservative player. (You have to guard against resteals.)

There is no shame in folding when you get caught. You are way ahead from all your successful steals. Part of the cost of aggressive play is getting caught and folding occasionally. You need to make sure, however, even with a weak hand, that you don't have the pot odds to call, even if you are behind.

In the late stages of an online tournament, there usually aren't a lot of chips separating the short stacks from the above-average stacks. Nearly everyone is on short chips. You will encounter situations where a short stack behind you or the blinds pushes all-in. If you are stealing, you probably expect to be the underdog. There are two competing considerations in deciding whether to call: (a) are you being offered pot odds to call, even with your weak hand? (b) if you lose, will calling cripple you? (The hard decisions are when you answer "yes" to both questions.)

If you are getting 2-to-1, you are generally getting good enough odds to call. Of course, based on your observation, if this is a super-tight player who has been letting you run him over and wouldn't dare make a move without a big pocket pair, you really aren't a 2-to-1 dog and you should fold. But otherwise, you are getting reasonable odds and you also don't want to get a reputation as someone who folds easily to reraises.

Then there is the matter of what happens to your stack if you lose. If calling with a weak hand and losing will reduce your stack to the point where you lose your ability to maneuver, you can fold.

Sometimes the value of your intact chip stack will be worth more to you tactically than the pot odds you are getting to call and potentially lose. If calling as an underdog and losing puts you in a position where you can't steal anymore, that would be devastating. It is okay to fold, particularly if you respect his reraise. Again, you can't make a habit of folding to reraises.

But I'm thinking of folding a hand like T-8o. You are not going to fold A-5s when you are getting over 2-to-1. Even if your opponent has a better ace, if his ace is unsuited, you aren't worse than a 2-to-1 dog. If you are up against K-Q, you are a favorite. If you are facing a pocket pair, you are still just a 2-to-1 dog. And you would never fold if you were getting 3-to-1.

Know who you are stealing from. You don't want to steal the blinds with a very weak hand when the big blind already has a lot of his remaining chips in the pot. In general, you want to steal from conservative players with medium stacks.

Say you raise with Q-8 in the short stack's blind. He has A-5o. That is a tough spot for a smart player to jam. A-5o isn't that much of a favorite over anything. So when you raise with Q-8, you still have folding equity. You have to rob people blind to win these tournaments, and win your gambles when they shove in on you.

I generally won't fold when I'm getting 2-to-1 or better. I realize I have to win some gambles to win a tournament, and I don't want anyone thinking they can push me around. I might lay it down if I know the player who jammed was super-tight, or if it was a super-satellite where losing would take me below the threshold that would force me to make a potentially bad move in the future.

Inside two tables—Once you get down to the last twelve or thirteen players, you face the first of two short-handed tables at the end of the tournament. This is a great time to accumulate chips if you know how to play short-handed. Become even more aggressive, setting yourself up to have a big stack when you get to the final table and have to be more patient.

You will encounter two general kinds of players: players trying to do what you are doing, and players waiting for a big hand to bust you (or just fold their way to the final table). You want to steal from the latter players and dodge their big hands. From your thieving comrades, you may want to try restealing. Restealing is better than stealing. It is much more profitable, but there is the risk that the original raiser actually has a hand.

Position is important. You want the other active players to your right. If an active player with a big stack is to your left, you are more likely to be the victim than the culprit of a resteal. Unfortunately you have no choice in the matter.

Here is how it works. You notice that the player to your right is stealing a lot. (You have to be observing the table. So many people are playing too tight in this situation that you can't randomly decide to scare someone off a hand. Your target could be the player who isn't putting chips in the pot at this point in the tournament without a monster, and you will probably know that by paying attention.) The active player raises. You don't know if he has a hand but he can't always have one. You have a decent hand, one you would steal with but not one you would normally play after a raise. If you reraise him and he was stealing, he will probably fold rather than play a big pot out of position.

You can't resteal from a player who has committed himself to play the pot. And if your stack is relatively short, he may be priced in to call you no matter what he has. If you have a medium stack and there is a big stack to your right, you are probably safe restealing unless he has a real hand.

You can't make this move too often, but you don't need to. One successful resteal is worth several rounds of blinds and antes. You need enough chips to raise him off a stealing hand, and he needs to have enough chips remaining to where it is not worth the risk to call.

Final table—At the final table, you suddenly go from five-handed to nine-handed. Take a deep breath. Realize that you can't raise every other pot anymore. But you can still pick up a lot of chips because you will notice a lot of opponents playing very tight. Each position means more money, and some players simply want to see if other players will get eliminated and they can move up.

That's not how you should play. You can't win the tournament when it is nine-handed, but you have to win every chip, and some of those chips will come when you are nine-handed. Folding your way to fifth or sixth place is nowhere near as profitable as taking some eighth- and ninth-place finishes by playing in a style that also gives you a chance at some first- and second-place finishes.

You have to be observant, particularly with the new players at your table. Which players are folding to reraises, and which ones are calling them? You want to find a good time to resteal from the former and get paid off from the latter when you have a big pair.

If you are one of the short stacks, it is really not in your interest to fold your way a couple spots up the payout list. You generally want to make a move anytime it gets folded to you in late position. If the big blind has a giant stack, always calls, and you have a terrible hand, naturally you should pass up that opportunity. But generally don't wait for a big hand to make your move if you have position. You can't just let yourself be blinded off. At some point, you have to gamble, and you are usually not going to be that big an underdog if you get your money in first. If you have nine or ten times the big blind and win a showdown, you will usually be in a position where you can start stealing and accumulating chips. Maybe you need to get lucky to do that, but one lucky showdown can be the difference between being anted away in an attempt to move from ninth to seventh, and having a real chance to win the whole tournament.

As soon as you get to the final table, look at the list of payouts. How many fifth-place finishes do you have to ring up to equal one win and a bunch of ninths? That should tell you all you need to know about why it is worth the risk of an early exit at the final table to give yourself a chance to win. Take what the table gives you. Stay away from the players your observations have given you reason to fear when they play a hand. But otherwise, take control of the table and realize that you need to take risks to win.

Conclusion

A good online poker player is a good poker player. You need to work on all elements of your game to succeed online and focus on the skills emphasized in online tournaments. First, bring your deep-stack stills into online tournaments, and then know when to abandon them. Second, learn to play the starting-hand game. Just being ahead of your opponents in evaluating your hand before the flop may be enough to help you finish in the money often. Third, learn to observe how your opponents play and how to adapt. Fourth, work on stealing: when it becomes important, when you can steal by raising and when by reraising, who to target and who to avoid.

Playing tournaments online can be very profitable. In addition, it is a relatively low-risk training ground for developing your game. Live tournaments emphasize some different skills, but there isn't any reason if you figure out the online game that you can't adapt it to major tournaments.

CHAPTER 11

Pot-Limit Hold 'Em

by Rafe Furst and Andy Bloch

If you make a few adjustments, you can adapt a lot of your no-limit hold 'em tournament game to pot-limit hold 'em. Many players don't make these adjustments, however, because they don't understand the consequences of the differences between the games. The main differences stem from two factors: (1) the limit on the size of possible bets, and (2) the lack of antes in pot-limit hold 'em tournaments.

Know the Pot

Initially, you need to understand bet-sizing. This may seem basic, but you have to be aware of several ratios during the play of a hand and throughout the tournament. Quickly knowing the size of future bets is important. You also want to be able to correct dealers and other players who don't have it right. The first pot-sized raise is seven times the small blind, or three and a half times the big blind. If, for example, the blinds are 100-200, the first raise would be to 700. Because there would now be 1,000 in the pot (100 + 200 + 700), the reraise would be to 2,400, or twelve times the big blind.

The standard reraise is computed as follows: the reraiser is calling the 700 bet, which makes the pot 1,700, and then raising by the amount of the pot (1,700 more)—700 + 1,700 = 2,400. This means there will now be 3,400 in the pot (100 + 200 + 700 + 2,400 = 3,400).

Remembering three and a half times the big blind for the first raise and twelve times the big blind for the second raise is important, and you want to compare those ratios with your stack. If you had ten times the big blind in a no-limit hold 'em tournament, you know you could get your chips in the pot, either assuring you would see all five cards or stealing the blinds and antes (though, remember, there are no antes in pot-limit hold 'em tournaments).

It's not so simple in pot-limit. Say you have 4,000 chips and the blinds are 200-400. In early position, you pick up T-T. In no-limit, with ten big blinds, you would move in. Even with a slightly larger stack, you might move in because a medium pocket pair is an especially tough hand to play out of position after the flop.

In pot-limit, however, as the first in the pot, you can bet a maximum of only 1,400. This may be enough to take the blinds, but you are in the vulnerable position of having—just barely—enough chips to fold to a reraise. What do you do if another player, in early or middle position, reraises to 4,800?

You can get all your chips in the pot, but you are now *calling* all-in. The extra 2,600 you couldn't initially get into the pot has forced you to make a difficult decision.

On the other hand, if you are the reraiser with those ten big blinds remaining, you are in a position to possibly take the pot from the initial raiser without a showdown. If the raiser makes it 1,400, you can move in your entire 4,000. You risk running into a bigger hand than if you put in the initial raise and were facing only random hands. The raiser could be on a steal, but he has shown strength by betting so he could also have a quality hand. But if you think, based on your opponent, the stacks, and the positions, that the raise may *not* signal a very strong hand, you may be able to induce a fold. It is a risky move but a lucrative one. If your opponent was stealing too, he was trying to steal 600 in chips. If you succeed, you will gain 2,000.

The ratios don't need to be exact. In that example, ten big blinds are typically enough to do the same job as twelve.

After the flop, the pot-limit structure also affects play. In particular, there are circumstances in which you would want the option to overbet the pot. For instance, let's say you have the best hand on the flop, but a vulnerable one. Your best play might be to overbet all-in to give your opponent(s) the worst drawing odds possible if they decide to chase you. In no-limit, you always have the option of overbetting the pot, but in pot-limit you don't; sometimes in pot-limit you will be forced to give your opponents proper odds to draw out on you. You need to keep this basic fact in mind when choosing starting hands and deciding how to play them.

For instance, let's say you have A-A in the big blind, the button raises and is called by the small blind. In no-limit, you may wish to raise less than the full pot in hopes of keeping at least one of your opponents in, knowing you can overbet the flop and freeze them out in most situations. But in pot-limit, the likelihood that both players will see the flop—and that at least one of them will pick up a draw with the proper odds to chase—is high. Therefore it makes sense to get as much money in pre-flop as possible while you have the advantage. In other words, you should force your opponents to make the biggest mistake possible while they are still making a mistake by calling. You will risk losing both opponents with your aggression, but this risk is outweighed by the benefit of winning a decent pot and not having to play the hand out of position against multiple opponents who have proper odds to call.

Starting Hands

There are two reasons why you should play tighter in a pot-limit hold 'em tournament compared with a no-limit event. First, there are never any antes in pot-limit, so you are playing for fewer chips already in the pot when you enter with a raise.

Second, the implied odds in pot-limit are not as good as in no-limit because it is harder to get all the money in on a single hand, especially early in a tournament or between tall stacks. In no-limit tournaments, you will play certain hands—low and medium pairs, suited connectors—specifically because you can win the whole stack of an opponent if you hit your hand on the flop. In pot-limit you may not get the same return from those hands, so you should make implied-odds considerations a lower priority.

You should use the hand rankings and percentages of playable hands in chapter 6 (or a different framework if you find something you like better). You would use the pre-ante percentages for playable hands, and consider lowering the suited connectors and low pairs when it seems unlikely you can win a big enough pot to compensate for taking a weak hand into the flop.

First Bettor versus Second Bettor

In no-limit, the first player to get all or most of their stack into the pot has a big advantage, due what David Sklansky popularized as the gap concept. In Sklansky's *Tournament Poker for Advanced Players* he used the term to describe why, especially in a tournament, you need a better hand to *call* a raise than you need to *make* a raise. This same advantage would exist in pot-limit except for the fact that most of the time the first bettor cannot get all their chips in the pot. In pot-limit hold 'em tournaments, unless the first player in the pot is very short-stacked, it is often the second person to voluntarily enter the pot who has the advantage of being able to shut their opponents out with a pot-sized raise.

Consider the following example. The blinds are 200-400 and you are on the button with 4,800, which is twelve big blinds. The cut-off, with 8,000, bets the pot, raising to 1,400. The pot now contains 2,000, or five big blinds. You can reraise to 4,800, putting yourself exactly all-in. If the blinds fold, the original raiser now has to call 3,400 more. Odds of 2-to-1 (3,400 to win 6,800) make this a difficult decision for the cutoff, but what does his stack look like? After his bet of 1,400, he had 6,400 left. It is difficult for most players to call off half their chips as an underdog, even if they think they are getting approximately the right odds to call.

You have to be aware of how the raiser is playing as well as—this might be even more important—how the table thinks *you* are playing. This is where cultivating a tight image in the early part of the tournament pays off. If your opponent gives you credit for any sort of hand at all, you can effectively resteal the pot with any two cards. If you are most comfortable with that style or you follow the advice here about playing fewer hands than your opponents, this is the dividend for that style of play.

Stop-and-Go After the Flop

After the flop, there is typically enough in the pot that the advantage shifts to the first player to bet. The stop-and-go play takes advantage of situations where the pot is big enough to make the first bet after the flop meaningful, particularly when that player did not have the opportunity before the flop to make a bet to shut out his opponent.

Let's say you are in the big blind with a middle pair like 8-8 and have ten big blinds left after posting your blind. A middle-position opponent with twenty big blinds raises the pot, and you decide that this is the time to make your stand; you figure to be a coin flip against likely overcards but with some extra money in the pot as a sweetener. You know your opponent has to call if you push before the flop. So instead, you just call the pre-flop raise (i.e., "stop") and decide that you are going to push all-in (i.e., "go") on the flop no matter what comes.

The interesting (and powerful) part of this play is that—assuming you were committed to playing for all your chips anyway—you can increase your chances of winning the pot without a showdown and be no worse off if you do end up in a showdown. This is a huge gain over simply jamming pre-flop. Why does it work?

If the flop misses your opponent—as it will a majority of the time if he started with two unpaired cards—the pot odds require him to have a 33 percent chance of winning to make the call. But with those two unpaired cards, his chance of making an overpair is just 25 percent. And remember, if he did hit a winning overpair on the flop, you are no worse off, since your only other option was to push pre-flop anyway. In all likelihood, an opponent with two high cards is going to call an all-in bet before the flop, assuming (correctly) that he is just a small underdog. But once he misses the flop, he is unlikely to call your all-in.

The really powerful part of the stop-and-go play is that it is no less effective even if your opponent knows what you are doing and can see your cards the whole time! Before the flop, had you pushed and your opponent could see your 8-8, he would have to call with K-J. After missing the flop, however, he no longer has the odds to call.

Playing the Short Stack

Obviously, you would prefer to have a big stack rather than a short stack. However, based on some of the dynamics described above, you can see how being short-stacked in pot-limit tournaments is not as bad as in no-limit. You can actually exploit some positive stack-size situations out of your short stack in pot-limit hold 'em. To do this properly, there are some short-stack "zones" that you should be aware of.

Experienced players are familiar with these zones in no-limit hold 'em. With ten big blinds or less, you are typically looking to push all-in. With approximately fifteen big blinds, you are looking to reraise all-in. Above twenty big blinds, you are no longer short-stacked. (Phil Gordon explains all this in detail in chapter 9.)

In pot-limit, the phase shifts occurs at smaller stack sizes than in no-limit. Although there are no hard-and-fast rules, the important concept is to consider the point at which you (or your opponent) would be forced to fold if reraised. For instance, if you had five big blinds and you entered with a pot-sized raise, you would have only one and a half big blinds remaining. You would have to call any reraise. If you had ten big blinds before the hand, there are situations where you could get away from the hand if you thought you were losing badly to a reraiser. Here are the short-stack zones for pot-limit tournaments; your mileage, of course, may vary.

- *Four big blinds or less*—Try to be first in with a pot-sized raise. Look for situations where you have a chance of successfully stealing the blinds, such as in late position against players who are unlikely to defend their blinds without a real hand.
- *Five to eight big blinds*—Be first in only with hands you are willing to call a reraise all-in with; assume anyone who came in before you voluntarily will call if you raise all-in behind them.
- *Nine to twelve big blinds*—Look to reraise all-in against an opponent who could lay down their hand (e.g., someone who has been loose-aggressive recently, or is likely on a steal in

late position); be very careful about putting any chips in the pot voluntarily as the first player.

With more than twelve big blinds, your options open up a bit more. You are in a similar situation as with twenty big blinds in no-limit.

Limping or Flat-Calling with a Big Hand

As already described, there is a big advantage before the flop to being the second person in the pot with a maximum reraise. You should consider limping or smooth-calling an initial raise with some of your biggest hands, especially when your opponents will be pot-committed on the flop, which will happen more often in pot-limit tournaments because the structure tends to create more short stacks than in no-limit.

When you start limping or smooth-calling raises, you need to mix up your play for deception. If you have the kind of table where you can expect to get action behind you, make two-thirds of your limps with great hands, and one-third with weaker hands when you want to see a cheap flop.

This is a strategy you can also use when you are short-stacked. If you have enough chips where an opponent thinks you can still get away from the hand, you can try limping or flat-calling. You aren't doing this to see the flop cheap: you *want* the reraise so you can get it all-in with the best hand.

After you succeed with this move, you may get the respect from the table to see flops with some hands that can't take a lot of action before the flop. Then you can limp with suited connectors and low pocket pairs.

Conclusion

Many years ago, you could probably expect the quality of play to be higher at a pot-limit hold 'em event than at a no-limit event at the same series of tournaments. Pot-limit was spread in cash games, while no-limit had a following primarily because they played it in the Main Event of the World Series of Poker.

If that was ever true, it sure isn't true anymore. No-limit hold 'em is the dominant form of tournament poker, and it is taking over the cash games, long ago eclipsing pot-limit and now rivaling limit hold 'em. Because record numbers of players are still entering pot-limit tournaments, the advantage goes to the player who can best adapt no-limit strategy to the pot-limit format, and who can take advantage of opponents who don't make the adjustment.

If you can adapt to the betting limitations of pot-limit hold 'em and understand the risks and opportunities of different stack ratios, you should be able to adapt your game and succeed in pot-limit hold 'em tournaments.

CHAPTER 12

Limit Hold 'Em

by Howard Lederer

With the increasing popularity of no-limit hold 'em in tournaments and, more recently, in cash games, many experienced players are neglecting their limit hold 'em game. New players are skipping it altogether. This is usually a mistake.

If you devote some time to limit hold 'em, you might be finding your game. We are all better at one game or another. If you play only no-limit hold 'em, you are narrowing your possibilities. Maybe you have the potential to be a decent no-limit hold 'em player but you could become great at limit hold 'em. Different poker games emphasize different skills, and if you ignore limit hold 'em you won't know if your temperament and strengths are best suited to that game.

In addition, to become a very good poker player, you have to learn all the games. Improving in one form of poker automatically makes you better at other games because you can take those skills to the other games and use them. For example, you can't be a good limit hold 'em player without understanding the concept of free cards—getting them and defending against them. The concept is arguably not as important in seven-card stud, but it comes up; you will play stud better once you develop that skill in limit hold 'em. For that matter, the concept of the free card comes up sometimes in pot-limit Omaha and no-limit hold 'em. A specialist in one of those forms of poker may not develop their free-card plays and defenses because it is not as important to those other games. That's an edge you have, even at *their* game.

Possibly the thing that is most missed in no-limit hold 'em these days is post-flop betting. The number one skill you are going to acquire in limit hold 'em is seeing how hands play out after the flop. When you are playing no-limit tournaments, you will see some pretty good players who just don't know what to do after the flop. It doesn't hurt them much because their game depends on being all-in by then. They become very good pre-flop players.

In limit hold 'em, however, as important as it is to play well before the flop, you cannot be a good player without knowing how to play after the flop. The nature of the limit game forces you to play hands all the way through. You will become a stronger post-flop no-limit player by doing that.

The very best no-limit players outplay their opponents after the flop. I developed my post-flop skills through years of playing limit hold 'em every day. I think many great no-limit tournament players would tell you the same thing. At the very least, if you follow my advice (both in choosing to play limit hold 'em and in how you play it), you will overcome the fear and unfamiliarity that so many relatively new no-limit players have about seeing the flop. If you don't develop those skills, that's a dangerous position to put yourself in during a no-limit tournament, having to put all your chips at risk because you are afraid of getting outplayed.

One particular concept I learned about post-flop play in limit hold 'em was actually responsible for my becoming a professional poker player. I grew up in a competitive family. We played games all the time. I was a good chess player growing up and understood, from chess and other games, the value of strategic thinking. But I didn't play much poker, and when I began playing in New York in the early eighties I was a consistent loser in low-stakes games.

Then I discovered a skinny book titled *Hold 'Em Poker* by David Sklansky. The book, with cards, chips, and a gun on the cover, was my introduction to concepts like semi-bluffing, check-raising, and, most important to me at that time, betting and raising to get free cards.

When I read about taking the betting lead with the worst hand to get the strategic benefit of a free card (which could save a bet on a more expensive street if your draw misses or provide a chance to see an extra card that wins several additional bets), it was like a light went on in my head. *You mean there is more to poker than playing any hand and winning when you get lucky and catch something?*

Limit hold 'em is where you learn all these marvelous concepts that can make the pursuit of poker skill fun and earn you money. I have been a strong limit hold 'em player for twenty years, playing and winning in low-stakes, medium-stakes, and high-stakes cash games (and, of course, in the limit hold 'em portion of high-stakes mixed games). After deciding during 2002 to devote myself increasingly to tournament poker, I won what was then one of the world's biggest annual limit hold 'em tournaments, the PartyPoker Million, in March 2003.

The great thing about limit hold 'em is that you never stop learning, and never stop refining what you have learned. In 2004, I released a DVD, *Howard Lederer's Secrets of Texas Limit Hold 'Em*. In this chapter, I will share those strategies, as well as expand on them and apply them to tournaments.

The Starting Framework for Limit Hold 'Em Tournament Play

Early in any poker tournament, in any game, you are just trying to play that game well. Tournament strategy comes in toward the middle to late portion of the tournament, when the blinds become significant in relation to the stacks and when making it into the money comes into play. Early on, you have to play good poker.

Your goal in the tournament from the start should be to control your stack and just hang around while you wait for your rush. A tournament isn't about winning the most hands or even winning the most chips. It is about surviving. When that rush happens late in a tournament, because you're able to hang around, that will often lead to a victory. At least 75 percent of my tournament wins have been of the "hang in there and be alive for your rush" variety. It has been rare for me to win a tournament by taking a big chip lead and dominating.

You hang around a tournament by being solid—showing people a nice, tight, solid game. When your cards are dry and you are not winning a bunch of pots, you can hang in there by stealing the blinds. If you build a loose image, it undercuts your ability to steal. You will need a rush of cards to survive, because your opponents will not concede when you show strength later in the tournament.

I can't say my style is correct, but I know it is correct for *me*. I know how to use it. It takes experience to know exactly how much you can get away with, but I know how to teach others to play that style and set up situations to take advantage of it.

There are some great players who have won limit hold 'em tournaments by being loose and playing a lot of pots. They make that style work for them. You can always try that style, creating a lot of action for yourself, but it is not a style I'm comfortable playing or, for most people, recommending. It might be a strategy that wins more tournaments, though success is not measured solely by tournament wins.

Maybe I could have won more tournaments going that way. But I am certain that I have won more money in total—even with the prize distribution weighted toward the top spots—by surviving until my rush. You cash more often when you play this way, and you finish second, third, and fourth more often. You can still win once you make the final table, even if you had to make it by clawing your way through the field on short chips without catching cards.

Every time you survive to the money and don't win the tournament, you have, by definition, taken advantage of the tournament structure. If you finished third, for example, you took advantage of the tournament structure because you ended up broke—zero chips—but they paid you a big check anyway.

The winner actually is the one that pays the biggest price for the tournament structure. The winner gets all the chips but does not get all the money. So the more times you survive, the more times you get that extra value in ending up broke and still getting paid.

The goal is always to win; I would never suggest not winning. But there are some players out there who are clear favorites to win a tournament. In a tournament of three hundred players, they might be in the top thirty to win it. The problem is, even though they win more than their share of tournaments, they don't cash nearly enough to make a profit from tournament poker. Those players come and go; they get their rush and win, but then they go through periods where they never even smell the money.

If you want to succeed over the long run, you need some very high finishes. But you also need those solid efforts where you never had a chance to win but you keep cashing checks. You keep hanging around, staying in the game, and then you are in action when your rush comes and you can take advantage. You get in that position by being perceived as a solid player. It keeps you from risking a lot of chips early and gets you the respect to steal when you need to survive later.

But you have to start building that image with a solid foundation at the start: both the start of the tournament and the start of each hand.

Pre-Flop Strategy

Unlike no-limit hold 'em tournaments, you cannot succeed in limit hold 'em solely by your skill at playing before the flop. But the way you survive in a limit hold 'em tournament is by playing strong cards (and, more important, by giving opponents the perception that you are playing *only* strong cards) and playing them aggressively. You need to be solid before the flop to take advantage of the great post-flop situations offered in limit hold 'em.

I have categorized playable starting hands in Groups A through E. The percentages refer to the percentage of the time you receive a particular hand or a better one. (There are 1,326 two-card combinations, consisting of 78 pairs, 312 suited duos, and 936 unsuited duos.)

Group A hands

You will receive a Group A hand 3 percent of the time.

A-A
K-K
Q-Q
A-Ks
J-J
A-Ko

Group B hands

You will receive a Group B hand 3.5 percent of the time.
You will receive a Group B or better hand 6.5 percent of the time.

T-T
A-Qs
K-Qs
9-9
A-Js
8-8
A-Qo
K-Js

Group C hands

You will receive a Group C hand 4.5 percent of the time.
You will receive a Group C or better hand 11 percent of the time.

Q-Js
A-Ts
K-Qo
J-Ts
A-Jo
Q-Ts
J-9s
A-To
K-Ts

Group D hands

You will receive a Group D hand 6.5 percent of the time.
You will receive a Group D or better hand 17.5 percent of the time.

7-7
K-Jo
Q-Jo
6-6
A-Xs
5-5
K-To

(continued)

(Continued)

Group E hands

You will receive a Group E hand 14.6 percent of the time.
You will receive a Group E or better hand 32.1 percent of the time.

T-9s
T-8s
9-8s
J-8s
Q-9s
J-To
K-9s
4-4
9-7s
Q-To
K-8s
3-3
J-9o
Q-8s
T-9o
A-9o
2-2
K-Xs
8-7s
J-7s
K-9o
Q-9o
J-8o
T-8o

You might be surprised that A-Xo doesn't make the list but hands like T-9o and 8-7s do. With these guidelines, you are playing up to 32.1 percent of the hands dealt. That means you are folding a lot in late position, even when no one has entered the pot. If you add too many more hands to the bottom of the list, your late-position raises aren't going to get much respect.

Hands like 8-7s play better than, say, A-3o from late position against one opponent. The reason is because if an ace flops, you can probably bluff successfully with 8-7s. You raised. The flop comes A-9-4. If the caller in the blind doesn't have an ace (or, probably, a nine), they are done. And they will lay down a lot of hands that would beat 8-7s.

But what happens when you raise and miss with A-3o? On an 8-6-4 flop, your bet is going to look like exactly what it is: an attempt to follow up on a high-card raise when you missed the flop. Now you are looking at a check-raise from an opponent with an eight, a six, a four, a made straight, an open-ended straight draw, a gut-shot straight draw, or two overcards. Are you prepared to put in a small bet to call the raise, and the big bet you'll have to call on the turn? Just to pick off a bluff or catch one of the three remaining aces?

You can play the texture of the flop better with medium connecting cards than with an ace, especially if you are facing one opponent in the blind. When you hit a single pair with the medium cards, you have to deal with overcards or overpairs, but you can also make straights and flushes with 8-7s; your only shot with A-3o is to hit an ace.

You should also treat these as *guidelines*. You have to play your situation, and especially pay attention to your short-term table image. If you have been folding a lot, A-8o in late position might start looking pretty good. If your opponents have branded you as too tight, and you really just haven't picked up any cards, raising with A-8o in late position is liable to be respected by observant opponents.

These are guidelines for very tight play. You should look for opportunities to expand these; that's where creativity comes in. Approximately 90–95 percent of the time, however, this is the way you should play.

The hand values differ from no-limit hold 'em in several important ways. First, you have to tighten up more in early position compared to no-limit, and you can loosen up more in late position. In the early stages of a limit tournament, you will have to show down more hands, and you are also limited to a single-bet raise. You shouldn't loosen up in early or middle position because of this, but actually tighten up. You need to start with a very strong hand if your opponents are going to hang around because you can't push them out by raising three times the big blind like you can in no-limit. If someone calls behind you, you also suffer from being out of position throughout the hand.

Conversely, in late position, you have a positional advantage through-out the hand. Opponents can't take it away by moving all-in.

Second, medium and small pairs go down in value. In no-limit hold 'em, you can do a lot more with them: limit the field, bet out a single opponent who missed the flop, or win a giant pot with a set. In limit hold 'em, however, a hand like 5-5 isn't worth nearly as much. Imagine a flop with two or three overcards, like K-Q-7 or J-T-3. Be-cause you raised in late position, an opponent who paired one of the top two cards has you beat and won't be bet out of the pot. If the player who called your raise from the blind has a gut-shot straight draw, they have ten outs to beat you and will call your bet on the flop. You are defenseless against a check-raise. And if you do hit your set, you won't get paid off like you will in no-limit. You can still play medium and small pairs, but they are less valuable in limit hold 'em.

Third, suited connecting cards move up in value in limit hold 'em. As I already mentioned, when you raise with these hands, you sometimes have a credible bluff when you completely miss the flop. In no-limit, suited connectors are tricky. When they hit flushes, they can get you broke against a bigger flush. They can hit two pair against a straight or a better two pair. In limit and no-limit, you can win big when you hit your hand. But a hand that might have gotten you broke in no-limit will cost you just a few bets in limit.

Aggression before the flop—If you can't raise, you usually should not enter the pot. Even when other players have limped or raised and you have position over them, it is rarely a good idea to call. If you are going to play solid starting hands, you need to make opponents pay for trying to outdraw you with inferior cards. You also need to narrow the field as soon as possible. With every chip in the pot, it is easier for an opponent to justify sticking around. Before the flop, when the pot is smaller, you need to make it a bad idea for opponents to put in two bets to see a flop. The second-best result you can achieve by raising pre-flop is getting heads-up against an out-of-position opponent playing two random cards in one of the blinds. The *best* situation, of course, is for everyone to fold; you have to raise for that to happen.

This is even more important in tournaments than in cash games. It is imperative as you get toward the money, and in the money, that you keep pace by stealing the blinds. You do that by cultivating a solid image, discouraging opponents from paying a substantial portion of their chips to (in their minds) get lucky against you. Even early in the tournament, when the blinds and bets are small in proportion to stack sizes, it is better to win small pots without confrontations.

Position, first to enter—In a ten-handed game, you have two blinds, and eight other players. Consider the first three players to act as "early position." The fourth, fifth, and sixth players to act are in "middle position." The seventh and eighth players (the "cutoff" and the "button") are in "late position." I will consider the play of the blinds, who act last before the flop but act first in the three subsequent betting rounds, separately. In a nine-handed game, like you will find in tournaments and cash games on Full Tilt Poker, consider positions 1 and 2 as early, 3–5 as middle, and 6 and 7 as late.

In early position, one of the first three players to act (or one of the first two to act in a nine-handed game), you should play only Group A and B hands. In middle position, one of the next three to act, you can expand your playable hands to include Groups C and D. If you are in the cutoff position or on the button, you can play Group A through E hands.

TABLE 12.1

First to enter, early position (6.5% of hands dealt)	
Pairs	A-A, K-K, Q-Q, J-J, T-T, 9-9, 8-8
A-Xs	A-Ks, A-Qs, A-Js
A-Xo	A-Ko, A-Qo
K-Xs	K-Qs, K-Js

First to enter, middle position (17.5% of hands dealt)	
Pairs	A-A, K-K, Q-Q, J-J, T-T, 9-9, 8-8, 7-7, 6-6, 5-5
A-Xs	All
A-Xo	A-Ko, A-Qo, A-Jo, A-To
K-Xs	K-Qs, K-Js, K-Ts
K-Xo	K-Qo, K-Jo, K-To
Q-Xs	Q-Js, Q-Ts
Q-Xo	Q-Jo
J-Xs	J-Ts, J-9s

(continued)

TABLE 12.1 ◆ *(Continued)*

First to enter, late position (32.1% of hands dealt)	
Pairs	All
A-Xs	All
A-Xo	A-Ko, A-Qo, A-Jo, A-To, A-9o
K-Xs	All
K-Xo	K-Qo, K-Jo, K-To, K-9o
Q-Xs	Q-Js, Q-Ts, Q-9s, Q-8s
Q-Xo	Q-Jo, Q-To, Q-9o
J-Xs	J-Ts, J-9s, J-8s, J-7s
J-Xo	J-To, J-9o, J-8o
T-Xs	T-9s, T-8s
T-Xo	T-9o, T-8o
9-Xs	9-8s, 9-7s
8-Xs	8-7s

You should stick to this fundamentally solid style 90–95 percent of the time. You have to use your poker skills to find the hands to play outside these guidelines. If you see a player you can take advantage of by playing additional hands, you need to do it. Finding a few hands to play that don't fit the framework also adds some deception to your game.

Getting reraised—After you have opened the pot for a raise, you should always call a reraise, unless there have been two raises behind you. If that happens, call only with Group A hands (A-A, K-K, Q-Q, J-J, A-Ks, and A-Ko).

You are almost always getting the right price to call a reraise. Here is an example to show you the math: The blinds are 25-50 and you make it 100 in the cutoff position, the button makes it 150. It is folded back to you. It is 50 more to you and there is 325 in the pot. You are getting 6.5-to-1 to call. You aren't that big an underdog with J-7s against A-A. The only time an opponent would be favored by more than 6.5-to-1 is when they have a pocket pair and you have one of that rank and an undercard (like A-A verus A-2).

Position, raised in front—If someone raises in front of you, you will have position over them for the rest of the hand, but you have to give the proper respect to their raise. Unless you are in the blinds, you should reraise or fold. I am not in favor of flat-calling behind a raiser in limit hold 'em.

The position of the raiser is very important. If I am on the button with A-9 and someone raised from early position, I don't even think about playing it. I wouldn't even play A-J after an early raise. But if I have A-J on the button and the cutoff position raised, I would reraise every time.

A reasonable early-position raiser will be playing hands in Groups A and B. How would my A-J fare against those fourteen hands? I would be favored against just two (K-Qs, K-Js). I would be a small underdog against three (T-T, 9-9, 8-8). I would split with another A-J. But against nine of the fourteen, I would get slaughtered. If I hit my ace, I would still lose to five of those nine hands. If I hit my jack, I would lose to at least four of them—more if a king, queen, or ten also showed up on the board.

But look at the range of hands you might be facing if the opening raise comes from the cutoff position. If the cutoff raises with hands in Groups A–E (32 percent of all hands), my A-9 is a favorite or in a coin-flip situation (for pairs below 9-9) against all but about 7.5 percent of the hands the cutoff could have. I am in bad shape only against the Group A hands, most of the Group B hands, and the three ace-better-kicker hands in Group C.

In addition, by reraising in position, your reraise represents an even bigger hand than you have, which you can use to your advantage on later streets. This also makes it difficult for the blinds to call, creating a lot of dead money in the pot. If your opponent makes it four bets, then you made a mistake but you are still going to call and see if you get lucky.

If the raise came from a player in early position, reraise with Group A hands and T-T. If the raise came from a player in middle position, reraise with the same hands and A-Qs. I might also reraise with any Group B hand depending on feel. Against a late-position raiser, reraise with Group A–D hands.

You always have to know your customer. If you don't know anything about an opponent, you should apply reasonable hand values and put them on a range of hands that they would play in that position. As you gather evidence to the contrary, you adjust those assumptions.

I don't put players on specific cards until late in a hand, but if I notice someone is not playing a reasonable strategy, I will adjust accordingly and take advantage.

This is why, even if you are a new tournament player, paying attention is vital. This is how you advance as a player, and it doesn't take much to put you on that path. You may not have the luxury, as in cash games, of playing many hours with the same opponents. You need to gather information quickly and respond quickly. If you see someone raise with A-4o in early position, you need to use that information right away. You want to target that guy. The next time he raises, if you have A-Jo, reraise him. Isolate that player and play a big pot with him, especially if you have position. You can't afford to miss opportunities like that. You need to notice this player is weak and find a hand to take advantage. If you wait for a hand based on my guidelines to take against this player, he could go broke and someone else will win those chips.

If your opponent who raised up front plays too loose, you should widen the hands you are willing to play against him. You have position and you want to exploit it, reraising with more hands than you would against a reasonable opponent. Here, a reraise helps isolate that opponent, plus it is a good investment because you may be starting with a stronger hand, and you have the benefit of position throughout the hand. If this player is not paying attention to their position (for example, opening with Group E hands from any position), you should be reraising with a hand that beats more than half those hands, like the hands in Groups A–C.

If the player who put in the raise is too tight and opens with only Group A hands, then you have to play just the hands that beat half those hands. Unless you have A-A, K-K, or Q-Q, you aren't going to play against that player. Against someone that tight, you have to forget about the idea of reraising with Group A and B hands.

Against tight players, your best strategy is to avoid playing hands with them. You beat them by winning their blinds because they fold too much. Against loose players, you want to isolate them and take advantage of good situations.

Don't flat-call a raise in limit hold 'em—I do not advocate flat-calling a raise in position in limit hold 'em. Some players make flat-calling in position an important part of their no-limit strategy. Even there, though I think it is a reasonable strategy, it is not one I use much. In very specific circumstances, I will flat-call a raise in position in no-limit. But in no-limit, you can win a big pot if you catch a big flop with a weaker starting hand. You can also bet enough to make a better hand fold if you sense weakness.

Limit hold 'em is not a bluffing game. It's a betting game. If you have a good hand in position, you want to put more chips in the pot. You want to put your opponent on the defensive. You want to set up to get free cards so you can earn or save more bets later. Limit hold 'em is not the game in which you want to take an inferior hand with position and try to get an opponent (who already showed strength by raising) off a hand.

Position, limped in front—Tighten up your starting hands a little, but do not follow the limper by limping yourself. The only time you should limp is when you are in late position, there are already at least two limpers in the hand, and you have a marginal hand that you would have raised if everyone folded to you, or you have a nice drawing hand like suited connectors.

You should not treat the prior limper like a raise, but you have to tighten up a little. If you understand why some of your hand values change, it will be easier to pick the hands to play and the hands to fold. First, it is very difficult to play a pot heads-up after someone limps. The limper will call a raise almost 100 percent of the time and the big blind, anticipating this, is getting 5.5-to-1 to see the flop. Second, now with two opponents, there is an even better chance that the flop will hit one of them if it does not hit you. Third, unless you are on the button, someone acting after you, anticipating that the limper will call and possibly the big blind as well, is getting 2.75- or 3.25-to-1 to call a raise and have position over you throughout the hand.

If I am in early position and a player before me limped, I will probably still raise with the same hands that I would play as the first in. Unless the limper is slow-playing A-A (a folly in limit hold 'em with so many players who limp after limpers) or has completely lost his compass, you are probably facing some kind of "multiway" hand such as suited connectors. The Group A and B hands play well against those suited connectors and your raise should scare most reasonable players out of the pot. You get the Group A and B hands only 6 percent of the time. You have to push them, especially against an opponent who is probably playing a nonpremium hand out of position.

In middle position, instead of raising with Group A–D hands, fold the Group Ds, and some of the marginal Group C hands after a middle limper or two. Raise with just the top half of the Group C hands. (Notice the kinds of hands you throw away in Group C when you do this: Q-Ts, A-To, and K-Ts. Those are the kinds of hands someone may think they should limp with up front. By folding those hands, you will be raising with the better hands.)

If you are in late position, you need to look first at the position of the limper and then if there is more than one limper. Against one limper, you have to use your judgment on whether they are limping with a "multiway hand" or whether they are trying to get away with playing a slightly weaker hand than they would be raising with in that position. If the limper is in early position, you have to give their call some respect. If they limped to play a hand that is playable in middle position, you should treat their action as a middle-position raise. If the limper or limpers came from middle or late position, you have to decide if they are slow-playing a monster hand or just trying to hang around to see if they flop something.

If you are in late position, especially with multiple limpers, there is little benefit to raising with a drawing hand like 9-8s. You aren't going to be able to buy the button or narrow the field with a raise, so you should be happy to limp in and see if you flop something. You need to remember that the limpers are likely to have medium connected cards, small pairs, random suited cards, or A-Xs, so be careful. The "something" you flop could amount to something *better* for one of your opponents.

Play from the blinds—In the big blind, you will be getting at least 3.5-to-1 to call a single raise. As long as the raise did not come from a player in early position (in which case you can give them credit for a very strong hand) you are going to call with a lot of hands. Mathematically, when you have nothing invested you would want to beat half the hands your opponents would play. But if you get to see the flop for half price and add in the dead money from the other blind, you don't have to be able to beat half their hands for a call to be correct. If the raise came from early position, reraise with Group A hands and call with Group B and C hands. Against a middle-position raiser, again reraise with Group A hands and call with Group B–D hands. If your blind was raised by someone in late position, reraise with Group A and B hands and call with Group C–E hands.

You need to defend your blinds vigorously, especially the big blind. Just as you want to make opponents pay for seeing the blind with random cards, you have to punish players who target your blinds. You should call a lot of hands from the big blind, but you should not reraise very often. You don't want opponents to be able to put you on a hand. Even if you are giving up some value by not reraising, you can more than make it back with the message you send. If you show down a big hand out of the blinds without reraising before the flop, how will opponents know when you are calling with a strong hand or a weak one?

Using my strategy, you are calling a lot of raises, sometimes with hands like T-T or A-Qs, where you may have the best hand and are giving up a little value by not reraising against a middle-position opener. But in the whole picture, you can call with much weaker hands and your opponent won't know if you have a strong hand or a weak one. If you reraise with all your strong hands, your opponents will know.

And you can get that value back later in the hand. The best way to defend your blind is to check-raise on the flop. You lose this weapon when you reraise before the flop.

In the small blind, you should reraise rather than call. Let the big blind play the role of table cop. You are playing from the worst possible position, you have to put in 75 percent of the raise, and you will likely have two opponents if you just call. If your hand is good enough to overcome all that, you should reraise. You also want to knock out the big blind.

Blind versus blind—It rarely gets folded around to the blinds, but if you play a heads-up tournament, or make it to the final two in a full-table tournament, you will need to understand the principles of blind versus blind play. When there are just two players at the table, the button has the small blind, so that player acts first before the flop and last on every later street. At a full table where everyone has checked, the small blind is out of position for the rest of the hand. Therefore, you can adapt some of the concepts I will describe in heads-up play at the end of the chapter, but note that important difference.

In the small blind, you should call with any Group E hand and a few more hands, like A-Xo, and raise with Group A–D hands. In the big blind, if the small blind limps, you should raise with the same hands, Group A–D. If the small blind raises, you have to call with a lot of hands. You have position, plus you have to make sure that this can't be an automatically profitable raise.

In any poker situation—not just in limit hold 'em—you have to act in a fashion that makes it unprofitable for an opponent to bet in a certain situation with any two cards. Blind versus blind situations are a perfect example. If the small blind raises, what kind of hands should I call with? At least half of all hands! If you aren't willing to call with half the hands you're dealt, then your opponent has a free shot to raise with any two cards.

Say you play only 40 percent of the hands after the small blind raises—30 percent calls, 10 percent reraises. Even if your opponent folds every time you reraise, it is profitable for him to raise with any two cards. The small blind's raise is a 1.5-unit bet to win the 1.5 units in the pot. For every ten times he does this, he wins nine units (six folds) and loses 1.5 units (when he folds to your reraise). Therefore, he is ahead 7.5 units on hands that end before the flop. He spends six units on the four occasions when you call, but now he is freerolling on the flop. Even if he checks and folds after the flop every time he calls his pre-flop raise, he will still win 1.5 units raising blind against your strategy. Needless to say, he should do better than that on the few flops he does see.

Play on the Flop

The flop is where the fun begins in limit hold 'em. This is where you accumulate chips and develop a full range of skills that will help in limit hold 'em tournaments and make you a better player in other games.

Limit hold 'em is about playing your position. When you have an edge, you have to push it. Although you sometimes do that by winning a pot, you are more often pushing your edge to win an extra bet or save a bet. In the long run the players who succeed in limit hold 'em are the players who are maximizing their profits; winning that extra bet or minimizing losses by saving that one bet on pots they lose. You need to feel good about the fact that you just check-called with a hand that a lot of players would have bet with and gotten raised. You lost the pot, but you saved yourself a bet. And that bet is going to matter over the long run. It's not about winning pots. It's about winning bets in limit hold 'em.

Being in position in limit hold 'em is where you earn your bets. In no-limit hold 'em, opponents can take away your position by moving all-in. They had to act first, but once they are all-in, the pressure is all on you and there will be no more betting after you decide whether to call or fold. In limit hold 'em tournaments, unless stacks are short, there tends to be betting all the way through. On every street, you get to take advantage of your position. That is why you can let position influence your starting hand even more in limit hold 'em compared with no-limit.

It is a truism to say there are too many possibilities for how hands develop to provide clear rules for post-flop play in limit hold 'em. But if you understand *why,* you will begin to understand how to evaluate the correct play after the flop from different competing considerations.

After the flop, you have up to five choices when it is your turn to act: check, bet, call, raise, or fold. Your best play among these possibilities can be determined by considering the following elements:

- Position, both yours and your opponents'
- Your action before the flop
- The amount of the chips in the pot
- Whether the hand is being played heads-up or multiway
- The action of opponents before the flop
- Your estimate of how the flop has affected your opponents' chances of having or drawing to the best hand
- Your estimate of how your opponents *think* the flop affected your chances of having or drawing to the best hand

- Your estimate of the *actual* likelihood you have the best hand or are drawing to the best hand
- The amount of chips you can expect will be in the pot if you win it
- What you know about your opponents by their action on prior hands
- What you know about your opponents by their physical appearance and actions
- The size of your stack in relation to the tournament average
- The size of your stack in relation to the blinds
- How close you are to the money
- The size of your opponents' stacks in relation to the tournament average
- The size of your opponents' stacks in relation to the blinds

The various ways in which these elements can combine to influence your decision is infinite. For example, you are dealt

in the position before the cutoff and open the pot with a raise. At this point, the most likely situation is that you will be heads-up against the big blind, the flop will be checked to you, and you will bet. But imagine all the things that could happen to change or at least significantly complicate the conclusion:

Variation #1: *The button reraises, the blinds fold, and you call. The flop comes*

Check the flop and go for a check-raise. Unless your opponent has A-A, K-K, Q-Q, or made an unlikely set, you probably have the best hand. There are a lot of hands that would have reraised you (A-K, A-Q, T-T, 9-9, 8-8) that will bet on the flop, so it can be a very profitable check-raise. Against most of your opponent's holdings, you have the best hand and, since your opponent three-bet you before the flop, it is almost certain he will bet the flop.

Variation #2: The cutoff position calls your raise, as do the button and the big blind. The flop comes

The big blind checks to you.

You should bet about half the time. Fold if you get raised; give it up if you get called. With blinds of 25-50, there would be 425 in the pot. It's worth a bet of 50 because you are getting more than 8-to-1. If none of your opponents has a king, there is a good chance you'll take the pot right there. If you are up against a pocket pair and they call—an opponent with 7-7 or 8-8 might not raise you here—you can catch a queen or jack on the turn.

Variation #3: The small blind reraises and you call. (Everyone else folds.) The flop comes

The small blind bets.

Given the implied odds, you should always at least call. You are getting 8-to-1 to call, plus the implied odds if you hit a ten on the turn. That alone justifies continuing with the hand. But it's poker;

there are a lot of ways you can win with this hand. You could be up against hands like T-T, 9-9, or 8-8, where a queen or jack could possibly win.

You should actually *raise* 20–25 percent of the time. Maybe that sounds insane, but if your opponent had Q-Q, J-J, or T-T, or one of those even lower pairs, he might just lose heart. You are getting 4-to-1 that your opponent has one of those hands and that he gives up, which is a reasonable price. A lot of other good things can happen if he calls your raise. You could get a free card on the turn and hit your straight or make a runner-runner flush.

Keep in mind that just because you call to see the turn, that doesn't mean you have to continue with the hand if you hit something. If you hit a jack on the turn and the player in the small blind continues to bet, you may want to throw the hand away. Unless you know that this player will keep firing at the pot with a weak hand, you have to respect the reraise before the flop and continued willingness to bet on the turn after you called twice and there are three big cards on the board.

Variation #3A: The same as Variation #3, but two of the cards on the flop are your suit.

Now you have twelve outs (the four tens—one of which also makes your flush—and other eight unseen suited cards), and possibly as many as eighteen if your opponent had a pair below jacks. Raise every time.

Variation #4: The player on the button, who has frequently been reraising in late position with what appears to be any playable hand, reraises. The blinds fold and you call. The flop comes

Check-raise in this situation, unless you're sure the flop hit him. You would always at least call, but you should raise most of the time. You can get your opponent to lay down a lot of hands this way. Mix up raises and calls, raising about 75 percent of the time and calling the remainder.

Most of these plays work best when you are playing against one opponent. If you play before the flop in the style I have described, you will usually be playing heads-up, either from the blinds when someone else has raised, against one of the blinds when you have raised, or against an opener after you have reraised.

Playing multiway pots after the flop—You have fewer plays available when a pot is contested multiway. That doesn't mean you have to abandon them, but you have to be careful. And you have to be on the lookout for opponents who don't properly adjust to multiway pots. You also need to know the strategies that are unique to multiway pots.

When will you be in a multiway pot? Based on the way I recommend you play limit hold 'em, you will usually be in one of the blinds, checking or putting in half a bet in a multiway limped pot. (You could also be in one of the blinds and call a bet from a middle-position raiser that was called by one or two players in late position, or where someone raised in late position after other players limped.) The next most likely situation is when you join the limpfest from late position. On rare occasions, one of your raises can draw calls behind you and from the blinds.

If you hit your hand in a multiway pot, especially in early position, you have to narrow the field. For example, say you flop two pair with A-T in the blind in a four-way pot on a flop of A-T-7. There is tremendous value in narrowing the field. Opponents with Q-J or K-Q are getting the right price to call a single bet to try to hit an inside straight draw. (Consequently, when you are on the other side of this play, note that it is correct for you to call a bet to see the turn to hit a straight.) You have to price them out of the pot.

The impulse for players who have not thought this through, especially if they are misusing the general advice about being aggressive, is to lead out with a bet. If you do that, your opponents are right to call, and if they hit, you have cost yourself a pot. If you lead out and get raised, that's great; it's just not very likely. Your opponent needs to have A-K or something like that to raise you.

You need to check and hope a player to your right bets so you can raise and make it two bets. If it was raised before the flop, you can generally count on the raiser betting. Even if everyone limped in, it is still likely someone will bet. Instead of allowing them a good call of one bet, you present them the unsavory choice of making a bad call or folding a hand they would have loved to see a cheap card with. If you have a hand, you always want to narrow the field.

Even if this strategy fails, you are better off checking (and failing to get a check-raise) than putting in a single bet that gets called. Your bet would not prevent opponents from chasing their inside straight draws, so you save a bet if they hit on the turn after it got checked around on the flop. If a blank hits on the turn, you can lead out with an upper-limit bet, which they will not be getting the right price to call.

If you are in late position with the same hand (A-T) and the same flop (A-T-7), you have to bet your strong hands if they are checked to you, both to avoid giving a free card and in hopes that someone will check-raise *you*. You are happy to get check-raised with A-T; less happy if you have some other kicker with your ace (other than a seven). Of course, even with the second-best hand, your opponent's check-raise should succeed in getting rid of the drawing hands, which is to your benefit. If someone bets in front of you, of course you should raise.

If you are in late position and you are the one drawing, check and take the free card. Bluffing and semi-bluffing have little value in multiway pots. Players attempt those plays too often against multiple opponents and they rarely work. Someone usually has a hand or a draw. With that same flop of A-T-7, if one player bets and another calls, the bluff is gone. You can start putting your opponents on hands. The bettor probably has at least an ace with a weak kicker.

If the betting goes bet-raise-reraise, players are approaching the nuts. You can look at betting patterns in multiway pots and believe them more. You can believe someone has a flush when there are three suited cards on the board and they made it three bets. You can start laying down big hands in multiway pots that you never consider laying down heads-up. And it is correct to do so. You have so much more information in multiway pots—not just an opponent's bet but how the multiple opponents are reacting to each other's betting.

You also have to be very careful about playing to less than the nuts in multiway pots. You don't want to be drawing to the ignorant end of straight draws. It is much more likely you will run into a better draw or a hand that has you beat if you get there. There is nothing worse than hitting your hand and still losing.

As I said before, it is probably right for you to call one small bet with an inside straight draw, but it has to be a draw to the nuts. Here is the math: if the blinds are 25-50, a four-way pot would contain 400 if the button raised and the blinds and a limper called. If someone bets after a flop of A-T-7, you are getting the right price—9-to-1 plus the likelihood of some additional action if you hit the straight—to call 50 with K-Q, K-J, or Q-J.

Mostly, in multiway pots, you need to narrow the field when you are in the lead and take what they will give you when you are drawing, based on your pot odds and implied odds. Other than protecting your lead, you need to play solid and take advantage of opponents who get cute with the strategies that work much better in heads-up situations.

Heads-up: keeping the lead—If you raise before the flop and it is checked to you, you are almost always going to bet. (This is less true if you raised in a multiway pot before the flop.) One of the few times I might check is if I raised with a good ace and the flop came something like 8♣7♣6♣ or 8♣7♣6♦ and I don't have a club. If you bet 100 percent of the time, you become a target for a free check-raise on the flop. By checking about 10 percent of the time when you raised before the flop, you will give your opponents an excuse to make a marginal laydown on the frequent occasions when you bet the flop with nothing.

Betting *nearly* all the time ties in with my pre-flop strategy. I am selective before the flop. Therefore, even though I bet almost every time after the flop, opponents have to give that bet some respect. Players are not going to put me on nothing, even though strong hands miss flops too. The more raises you put in before the flop, the less success your bets will have after the flop. People are less likely to assume that you've got it this time and fold. They look for reasons to fight back.

You have to occasionally show opponents that you can check, even when you opened before the flop with a raise. There aren't many situations in which I recommend slow-playing a big hand, though checking occasionally when you miss the flop sets those plays up. On that 8-7-6 flop, opponents are going to have to ask themselves, "Did he have A-K? Or T-9? Or 8-8?" But that's secondary. The main reason you throw in a check is to give credibility to the times when you miss but still bet. If you raised before the flop, check on the flop, and fold to a bet on the turn, an opponent who watched you do that will give you credit for hitting the flop when you follow up your pre-flop raise with a bet next time. But you don't have to have a real hand; all you need is the image of a solid, aggressive player who doesn't bet all the time.

I don't look for spots to check, but it is profitable overall if opponents know that I will occasionally do it. It may not even be profitable to check in the 10 percent of the hands in which you do it following a pre-flop raise and a missed flop. But if you pick a few spots, like the example with 8-7-6, or where you raised in late position with 5-5 and the flop is A-Q-T, you will benefit. Apart from avoiding a check-raise or a call on a hand where you are already beat or you could be if any eight, nine, jack, or king hits on the turn, opponents will respect your bet on the flop *next time*.

I like to get people to submit to me. I am parlaying my selectiveness before the flop into extreme aggressiveness after the flop. This is particularly important in tournaments, where you have a limited amount of chips and you need to keep accumulating them just to keep pace with the rising blinds. The deeper you get in the tournament, the more important it is to win pots with bets on the flop.

The most successful player is the one who makes the series of decisions that leads to the most profitable outcomes, not the one who makes the most correct decisions. I may not play a big chunk of hands that are very marginally profitable. So let's say I play 25 percent of the hands and another player plays 35 percent of the hands. If they are a very skilled player and show a profit on those hands, someone could argue that 10 percent of the time I am folding a hand that I could turn a profit on.

That would be a mistake. What about the size of my profit on the 25 percent of the hands I play? By folding those marginal hands, I am making my playable hands more profitable, outweighing the possible profit I could squeeze out of those hands I folded. Maybe it would be slightly profitable to bet at a flop of 8-7-6 since I'm getting 3-to-1 to take the hand right there. But it makes my other bets much more profitable if I "miss" that bet. It will dawn on my opponents that I can't always have the best hand after the flop if I never check. I need my bets to mean something. I don't have to check very often to convince them of that.

Heads-up: losing the lead, semi-bluffing—If someone has taken the betting lead pre-flop (raising your blind or reraising your open), you should check to them on the flop almost all the time. This allows you to recapture position, forcing them, in a way, to act first. Even if you hit your hand on the flop, check. If you tend to bet when you hit the flop and check when you miss it, your opponent is getting the maximum benefit from their position. They are able to gauge the strength of your hand based on your action.

If you always check, you are a blank slate. They have to decide whether they want to bet without regard for your actions. That way, you reveal the strength of your hand only after they have bet.

You have to check-raise if you catch any piece of the flop. If you hit the flop and they missed, by check-raising you will win at least one more bet. If you pair any of the three cards on the board or are drawing to a gutshot straight or better, check-raise. That includes a lot of hands. You should do that 100 percent of the time with these hands, unless you get a strong vibe that your opponent caught something big.

Very often, this check-raise on the flop is a semi-bluff. If the flop came

and I check, I know my opponent will bet with a huge percentage of hands. If you are the pre-flop raiser in late position, that is the way you should play it. If I have 9-8, I am going to take a crack at winning the pot right there.

Am I going to check and call at 4-to-1 or 5-to-1 and hope I hit something? Or am I going to check-raise and possibly get my opponent to lay down a lot of hands that have me beat? If I win the pot on the flop occasionally, this is a profitable play. In addition, I am building a bigger pot that I will certainly win with a ten and possibly win with an eight or nine.

This play also allows me to maintain my aggressive stance. I want opponents to know that I will check-raise with a lot of hands. From the big blind with a flop of J-7-4, I don't need to be holding 4-4 or A-J to check-raise. My check-raise doesn't mean I have a huge hand. It just means I have something—at least a pair or a straight draw. If an opponent defends by reraising, I have enough to at least call and see the turn. But if my opponent has no pair and no draw, he is in an uncomfortable position.

Over time, other players will see me check-raise a lot and start to give me free cards on future hands. My opponent, who raised my blind, may now start checking behind me on the flop. (Maybe that opponent will go further and stop trying to steal my blinds.) Every once in a while, you will have K-9 and completely miss a flop like J-7-4. You would check-fold this hand but your snakebit opponent checks, telling you that the flop missed him too. If a king or nine hits on the turn, you pick up a pot you would have otherwise lost. Or you might bet even if you miss and pick up a pot with nothing, a pot that should have been your opponent's.

If my opponent calls my check-raise, I will continue betting on the turn 90 percent of the time, no matter what comes up. I have to take one more crack at it. I have to make him lay down A-K or a similar hand. If an obvious scare card hits the board—an ace or a king are the most likely candidates if the flop was all lower cards and the bettor did not reraise me—that might be a spot where I consider checking. I would also consider checking with my strongest hands, like if I flopped a set.

That way, I am almost always putting pressure on my opponent by betting the turn when I have "accused" him of having missed the flop. And the few times I don't bet the turn are divided between the situations where I have a great hand and those where I am pretty likely beaten. Generally, you don't want to use strategies that require you to play a certain way with only certain cards. You always want to counterbalance it by playing the same way with much different cards.

The key to keeping opponents off balance is to build your game around profitable plays that are masked by identical-*looking* plays with much different cards. Every time you find a good strategy, you have to find a much different situation in which you will appear to play it the same way. If you are in the blind and the flop comes A-T-7, your check-raise is almost impossible to correlate with a hand. You could have K-Q, K-J, 9-8, J-9, A-X, T-X, 7-X, T-T, 7-7, A-T, A-7, T-7, or any pocket pair above eights.

The check-raise is one of the most powerful and important weapons you have in limit hold 'em. If you don't check-raise frequently when you are out of position, without the betting lead, your opponent gets the benefit of position by using the information you provided by your check. Checking is the weakest thing you can do in poker, and if you put some teeth into it by check-raising a lot, your opponents will not know whether your check is a show of weakness or a show of strength. That is exactly the way you want it.

I am not a proponent of making a complete bluff on the flop. There are certainly flops where the texture of the board has you thinking, "I bet that flop didn't hit him." But if you can't check-raise at least as a semi-bluff, give up the hand. If you play the way I have described, you are already check-raising with all pairs, all gutshots, and all flush draws. There is enough aggression and enough bluff in this style of play without looking for naked bluffs based on the texture of the flop. (There is one exception, which I describe when talking about the bubble.)

Likewise, I think it undercuts your strategy if you lead out and bet the flop, either as a bluff or with a hand. The check-raise is such a powerful weapon that you undermine it by trying to take away the betting lead with a single out-of-position bet on the flop.

Free cards—Betting and raising to get free cards, as I explained in the introduction to this chapter, is the concept responsible for my becoming a professional poker player. You can build your whole game around this play. It is the fundamental play in limit hold 'em, the play from which all the other post-flop plays are derived. Once you are willing to raise without having a really strong hand, everything else is possible.

To use the concept of free cards, you need position and the betting lead. Unless you are calling from the blind, this will frequently be the case. You are coming in raising, trying to keep players behind you out of the pot. Frequently, you will be heads-up against a caller from the blinds and it will be checked to you after the flop.

If, for example, you raised in late position with Q-J and the flop is

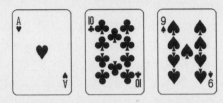

you have to bet if it is checked to you. First, you can win the pot right there. Second, if you get called, you will often get a free card on fourth street and see both the turn and river cards for the one bet on the flop. You are begging to have the pot taken away from you if you don't bet, and you make yourself very easy to read if you play the flop differently with a pair than with a draw. There are so many reasons you have to bet the flop almost all the time; getting a free card on the turn if you need it is one very important reason.

If you don't bet your draw when it is checked to you on the flop, you miss the small bet if you hit your draw. You will often face a big bet into a small pot on the turn when you miss. It's simply a disaster to not bet a draw if you had the betting lead and it is checked to you on the flop.

Even when you are in the betting lead, they will still try to take it from you sometimes. If the pre-flop caller tries to take the betting lead, you should raise if you have any piece of the flop—any pair, an overcard, or a gutshot straight draw. You want to discourage the players in the blind from betting you out of the pot when you miss the flop, because that happens pretty often. You are going to have to call enough so they can't make that play profitable regardless of their cards. Playing back at them to get a free card is part of that strategy.

Say a player who tried to take the betting lead has a decent pair. Does your raise mean you are on a draw, or does it mean you have something much better? The player out of position generally will call and then check the turn.

With your Q-J in late position, imagine you get called by the big blind, who holds T-8. With that same flop of A-T-9, many players with T-8 will bet out (though I think the better play is to check-raise). If the big blind bets, the proper play is to raise. The player with T-8 isn't going to fold, but he isn't going to bet the turn after you raise either. Did you raise with an ace? Two pair? A straight draw? With your Q-J, you are going to get a free card on the turn.

You spend one extra small bet to save a big bet on the turn. If you actually hit your hand with a king or an eight, you made an extra small bet by raising on the flop.

You gain so much by making some of your raises without a made hand. If you raise only when you have a big hand or when you are on a complete bluff, even though you are mixing up your play, you are still making it easy for opponents to play against you. All they have to do is decide whether you are bluffing or not. But when you start raising with draws to take advantage of the one-bet/two-bet structure, your opponents have no idea what your raises mean.

On one hand, you could raise on the flop and take a free card on the turn. The next time you raise on the flop, maybe you have a big hand. So if your opponent tries to take away the free card on the turn, they'll just get raised. You are playing aggressive poker so you are going to raise on the flop with good hands, draws, and a few bluffs. (By approaching the game this way, I make slow-playing a strong hand a very small part of my game. I would rather play aggressively all the time and get a lot of folds and some action on my strong hands. Otherwise, I have to play a lot of hands slow to make up for all the times I'm calling with draws to disguise the strength of my hand when I call with a big hand. If I call with my draws, and raise with very strong hands and fold with very weak hands, then I become easy to read.)

When you start calling with draws or mediocre hands on the flop, unless you want to be an open book, you have to also call with some strong hands to make your play indistinguishable whether you have a strong hand or a draw. In every situation in poker where you want to act in a particular way, you have to find different types of hands in which to act the same way. If you don't mix it up, you can't win at poker. Opponents will correlate your actions with your hands. If you want to slow-play, then you are choosing, for a lot of your hands, to play passively. You lose all the benefits of aggressive poker when you do this: extra bets when you bet your strong hands for value; action on your strong hands because they never know if your bet is based on strength, a draw, or a bluff; a payoff for hitting your draw because they can't put you on a draw if you play aggressively all the time; the ability to get free cards; and getting your opponent to fold a better hand when you bet with nothing.

In contrast, when you play aggressively, betting or raising in position on the flop, your opponent has little idea of where he stands on the turn, unless he has a very strong hand. Because you are playing your strong hands just as aggressively as your draws, you could have a strong hand, a hand where you just made your draw, or the same draw you had on the flop. They can't bet with confidence that you will fold because you are weak, and they can't check-raise for the same reason. And because you are capable of raising on the flop to get a free card, they can't afford to check with their strong hand and let you draw.

If there is a 30–40 percent chance you are on a draw and looking for a free card, it is hard for them to go for a check-raise on the turn. Now when they check, it means they are checking because they are not strong. (Otherwise, they would have bet because they don't want you drawing for free.) This lets you value-bet a lot of hands. Now you have more confidence that a hand like top pair/weak kicker is good and will be paid off by second pair and busted draws on fourth street.

Opponents have to call you down with second pair because you could easily be on a draw. Sometimes—maybe 20–25 percent of the time—you will bet the turn on a draw even though you could have gotten the card for free. To choose those situations, you really have to use your poker skills to decide when to turn this play into a semi-bluff, trying to spot when an opponent is weak and will lay down a hand. This style of play, however, accommodates all these strategies and keeps opponents constantly guessing.

The more your opponents have to guess, the greater the disparity is between the amount of information you give away and the amount they give away. When they recognize that you could be playing drastically different cards in the same way, they have to be much more straightforward with their play. They can't show strength when they are weak, because they are reacting to a play you could have made due to your strength. And when they are strong, they can't slow-play or trap because they could lose bets or give you the free cards to beat them.

That is why you need to build your entire game by looking at every street and have every play available. If you called a raise before the flop out of position from one of the blinds you don't need to try to take away the betting lead if the flop hits you. You should almost always check to the raiser. If they bet, you will sometimes call, sometimes fold, and sometimes raise. When you have position and the betting lead, you will almost always bet, but not always. When you have position on someone with the betting lead and they bet, you can find situations for raising, calling, and folding.

Make every possible play a part of your game and think about when to use them. Figure out how often you want to choose one action over another in a particular situation. If you ever decide that it's *always* right or wrong to act a certain way, then you are giving information away. Someone could argue that you don't give away information if you always do the same thing (for example, always betting the turn after betting the flop in position).

The problem with that, however, is that you have position over your opponent and you are not forcing them to give you information. You have to check occasionally to make an opponent give you information. If you always bet on the turn, your opponent effectively takes away your positional advantage. Your opponent will always check, making you act first. If there is a chance you will check the turn—and it doesn't have to be a very big chance—your opponent can't risk checking a moderate-strength hand and letting you draw for free.

Play on the Turn

We can divide up important concepts about playing fourth street into three situations: heads-up, in position (which should be the majority of the time); heads-up, out of position (usually when you called a raise from the blinds); and multiway (which will come up more often early in tournaments).

In position, when to bet—Most of the play on the turn revolves around free cards. You are almost always keeping the betting lead after the flop when you have position, either because you have the best hand and your opponent is paying you off with a worse hand or a draw, or because you are drawing and semi-bluffing.

Whichever it is, your opponents won't know, because you play both kinds of hands the same way on the flop. The turn is about betting your good and decent hands and continuing to make the draws pay. It is also about taking the free card when you need it. But you can't always play it that straightforward. You will become too easy to read. The skill you need to develop on the turn has to do with mixing up your play as well as responding to the plays opponents will try to use against you.

If you are still drawing, you can't always take the free card. If you bet only when you have a hand and check whenever you have a draw, you hurt yourself in two ways. First, you make yourself predictable. Opponents will have an easier time checking and folding on the turn when you bet and can bluff at you on the river with even worse hands than yours when you check the turn too often.

Second, you lose some profitable semi-bluffs. An opponent in the big blind with a hand like 9-8 might check-call your bet after a flop of A-T-8. If you have J-9 and the turn is a king, that free card you get if you check is only 25 percent likely to help you, and a bet could get your opponent to lay down what is now the best hand.

You can't lose your nerve on the turn. You have to bet some of your draws and almost all of your made hands. When you raise with a hand like A-Q and the flop makes you top pair, every street on which you get called makes you feel more vulnerable. The turn will test your nerve; you have to bet.

Here is an example that will cover a lot of circumstances. You have A♦Q♣ in late position and raise, getting a call from the big blind. The flop is

The big blind checks, you bet with top pair/second kicker, and the big blind calls.

Let's use several hypothetical turn cards:

Turn A: 7♦ (a blank)
Turn B: 8♥ (a third heart)
Turn C: T♠ (a second ten)
Turn D: K♣ (a possible second pair or straight)

After each of these turn cards, your opponent bets at you. What could that mean, and how should you respond? Turn A is unlikely to have helped your opponent, unless he had A-7, T-7, or 7-7. Turns B, C, and D could have made his draws if he was drawing.

I advocate raising almost all the time after that bet. Your opponent is most likely making a defensive bet to protect an inferior hand. Your opponent knows that you will bet the flop to pick up a free card. The bet at you on the turn does not mean your A-Q is no good. If you bet only when you had a big hand on the turn, your opponent's lead-out bet would signal that he too has a big hand. But he knows he has to defend against giving you the free card, so he will bet with a lot of marginal hands. (Of course, you need to know your opponents. A good, observant player will play against you this way, but for other players, that bet could mean something entirely different.)

You need to get the extra value when your opponent is drawing or incorrectly guessing that you were going to check to get a free card. If you just call, you aren't punishing your opponent for drawing or making that play. In fact, if you just call with good but not great hands, it is a very smart play by your opponent. If you just call, you aren't punishing an opponent who mistakenly thought you were drawing. Because you will make the exact same play when you *are* drawing, you don't want him betting in this situation. You have to raise, both to get the extra bet and to convince him not to bet the turn in the future.

It is important to make the draws pay, important enough that you don't need much of a hand to bet. Say you raised with K-T instead of A-Q and made second pair on the flop. You would play it the same way with second pair as with top pair if it was checked to you.

After Turn A, you would definitely bet if it was checked to you and raise if it was bet to you with A-Q or K-T.

After Turn B, with either A-Q or K-T, you would bet if it was checked to you and call if your opponent bet. If your opponent made a flush and checked, you will have to pay off on the turn and river.

Occasionally, you will get reraised and it will cost you, but here is what you gain: if your opponent has a low flush, he may call and check the river, so you won't pay any more for a showdown than for calling twice. If one of your cards is a heart, any flush your opponent could have would probably be low. If you make your flush on the river, you get an extra bet. If you don't, it gets checked down. If your opponent is betting something other than a flush or representing a flush, you may get him to lay down the better hand. (This is assuming you had second pair, not top pair/second kicker. He might lay down a weak ace, but he won't lay down ace-king or two pair.)

Unless you know this opponent wouldn't be betting without making the flush—and he would lead out instead of going for the check-raise—you have to view his bet as suspicious. If you just assume your heads-up opponent has a flush whenever three of one suit appear, you will be easy to bluff.

Bluffing the flush on the turn by leading out with a bet is not a play I would usually consider making, but a lot of players will. A super-aggressive player who has something like ace-rag or second pair/weak kicker may want to test you, thinking he has some of your hands beat and may get you to lay down a better hand.

If he doesn't have a flush, what is he going to think when you raise him? You probably have the better hand anyway, but now he has to worry about putting plays on you. Too often, you will have a good hand but not the nuts when you are heads-up. You want the players who act like they always have the nuts picking on someone else.

With Turns C and D, you want to bet if they check and raise if they bet. If you had K-T and made trips with Turn C, fight the urge to slow-play. I am not generally in favor of slow or timid play, and this example illustrates why. If you check here, there is some chance your opponent will bet the river and you can raise. But it is more likely that your opponent is going to check-fold or hit a card that allows him to check-raise and beat you. You aren't far enough ahead with trips to give a free card, and most of the free cards that will give you action on the river make straights and flushes to beat you. With K-T, you still need to make the draws pay, plus you can get action from some inferior made hands. If you have A-Q and your opponent made trips, you have to take your medicine if you get raised or reraised. Your opponent is much more likely to be in the hand with something other than a ten, and you have to play it that way.

After Turn D, your opponent makes a hand that beats you only if he had Q-J or K-T (if you had A-Q). You need to bet or raise because there are many more hands your opponent could have where you need to make him pay for drawing or get him to pay off with second best. If your opponent has two hearts, you need to bet. If your opponent has K-J, he was sticking around for the gutshot draw and hit enough to stay with the hand. You have to charge him.

In position, when to check—You should take the free card when you are drawing about 80 percent of the time. As I already explained, you can't always take it.

When should you bet your draw? That is the beauty of poker. You have to make a judgment about when your opponent is ready to lay down. This is where your observations about how your opponents play, combined with the texture of the board, can pay off. You are mostly betting in these circumstances to keep other players from reading you, and if it costs you a bet, you expect to make it up on other hands. But the real poker skill is in picking the right spots, so the play becomes profitable right now.

If you bet and hit your draw, you will make the bet your opponent called on the turn; he might even decide you wouldn't have bet the turn when you could have gotten a free card and bluff-raise you, allowing you to make three bets on the river if your draw hits. You are also looking for situations where your opponent may lay down a weak hand that beats you if you don't make your draw.

Because you are betting sometimes with nothing but a draw, you also have to check sometimes with a pair. You should do this about 10 percent of the time, choosing your marginal hands. With the board we just used as an example, say you raised with 9-9. With Turn A, you would probably still bet to keep your opponent from drawing for free, but with Turns B, C, and D, you might choose to check. With Turn B, if you had the nine of hearts, you could make a flush on the river. You will occasionally hit a nine on the river or, with a slightly different board (like A-T-6 with Turn A or B), make a straight.

Pocket nines still have value against opponents on the draw or who will fold second pair on the turn, so you wouldn't always check. But if your poker skills tell you there is a decent chance you are against ace-rag or a ten who will call you down, it becomes a checking situation. If your pocket pair is much lower, the case for making this one of the 10 percent situations for checking is even stronger. If you raised with 4-4 and your opponent is still in the hand, either you are beat or the only way you will win is if it gets checked to the end.

Out of position—The most common situation where you are out of position on the turn is when you called a raise from the blinds and check-raised the flop. (You should have either raised or folded on the flop.) If you were reraised on the flop, you would have almost always called for value. What you do on the turn in that situation is dictated by the strength of your hand or the odds the pot is offering you to draw.

The trickier situation is when you check-raised the flop and got called. Remember, you are check-raising with just about anything: any pair, flush draw, or gutshot straight draw. If your draw came in, you are in great shape and your only concern is getting paid off. The hard part is when you don't have an especially strong hand. You are out of position, you have the betting lead, and you have to figure out what to do with an ever more threatening board and an opponent who started the hand by raising and has position on you.

It is important, if you have middle pair or better, not to lose your nerve. You have to bet. So often, when your opponent just calls and doesn't three-bet, he whiffed with a couple high cards, his own middle pair, or a draw. You don't want to give your opponent a free card, and you want him to fold middle-strength hands that might have you beat. Remember, you have shown strength and the board looks increasingly threatening to him too, if he has a middle pair.

You are building a game where it is not easy for opponents to read you. Therefore, you have to continue betting some marginal hands on the turn. If you have the best hand or your opponent is drawing, it's clearly the right move. Even though you sometimes cost yourself an extra bet when your opponent has a better hand, you more than make it up in other ways. Opponents have to pay you off when you bet your big hands because they know you don't need a big hand to bet. If you don't bet the turn in marginal situations, you are inviting your opponents to take advantage of you.

When will you check the turn after check-raising the flop? There will be some situations where you feel it is hopeless to bet, either because you feel this particular opponent called your check-raise to raise your bet on the turn, or because the board is really brutal. If you have nothing but a gutshot draw, you might check it two-thirds to three-quarters of the time.

Why not always check when you are that weak? Because an opponent with overcards or a middle pair may fold.

If you check sometimes when you are weak, then you have to check sometimes when you are strong. You shouldn't do this too often, but occasionally find situations where you have two pair or better where you are not risking a free card that makes an opponent a straight or a flush. If you check and your opponent bets, check-raise. You didn't make this play to only call when you induced a bet. Playing in the style I describe, you should get action on your good hands. You are doing it to signal that your check is not a license for opponents to bet and, once again, you aren't a free check-fold when you check.

In position after a check-raise on the flop—When you are in position and you've been check-raised on the flop, you have to know who you are up against. If they are a traditional-style player—where they check-raise with big hands, lead out with small hands, and check with weak hands—you need to give their check-raise a lot of respect. If they don't make that play that often, it's okay to make some tight laydowns on the flop or the turn. You want to reward their strategy of playing too tight and too straightforward. You can lay down middle pair and get away from a lot of hands that you wouldn't lay down against someone playing a more aggressive style.

If you are playing against someone who plays like I am recommending here, you are going to have to make a judgment. (This is why it is a powerful way to play. Even if you know exactly how this opponent is playing, you don't have an easy response.) If you are aware of all the types of hands that kind of player could check-raise with, maybe up to half of them aren't even a pair yet. You are going to have to play a lot of hands in the face of check-raises. You're going to have to play A-K and see if you can spike a card on the turn. You are going to play your pairs. Maybe you can throw away something like bottom pair on a real dangerous flop where you are behind if your opponent caught any piece of it and the draws make it likely that you can easily lose even if you are ahead—like a T-9-8 flop where you raised pre-flop with 5-5. Even drawing hands can be favorites against you (especially if there were a couple suited cards on that flop), so maybe you lay down that hand.

If you get check-raised and call, it is important to bet the turn if the check-raiser doesn't bet. Even if you have nothing but overcards, you have to guard against players using this tactic to get themselves a free card out of position.

Multiway on the turn—The advice I gave about multiway hands on the flop applies to the turn as well. You have to play more straight-forward, folding without a great hand or draw, calling with the right odds on a great draw, and raising (or check-raising if that is an option) whenever you can narrow the field. You have to give a lot of respect to people taking action; they are going to tend to have it.

A situation that comes up when you are still multiway on the turn is where some players have made hands and some are still drawing. For example, if four players see a flop of A♦T♠9♠ and they all called a bet on the flop, they could have some of the following hands: A-K, Q-J, T-9, two spades, A-A, T-T, or 9-9. (By the way, it would be a mistake for anyone with top pair/top kicker or better to fail to raise or set up a check-raise, even if there was a good chance they were facing a superior hand.) If the turn is a blank (like the four of clubs), the drawing hands are still getting the odds to call one bet. At the 50-100 blinds level, the pot would have at least 1,200, so a player trying to hit eight or nine outs on the river is getting the right price to call 200 in a pot of at least 1,400 and maybe more, plus the implied odds of at least one bet on the river.

But is it just one bet on the turn? If you have T-9, A-K, or a set, you have to try to make it more than one bet. If you were in the big blind with T-9 and led out, you have to avoid repeating your mistake on the flop and check, figuring at least one of the three players after you isn't on a draw and will bet. Then you can raise and the draws won't be getting the right odds to call.

Likewise, if you are the player who followed a couple limpers with Q-J, you have to decide before you call a bet on the turn whether it will get raised behind you. This is where it pays to be observant. You have to ask yourself whether a couple of these players are aggressive enough and/or have strong enough hands to punish the draws by putting in capped raises on the turn. You also have to discount the value of your hand by (a) any draws to less than the nuts, and (b) the likelihood that your opponents have some of the cards you need to hit your draw.

Play on the River

The overriding difference between playing on the river and other streets in poker is that, all of a sudden, the free card is no longer a factor. So much of limit hold 'em is about free cards—that extra bet you make or save is the main way in which your stack grows—that now you have to shift gears on the river. It is no longer about controlling the betting to get free cards, or misdirecting opponents into thinking you are trying for free cards, or preventing them from getting free cards.

Very simply, you have to focus on what good things can happen if you bet. There are only two, and this is true in every form of poker: (1) You can get called or raised by a worse hand and win a bigger pot, or (2) you can get a better hand to fold.

That's it. Nothing else good can happen if you bet on the end. Everything else is neutral or negative. Getting the better hand to fold on the river is a rarity in limit hold 'em. If there has been betting all the way through, a player is getting better than 6-to-1 to call the last bet. Most players, in any close situation, will call. Because of that, you need to maximize your chances of (1) occurring by collecting one more bet in many marginal situations.

Managing your stack also depends on knowing when not to bet. People tend to bet too much on the river. They do what I call "bluffing with the best hand," betting a hand like ace-high or bottom pair. For example, you are in the big blind with A♣J♦ and you call a late-position raise. The flop is

You check-raise the flop with an overcard and the gutshot draw. The turn is

Bet-call. The river could be just about anything that leaves you with nothing better than ace-high—a blank like the

If this happened at the 25-50 blind level, the pot would have 625. If you check and the original raiser was on a busted draw like K-T or A♦8♦, it is pretty unlikely he will bet. But if he had 8-8, it costs just 100 for a shot at a pot of 725. It doesn't happen that much that a player folds any pair on the end getting those odds. If you bet, the busted draw will fold, but would check if you checked, and you will win the same pot in a showdown. The pocket pair will call your bet and you will lose an extra 100. You need to be selective about your betting on the river.

Instead of betting, you can check. You can save a bet against the 8-8, who is likely to check behind you. If the player behind you bets, there has to be at least a 1-in-7 chance he has a busted draw and you should call. If he has 8-8, you lose a bet (the same bet you would have lost if you bet). If he has A-8 or K-T, you win the pot and get that extra bet.

If you are going to bluff, make sure it is *really* a bluff. You need to bluff sometimes so your bet doesn't always signal a strong hand; you want people calling you with any pair on the end. (Indeed, if opponents think your bet signals a strong hand, you definitely want to make some bluffs.)

In addition to betting very strong hands and bluffs, you have to bet some medium-strength hands. If you have top pair with a good kicker, you should bet the river if the board is not particularly scary. If you bet only very strong hands and complete bluffs, your opponents have a very easy decision calling with a marginal hand. They are getting better than 7-to-1 to call and it is simply not 85 percent likely that you have a super-strong hand.

So you are betting all your strong hands, some bluffs, and a lot of your medium-strength hands. How do you decide, especially in those medium-hand situations, when to bet? You need to put your opponent on a range of hands and decide, for each hand in the range, what play is correct. This analysis is helped significantly by your observations of what kinds of hands your opponents play and how they play them.

But you don't need to have years of experience at the tables or the intuition of a world-class "feel" player. You are mostly using logic and math. Often, with most of the hands your opponent could conceivably have, the decision is the same, so you won't have to pick one particular hand.

Here is an example of the process. You call a late-position raise from the big blind with A♣T♠. The board is A♥8♦5♦2♠8♣. You check-raised the flop and were called. It went bet-call on the turn. With the eight on the river, the draws miss but someone with an eight makes a set. Your ace looks decent. Do you check or bet?

Look back on the hand and figure out what your opponent could have and whether checking or betting is better for each possibility.

Ace with a worse kicker—This is one of the more likely hands you are facing, but probably only about 15 percent likely. If you knew you were against an ace with a worse kicker, of course you would bet. If you check, there is a chance an ace with a worse kicker would bet and you would earn the same amount by checking as by betting.

Ace with a better kicker—You are probably in for one bet. If you bet, you may get raised, but your opponent will most likely call. If you check, the better ace will probably bet. It is clearly wrong for you to bet.

An eight—If you bet, your opponent will raise and you will have to pay off. If you check, your opponent will bet and you will have to call. Checking is clearly the right play.

Busted straight draw—If you bet, 6–7 will fold. If you check, there is some chance this player would bluff at the pot, and you would call. Checking is clearly correct.

Busted flush draw—Same analysis.

As you can see, we don't even need to narrow down your opponent's hands. You can figure out a play that works best against a variety of hands, even if you can't figure out which hand your opponent has. That's the beauty of poker, being able to reason your way to a decision even though, until your opponent shows his hand, you have almost no idea what he has. In this example, checking is right against nearly every hand, and not very wrong in the relatively unlikely case that betting is arguably better.

This situation comes up fairly often, but it is simpler than the situation when some of the draws hit. If your attempts to make an opponent fold a draw failed and he didn't try to take over the betting lead earlier, you have to say there is a decent chance his draw came in. That doesn't mean you should fold. If we take the example I just explained and change the river card to the three of diamonds, an opponent drawing to a flush just hit. If you are out of position and check, you have to call. It is too easy a bluffing situation if he was drawing for the straight, missed, and thinks you are so scared you will fold. You are scared, but not *that* scared. You only have to be right one time in seven for that call to pay off, plus it sends a message to opponents that they can't bluff you.

Most of the time, you will be the first to act, either because you are out of position or because the other player checks. When someone bets, either leading out or after you check, you have to be stubborn about calling them down. Remember, the pot is laying you better than 7-to-1. Even if you have ace-high and can't beat anything but a bluff, you have to stand your ground and call. If you are pretty sure your opponent won't bluff at least 15 percent of the time, you can fold ace-high. But you are going to beat bluffs with some weak hands— especially if you check-raised after the flop and now check the river.

Tournament Strategy—The Bubble, Big Stacks, Short Stacks

I generally don't play much different on the bubble or short-stacked (or against short-stacked opponents) in limit hold 'em tournaments. I make my adjustments based on how my strategy is working. Of course, if you or your opponent is so short-stacked that there are barely enough bets to complete the hand, you have to tighten up. Getting people to fold is no longer a consideration, so you will probably have to show down a hand. But that doesn't happen until you or your opponent get down near four big bets.

That said, you will frequently have the opportunity to open your game a little bit as the tournament goes on. If you find, as is often the case, that players are getting more timid and your solid image is getting respect, look for situations to take advantage of later in the tournament. You are less likely to exploit the short stacks (because many of them will be looking for a hand on which to make a stand) or the biggest stacks (who are less likely to be intimidated). The best targets are the medium stacks, even if you are a medium stack yourself. The aggressiveness I recommend isn't just a strategy for when you have everybody outchipped. It can be a strategy when you are in the same boat with most of the players later in the tournament, feeling vulnerable if you lose a couple hands. If you sense the table is shutting down a little bit and your raises are getting respect, some of those blinds and opening raises are there for the taking.

I remember a World Series event early in my career when it was getting near the bubble and the players at my table were letting me pound on them. I had probably stolen the blinds in six out of six attempts over a period of less than two rounds. I picked up J-9, raised, and was called by the big blind. The flop was A-T-7. All I had was a gutshot draw, but I bet—if the positions were reversed and I was in the big blind, I would have check-raised with that draw—and he called. I got lucky and hit my eight on the turn. It went check-bet-call on the turn and river. I turned over my J-9 and, instead of mucking, my opponent turned over A-K with this look of *What kind of an idiot are you?* on his face.

A lot of people aren't going to get what you are doing, which is great. First, I was running over these guys. If I never hit my gutshot draw and got check-raised and had to give up the hand—which should happen sometimes—the move was still profitable for all the times it worked. Second, this guy didn't realize that he was so completely cowed that he didn't check-raise me to get me to stop. There simply are not enough chips to be won by calling someone down when they try to run you over and you have something.

You can't accumulate enough chips to survive by always waiting for a good hand to fight back. You are going to have to fight back sometimes with marginal hands and semi-bluffs.

The beauty of my strategy is that you don't need a big stack to execute it. If you have enough chips to comfortably bet through the hand, that is enough for it to work. This isn't like no-limit hold 'em, where a bigger stack can put your entire stack at risk. Avoiding trouble in a limit hold 'em hand means staying away from losing four big bets on a hand—a raise before and on the flop, and a big bet on the turn and on the river. At the 100-200 level of a no-limit tournament, if I have 1,200, all I can do is push in or fold. I barely have chips to make the big blind fold, and my blinds can be attacked by anyone with a bigger stack.

In limit hold 'em, however, with 1,200 in chips in the big blind, I can call a raise, check-raise the flop, and bet the turn and river, executing my strategy as well as if I had 10,000 in chips. If my opponent thinks he has too many chips to respect four big bets, I should be able to learn that pretty quickly (as should you) and take advantage.

You aren't short-stacked yourself until you get to about four big bets. When that happens, you have to look for an opportunity to win a showdown. You have to play bigger cards in the limited time you have left. K-9o suddenly is better than T-8s. Ace-rag goes up in value; suited connectors go down. You can't tighten up too much, though. Look for a heads-up situation if you can. Either be the raiser in late position or find a spot where your hand in the blinds might hold up.

In short, in limit hold 'em you usually can't bully people with your stack or be bullied by them. It always pays to know your customers, though, so you have to pay attention to who can easily be bet out of a pot and who will never fold. I am comfortable saying my style of play works in most situations. My tournament success has been based on it, but you have to adapt to your circumstances.

There is one play I will use against certain opponents, especially as we near the money. An opponent in middle or late position raises your big blind and you call. The flop comes ace-rag-rag. In addition to all my other check-raising criteria, it is just too tempting to check-raise here with nothing. You are literally getting 3.5-to-1 that your opponent won't be able to call. It is a powerful play in tournaments once the blinds and limits have risen and everyone is feeling a little short-stacked. At fifteen times the big blind, people just aren't ready to cripple themselves with T-T after an A-7-3 flop when you have check-raised. To make this kind of play, you have to pay attention to the comfort level of your opponent. But if you pick your spots, it is a very profitable play.

Short-Handed Play

You need to understand short-handed play for the last few tables of a tournament as well as to participate in the growing number of six-handed-table tournaments at the World Series of Poker, on Full Tilt, and elsewhere. You will frequently find opponents who significantly over- or underadjust, either playing more than half their hands in late position or waiting for premium hands (usually expecting, incorrectly, that they need big cards to take down their overaggressive opponents).

The only adjustment you need to make is to modify the definition of "early," "middle," and "late" position for starting hands.

- *Early position*—There is no early position short-handed.
- *Middle position*—The first two players to act after the blinds should play the hands in Groups A–C.
- *Late position*—The last two players to act before the blinds, the cutoff and the button, should play the hands in Groups A–E.

Heads-Up Play

You have to be super-aggressive when you are playing heads-up. The basics of heads-up strategy are pretty simple:

- You have to play nearly every hand;
- You raise on the button (your small blind) 95 percent of the time, and even if you "tighten up from that," you raise with all connecting cards (even cards with a couple gaps count here), all suited cards, and any card ten and above;
- You call with almost all the same hands in the big blind, maybe a few less because you are out of position, and reraise with any hand you would play in middle position at a full table;
- Don't bother with trapping and slow-playing, but occasionally just call raises, rather than reraising, with some of your strong hands, so your reraises won't telegraph your cards; and
- Adjust.

The last element is the most important, and the most difficult to reduce to a simple explanation. Heads-up is all about adjusting to how your opponent plays. If I don't know anything about an opponent, I will start out raising the first several hands no matter what I have. I need to find out if this guy understands the basics of heads-up play. You will frequently find a player who is skilled enough to *get* to short-handed play but who doesn't have the experience to succeed at it. That player will fold too much and I can chip away at him enough by stealing that I never have to play a pot with him. I will be very quick to fold when he makes a stand, because he isn't doing it often enough to make up for the blinds he loses by folding too much. I can fold to that opponent because his play on that hand is screaming, "I have a big hand here!"

If your opponent will reward you for being a complete maniac, go for it. But you could find the opposite situation. If your opponent responds by trying to be more aggressive, you can't back down but you can get paid off more on your good hands.

Remember, in poker, only two good things can happen when you bet: you can get called by a worse hand, or you can get a better hand to fold. You are going to bet *a lot* heads-up. Which of those two is going to be the potential source of profit against this particular opponent? If you always think about it that way, you will more quickly understand how to respond to your opponent.

Then figure out how the other player is getting good things to happen on his bets. Are you paying off with the worst hand too often? If that doesn't seem to be happening and you are not wiping the floor with this guy, then it's possible you are folding to a worse hand too much. Be suspicious of the other player's aggression, and when you realize you are calling with the worse hand too much, be less suspicious.

Heads-up, it is all about being aggressive and adjusting to your opponent's level of aggression. Whoever learns best to take advantage of all the marginal situations that develop heads-up is the player who will win. If you start aggressive and look for ways to adjust, you can succeed.

Conclusion

I became a professional poker player in limit hold 'em, and it is one of my favorite forms of poker. Like no-limit hold 'em, it rewards aggressive play. Unlike no-limit, however, you can't shut opponents out with aggressiveness, nor can they shut you out. You play aggressive poker and you definitely win against opponents who don't play aggressive poker. Against aggressive opponents, your wins and losses will be defined by how you play after the flop. Will you check-raise whenever you catch something? Will your opponent throw away superior hands when you both miss the flop? Will he pay you off by putting you on a draw when you have the better hand? Will you fire another bullet after you check-raised, with either a decent hand or nothing but a draw? When you were the aggressor, will you bet the turn sometimes with a medium pair or a draw? When your opponent check-raises the flop, will you stand your ground in the right number of situations with medium hands? On the river, can you get a call with a decent hand, but hold off betting when the situation suggests that inferior hands will fold and superior hands will raise?

All these close situations are where a good poker player thrives. You should regard this chapter as a tool for becoming a good poker player in limit hold 'em tournaments. Take these guidelines to the tables and learn how they work. With experience, you should become a better limit hold 'em player and, more important, a better *poker* player.

Structure of Limit Hold 'Em Tournaments

This was the structure of the $1,500 buy-in limit hold 'em event from the 2005 World Series of Poker, along with the number of remaining players and average chip stack. There were 1,068 starting players.

TABLE 12.2

Level	Players	Blinds	Limits	Average
1		25-25	25-50	
2		25-50	50-100	
3		50-100	100-200	
4		75-150	150-300	
5		100-200	200-400	
6		200-300	300-600	
7	230	200-400	400-800	7,000
8	160	300-600	600-1,200	10,000
9	115	400-800	800-1,600	14,000
10	100	500-1,000	1,000-2,000	16,000

TABLE 12.2 ◆ *(Continued)*

11	74	1,000-1,500	1,500-3,000	21,600
12	54	1,000-2,000	2,000-4,000	30,000
13	34	2,000-3,000	3,000-6,000	47,000
14	28	2,000-4,000	4,000-8,000	57,000
15	17	3,000-5,000	5,000-10,000	94,000
16	12	3,000-6,000	6,000-12,000	133,500
17	8	4,000-8,000	8,000-16,000	200,250
18	7	50,00-10,000	10,000-20,000	229,000
19	3	10,000-15,000	15,000-30,000	534,000
20	2	10,000-20,000	20,000-40,000	801,000

Notes on This Structure

1. This was from the fourth event of the 2005 Series, $1,500 limit hold 'em. I did not play the event. The limits and blinds at each level are according to online and onsite materials from the tournament. The information on the number of players comes from CardPlayer.com. Some of the information about the number of players left is approximate (i.e., it could have come from the beginning, end, or middle of a particular level, though it is mostly from the beginning of the level). This was also the basic structure for the 2006 World Series limit hold 'em events.

2. This event started with 1,068 players. Players started with 1,500 in chips, so there were approximately 1.6 million chips in play. Levels lasted one hour. As of the first break, after two hours, approximately 10 percent of the field had been eliminated.

3. The event paid 100 places. During level 10, the last level of the first day, the tournament was down to 100 players.

4. The tournament ended during level 20. Level 21 would have had blinds of 15,000-25,000 and limits of 25,000-50,000. Level 22 would have had blinds of 20,000-30,000 and limits of 30,000-60,000. Level 23 would have had blinds of 20,000-40,000 and limits of 40,000-80,000.

PART III

TOURNAMENT OMAHA

CHAPTER 13

Omaha Eight-or-Better

by Mike Matusow

An Omaha eight-or-better tournament is really two different tournaments. The first part takes place during the first few levels. Blinds are low, a lot of people limp into multiway pots, and a lot of hands are shown down. Then the tournament changes completely. The first person in the pot is always raising. Most hands are played heads-up. You don't see as many showdowns. I believe the first part of the tournament lasts three levels in the World Series structure, but use your own judgment based on your chip stack and your table, based on the advice I give you about playing each part of the tournament.

If you want to do well in an Omaha tournament, you have to learn how to play both parts of the tournament. Raising and throwing around chips in the early levels doesn't help you narrow the field. And you're just asking for trouble if you limp or call raises in the later part of the tournament.

You also need to learn patience during that second part of the tournament. You don't win an Omaha tournament by outplaying people. You win by knowing the right hands to play in the right situations, how to bet them, and how to play against the people at your table. If you don't catch the cards, it's just not your day. Unless a guy is really bad, I'm not going to beat him if his cards are a lot better. You have to set yourself up to win when you pick up a hand, and you have to take advantage of situations where you can win extra with that hand. It's not about pushing people around with your chips (though, as I will explain better, you can play with a little more freedom as the big stack). That just doesn't happen in limit poker, and it sure doesn't happen in Omaha eight-or-better.

Part of what makes a great Omaha player are things I can't teach you. Things like knowing when the flop misses your opponent and you can take the pot away with nothing. The best Omaha players in the world can do that, and you can't teach it. You have to play a lot of poker—that's the only way to learn.

But you can go far in tournament Omaha without a lot of experience. Tournaments like the World Series of Poker are so big that a lot of people enter who have almost no experience at Omaha or any form of limit poker. Even against experienced players, there are some things you can do to build your stack and stay out of trouble.

Tournament Structure

The basic structure of World Series of Poker Omaha events is one-hour levels, limits that increase 25–100 percent per level, and 2,000–5,000 in starting chips, depending on the buy-in. In 2006, each of the Omaha events had this structure:

TABLE 13.1

Level	Blinds	Limits
1	25-25	25-50
2	25-50	50-100
3	50-100	100-200
4	75-150	150-300
5	100-200	200-400
6	200-300	300-600
7	200-400	400-800
8	300-600	600-1,200
9	400-800	800-1,600
10	500-1,000	1,000-2,000
11	1,000-1,500	1,500-3,000
12	1,000-2,000	2,000-4,000
13	2,000-3,000	3,000-6,000

TABLE 13.1 ◆ **(*Continued*)**

Level	Blinds	Limits
14	2,000-4,000	4,000-8,000
15	3,000-5,000	5,000-10,000
16	3,000-6,000	6,000-12,000
17	4,000-8,000	8,000-16,000
18	5,000-10,000	10,000-20,000
19	10,000-15,000	15,000-30,000
20	10,000-20,000	20,000-40,000
21	15,000-25,000	25,000-50,000
22	20,000-30,000	30,000-60,000
23	20,000-40,000	40,000-80,000

Early Tournament Strategy

Early in the tournament, you see a lot of people entering pots limping. Sometimes they are doing it because they don't have any idea of how to play the game. Sometimes they are doing it because it's the correct thing to do. In the first three levels, don't fight it. The limits are too small to keep people out of hands, so it's not worth trying. More important, you are getting great implied odds in a multiplayer hand to scoop a big pot. Even half of a four-way pot can put you ahead early.

You can and should play a lot of marginal hands in the first three hours of an Omaha World Series event. What's a marginal hand?

High-only hands like Q-J-T-9 or K-Q-J-T or Q-J-T-T are marginal hands. You don't want anything to do with high-only hands later in the tournament. Early, you can clean up with them. Unless you are at a table where players are reraising each other like crazy, or they go the other way and are so tight that the hands are played heads-up even when it costs just 25 to call, you want to see a lot of flops.

Playing these high hands, there are a few things you should watch out for. First, with a high-low board like T-8-3, you are probably playing for just half the pot. You can't afford to play less than the nuts, or draw to less than the nuts, for half of a multiway pot. You are too vulnerable to the other three or four players making high hands, even if they are all chasing the low with A-2. Don't get trapped for a bunch of bets for half, especially when two guys both have A-2, start a raising war, and one of them has a set while you are calling off chips with top two pair, or one of them has the ace-high flush while you have a lower flush.

Second, although you generally want to avoid calling raises before the flop, if there is a lot of action in front of you and you have a high-only hand, see the flop. If four guys come piling in for two bets, there's a good chance the aces are all out, so no one's going to make a higher pair on you, and most of the low cards are out, so the flop could come high and hit you just right.

What is a marginal low hand?

You could play just about any suited ace with a couple of low cards, like A-4-5-Q. It's 25 chips and you can win a big pot if the flop comes just right. Now, that doesn't mean you should call a raise with it. In the first few levels, if you see a raise, that means you are up against A-2 or A-A and you are behind. Your hand will be contingent on your opponent getting counterfeited or hitting some kind of long-shot lucky flop like 2-3-6.

Think of it like holding A-Q in hold 'em. It's a strong hand, but if someone in early position raises, chances are they have A-K or a pair—especially in a limit game.

This makes position important during the early part of an Omaha tournament—sometimes. If your table is very tight or very loose, you don't want to play a marginal hand in early position. It's not worth it against one opponent, or against a crazy table where people behind you are putting in multiple raises. With a table full of limpers, position hardly matters at all before the flop. You are generally assured of seeing the flop for just one bet. Even if you and a bunch of players come in and you get raised, for just one more bet, you get a shot at hitting a lucky flop and taking down a big pot. But even at this kind of table, watch how they play after the flop. If the field quickly narrows or guys start firing chips like crazy—again, if the table is very tight or very loose—you have to play with more discipline in early position. Until you have the table figured out, assume that position matters, even in the first three rounds.

In early position, you want to play quality low hands, quality two-way hands, and quality high hands. By "quality low hands," I mean A-2, though having a third wheel card makes the hand much better. A quality two-way hand has A-2 with something to help on the high side, like another ace, being double-suited, or a high card or two for making high pairs and straights. "Quality high hands" are four high cards close together. It is better if there are no gaps and if you have two cards of one suit or are double-suited.

Depending on your table, you have to decide how much to open up in middle position. At some tables at the beginning of a tournament, you will see half the table limp into every pot and no one ever raises. You can play a lot of hands in middle position (and maybe even early position) at a table like this.

Figure out how your table works: Does anybody raise? Do a lot of people limp? Whose raise means A-2 and whose means A-A? Who just calls with A-2 or even a super-strong hand like A-2-3-K double-suited or a similar great hand? Because a lot of hands get shown down early in most Omaha tournaments, you can see what hands your opponents started with.

In late position, play just about anything you can get away with. Any suited ace with a low card. Anything double-suited. Any three low cards. The goal is to see a flop for one bet and release the hand unless you catch the nuts or are drawing to them. The two biggest problems you will run into playing this way in late position are (1) catching enough of the flop to tie you to the hand, and (2) doing this too much and, without even getting into any big pots, having your stack get small. Usually, if you stay away from (1), then (2) shouldn't become a problem.

Regardless of your position or your cards, you shouldn't be raising early in the tournament. Let's say you are at a ten-player table during the second level and are fourth to act. One person limps in front of you. You have A♣2♣4♥6♥. There is 125 in the pot. You don't raise here. First, even if you could succeed in taking the blinds, all you get is 125. You are holding one of the best possible hands. You need to make more from it than that. Second, you won't succeed in taking the blinds. You will get one or two calls, maybe win a little larger pot, and possibly lose more when the flop comes 8-T-J with none of your suits and you have to fold to a bet or a check-raise.

By raising, all you really do is scare off hands you can beat. You want to be against high-only hands. You want to be against A-2 with no other low cards (though your raise won't scare them out anyway). You want to be against A-3. Keep those people in the hand, at least for the flop. You want to scoop a big pot, or win half a big pot and trap someone in the middle, or be able to get away cheap from a bad flop.

Even a pair of aces isn't worth a raise early in an Omaha tournament. No one will fold and a pair of aces doesn't play well in a multiway pot, especially if your raise helps make the pot big enough that everyone wants to keep drawing. The only conceivable time to raise would be if you are on the button with five or six players limping ahead of you and you have A-A-2-3 double-suited. Your raise will make the pot bigger and probably won't get anyone to fold.

But even then, you should probably limp. If you raise, there is a good chance everybody will check to you on the flop and you may not get more than one bet on any street. If you just call before the flop, there is a good chance someone in front of you will bet the flop. Someone else could even raise on the flop in front of you. Now you can get a second or third bet in on the flop when you hit, and you avoid getting check-raised after a flop where all you have is a pair of aces.

After the flop, you are going to usually play a lot less aggressive than in hold 'em. In hold 'em, you usually want to bet people out of multiway pots once you have a hand so you don't get unlucky. In Omaha, you want all those people, because once you get a nut low made, you've already locked up half (or a quarter, in which case you definitely don't want to be raising). You are freerolling for the other half, so why get people out? Even if you don't have protection from being counterfeited, the only card that can beat you on the river is a deuce, so why raise to keep someone from hitting a three-outer? With the nut low, you want people in.

There is one time you should raise with a low hand in Omaha, though it is not a play I recommend unless you know the players in the hand really well. You raise when you have the *third*-nut low when someone behind you has the *second*-nut low. You do that to put pressure on the better hand to get him to fold. For example, you have 2-3-4-J double-suited in late position. By the turn, the board is 4-5-J-Q. If it is bet to you, you raise to get the player with A-3/no pair to fold. That player should fold—he doesn't have a two-way hand and he has almost nothing invested in the pot.

There are a few situations where you want to raise after the flop with a high-only hand. If there is only one low card on the board, you want to raise to keep someone from sticking around and making a backdoor low. If the board is J-8-8 and you have jacks-full, you raise if someone bets out. If the bettor has an eight, you can win a big pot. In addition, you don't want to slow-play and let someone with a low hand hit running babies and take half the pot.

If you have the nut high, you want to raise to punish the low cards, but not only if you are way ahead with your nut-high hand. Let's say the board is J♠8♠7♥ and I have Q♣J♦T♥9♠. If someone bets, I will just call. Raising is not going to chase anyone out of that pot and it is just too likely that I am putting more chips into a pot I can lose. If the turn is a baby spade, I am going to throw the hand away. If it comes a baby non-spade, I still have to be careful about calling. Half the pot is gone and there is still the flush draw out there. I have just the two small bets invested in the pot. If it has been bet and raised by the time it gets to me, it's going to cost me at least three big bets to show my hand down, and maybe more.

After the flop in these early-tournament multiway hands, you constantly have to be on the lookout for situations where you can lose a big hand with the high nuts. Let's say you have K♥K♦Q♠J♠ and the flop comes K♣8♠6♠. Even though you have the top set and a flush draw, you do not want to put a lot of pressure on this pot. You have to worry about straight draws, low draws, and even the nut flush draw. If someone bets, you call and see what happens behind you and on the next card. If the turn is a baby spade, you have the third nut flush, but you have to fold if it is bet and raised in front of you. You have nothing invested in this pot, you are closed out for half, and there's a good chance you are chasing with the second-best high hand. If the turn is a seven, you are looking at the same decision: calling a bunch of bets for half when you are probably behind.

Finally, you have to learn when to shift gears. As I've explained, that usually happens after the first three levels. But sometimes you have to change your strategy because it's not working out to play so many hands. If it's just not your day to catch cards, you can give away all your chips gambling. You have to play tighter, sticking with only quality starting hands. If I start with 2,000 chips and I lose 500–600 playing this way, I'm probably going to tighten up. Everyone else will still be limping and playing loose, so I can't play exactly like I describe the right way to play later in the tournament, but I know I can't keep gambling on catching a flop or hitting enough of the flop to keep drawing.

Late-Tournament Strategy

After the first three levels, no matter how many chips you have, the strategy changes. Once the blinds go up, you attack with playable hands, raising and getting heads-up. It costs three and a half bets for someone to call you down from a pre-flop raise to showdown. When the limits are 100-200, that's 700 chips. If you start with 2,000 chips in a World Series event, not that many people will be eliminated by that level, so the average stack will be under 3,000. If you raise, you aren't going to get four callers willing to call off 20–40 percent of their chips.

After the first three levels, the blinds and limits start getting high. There is enough money in the pot at the beginning of the hand to make it worth winning. And at the higher limits, you can't afford to bet through very many hands without winning a piece of the pot.

This is what you have to do: (1) forget about high-only hands; (2) come in raising or reraising; and (3) play your position. There are exceptions to these, but if you understand why you need to follow them, you'll understand when to ignore them.

Late-Tournament Strategy—Come in Raising with Low Hands

Give up the high-only hands—After the first three levels, one of the biggest mistakes players make in Omaha tournaments is playing high cards. There won't be many hands where four players see the flop. It will almost always be heads-up. Two-thirds of the time, the board shows a three-card low by the river. You can't afford to play heads-up with no shot at half the pot two-thirds of the time. You can do that in a four-handed pot, especially because all those other players probably have a lot of the low cards and the flop is coming high. Heads-up, you want a shot at scooping. You can't count on that without a low hand.

Patience—You aren't going to get great hands a lot. That's why you need patience to go far in an Omaha tournament. You have to get dealt certain cards. If you get very short-stacked, you are going to have to make a move, but generally you aren't going to play a lot better than the cards you get. You can get some extra bets and save some extra bets, but you are mostly going to make a lot off players who aren't patient or who think they can outplay you. You aren't going to win an Omaha tournament outplaying anyone. Most Omaha players play too many hands and you can take advantage of that.

So what are the best hands?—Obviously, you need A-2, but the best hands have something more. Another baby keeps you from being counterfeited. Suited cards, especially the ace, give you a chance to make a flush. A high card or two gives you the opportunity, along with the ace, of making top pair, top two, or a straight. Some people say the best hand is A-A-2-3 double-suited. Double-suited A-A-2-K, A-2-3-K, and A-A-2-4 are all up there with it. Hands with four low cards are all playable from all positions, even after a raise—any A-2-3 or A-2-4, like A-2-3-6, A-2-4-6, A-2-4-7. Of course, being double-suited is a bonus.

Raising—In the first three levels, you limp with anything and everything. After that, you want to enter raising. That includes reraising if someone raises in front of you. If your hand is good enough to play against someone who is showing enough strength to be raising out of position, you want to be heads-up with them. If I am in late position and someone has raised and I have A-2-4-Q or A-2-4-K, I am three-betting that hand every time. I want to isolate and, as in every form of limit poker, I recommend that you generally don't follow a raise by calling. You three-bet it.

Aces—You are going to play any A-A late in a tournament, three-betting if you are not the first in the pot. Even if you have no low hand, like A-A-9-Q, you want to play aces and play them fast. In a multiway pot, A-A can get you in big trouble, but heads-up, they make a powerful starting hand. That said, if you three-bet with A-A-7-8 and the flop comes K-3-4, you bet the flop but be prepared to check the turn if another wheel card rolls off. You could even check the flop. If the turn is a five, maybe you fold. If an eight comes on the turn, your aces are probably still good for high and you can call. You are getting just half the pot but it is very unlikely you will get scooped.

You have to be willing to slow down and maybe even shut down if your A-A is a one-way hand and there is a three-card low by the turn. You have to be willing to lose just those small bets if you get a bad turn card, because you don't have a low and your high hand may no longer be good. Of course, if it comes K-Q-9 on the flop, they may try to outplay you because they think you three-bet with A-2.

Throwing away A-2—Against good players, you have to respect their early-position raise. That's where the discipline comes in. So many people who play Omaha eight-or-better think A-2 is magical. If someone raises in front of you in early position after the first three levels of the tournament and you have A-2-7-J, you throw it away. A-2-8-9, unsuited? Fold. You have to be prepared to pass with A-2 when you have nothing to go with it. Obviously, if you are against an opponent who will raise with a K-K or A-3, or has a very short stack and you think he is just trying to get the blinds or all his money in on a decent hand, you will play your A-2-7-J. You need something more than A-2 if you are in early position or someone has already entered the pot, like another wheel card, a suited ace, or high cards—and you want to have a combination of those.

A friend of mine, a pro who has won a couple of hold 'em bracelets, was down to the last few tables in a 2006 Omaha event and we talked about strategy during a break. I told him, "If you pick up A-2-5-5 and someone raises, that's a horrible hand. At best, you have half the low and 5-5 for high."

So what did he go broke with? A-2-5-5. Sure, it was just luck that he went out with the exact hand I warned him about, but he came in after a raise, and hit a flop like K-J-5. He had to hit perfect, and even after getting that lucky he put himself in a position where someone else could get lucky against him.

Playing a big stack—A-2 is a little different if you have a lot of chips. If you get to the later part of an Omaha tournament and you have a lot of chips, you modify all this advice I've given. You can afford to see a flop with A-2 and outplay people. You can also flat-call raises. You need chips and an ability to outplay your opponents after the flop, but if you have those, you can open up a little bit. Even then, I emphasize that you are opening up only *a little*. It's still a mistake to play A-3 and high-only hands. You aren't going to get the action you would get in the first three levels. Therefore, you won't get paid enough to play that way.

You don't use a big stack to push people around as you would in other forms of poker. Apart from flat-calling a raise with a weak A-2, it's not worth it to play much different just because you have a lot of chips.

Late-Tournament Strategy—Play Your Position

Position is not as important in the early levels of an Omaha tournament as it is in other forms of poker. Unless you are at a table with a lot of raising, your goal is to see a lot of flops cheap and hit something big in a multiway pot. But when the blinds and betting limits start rising and it costs a decent portion of your stack to play a hand through and lose, position becomes extremely important. A lot of players get crippled or eliminated because they ignore this or are too slow to pick it up. You are better off adjusting too early in a tournament than too late.

Most Omaha players play too many hands and they play them in the wrong positions. If someone in early position raises, you have to be prepared with pass with A-2.

When you are in early position, you need a premium hand to play. You have to be careful, even as the first person in the pot, that you don't overvalue your hand just because it has A-2. For your hand to stand any kind of action, you really need A-2-wheel-paint to play: A-2-4-J, A-2-5-Q, hands like that. A hand like A-2-7-J or A-2-6-9 isn't really playable from early position after the first three levels of an Omaha tournament. Unless you get extremely lucky, you can get only the low half of the pot. You are probably an underdog to anything that calls you out of the blinds for the high half. And where are you if you get reraised?

After the first three levels, you want a scooping hand. Getting half the pot is your fallback position, not your goal. Up front, you can't risk having the second-best hand if someone calls or reraises behind you, and you can't afford to let a random hand out of the blinds be a favorite for half.

If your table is tight and you have chips, you can expand your hand selection. Near the bubble, a lot of players are afraid to play a hand. As you get into the money, a lot of players are afraid to play because they can move up in the money by folding. With a table of those kinds of players (or if the players who *don't* play like that have already folded), I will raise with any A-2 or A-3. (I haven't talked much about having the ace suited or being double-suited. It's not a requirement, but being suited or double-suited makes the hand much better. I don't really like making plays before the flop without at least the ace being suited.)

Against a tight table, if I raise in early position, look at what kind of a hand they need to come in against me. A-2 alone wouldn't be enough for a good player to come in after a raise. If I raise with A-3-6-J with the ace suited and someone calls (or raises) behind me, I have the benefit of knowing what they have and they don't have any idea what I have. They have A-2 and one other low card. If they didn't three-bet me, I can almost guarantee their hand is something like A-2-5-J or A-2-4-J. If you know what their cards are, you are in position to pound them if their flop doesn't come.

In late position, you don't really loosen up too much, and you don't play the stealing game that you play in some other forms of poker. You can't steal in Omaha tournaments like you can in those other games, so being the first to enter the pot in late position doesn't give you license to pound people. If I'm the first in after almost everyone folds, there are two ways in which I'll loosen up. First, any A-2 becomes playable. I don't need the extra features that I would insist on up front when I play A-2. Second, I will raise with a hand with three babies. If everyone has folded and I'm in late position, that tells me that the aces are live and a flop is coming low. For all those people in front of me to fold, they had to have a lot of unplayable hands, which mostly means high cards. The low cards are live, the aces are live, and I can play a hand like 2-4-5-Q.

As I already mentioned, you generally don't call raises late in an Omaha tournament. Either you reraise or fold. (Later in this chapter, I will describe the specific exceptions.) If you reraise, of course you need a better hand than the raiser has. Unless you know the player who raised is a maniac, you need one of those premium A-2 hands with flush possibilities, wheel possibilities, and high-card possibilities. If your opponent is a reasonable player, he for sure has an ace. If you are heads-up and an ace hits the board, how will your hand stand up high or low? If you have a king in your hand, you are in good shape if a pair of aces takes the high. If you have some other wheel cards, you can still make a low. If you have A-2-7-J, you're screwed, which is why I tell you to throw that hand away in early or late position.

If you have a lot of chips and the raiser doesn't, you could three-bet with one of the unplayable A-2 hands (A-2-5-9, A-2-6-9, A-2-6-8, etc.). The reason you make this play is to test the raiser after the flop. If the flop comes high, you can bet and get him to fold if he has enough chips left. It pays to know your opponents here. If you made it three bets before the flop and he made it four, that means he is probably getting all his chips in no matter what. But if you three-bet and he just called, he could be the type of player to throw away the hand after the flop and wait for another opportunity.

But if you have a stack and the raiser does too, you need a monster to get involved. You want A-A, or A-2 double-suited with some combination of another baby and another high card (preferably a king). I might three-bet on the button with A-3-4-K double-suited. Unless the raiser has A-A, the A-K keeps me from being a dog to much of anything on the high side.

Unless you have one of the best possible Omaha hands, you should be very careful about coming in after any raise later in an Omaha tournament. (The exceptions would be calling one bet from the big blind, playing short-stacked opponents, and playing against players who you know are raising without great hands.) It is so easy to get trapped with the second-best hand in Omaha.

I was playing in an Omaha tournament at the Bellagio a few years ago. I was in the big blind with A-3-5-K double-suited. It was raised and reraised and I called the two raises. I got scooped. I was against A-A and A-2, which is exactly what I was supposed to be up against late in an Omaha tournament against good players. Naturally, the flop was K-6-4, but I put myself in that situation. Here I was with the perfect flop and I *still* needed help to win either side.

Play in the blinds—You don't play as loose in the blinds in Omaha as you do in hold 'em. In no-limit forms of poker, you can call raises a lot because you aren't giving away anything about your hand and you can win a huge pot if the flop hits you just right. Even in limit hold 'em, you can call a raise with a pretty weak hand and try to out-play your opponent after the flop. It doesn't work that way in Omaha because once a player voluntarily puts chips in the pot, he is repre-senting that he has enough of a hand to win in a lot of ways. If you call a raise out of the blinds with a garbage hand and hit something on the flop, the raiser could have you beat on that side and have the other side locked up. You have to get extremely lucky to scoop a pot from a raiser when you have nothing before the flop.

To decide whether to play from the blinds after a raise (especially the big blind—from the small blind, if someone raises, you should play pretty close to the way you play in early position), it depends on where the raise came from and how many people called. Early in a tournament, if it has been raised and three or four people call, this is a good time to call a raise with a hand with three or four high cards, like K-Q-T-9, K-J-T-8, or even a seven and three paint cards. I'm calling here because with three or four people calling a raise, they all have low cards and the flop is coming high.

Later in the tournament, it is more likely to be just me and the raiser if I call, or maybe one other player. If it's just the raiser, there is a good chance the aces—or most of them—are live, so I could call with a hand with three wheel cards. I could make two pair, or flop an ace and a wheel card. I'm not calling a raise when I'm in one of the blinds with a high hand. I want to do that late in a tournament only in the rare situations where several people have called a raise and I know the flop is coming high. Here, it's the opposite situation: everybody fold-ing had high cards or mediocre high and low cards. That means there is an excellent chance the flop is coming low. Without a good starting low hand or three babies, I'm probably giving up half the pot before the flop. The raiser had to have a good starting low hand.

Omaha is ridiculously card-dependent. You pick up chips in Omaha by making extra with your good hands and getting away from bad hands. You don't do it by pushing people around and betting them out of pots.

"Knowing" What Cards Are Coming

In Omaha, unlike hold 'em, most of the deck gets into play. Especially because the game of Omaha is so ace-dependent, and so many players play any hand with ace-baby or ace-suited, you have to keep track of where the aces are. Find out who plays only when they have an ace. If you can identify where the aces are, you can play more marginal hands.

Let's say everybody folds to you on the button and you have 2-3-4-6. That's a monster hand when aces are coming on the flop, and it's pretty likely they are coming. Everybody folded so it's unlikely many aces came up. Ten-handed, that means twenty-eight cards have already been removed from play, plus your four, with no playable aces. The aces must be in the big or small blinds, or they're coming.

If you get this same hand in early position, don't even consider playing it. You've got seven or eight people playing after you and all the aces are out there. Even early in a tournament, you shouldn't play that hand. It is exactly the kind of hand you could lose a lot of bets with.

You can occasionally find the opposite situation: all the low cards are out of the deck because several players put in two or more bets to see the flop. If you are in late position, you definitely don't want to play a low hand. A-2 without good high prospects should be mucked. In fact, this might be the time, even late in the tournament, to play a hand like Q-J-T-9.

Because everyone is playing low cards and everyone is playing aces, you can make some very smart laydowns with hands everyone else will play and get trapped with. One time, I was in the big blind with A-2-3-6, one of my favorite starting hands. It went call-raise-call-raise. I threw it away. I didn't want to call two more bets (or make it four bets, or call and expect to call a third raise because the original raiser was going to cap it). Of course, the flop came Q-J-T.

That's why I say patience is so important in Omaha. You can wait a long time for a hand like A-2-3-6, but you have to throw it away when the other players are screaming that all the low cards are out. That great low hand of yours is garbage.

Let's say the player under the gun raises and two tight players call the raise. You are on the button with K-Q-J-T or a similar high-only hand. Don't follow my usual advice of throwing it away. *Three-bet it! All the low cards are out.* The baby cards are gone. The flop is coming high.

When you get one of these situations where you know what is coming on the flop, you can occasionally make a big score in an Omaha tournament. These situations don't come up too often, but you have to watch for them. One time, it was three bets cold to me on the button and I had K-Q-T-6. I made it four bets and scooped the pot.

Everybody was complaining that I was an idiot. I just said, "One day, you guys will figure it out. It'll all be out in my book."

Think about it: four people are in for a double raise. There is no way sixteen baby cards aren't out. I *flopped* the nuts that time, by the way. This kind of thing doesn't happen a lot, and sometimes it goes wrong even if it is set up and you notice it. If that happens, you have to throw your hand away on the flop. But every so often, you can tell what cards are coming by the other players' actions and get rewarded for being right.

You can take advantage of the same kind of thinking when you raise and get flat-called. In the example I described before about playing A-3 at a tight table, you can pretty much figure out your opponent's hand a lot of the time. Say you raise under the gun with A-3-6-Q. (You can do this, but only with a big stack and a tight table.) A small to medium stack flat-calls you. He probably would have three-bet you if he had A-A or A-2-K. For sure he has A-2, but now you are talking about a limited group of hands: A-2 and some low card (but probably not a three) and some high card (but probably not a king); A-2-5-J, A-2-4-J, A-2-4-T, A-2-5-Q, and a few other combinations like that.

Knowing what your opponent has allows you to do a lot after the flop. You are behind, but you can get away from a losing hand immediately and outplay the other player based on hitting your hand or him missing his.

When to Limp Later in a Tournament

After the blinds and limits go up, you should be playing aggressive poker and coming in with a raise or reraise. There are two exceptions. The first exception is when you get a hand like A-2-3-4, A-2-3-5, A-2-3-6, A-2-4-5, or A-2-4-6. In early position, I want to limp with that hand. If I can encourage a few extra players to call and a couple babies flop, I could win somewhere between half and all of a multiplayer pot. I even want to limp in middle or late position. If I can get the button to limp (or raise) behind me or get the small blind to put in the half bet, it's worth it.

The second exception is when you are short-chipped. When you are short on chips, you never raise and you never bet when you flop a low draw. If you have position and it is checked to you, you check. Even when you have a pair and a low draw, you don't play aggressive. If you miss completely, either on the flop or when your draw doesn't come in after the flop, you want to be able to fold. Why be in a rush to pot-commit yourself when you probably won't chase people out of the pot anyway and you have to hit a draw no matter what? (The exception to this would be A-A-baby. You are happy to isolate with that hand and you don't care if anyone comes in after you. You already have a made hand if it's heads-up and an opportunity to scoop.)

Late Tournament Play—After the Flop

If you play the kinds of hands I recommend, most of your decisions after the flop will be pretty straightforward. You will generally be heads-up and should be in contention with a high flop or a low flop. The most important thing is to be careful about someone trying to outplay you. With a high flop, if you have anything, you shouldn't let yourself get pushed around by an aggressive player.

Scotty Nguyen is one of the best tournament Omaha-eight-or-better players in the world, and we got into a hand where I raised and he three-bet. I had A-J and a couple babies. The flop came J-9-7. I bet, then three-bet when he raised me. The turn came a ten. I bet, then called when he raised me. The river was a blank. He bet and I called. My pair of jacks won it.

You have to know your opponents to succeed playing like that. A good player who plays like I recommend is generally loaded with low cards, and you will be too. On a high flop, that player may have nothing and figure you have nothing too. It doesn't take much to call down someone in that situation and have the best high hand. You need to know who you are up against. Against someone you know nothing about, they could be playing anything.

A lot of post-flop play later in the tournament comes from knowing your opponents and comparing the hands they play with the board. You have to put in a lot of hours to read opponents as well as an experienced pro, but there is plenty you can do just by paying attention. I have already explained how a smart player *should* play. How are your opponents playing? If they play that way, you know the kind of hand they need to raise or reraise, and the kind of hand they will flat-call you with.

If they have a big stack and are playing a lot of hands, you can't give them credit for the same cards. They could be playing a high-only hand, or a hand like A-K-K-X or an ace with another high pair. You shouldn't be playing those hands, but top pair/top kicker, like in that hand I described against Scotty Nguyen, isn't good enough against someone who plays that way. You are going to take advantage of that player in other ways: making a low out of just about anything, or making a high hand out of two low pair.

Conclusion

The key to winning in Omaha eight-or-better tournaments is to see a lot of multiway flops early and to narrow the field with premium cards later. Early, if you get away from trouble hands on the flop and stick with the hands where you are a huge favorite to win half, or you have half in the bank with a freeroll for a scoop, you need only a few good hands to build a stack. After the blinds and limits get higher, you have to be patient and exploit opponents who aren't patient. Isolate and get those players to fold, or start with better hands against them and get them to hold up. You are at the mercy of the cards a little bit in Omaha tournaments, but just knowing that puts you ahead of a lot of people.

CHAPTER 14

Pot-Limit Omaha

by Chris Ferguson

Playing Philosophy

Pot-limit Omaha (PLO) is an "action" game. It is more popular in Europe than in the United States, but its popularity in the United States is on the increase. It is one of the favorite games of high-stakes players because of the propensity for big pots to form. The action and popularity of PLO have combined to make it a thriving form of tournament poker despite the overwhelming emphasis on no-limit hold 'em. As more European and high-stakes cash players have entered World Series events, tournament organizers have accommodated their interest. Because chips move in the game, it is catching on for some of the same reasons no-limit hold 'em is popular.

If you like to gamble, you will probably enjoy pot-limit Omaha. And if you like to have the best of it *against* people who like to gamble too much, pot-limit Omaha might be the game for you.

One reason to learn pot-limit Omaha is that it is not well understood by a lot of players. By learning how to play it, you get in on the ground floor of an increasingly popular game. Even if you are just looking for some variety from hold 'em, PLO is a great game to try. It will hold your interest if you find that limit poker is boring or doesn't have enough action. It has the novelty of being a different form of poker to new players, yet it gives the thinking player an opportunity to get an edge over all the other players coming to the game.

The obvious difference between pot-limit Omaha and no-limit hold 'em is that you start with four cards instead of two. Of course, everybody knows that, but a lot of players take their hold 'em game and modify it for PLO without grasping the consequences of this.

Six hands instead of one—Your four starting cards form six two-card combinations. The more attractive combinations you have, the better your starting cards. Don't be one of those players who acts as if he is the only one given four cards, and overvalues his starting hands, finding something good in every hand. One thing to keep in mind is that starting hands in Omaha are closer in value than in hold 'em. This doesn't mean you should play more hands. In fact you should play fewer hands from early position because you can expect more players to play against you with position. You must, however, be prepared to call more often from the big blind and call reraises more often.

A-A, K-K, and Q-Q are monster starting hands in hold 'em. Those big pocket pairs do not necessarily make strong pot-limit Omaha starting hands. You want four cards that work well together. For example, Q♣Q♦8♦4♠ doesn't even make six starting hands; it makes just four: Q-Q, Q-8s, Q-4o and 8-4o (Q♣8♦ is dominated by Q♦8♦, and Q♣4♠ is equivalent to Q♦4♠). Only one of those four, Q-Q, is a good combination. Q-4o is unplayable, and Q-8s and 8-4o will at best make you non-nut straights or flushes. This hand should be routinely folded before the flop.

Compare that with a hand that doesn't contain a monster hold 'em combination like Q-Q but has four cards that work well together to make six playable starting hands. For example, J♠T♣9♠8♦ gives you a chance of hitting a flop based on J♠T♣, J♠9♠, J♠8♦, T♣9♠, T♣8♦, and 9♠8♦. None of these is a powerhouse combination, but they are all playable, especially because you get to play them all at once and because they are good "sneaky" hands. They can turn into power-houses or become great drawing hands. Another nice thing about these hands is that, when they miss the flop, they can easily be folded.

What about K-K versus Q-Q? In hold 'em, K-K is a huge fa-vorite over Q-Q, and unless the player with Q-Q catches another queen, K-K will almost certainly hold up, maybe even winning a big pot. In Omaha, though, all the combinations made by the other two cards can make Q-Q a slight favorite over K-K. Q-Q-A-J double-suited is a small favorite over K-K-8-4. The pocket-queens hand is also a much better hand to play after the flop. With the bets escalating, you want your decisions to be as clear-cut as possible after the flop.

The problem with valuing pocket pairs too highly occurs most often with A-A. You are obviously in great shape in hold 'em with A-A. In Omaha, you mostly have to play A-A, but there are a lot of situations where you find yourself hating your hand after the flop.

If you can move yourself or your opponent all-in (or get one of you pot-committed) before the flop in PLO with A-A, by all means do it. Against one opponent, you could be as much as a two-to-one favorite, and you are probably not an underdog. You don't have any problems with how A-A plays post-flop, because there is no more betting. But if you can't get yourself or your opponent all-in or pot-committed before the flop, a hand with A-A is still strong, but not automatically one you want to raise with.

Compare pocket aces with some hands that can make a lot of straights and flushes:

- A♣A♠2♦5♥ versus J♦T♥9♥8♦. (The aces are an underdog, 49.3 percent versus 50.7 percent.)
- A♣A♠2♦5♥ versus Q♦T♥8♦6♥. (The aces are an underdog, 49.6 percent versus 50.4 percent.)
- A♠A♣K♦Q♣ versus J♦T♥8♦6♥. (The aces are a favorite, 55.6 percent versus 44.4 percent.)

In the first two examples, the A-A hands are actually a small underdog, even against the hand where the cards aren't consecutive. (I refer to hands like Q-T-8-6 as "skip-straight hands.") In the third example, the aces have big companion cards and also block some of the straights the J-T-8-6 hand could make. Even so, they are not a gigantic favorite. In all these situations, the straight and skip-straight hands play better after the flop. The hands those starting combinations make will beat aces and more frequently be the nuts. They are also easy hands to throw away when the flop doesn't hit them. That's another huge advantage of these hands.

PLO, not NLO—Because starting hands are closer together in value, Omaha-high is played pot-limit instead of no-limit. If you are an eighty-twenty favorite (like you are before the flop in hold 'em with pair-over-pair), you don't have to bet much for an opponent to be making a mistake to call. But if you are a fifty-five-to-forty-five favorite, you have to make a gigantic bet to give an opponent bad pot odds to call. Because this situation arises so much more in Omaha, no-limit Omaha would be characterized by a lot of all-in betting. An A-A hand would be easy to play in no-limit Omaha. You would move all-in no matter how many chips you had. Because aces are so difficult to play after the flop in Omaha, you are happy winning a smaller pot with them.

Playing pot-limit instead of no-limit has several consequences. First, you may not get the opportunity to bet opponents off hands pre-flop because you can't bet more than the pot. Second, there are a lot fewer situations in PLO compared with hold 'em where it is a mistake to call a reraise after you raised pre-flop.

There are a few other aspects of pot-limit Omaha you should immediately be aware of:

Play straightforward—You should play straightforward more often in pot-limit Omaha than you would in no-limit hold 'em. The turn and river often change the entire complexion of the hand, bringing straight possibilities, flush possibilities, or full house possibilities. Many more weak hands become strong so it isn't as necessary to feign weakness by slow-playing a strong hand. For the same reason it is more important in Omaha when you have a hand to protect it by betting. You are usually giving your opponents a lot of outs to win if you don't bet. In addition, even when you have the unbeatable nuts, it is more likely that your opponent *thinks* he has a lot of outs, so you don't need to hide the strength of your hand.

Slow-playing and check-raising have a role in PLO, but a smaller role than in no-limit hold 'em. You slow-play because you want someone to make the second-best hand. It is rarer in Omaha that you can do that without the danger of your opponent making a stronger hand than you.

Position in PLO—When hands are close in value, position becomes more important. In late position, you can play more starting hands. After the flop, you benefit from the information your opponents give you based on their actions. You can also bet or raise to protect your hand, or take a free card if you think you need it.

The important exception is when you or an opponent is all-in. Position is meaningless when there is no more betting. Therefore, the bigger your stack, the more importance you should give to your position (or lack of position). With only a small number of chips left to bet, position should play less of a role in your decisions.

Tournament Structures

This was the structure of the World Series of Poker $1,500 PLO events in 2006:

TABLE 14.1

Level	Blinds	First raise
1	25-25	50-100
2	25-50	100-175
3	50-100	200-350
4	75-150	300-525
5	100-200	400-700
6	150-300	600-1,050
7	200-400	800-1,400
8	300-600	1,200-2,100
9	400-800	1,600-2,800
10	600-1,200	2,400-4,200
11	1,000-2,000	4,000-7,000
12	1,500-3,000	6,000-10,500
13	2,000-4,000	8,000-14,000
14	3,000-6,000	12,000-21,000
15	4,000-8,000	16,000-28,000
16	6,000-12,000	24,000-42,000
17	8,000-16,000	32,000-56,000

TABLE 14.1 ◆ (Continued)

Level	Blinds	First raise
18	10,000-20,000	40,000-70,000
19	15,000-30,000	60,000-105,000
20	20,000-40,000	80,000-140,000

Rebuys—I think you should play the same in a rebuy tournament as one that does not have rebuys. If your opponents play differently, then you should adjust. If they are playing liberally, gambling more, and rebuying a lot, then you shouldn't try to bluff them off a hand. In general, however, your best money-management strategy would be to treat your original buy-in as if you could rebuy whether you intend to or not. That's how I play all tournaments in the early rounds. If it is within your budget, you should be prepared to rebuy. If you think you have a positive expectation in the tournament and that hasn't changed, rebuy.

Starting Hands

The best starting hands in Omaha contain four coordinating cards. There are different ways the four-card combinations can coordinate, and you generally like four tightly coordinated cards (like T♦9♦8♠7♠) or a combination of connections between them. For convenience in this discussion, I have put labels on the different attributes—"straight possibilities," "flush possibilities," "pairs"— but they aren't equal in value nor are they exclusive to one another.

Any hand that is in more than one category improves its value. For instance, A-A in pot-limit Omaha, though great for moving all-in with, can be little more than a marginal hand if the other two cards don't mesh. If the side cards are suited with the aces, however, the hand becomes much more powerful. I am using the designations merely to organize starting hands. A lot of the time, the features of the hands cross categories, such as straight-and-flush hands (e.g., J♣T♠9♣8♠) or straight-possibility hands with a pair and two to a flush (e.g., T♥T♦8♣7♥).

In PLO, you are much more vulnerable to the nuts than in no-limit hold 'em. Therefore, it is important that your straights be nut straights and your flushes be the nut flushes. If you have 8♠4♠ in the big blind in hold 'em and the flop is 7♣6♥5♦, the only hand you have to pay off is 9-8. If you are heads-up against a pre-flop raiser, you aren't too worried he has 9-8.

Heads-up in Omaha, you are facing the six two-card combinations of your opponent. Imagine seeing a flop of 7♣6♥5♦ with six hold 'em opponents and getting action. You would be vulnerable with less than the nut straight. That's what seeing the flop heads-up in Omaha is like. In a four-way pot, you are up against eighteen two-card hands, six for each of your three opponents. If you don't have the nuts, they are likely out there against you.

I don't like the pair-hands very much, and here's why. First, you don't even start with six two-card combinations when you have a pair in your hand. Pair hands have only four two-card combinations. Second, unless you are in that situation where you can get all-in against one opponent and you have A-A, playing pairs can lead you into some very difficult post-flop decisions. Third, it is extremely difficult to make the nuts with a pair. If you make a set, you need to worry about a higher set. By the time all five cards are out, it is likely that the board will make a straight or flush possible. You are really playing in those situations to make a full house. Therefore, you need the board to pair and if it does pair, you have to worry about higher full houses. Because of the likelihood that you can make a full house without a pair, you are better off playing connecting cards that make straights and flushes and, almost by accident, full houses.

Straight possibilities—My favorite starting hands are hands that can make straights. The best hands in PLO are hands like T-9-8-7, 9-8-7-6, and 8-7-6-5. Even skip-straight hands like 9-7-6-5 and T-8-6-4 are playable. Those starting cards make a lot of great combinations after the flop, making either straights or big straight draws. They are also easy hands to get away from after the flop. Unless you hit your great hand or a great draw, you will usually have an easy decision to fold.

A hand like A-K-Q-J is very strong. It will make fewer straights than a hand like T-8-7-6, but the straights you make are always the nuts. In addition, all those high cards are very strong when no one makes a straight or better. Also A-K is a good combination to have for a starting hand. Unlike A-A, you know you have to improve your hand for it to have any value. A-K can improve in more ways than A-A, especially when you have two other high cards to go with it.

Flush possibilities—In a few paragraphs, you will read about how difficult it is to play A-A hands in Omaha. The exception is when one or both of your aces are suited with another card in your hand. If you don't have suited aces, flush hands can be tricky to play even after you make a flush. I would much rather play the straight-possibility hand with no suited cards, like Q♣J♦T♥9♠, than a double-suited hand without an ace that has limited straight draws, like K♦T♥6♦2♥. Some players will play any double-suited Omaha hand. I think that's a big mistake. I don't think a double-suited hand is generally playable unless it includes at least an ace, is composed of high cards, or has some straight possibilities, or some combination along with a pair.

Straight-only hands are superior to flush-only hands, especially if the flush-only hand does not contain an ace. A flush beats a straight, of course, but you can frequently get away from your straight when a possible flush appears. In every other way, trying to make a straight is better than trying to make a non-nut flush. First, you will flop more straights with four connected cards than you will flop flushes when double suited. With suited cards, you are more likely to be *drawing* to a flush after the flop rather than having a made hand. Second, you are more likely to hit a straight draw than a flush draw after the flop in Omaha. If you are holding T-9-8-7 and the flop comes K♠8♠6♣, a player with a spade-flush draw has nine outs. You will make a straight with any ten, nine, seven, or five, for thirteen outs. Third, you have a difficult decision on every street with a low flush.

Pairs—Paired cards are easily overrated by players switching from hold 'em to Omaha. An overpair will win a lot of pots in no-limit hold 'em, including some big ones. A small pair that makes trips will take down a lot of big pots. An overpair in Omaha sometimes wins the pot; but if it does, it will be a very small pot. Small sets always have to dodge a lot of bullets to win a big pot.

With a pair, you are drawing to just two outs to improve, and even then, your set will be at the mercy of the board making possible straights and flushes. Unless your pair matches the high card on the board, you could be against a higher set and be drawing almost completely dead.

I will play A-A but it is potentially a very dangerous hand in pot-limit Omaha. If the hand does not have something else going for it, like straight or flush possibilities, it won't play well after the flop. And, unlike in hold 'em, if you miss the flop, A-A is generally reduced to little more than a bluff-catching hand. You don't want to get married to aces in hold 'em but they can be a complete disaster in pot-limit Omaha.

I don't like K-K unless I'm very short stacked, though I will play it in combination with straight cards, like K-K-Q-J, K-K-Q-T, or K-K-A-T. Being double-suited also helps. I will play a hand like K♣K♦8♣4♦, but it isn't a monster like some people think. Paired cards lower than Q-Q are not worth playing unless they are also have strong possibilities for making straights. Most of the value of T-T-9-8 is in making a straight, not a set. Your set is vulnerable to higher sets, straights, and flushes. If you make a straight, you can better find out where you are in the hand, and potentially beat a lot of hands that will call your bets.

You may find yourself playing lower pairs because the pair co-ordinates with the other two cards, like 7♣7♦6♣5♦. You have to be careful playing this hand if you make a set and aren't drawing to a straight or a flush. If the flop is Q♠T♥7♦, you are in a dangerous situation. Not only do you have to worry about straight draws but higher sets. Even if you make a full house—say the turn card was the queen of hearts—it's scary because your full house is beat by a player with Q-Q, T-T, Q-T, or Q-7.

Playing double pairs—Some players put a premium on double pairs, like K-K-9-9 and 6-6-5-5. True, about one time in four, you will make a set. But you are probably going to have to fold to any bet the other three times (except in the rare situations where you play 6-6-5-5 and the flop is 4-3-2). You won't necessarily win a big pot, or win at all, when you flop your set.

Double-paired hands are probably stronger than single-paired hands. Going from six two-card combinations with an unpaired Omaha hand to four with a paired hand is a significant disadvantage. Going from four combinations to three when double paired is, relatively speaking, not as bad. The two pairs that work well individually more than make up for this, but this isn't the powerhouse it looks like.

If you play K-K-9-9 and your nine hits, there are a lot of flops in which you could be making crying calls to the end or folding. If there are two suited cards on the flop, especially if your cards are not of that suit, you have to fend off flush draws. (If the flop comes all one suit, then you may already be facing a flush.) If the other two cards on the flop are close in value to the nine (e.g., Q-J-9, Q-T-9, J-9-8, T-9-6), you could already be beat by a straight. (If the flop is bigger than nine-high, you may be beat by a higher set.) With a set, you will have seven outs to make quads or a full house on the turn and, if you miss, ten outs on the river. That is a difficult spot to be in: playing a hand that will hit on the flop 25 percent of the time and even then may require you to dodge bullets to win.

Making a small set will frequently either win you a small pot early in the hand or force you to make difficult decisions on the turn and river. I like playing in a way that minimizes the number of difficult decisions I have to make, and maximizes the number of difficult decisions my opponents have to make.

Playing aces—Think about A-A-X-X against T-9-8-7 double-suited. The straight hand is probably a slight underdog depending on the other cards in the A-A hand. (It could actually be a slight favorite.) But how will those hands play after the flop? With the straight hand, if you miss it, you can get away from it. With the aces, if someone bets, I don't even like making that first call very much. If that first call isn't already a crying call, any future ones surely are. Those aces might already be beaten, and if they aren't, the bettor surely has a lot of outs against you. You are either a small favorite or a big dog. Aces will win, but they either hit their lucky flop or you get a quick fold. You can beat some lousy hands, but not many good hands. T-9-8-7 beats a lot of good hands.

If you have a chance to move all-in with aces before the flop (or get pot-committed), you should always take it. Because aces are almost always a favorite before the flop and are likely to get outplayed after the flop, you should pot-commit yourself to the hand before the flop if you can. If you can't do that, you should play them much more cautiously.

The two situations in which aces make a strong hand are when the aces are suited with your other two cards and when you are short-stacked. Aces create a lot of difficult decisions later in the hand. The fact remains, though, that you will usually be a favorite before the flop. If you can commit your chips with aces, do it. If someone else has raised, reraise if you can get pot-committed (i.e., bet at least one-third of your chips). Sure, you are telegraphing your hand, but you are telegraphing a hand where you want them to fold, and where there really aren't going to be any more decisions on the hand. You love aces in that situation. (You should also be reraising with hands other than aces. It is rarely a good idea to make a certain play with only one kind of hand, and if you reraise sometimes with 8-7-6-5, you may take away a pot where you miss the flop and an ace falls, or get an opponent betting into your made straight with two pair because they think all you have is the overpair.)

But if you have a big stack in front of you and have to bet all the way through, aces don't play very well. With a big stack, you should routinely be folding aces after the flop. In fact, you probably should not reraise with aces if you have a lot of chips. Opponents will expect you to have aces, and if they call, you have limited means of improving plus you have no idea how the flop hit them.

Pre-Flop Strategy

Position—Because pot-limit Omaha hands are similar in value, position takes on greater importance. Compared with hold 'em, you actually want to play tighter in early position. There is no hand in Omaha like A-A in hold 'em, where you can be a big favorite over anything else. Every Omaha hand is a drawing hand. Even if you are playing premium hands that can stand a reraise, you are paying a high price to, essentially, hit a draw.

Therefore, if you are in late position and no one has entered the pot, you can open up your hand selection. In chapter 6, Andy Bloch described the percentages for hands to play by position in no-limit hold 'em. In a game without antes, he explained why you play 11 percent of your hands under the gun (in a ten-handed game) and 45 percent on the button (if no one has entered the pot). In Omaha, you should play even tighter up front and open up a little more on the button. Many Omaha players will be surprised by this.

How much to bet—To protect your starting hands and to give your opponents the opportunity to fold, you should always enter the pot with a raise if it is folded to you. I recommend always making a pot-sized raise. Because hands are closer in value in Omaha I don't believe in small pre-flop raises as I do in hold 'em. As in no-limit hold 'em, you don't want to give away information about the strength of your hand by calling with certain hands or by betting different amounts that could indicate the strength of your hand. Always raising in Omaha is not as important as in hold 'em, but it is still the right way to play.

You should follow the same advice after the flop: bet approximately the size of the pot, when you decide to bet.

Play from the blinds—Call more raises from the big blind in Omaha than in hold 'em. Because hands are closer in value, it should take more to make you fold after you have already put in a bet. Unless your hand is extremely weak (like three of a kind), you should usually call a raise and see the flop when you are in the big blind.

Late in a tournament, you might lay down more hands, even in the big blind, if you are on a short stack and close to the money. There is some value in those hands, but it may not be worth putting your tournament on the line if you are on a short stack.

Three of a kind—Three of a kind should always be folded, except for three aces in rare situations. One of the things that makes three of a kind so incredibly weak is that you have only two starting combinations—a pair and one of your three of a kind with your side card. You are drawing to one card to make a set instead of two. Therefore, you should fold this hand before the flop.

Limpers—If people limp in front of me, I don't mind limping behind. If I think I am unlikely to get raised, I will even expand my playing hands. The question, therefore, is whether to follow limpers by limping or raising when you have a playable hand. You have to ask yourself some questions: Can I commit myself to the pot and do I have a hand with which it makes sense to do that? Can I get my opponents to fold? Do I have the kind of hand that plays best against one opponent or multiple opponents? How likely am I to make the nuts? In general it is very difficult to get opponents who limped in to fold for a raise. It's even tough to get players who raised to fold for a reraise. This is a big difference between hold 'em and Omaha.

You have to weigh the answers to all these questions based on the circumstances. In general, though, you don't mind playing a multi-way pot when you can make the nuts if you hit your hand. Hands with straight possibilities, though they contain some risks, can win you a giant multiway pot. A pair of aces, unless they are both matched with a card in your hand of the same suit, will not likely make the nuts. That makes aces a better hand heads-up, but unless you are short-stacked, you may be risking too much of your stack on some very difficult post-flop decisions. With a deep stack, if you play A-A in a multiway pot (unsuited or with just one possible flush draw), you might be better off just limping along to see the flop and try to hit a set. If someone raises behind you and you can commit your stack for a reraise you should definitely do so.

Raised in front—When you follow a raiser into the pot, you also have to make the decision of flat-calling versus reraising. In general, I don't reraise as much in Omaha as in hold 'em. I like having and keeping my positional advantage. I don't want to let my opponents take away the value of position by moving in on me, unless I have aces. If I let them move in or bet the majority of their chips, I can't use my positional advantage anymore. When reraising, weigh losing that advantage against what you hope to accomplish by reraising. For instance, when you have aces and a short stack, you want to get your chips in while you are a favorite. That is more important than the value of position.

There is value in mixing up your play by flat-calling occasionally and sometimes reraising, but mixing up your play is not as important in Omaha as it is in hold 'em. In hold 'em, whenever you reraise, you are usually telling opponents you have a very narrow range of hands, like A-A, K-K, Q-Q, or A-K. The premium hands in Omaha are much more varied. The first instinct when someone reraises in Omaha is that they have A-A, but there are many other hands with which you could reraise, like double-suited Q-J-T-9 or even T-9-8-7. You don't want to always be reraising with these hands, but if your opponents recognize you *could* (which probably means you sometimes *do*) reraise with them, then your reraise does not give away that you have a narrow range of hands, as it might in hold 'em.

I will sometimes reraise with my strongest drawing hands. I don't even mind if someone moves over the top of me on those hands because I can't be a very big underdog. I would rather play a smaller pot and outplay them after the flop, but it is a concession I sometimes make to mix up my play.

To call a raise, you need a hand about as strong as your opponent needed to raise in the first place. If the player under the gun raised, I would need a hand much stronger than I would need if he raises from the cutoff. So if you have a playable hand, do you call or reraise?

One thing to keep in mind when someone raises in front of you is that position is more important in Omaha than any other game. Your playable hand, in position, is still playable, even if someone else has shown strength. But that advantage usually translates into calling rather than reraising, particularly if reraising allows my opponent is to get pot-committed or move all-in.

If the players have very large stacks, I believe you should reraise rather than call behind a raiser. Position does not lose its value there. In fact, it gains value with really huge stacks because the pot is growing, and my opponent can't take that advantage away by getting one of us pot-committed or moving all-in. I will rarely call a raise if the stacks are really big and I have position. I will reraise instead. I am not so likely to reraise when my opponent can come over the top for a large percentage of his remaining chips and make us pot-committed. Let's say the blinds are 50 to 100. If the raiser bets 300, my natural reraise would be to 1,050. If one of us has 10,000 or less, he can raise again, this time to 3,200, and pretty much pot-commit the shorter stack or at least minimize the advantage of position. Therefore, if I can reraise to less than 10 percent of the smaller of our two stacks, I am much more likely to reraise than flat-call.

Playing After the Flop

Before the flop, most playable hands are pretty close in value. With each street, they move further apart. After the flop in Omaha, the range of values of different hands is probably similar to before the flop in hold 'em but not as close as after the flop in hold 'em.

Position—Your position is extremely important after the flop. It is more dangerous to give free cards in Omaha than in hold 'em. Generally, your opponent is going to have more outs to beat you. Because giving free cards is dangerous, the first player is forced to play more straightforwardly. The second player, therefore, has a better idea of the first player's hand and can act accordingly, but he too should not get too tricky.

In hold 'em, an early-position raise generally means you are facing one of a small number of premium hands. A player raising in early position in Omaha could have such a wide range of hands that you can't assume that a particular flop hit or missed him.

Heads-up or multiway—In Omaha, you have to play much more straightforwardly in multiway pots as well, but you need to tighten up considerably. Heads-up, when you bet, you are saying, "My hand can beat yours, and even if it can't, I can try to bluff you." If five people see the flop, that bet says, "I can beat the best of four other hands." That's a pretty strong hand.

With four cards instead of two in Omaha, each player has six two-card combinations instead of one. Against four opponents, you are facing twenty-four potential hands, not four. Top pair/top kicker is useless against that kind of competition. Two small pair without a draw is pretty junky. You don't want those hands anymore.

Multiway, trips could be worth just a crying call. Imagine having a six with a flop of 6-6-J. If someone bets into you, there is a decent chance you are facing someone with a six. Against four opponents, there are sixteen cards out against you, over one-third of the remaining deck. If you were intending on betting your six without a good kicker, there is a good chance you are facing a better hand.

Note that if you have an overpair, like a pair of aces, it's twice as likely that another six is out there, compared with when you have a six and are concerned about your kicker. That's why a six with a bad kicker is a better hand, plus you are more likely to make a full house. This is a good example of why A-A doesn't play well multiway. With a pair on board this isn't that bad a flop for A-A. It will never lose to any two pair hand, and still it isn't very strong. Against four opponents playing random cards, there is a 58.99 percent chance that one of them has a six. There is only a 35.56 percent chance the six is out there if you have a six.

With pocket aces, I don't even make a crying call. If I have a six and three other low cards, I will probably make the crying call. I have nine outs to make a full house (unless I have a pair in my hand). If I don't make a full house or quads on the turn and my opponent bets again, I'll fold, though I might call another bet with 6-A-X-X. What if you have A-A-X-X and the flop is 6-6-6? Now you have a monster, right? Your opponent needs quads to beat you. Against four opponents there are sixteen cards out against you, therefore you should win only about two-thirds of the time.

When you miss the flop—When you miss the flop and your opponent bets, you can fold. But what about when you are the aggressor? If you raised before the flop and were called by only the big blind, you should generally bet if it is checked to you. Against multiple opponents, you want to have something to bet. Bluffing does not play as large a role in Omaha, especially with multiple opponents. With four opponents and their twenty-four two-card combinations, somebody is likely to have a big hand or be drawing to a big hand and call you.

Leading with a draw—If I led the betting and have a really good draw, I am almost certain to bet it. With a marginal draw, I might go for the free card myself. I don't like getting raised off my marginal draw because I hate laying down a hand that has a lot of value. A wrap straight draw can be a favorite over a set. With a draw like that, I don't mind getting raised by someone with a set. I'll move in after a raise if my draw is good enough.

Betting your draw is known as semi-bluffing. You would like your opponent to fold so you can take down the pot without having to hit your draw. You can put a lot of pressure on opponents at this point. Often opponents recognize that their hand, even if leading, is so vulnerable that they fold. You need to bet your draws occasionally to get opponents to fold. This is part of the value in playing the hands with straight possibilities and drawing hands in general. If you bet and they fold, you've won whether you would have hit or not.

Slow-playing—There are three reasons to slow-play in pot-limit Omaha:

- Your opponent is drawing slim to beat you
- You have the deck crippled
- You might already be behind

Any combination of these reasons makes the case for slow-playing even stronger. Giving a free card can be very dangerous in pot-limit Omaha, so it can be risky to slow-play in the wrong situation. Slow-playing doesn't play as large a role as it does in hold 'em.

There aren't many situations where you are so far ahead on the flop that your opponent can't catch up, but you can afford to give a free card when that happens. If you make the top full house, you can give a free card, especially when there are straight or flush draws on the board. If you have K♥K♠J♥T♦ and the flop is K♣7♣7♦, the only way an opponent could catch up is if he had A-A and he turned an ace or someone with three sevens catches a fourth. If someone has a seven, you should get action from them on the turn and maybe the river too, so you will get paid by them whether you bet the flop or not. But if you give the flush draw a chance to hit, or someone with a pair a chance to make a lower full house, you may get a lot more action on the turn that way.

You don't need a pair in your hand for this kind of situation to occur. In fact, because you are avoiding pairs and frequently playing cards close in value, you may be more likely to get action when you make the top full house without a pair in your hand. With a hand like Q-J-T-9 and a flop of Q-Q-J, you might have opponents with straight draws as well as flush draws if the jack and one of the queens are suited.

Another time to slow-play is when you have the deck crippled. A classic case would be a flop of K-J-J and you have K-J-X-X. There are not a lot of scare cards left in the deck. Again, the only way a free card can beat you here is if your opponent has A-A (or A-J) and an ace comes on the turn.

Generally, when you make three of a kind, you don't want to give a free card to someone on a flush to straight draw. For example, if you have T-T and the flop is T♥9♦5♦, you need to play your top set for as many chips as you can. You have to make your opponents pay the maximum to draw against you. You may even get a lot of action from a player with two pair or a lower set.

But if you flop three of a kind and there aren't flush or straight draws, you can slow-play it. In fact, not only is checking unlikely to give someone a card to beat you, but you could be behind to a three of a kind with a better kicker or, with a pair on the board, to a full house.

With trips and no possible draws, you are either far ahead or far behind. In either case, it doesn't hurt you to check. You usually want to play three of a kind fast because of straight and flush draws. But without those draws, your opponents aren't drawing to very many outs if you give a free card.

With a flop of A-A-K and A-K-X-X in your hand, you can give a free card because you are obviously in the lead and it is impossible for your opponent to catch up. With a hand like 4-5-6-7 and a board of 4-4-T, you might have the lead, but you can also be behind. Because there are only a limited number of cards that can beat you, it makes sense to check if you are ahead or behind.

The best hands to slow-play are those where you are ahead and are unlikely to be caught, or are behind and unlikely to catch up. If you are in one situation or the other but don't know which, slow-playing is a good idea.

If you clearly have the lead, like

with a flop of

you can afford to give a free card, but you have to start betting at some point. If your opponent has a four and can't get away from the hand, you want to make him put in the maximum.

One problem with slow-playing in that situation with T-T is that an opponent with a four may slow-play too and save himself some chips.

When you have a four and the flop is 4-4-T, you are in the same position as in hold 'em with a weak ace and hitting an ace on the flop. If you start betting that ace, you are most likely to get called by hands that beat you. But if you check it down, you may have to pay off just one bet if you lose and the bettor on the end could be bluffing or betting because they think second pair is good. You couldn't get that player's chips in the pot if you bet the flop or turn, and you would hate betting A-5 and getting action from A-J. The way to win the most (or lose the least) is to check-call in those situations. The same is true with a weak three of a kind in Omaha.

But with T-T, you want to push the player with the four into losing the most possible, so you bet. Maybe the four will call once, hit a full house, and you can make two more bets.

It may look like you have the deck crippled, but you really don't. It is very unlikely you could get a player with a ten to call you anyway on the flop. The only way you will get a lot of action from a player without a four is if the free card makes your opponent a full house. In that case, an opponent with 5-5 could catch a five and pay you off on the turn and the river. But if your opponent has an overpair—there are four overpairs and seven underpairs in this example, and if your top full house was lower, the ratio becomes less favorable—you are giving a free card that can more easily beat you.

Check-raising and free cards—If you are out of position, either because you called from the blind or were reraised after you made a pre-flop raise, you should frequently check to the raiser. Most of the time, the player who raised will bet the flop because they are expected to. But whether you are the raiser in position or the player in the blind, you need to consider how to maximize your profits and minimize your losses when faced with this recurring situation.

When you are out of position you don't mind having a raiser who always bets the flop. If you know the raiser will bet the flop, you have effectively taken over position for that round. You can just check, the raiser will automatically bet, and then you could fold, call, or raise. You obviously fold your worst hands, but you need to mix up your calls and raises, sometimes raising with the strongest hands and sometimes with weak hands, preferably draws.

When I am the raiser in position, I'm generally going to make a continuation bet, but I won't automatically bet. In hold 'em the reason for the continuation bet is that the raiser has shown a lot more strength than the caller. Because of this the caller is likely to fold, so why not bet and give them the opportunity? Because hands are closer in value in Omaha, the caller is not as likely to fold, and the continuation bet becomes less useful. It can be dangerous giving free cards, but I have to find some hands to check when the player in the blind checks to me. I don't want to give up position and have to commit a pot-sized bet if my opponent has a great hand. If I don't automatically make a continuation bet, my opponent is at risk of giving me a free card by always checking to the raiser. If my opponent has a medium strong hand— something that's leading but vulnerable to free cards—he'll have to bet if he knows I'm capable of checking. Now his bet tells me a lot and I can respond appropriately. And I still have position for the turn.

When can you risk giving a free card, either as the player in the blind who hit the flop or as the raiser with position? What kind of opponent do you have? If I am in the blind and my opponent checks a lot, I'm going to have to bet if I think my hand is in the lead but in danger of falling behind on the turn.

Check-call or check-raise?—I don't mind check-calling, because I think it is a strategy that works well against good players. In position, good players like to put pressure on their opponents. If they bet without an extremely strong hand and I check-call occasionally with strong hands, they can't automatically bet and take the pot away when I check again on the turn with a strong hand. They can't know I didn't hit a draw or am slow-playing. Do they want to risk a second bet and the possibility that I'll check-raise what is now a very large pot?

Check-calling also has some utility against players who play their good starting hands too fast, betting them to oblivion, keeping the lead until their hand only has value as a bluff. If you have any idea that your opponents play this way—and it is a common way to play, taking hold 'em-style aggression into a game where most flops *don't* miss everybody—you have to call them down a little more often.

Sometimes I will check-raise with a draw and sometimes check-call. I want to mix it up to make it difficult for opponents to put me on a hand. My stack size may weigh toward one move or the other. With a big draw I want to be the one moving all-in or pot-committing us to the hand, giving my opponent a tough decision. A lot of the value of the draw is getting my opponent to fold. With a monster I try to induce my opponent to move in thinking he's giving me the tough decision. Check-raising all-in or pot-committing us takes away my opponent's advantage: position.

There is no manual on when to check-call. It's a weak move that signals weakness. Unfortunately it's risky to do it with a big hand, which is exactly why it is such a sign of weakness. An example of when I might check-call would be when I have top pair and overcards and the board doesn't look too scary. If I have a pair and some of my weaker draws, I might check-call and see another card.

Another check-calling example would be the hand I described earlier, holding a four with a flop of 4-4-T. Check-calling the flop seems reasonable, but the problem occurs on the turn. I'm hoping my opponent finds my call as troubling as I find his bet and we check it down. But what if he bets the turn as well?

You have to be willing to call some bets on the turn when you check-call the flop. Otherwise, your opponent can just bet you out of the pot if he fires two bullets at you. Those trip fours are a good example of a hand you don't mind check-calling with. If I can pot-commit myself, I'd prefer doing that, but if that's not the case, check-calling might be the best option.

Taking over the betting lead—In Omaha there are more multiway pots and the idea of always checking to the raiser pretty much goes out the window, especially in multiway pots. It is harder for the raiser to keep betting without a real hand because he has several players to act behind him. Since you can't rely on the initial raiser betting as in limit hold 'em, you can't simply always check it to the raiser.

Whether heads-up or multiway, there are some interesting hands where I am confident I am ahead but I won't know if I'm ahead after the turn. For instance, I could have a straight draw and a non-nut flush draw. I have enough outs that I am probably ahead at this point in the hand, especially if I also have a pair. What I don't know is whether I'll still be ahead if I actually hit one of those outs. I could make a straight but not the best straight. I could make a non-nut flush. I actually want to put a lot of chips in on the flop, and not wait for the turn.

This is a good time to take the betting lead whether you are in or out of position. You should avoid difficult decisions and force your opponent to make difficult decisions. You are in the lead or have a lot of outs. Bet. If you don't get your money in now and hit your non-nut flush, for example, your opponent can put a lot of pressure on you by betting. You want to be the one putting on the pressure, so bet while your hand or your draw looks best.

Another time to take the betting lead is when you make top two pair. The nice thing about this hand is that you're less worried about your opponent having a set because you have two of his cards blocked. If you flop a wraparound straight draw with no pair, your opponent has six two-card hands and any one of them can be among the nine pairs that make a set. If the flop is

there are three pairs of kings (i.e., K♦K♥, K♦K♠, K♥K♠) that your opponent could have to make a set. There are also three pairs of jacks to make a set of jacks, and three pairs of sevens to make a set of sevens. There are 1,176 two-card combinations left in the deck. There are nine pairs that make a set, about .75 percent. A four-card hand contains six two-card combinations, so an opponent has about a 4.5 percent chance of having a set.

But if you have

for top two pair, your opponent has just one pair of kings (K♦K♠) and one pair of jacks (J♣J♠) plus the three pairs of sevens to make a set. You are much less likely to be betting into a hand that kills you, about 3 percent.

I don't mind getting a lot of money in with top two pair. I won't call a couple raises in front of me, especially when the action is telling me that I'm already beaten. But I would usually check-raise one opponent with that hand, or lead out if I thought my opponent might check. If my opponent is paying to see the turn, it is extremely unlikely he has a set of kings or jacks. It's more likely he has a wraparound straight draw or a flush draw or some combination.

Pot-limit Omaha is more of a feel game than no-limit hold 'em. In hold 'em, there are more situations where one play is superior and you want to be making that play. A lot of Omaha is about outguessing your opponents. If the game has been pretty active and I am sure someone is going to bet, I'll check my top two pair with the intention of raising. (If there is a bet and a raise when it gets to me, I'll just lay it down and probably save chips that way.) On the other hand, if people are slowing down, then I'll just bet out. Top two pair is vulnerable to draws so that you can't afford to give a free card that can make someone a straight or a flush. If you are against three opponents, half the deck could make one of them a hand that beats you and your hand may not be worth a crying call on the turn.

I will play top set more aggressively than top two pair. With top set, there is no limit to the amount of money I want to get in the pot. Bet, or check-raise. You have to bet if there is any realistic likelihood it will get checked behind you. Top set is not a hand where you want to give a free card. You don't have the deck as crippled as you do with top set in hold 'em because few people are willing to lose that much with just top pair. You're hoping someone flopped a lower set.

Bluffing—In general, you don't need to bluff very often in Omaha. There is, however, a lot of semi-bluffing, betting with a draw. You generally don't want to consider making a complete bluff in Omaha, especially at a multiway pot. You will find yourself getting called most of the time. There are too many good hands and too many good draws out there to scare everyone away. With so many potential draws, you generally aren't getting the right odds for a complete bluff to succeed. You want to be drawing to something because of the likelihood your bluff will get called. Betting your draws is known as semi-bluffing.

There is one situation in which I frequently bluff in Omaha (and occasionally in hold 'em): when there are three to a suit on board and I have the ace of that suit but not another of that suit so I can't make a flush.

For example, if you have the ace of spades and there are three spades on the board, this is a good time to bluff. (In hold 'em, this would be a semi-bluff. Not so in Omaha where you need two of a suit in your hand to make a flush.) You know your opponent doesn't have the nuts. Check-raising is often the right play if you decide to bluff. It really puts the pressure on. If you bet, your opponent will call with smaller flushes. But if you check-raise, your opponent really has to think he is in trouble. Unless he is already pot-committed, he is going to fold most hands.

When there is a two-flush on the board, I don't like this bluff so much. You need other value in your hand because the opponent with the non-nut flush draw is going to have something else to call you. You may be going out on a limb against an opponent if you are beat. If the flush does come, at least now you have a credible bluff. Your opponent is going to put a lot of pressure on you if he has a set and correctly reads that you are representing a flush draw. He's going to feel pretty good reraising you with the better hand.

Pot odds—Pot odds are a very important concept in all forms of poker. The time when they are most relevant is when an opponent has moved all-in or committed almost all his chips. The pot odds are the ratio of the amount of money you have to put into the pot to call compared to the amount you win if your hand wins.

For example, suppose the pot is $10 and your opponent moves in for $10. If you call and lose the hand you will lose $10, if you win you will win the $10 in the pot and the $10 your opponent bet for a total of $20. In computing pot odds we ignore who put in the money that comprises the pot. Thus you are getting $20-to-$10 or two-to-one pot odds. To make a call correct in this case you need to win the hand at least one time in three.

Now comes the hard part: What are my chances of winning the hand? I don't put an opponent on a hand so much as a range of hands. What is the chance my opponent has a set? Two pair? A nut flush draw? An overpair? I assign them percentages and estimate how likely I am to win against each hand. Let's assume I have a big straight draw, where twelve cards will make me a straight. Maybe all my straights are good unless my opponent has a set and hits a full house.

I need to estimate a lot of things, but that's why I pay attention to the kinds of hands my opponents play. At the end of this, I might conclude that there is a 25 percent chance that I have a 50 percent chance of winning, and a 75 percent chance that I have a 30 percent chance of winning.

What's my approximate chance of winning? $(.25 \times .5) + (.75 \times .3)$ or about 35 percent. This is greater than one-third so I would probably call. It's close, though, and all I can do is estimate. If the circumstances were slightly different and I estimated that 25 percent of the time I had a 75 percent chance to win (instead of 50 percent), my overall chance would be 41.25 percent and I would definitely call. A vital aspect of pot odds is that you don't need to be a favorite; you just need a likelihood of winning greater than the size of the bet (compared to the total pot) that you have to call.

Once you settle in at a tournament, what keeps you busy is preparing for these moments. This is why you pay attention to your opponents, the hands they play and how they play them.

I will do this same kind of analysis in no-limit hold 'em before the flop. Say I raise with 6-6 and my opponent moves all-in. To keep it simple, assume I completely discount the possibility he has an underpair; I am facing either an overpair or overcards. If I eventually put my opponent on a 40 percent chance of an overpair (in which case I have a 20 percent chance of winning the pot) and a 60 percent chance of overcards (in which case I have a 55 percent chance of winning the pot), I have a 41 percent chance of winning the pot. If I have to put in 41 percent of the pot to call, it's a toss up and I'll probably fold. But if I have to put in less than 41 percent of the pot, I will call.

Drawing to less than the nuts—To draw to a non-nut flush, you need some other value in your hand, like a straight draw or one or two pair in your hand. The same is true of your weaker straight draws.

Playing those aces after the flop—What do you do with aces after the flop? We can skip many situations that arise because they are obvious: when you are already pot-committed, when you pick up an ace on the flop, and when one or both of your aces is suited and you flop a flush or a flush draw.

The difficult situations are the majority of the time when your hand does not improve. In general, you want to bet to protect your aces, but lay them down if you encounter any resistance.

When you have a chance to put in the first bet on the flop, you will generally bet if you raised pre-flop and have one opponent. Otherwise, you have to decide whether to bet based on what the flop looks like and the number of opponents. If you have two opponents and a dangerous flop—clustered cards like 8-9-J and/or a couple of suited cards—you should check and fold. If someone else bets, it is unlikely those aces are still good, and even if they are good at the moment they are likely to be an underdog to a huge draw.

On the other hand, if the flop comes something like 4-4-T, aces still have value. In fact, giving a free card isn't too dangerous here. The only cards likely to beat you are another ten if an opponent has a ten in his hand, or a card that makes a set if an opponent has a pair in the hand. You can beat all two pair hands.

After the flop in Omaha, a pair of aces plays like a pair of sevens in hold 'em. In a multiway pot after a flop like 8-T-J, sevens aren't worth much in hold 'em, and aces aren't worth much in Omaha. With a flop like 4-4-T, however, they might still be good. (Obviously, giving a free card in hold 'em with 7-7 with that flop is a lot more dangerous than giving it in Omaha with aces.)

Playing the Turn and River

When your set is facing a potential straight or flush—If you played it right, you bet the maximum with your set on the flop but got called. Now a potential straight or flush gets there on the turn. Occasionally you need to fold your set on the turn. Keep in mind though that the set has now become a drawing hand. If you are up against a straight or flush, you have ten outs to hit a full house. If I have bottom trips, I might not like a threatening board and someone betting at me as much. I will fold bottom set more often because I might be up against a higher set. With top set I like my hand a lot more since my opponent could be drawing nearly dead if he happens to have a lower set.

Taking over the betting lead on the turn—When you have those bottom trips and the board doesn't show a possible straight or flush, check-calling the flop and betting the turn is an underused play in Omaha. If you have one of those hands where you don't know if you are ahead or behind, you might want to try betting out on the turn. Especially if this pot-commits you, betting eliminates your opponent's positional advantage and puts him to a tough decision. I don't think about implied odds as the hand progresses, but here is a short-cut for many decisions you will have to make if you are drawing to a hand with one card to go. Generally, you need to be drawing to more than ten outs to win to call a pot-sized bet on the turn. Thus if it becomes nearly certain I'm up against a straight or flush I fold my lower sets but call with top set.

If I am first to act, I am more likely to bet my draw. If I am second to act, I can get a free card by checking; I can also get raised if I bet. It's true that by acting first and betting, I can also get raised, but I'm giving up more by checking out of position than in position. If I check when I'm first to act, I lose my chance to win the pot right there and I still may not get a free card. With a strong draw, I will almost definitely bet the turn when I am out of position. I can't be far behind and a lot of the equity in the hand comes from getting my opponent to fold. With a weak draw, I am more likely to check when out of position to ensure that I get a free card.

Tournament Strategy

How many bets are left?—In all forms of tournament poker, it is important to know how many bets are left between you and your opponent. Look at the size of the pot. If the smaller of your and your opponent's stack is the size of the pot, then there is only one bet left. If the smaller stack is four times the size of the pot, then there is room for two pot-sized bets. The smaller stack needs to be thirteen times the pot for there to be three pot-sized bets left. It is important to be aware of this for many reasons. It is important to try to manipulate the pot in an attempt to be the player to move all-in. Anytime there are two bets left (the smaller stack is four times the pot) making a pot-sized bet allows your opponent the opportunity to move all-in. Be prepared for this anytime you make a pot-sized bet in that position. I don't like betting a draw in this situation; I would rather go for a check-raise where I can move in myself.

Short-handed play—I constantly hear top players say you need to loosen up and play a lot more hands when playing short-handed. It is true that you will be playing a lot more hands but you absolutely don't need to loosen up! At a short-handed table, you should generally play the same as at a full table, based on the number of people left to act. If I am playing four-handed and I am first to act, I play the same as I would at a nine-handed table where the first five players folded. The only difference is that four players with unplayable hands have folded in one case. This has only a slight effect on the hands you are likely to be up against, which I generally ignore.

Stealing near the bubble—You need to be aware of chip positions, especially when you get close to the money. You lose very little value by folding marginal hands because a lot of hands are close in value. Why would you, with a short stack, want to play a pot when you are close to the money? Say you have a 51 percent chance of winning 1,000 and a 49 percent chance of losing 1,000. If you have 1,000 in chips, you're not getting the right odds in this situation. Even if you had a 55 percent chance, you wouldn't be getting the right odds, when you can hang around a little longer to make the money.

Because the short stacks don't want to get getting involved in pots, the big stacks can put a lot of pressure on them, even more than they can in hold 'em.

If you, as the big stack, put pressure on the short stack and lose, you soon may become the short stack. Then you have to switch gears, but it's worth a try anyway.

This applies only when you are very close to the money, or at a time after making it into the money where sticking around is especially valuable such as when there is a large increase in the pay-out. As a big stack, you can apply a lot of pressure. As a short stack, you can't take a lot of pressure.

Short-stacked—If you make a pot-sized bet and your opponent can make a pot-sized reraise to put you all-in, you are definitely short-stacked. That amounts to about twelve times the big blind. With a stack about this size you can get pot-committed very quickly. At stack sizes less than about eighteen times the big blind, you should evaluate your starting hands in a slightly different way. You want big cards. You still don't mind a straight hand like 8-7-6-5, but you don't have to worry about making hard decisions later in the hand. You can get all or almost all your chips in the pot while you are probably the favorite. You also have a chance to win the hand with the raise and pick up the blinds.

If you are short-stacked, you still want to raise with the straight hands, but you aren't as anxious to get yourself pot-committed if you can help it. Part of the value of those hands is in being able to outplay your opponents after the flop. That is obviously not going to happen if there is no more betting. You won't like getting reraised—you'd love that with high cards—but that's okay. If you have to get all your chips in, you are giving yourself a decent chance. The straight hands play well against big cards—just not as well as when there is post-flop betting.

If you are already facing a raise, you want to reraise with big cards. With a straight hand, you are more likely to just call the raise. All the reasons why big cards and pairs can get you in trouble become less important. You don't have to worry about making difficult decisions later in the hand. You can get all your chips in (or be pot-committed) while you are probably the favorite.

With a small stack, a pair of aces is a really good starting hand, as is a pair of kings. High pairs go up in value. You don't have to worry about whether to make a tough call on a later street. 7-8-9-T is much better than most hands with K-K, but a lot of the value of 7-8-9-T comes from decisions you make after the flop. When you are all-in, you don't get that benefit with the straight hands anymore.

Conclusion

You have to be willing to gamble to succeed in pot-limit Omaha. The hands are closer in value and it is harder to bet people out of the pot. You need to be willing to put pressure on your opponents when you have the slightest of advantages. You also need to be willing to call reraises frequently before the flop. If you recognize this and make plays that both maximize your chances that opponents will fold and get your chips in as a favorite, you should do very well in the long run.

PART IV

TOURNAMENT STUD

CHAPTER 15

Seven-Card Stud: Tournament Hands

by Keith Sexton

Playable Hands on Third Street

Often the biggest decision you'll make in a hand of seven-stud is whether you're going to put any money in the pot on third street, or whether you're just going to throw the hand away right there. When I play a hand of seven-card stud, I'm looking for a hand on third street that falls into one of the following general categories:

- *Small and medium pairs*—This includes all hands that contain a pair, 2-2 through 9-9.
- *Big pairs*—I consider T-T and up a big pair.
- *Rolled-up trips*—These don't come around too often, but when I start on third street with three of a kind, I'm obviously playing.
- *Three flushes/three straights*—Drawing hands are often playable.
- *Three big cards*—Here, I am looking for cards that give me high-pair and straight possibilities.

In the remainder of this chapter, I will show you when and how I like to play these hands on third street. Then I will go on to describe some typical situations that come up with each of these hands on later streets and show how you should think through and react to what you're seeing.

For the most part, the advice here will work for both cash games and tournaments. Most of the time, the best play in a stud ring game would be the best play in a stud tournament. But there are exceptions, and I'll make note of some of these as I go through the chapter. Also, my friend David Grey—who is a fantastic stud player—in chapter 16 explains the differences between stud cash games and tournaments and also points out how some hand values change over the course of a tournament.

Small and Medium Pairs

The first thing to consider when looking at 2-2 through 9-9 is whether all of your cards are live. Say I have 6-6-4 and one of my sixes is out. As far as I'm concerned, that hand is complete garbage. I'll normally just throw it away. Even if one of the fours is dead, I normally muck the hand. So the first consideration is whether all of your cards are live. If they're not, look to muck it right there.

Usually with a small or medium pair, if my cards are live I want to see what develops. When I have 6-6 and I'm in early position with a couple of overcards showing behind me, I will usually call the bring-in (limp) and see what happens. If there is a single raise behind me, I'm going to call that raise and see what comes on fourth street. If there is a raise and a reraise after I limp, I'll fold. But if there is a single raise before the action gets to me, I'll usually call the raise and go from there.

These are general guidelines. At times you will need to think very carefully about whether you should put money in on third street. For example, if a very tight player raises with a king in early position, you may think twice about giving him action with a small pair. Or if there is a raise in front of you and some big cards and aggressive players behind you, you may consider mucking for the single raise. In some of the more complex situations, there are a few factors I consider before I decide how and if I'm going to play my hand. These include my kicker, my position, whether the pair is split or concealed, and the previous action.

The kicker—The quality of my kicker will often help me decide whether to play a small or medium pair. A bad kicker may push me toward a quick fold. For example, say that I am in early position with (6-3)-6. (For the purpose of this chapter, I will put the hole cards in parentheses. A hand with X-X is simply displaying what the hand looks like to my opponents or, in the case of my opponents' cards, to me.) I look around the table and see 8-T-Q-A. If there are a bunch of very aggressive players at the table holding these cards, I'll usually just muck my hand right here.

But other kickers will push me toward playing the hand. A good kicker is one that gives me two of a suit and is connected to my paired cards. So if I have 6♣6♦, I'd feel pretty good about having the seven of diamonds or the five of clubs as a kicker. I'll definitely limp from early position with big cards behind me so that I can see what develops, or I'll call a single raise. You would be surprised how often you hit running cards of your suit or connected cards, and then by fifth street you have a pair and a nice draw—which is a pretty big hand. Note that I'm never calling two raises cold with 6-6 and any sort of low kicker.

When starting with a medium pair, a high kicker also has a lot of value. If I start with 6-6-A and all my cards are live, then I'm definitely looking to play the hand beyond third street. I'll have no problem calling a raise with this hand, and if I'm in favorable position, I'll look to complete myself.

I'm still not going to call two bets cold with 6-6-A. There are pros who believe you can call two bets with that sort of hand, but I'm not in favor of it, and for beginning and intermediate players, mucking the medium or small pair for two bets is almost certainly the best play.

Split versus hidden pair—A hidden pair is a far better hand than a split pair. To understand why, consider how the hand is likely to play out if you make trips. If you have (9-7)-7 and play beyond third street, your opponents are going to suspect that you have what you appear to have—a pair of sevens. When you make trips on fifth street (showing X-X-7-Q-7), you'll have the lead and will bet out and at that point, about 90 percent of the time, your opponents are going to fold. So if you have a split pair and make trips, you will not win a big pot most of the time. But if you start with a hidden pair like (7-7)-9 and make trips on fifth, your board looks less dangerous (X-X-9-Q-7) and now you have a chance to get in some good raises and win a nice pot, as others will have a hard time putting you on trips. And if you do happen to pair your door card and bet, you have a chance to get a player with an overpair to fold.

When to raise with middle/low pairs—There are situations when a medium or small pair is worth a raise. When I'm in middle position and there's only one up card higher than my pair behind me, I'm going to go ahead and complete. So if I'm in middle position on third street with (6-7)-6 and behind me I see two fours and a ten, then I'm going to raise. If I get reraised by the ten, I'll just call and see what develops by fifth street. In this kind of situation I'll usually raise even if a six is dead. However, if I complete with my 6-6 while one of them is dead and a tight player reraises me, I'm not going to even call the extra bet; I'll just muck it right there.

Playing a Small or Medium Pair Beyond Third Street

I can't cover every possible scenario you'll encounter beyond third street, but to give you an idea of the decision-making process, I'm going to go over some of the more typical situations that come up with 2-2 through 9-9.

When you both catch rags on fourth street—To start with, say that I have (7♦6♦)7♣, and that I called an opponent's raise on third street from a player who had a queen up. On fourth street, I'm going to be calling a bet almost 90 percent of the time. Even if he had the queen of diamonds and caught the king of diamonds—a card that seems to be a perfect match with his hand—I will call and take another card off and see what happens. About the only time I am folding on fourth street is if he hits an open pair. If we both hit what appear to be blanks—which is the most likely scenario—then I will definitely call if he bets.

Let's say that on fourth street, I catch a ten of hearts to go with my (7♦6♦)7♣ and my opponent gets a four of spades to go with his queen of diamonds. Clearly, I will call if he leads. If he checks, though, now I have a decision, and I'm relying on my feel for this opponent. If I feel he's weak—that he missed on some hand with three high cards or three of one suit—then I'll bet. If I feel he is looking for a check-raise, then I'll check. Most of the time, I'm going to bet here.

Fifth street with random boards—Now assume on fifth street that neither of us catch a card that appears to offer any help. I have

and my opponent, who raised on third street and bet on fourth, shows

He bets again on fifth. Now I'm facing what I think is the toughest decision in all of seven-stud—what to do on fifth with a small pair against an opponent who bet on fourth and fifth. If this happened in the third level of a World Series $1,500 stud event, there would be at least 230 in the pot after the other player bets and I would have to decide whether to call 60. (At the 30-60 level, antes are 5 and the bring-in is 10, so the pot would contain 40 [antes] + 10 [bring-in] + 60 [third street raise and my call] + 60 [fourth street action] + 60 [my opponent's fifth street bet].) By this point, there are quite a few chips in the pot, and I hate to just leave it to someone who may not even have me beat. But the problem is that if I call on fifth, I'm definitely going to call on sixth street, unless he makes an open pair bigger than my pair. And if he's got the heart to bet on seventh street, I will call there as well, even if my sixes haven't improved. There are almost no circumstances where I would call on fifth street and fold on sixth or seventh. So when I make the call on fifth, I am committing to three big bets, which is a lot of chips. In a tournament, those bets can be crucial to maintaining your stack. (To call down from fifth street, I have to pay 180 chips, to win 350.)

So how do I make the decision as to whether to call or not? In a tournament I'm more likely to throw away the hand. But in a cash game, and even in tournaments, I'm looking to get some feel for where I stand. I'll look at dead cards. If I caught a four on fifth street and I remember that two fours were folded on third, then I'm more likely to fold. However, if he catches that four and all my cards are live, then I'm going to lean toward continuing with the hand. As you're learning stud, the liveness of your cards and your opponents' cards should be an important factor in determining whether or not you're going to call on fifth street. If you're very live, and he is showing dead cards or less-than-live cards, then I think it's appropriate to call even in a tournament.

I'm also looking at my suits. If I've picked up a three flush, I'd lean toward continuing. If I didn't and my opponent picked up a card suited to his door card, that could push me to fold.

As David explains in chapter 16, surviving and maintaining your chip stack has a value that doesn't exist in cash games. That is why I am less likely to call down a medium pair in a tournament, but those tournament issues may not concern me much if the limits are small relative to my stack.

Fifth street, when an opponent catches two high cards—Using the same example of (7-6)-7, you get a deuce and your opponent gets a ten on fourth street. Then on fifth, you get a three and he gets a king. This is an easy fold if he bets into you. Even if you happen to be ahead at this point, you're a very small favorite, which makes this a very tough situation.

Sixth and seventh streets with a middle pair—As I already mentioned, the big decision comes on fifth street. If you call on fifth, unless your opponent picks up an open pair higher than your pair, you need to continue. Using the example from the previous section, it costs you 120 to call bets on the last two streets, to win 410, so you are getting nearly 5-to-1. If you catch yourself folding on sixth street in seven-card stud, then you're playing bad. When I grew up playing, if a guy folded on sixth street and nobody made a bigger pair than he had, then you knew he called on five with no pair or no draw. And you kind of snickered to yourself because you knew the guy was out of line.

And if you call on sixth, you need to put in the final bet on seventh. At that point, you are getting great odds to pick off a bluff. Using the same betting amounts, calling the bet on the end costs you 60 and the pot is 470, or almost 9-to-1. You have to call at the end even if all you can beat is a bluff.

When you catch a scare card on fourth street—Sometimes you will catch a card on fourth street that could really put some fear into your opponent, even if he has a hand like a big pair. Say you start with the same (7♦6♦)7♣ and your opponent raised with the queen of diamonds as his up card. Now on fourth street he gets a card totally unrelated to what he's showing, like the three of spades, and you catch the eight of clubs. Now you can think about playing the hand as though you've picked up a monster draw. If he checks, you can definitely bet. If he check-raises, you want to call.

If he bets out on fourth showing X-X-Q♦3♠ and you show X-X-7♣8♣, take stock of the player before you act. If the player is weak—the type you can push around and force into a fold on fifth street—consider raising. However, there's also a very good reason not to raise here. When a novice player bets out with Q♦3♠ after you caught a card that seems to match your hand perfectly, then you have to give a weak or inexperienced opponent more credit for having the hand he is representing. You can more confidently put this guy on Q-Q, a hand that he is not going to give up on so easily. It is far less likely that he started with three spades or T-J-Q. For this reason, I will frequently just call my opponent's bet.

There are players who will raise every time they show something like 7♣8♣ on fourth street. But the scary thing about that play is that a good player—or even an average player—will reraise in that spot, making you put in three bets when you have nothing more than 6-6. After all this action on the turn, there's no chance that you will bluff your opponent off the pot. He will see all that money in there and be committed to seeing it through to the end.

However, if he checks to you in this situation, you must bet. You have an opportunity to take down the pot right there, and you can't let that opportunity pass you by. If he calls and catches a blank on fifth street, you should bet again. I think betting on fifth is crucial, because in my opinion, the worst thing you can do in stud is fail to bet when that bet would have won you the pot. Don't worry about being check-raised. It happens. Getting check-raised isn't as bad as missing out on a chance to win a pot, especially when you're holding a hand as vulnerable as 6-6.

Fifth street with a heavy-drawing board—Now let's move forward with this hand, where you picked up a connected card on fourth. Say that you pick up a card that gives you a pair and an open-ended straight draw on fifth. You have

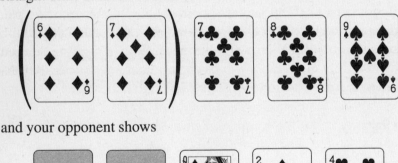

and your opponent shows

He raised on third, bet out on fourth, and then bet again on fifth. You can pretty well assume that your opponent has a pair of queens, but even still, this is a spot where you definitely want to raise. There are a few reasons for that. First, a pair and an open-ended straight draw is a slight favorite over a higher pair, and you want to push your advantages. Second, 99 percent of the time, the player with queens is just going to call your raise. If he happens to have trips or two pair, he may reraise, but that's okay, because you still have a solid draw. But if he has only a pair, he is probably going to call and then check on sixth street. At that point, you can check behind and take a free card if you don't improve.

Another good reason to raise here is that you really don't know exactly what your opponent has. If he had something like 7-7, he may look at your board and decide it's not worth it, and just dump. So you will have gotten a better hand to fold.

You also might hit something that gives you an open pair on sixth street. Say you catch an eight on sixth. You raised on fifth, then picked up an open pair and bet out with a board that shows

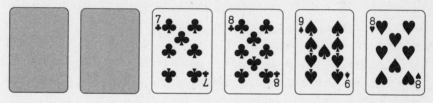

He's got to think, "Did he have a straight, or stumble into two pair, and now he filled up?" A lot of guys, myself included, might just fold queens there. It would be a mistake, because I'd be getting the right odds to take one off and try to catch two pair on the river. But that board is just too scary for a lot of players to continue.

Big Pairs

When I talk about big pairs, I'm referring to T-T, J-J, Q-Q, K-K, and A-A. If a queen or a king raises in early position, before the action gets to you, then you can treat T-T and Q-Q more like medium pairs. If you have a ten up on third street, and it's the highest card showing, then you treat it like a big pair. In the following discussion, if I don't say otherwise, assume I am talking about playing split big pairs. Following that, I will discuss how I like to play hidden big pairs, which is a bit differently.

Playing a split big pair on third street—Generally, the idea with a big pair is to play it in a straightforward way. Say I have a split K-K.

If I am the first one to act, I am going to raise. If someone raises before me, I am going to reraise. The common exception to this is if someone with an ace raises in front of me. In that case, I'll just call.

The idea behind playing big pair so aggressively is that you want to narrow the field. I prefer to play my big pair against just one or two opponents. When several people are in there against your high pair, you usually need to make a pretty big hand in order to win the pot. K-K doesn't win frequently in a four-way pot.

When the third street raise fails to narrow the field—Here is a situation that sometimes comes up with big pairs: Say there's a limper to me and I complete with my king showing. Three people, including the limper, call my raise. Now on fourth street I want to make a quick judgment as to what my best play is—whether I want to bet or look to check-raise. There are two advantages to the check-raise if I can get it in: first, it allows me to get more money in the pot while I am ahead, and second, it helps me narrow the field and knock out some of the drawing hands.

To get in that check-raise, I have to analyze what my opponents have caught. If it appears that no one caught a card that would have helped them—if they're not connected in any way to the door card—then I will abandon the check-raise idea and just go ahead and bet. I would hate to see it checked around, because giving a free card when so many people are probably on draws would be a very big mistake. You need to give these players a chance to fold when they don't connect.

When the player to my immediate left appears to have improved, I will bet again on fifth street. Let's say that he had a seven of diamonds on third street and caught a five of diamonds on fourth. Again, in this spot I would lead out and bet. I want to give this guy a chance to raise and make it very expensive for the rest of the field, particularly if the other players didn't appear to catch anything.

But now let's say that on fourth street the board looks like this (with the order-to-act on fifth street being me, player 1, player 2, player 3):

Me:

Player 1:

Player 2:

Player 3:

In this spot, I think I've got a pretty good chance of getting in a check-raise. If player 3 caught a four flush or four straight, which seems likely, he will probably bet because he wants to get some money in the pot while he has a big draw. Plus, he would want to prevent players 1 and 2 from catching helpful cards. When player 3 does bet, that is the perfect time for a check-raise. At that point, the other players in the hand will probably have to fold.

The check-raise on fourth is a very important play, and it's one you should be on the lookout for.

Fifth street against a large field—After check-raising or betting out on fourth street, you need to stay aggressive on fifth. So bet. At this point, you will almost certainly lose at least one of the other players, as someone will have failed to connect with his draw.

Don't look for the check-raise play on fifth street. At that point, the chances are too good that your hand is no longer best. Just bet and see what happens.

When an opponent makes an open pair in a multiway pot—When an opponent makes an open pair, you are going to lose the lead. How you should react to the open pair will depend on whether the opponent paired his door card or hit a running pair. Say one player called on third street with a five, and by fifth street his hand is X-X-5♥9♦5♣. He is probably going to bet out. At this point, I'm probably going to just call his bet. There is too much money in the pot for me to just give up. I've got to hope that he's got something other than trips. But I wouldn't put in a raise in this spot. It is tempting to try to narrow the field by raising, but the chances are too good that the open pair will three-bet, which would be terrible.

However, when an opponent hits a running pair, I'm going to consider raising with my kings if he bets out. In a four-way pot, where one opponent shows X-X-5-9-9 and bets, I may raise to narrow the field. At that point I'm going to assume that he's got something like two pair, nines and fives. Even though I'm behind, I have decent odds against that hand. And I would hate to give the straight or flush draws behind me good value on a call.

When fifth street improves more than one opponent—Usually, I'm going to stick with my kings to the river. (Remember the tournament math I shared earlier: I will get 5-to-1 to call on sixth and 9-to-1 on the end, or even better odds when there is additional dead money or raising on some streets.) In general, things are going to have to get pretty bad for me to fold. But there are circumstances when things look so scary that I may just dump the hand on fifth street. For instance, say that on fifth street my split kings have not improved. One of my opponents paired his door card and is showing X-X-5-9-5 and another player in the hand now has X-X-Q♦6♦8♦. The guy with open fives bets into me. Now I've really got to think he caught trips. He'd have to be a maniac or a fool to bet into two players—one representing kings, the other with a possible flush—without a big hand.

Even if this player doesn't have trips, I have to be very concerned about the other guy in the pot. If I call a bet on fifth, I could very well get raised if the other player is aggressive and caught a flush or even a pair and a four flush. In this spot, I may look at the board, remember that I put in only two small bets, and decide to fold. I would definitely be more inclined to fold in a tournament than I would in a cash game.

Playing a big pair heads-up—Normally, when I have kings and I'm playing heads-up, I'm going to be betting all the way, including seventh street. I'm going to assume that I've got the best hand until my opponent gives me a reason to think otherwise. But there are times when my opponent will signal that he has a better hand. For example, say I have my split kings and I bet on fifth street. My opponent then raises with a board showing X-X-6-8-9. At that point I will just call and see what comes out on sixth. If he gets a five or a ten and appears to have made a straight, I'm going to check to him, with the idea of calling him down on sixth and seventh. However, if he gets something that doesn't seem to help his hand, like a queen, then I'm going to lead out again on sixth street because I don't want to give a free card to someone who has nothing but a draw.

If I get raised on sixth, I have to assume that I'm behind, but I'm still going to call my opponent down and hope that I make two pair or trips on the river—and hope that it's good.

It may seem that you ought to fold a pair of kings when things have gone that badly, but you have to remember that this is limit poker, and by the river you will be getting odds of at least 9-to-1. There are maniacs in the world, and fools. Occasionally, someone will be raising on a very powerful straight and flush draw. After missing on the river, he will bet because he knows it's the only way he can pick up the pot. The bottom line is that you'll catch someone getting out of line frequently enough to make calling on the river the right play.

But they refer to it as a "crying call" for a reason.

When you hit an open pair—If you raise with a big pair and then hit an open pair on fourth street, there's really no point in trying to be deceptive. If you make something like open queens after raising on third street and then check, you might as well turn your hand over and show him the trips. There's simply no way any reasonable player is going to give you action. Just bet and don't worry about your opponent folding, which is what he is going to do most of the time. All you can really hope for is that he has a big pair in the hole and is feeling stubborn.

In fact, I'm going to bet out my open pair on fourth street no matter what I have in the hole. Say I called a raise from a king, showing a five of clubs and two more clubs in the hole, and I pick up a five of diamonds on the turn. I am going to lead out there. I may force a guy who started with three big cards to fold right there, or I may get a weak player to fold K-K.

This play is even more likely to work in tournaments than in cash games. People are more likely to lay down hands, especially when they have below-average chips and the limits are getting steep. The exception is when they are very short-stacked. The player with just a couple bets left in his stack and no pair may fold, but a player in that situation with K-K is definitely not folding. Other than that specific situation, take the opportunity when you hit an open pair to play it aggressively.

Playing a hidden big pair—When I start with a hidden big pair, my third street play is going to be determined by a couple of things: the previous action and my up card. When I have a small up card, like (K-K)-4, then I may have the opportunity to play the hand deceptively. So if a jack raises and it's folded to me in late position, then I'm likely to just call and conceal the true strength of my hand. At that point, I am probably going to be playing the hand heads-up, and I like having the opportunity to keep my opponent in the dark about my hand.

The situation changes some if there is a raise and a call to me. At that point, I'm probably going to reraise, even though it lets everyone know exactly what my hand is. If it is folded to me in late position, I'm going to raise, because I could have a lot of hands other than a hidden big pair.

An interesting situation comes up when it's raised in front of me but there are still a lot of players behind me. At that point, if I look around the table and see an ace and a queen behind me, I will definitely just call. I'm hoping that the queen will reraise and I will get a lot of money in the pot as a nice favorite on third street. If I get a reraise from an ace, then I will probably call and see what develops, knowing that I could be against a bigger pair.

The situation is quite different when I have a big door card, like (K-K)-Q or (K-K)-A. When I'm showing these sorts of cards, then I will play the hand as I would if I had a split pair of that rank.

Hidden pair on later streets—The best situation you can find yourself in with a hidden big pair is when a big card, like a jack, raises on third street and you call in late position with a little card showing. Playing heads-up, you both catch cards that don't seem to help on fourth. At that point, when your opponent bets again, just call. Wait for the big bet on fifth street to put in the raise.

If you're in a multiway pot, it is best to play a hidden big pair fast. After third street, a hidden big pair will play similarly to split big pair.

Rolled-Up Trips

I don't usually slow-play rolled-up trips, especially low trips. In the past I've found out that you get burned pretty badly by doing that. You start with rolled-up threes, fours, or fives, and you slow-play. Then down the road someone pairs his door card and you end up losing a really big pot.

Normally, I play rolled-up trips, especially small ones, as I would a hidden big pocket pair. The same sort of dynamics apply as when you have a hidden big pair. If I have, for instance, rolled-up threes, I might call an early-position raise, limp if I'm the first one in the pot, or reraise if there has been a raise and a call to me. Like with hidden kings, the play depends largely on the position, previous action, and the door cards. When you reraise with a three up, everyone is going to put you on a big pocket pair, so you might as well raise and let them believe you have A-A in the hole. That way, if they catch two pair, they will definitely call you down. On the occasions when I do decide to slow-play on third street, I'm definitely going to get aggressive on the turn. I'm hoping that I catch a suited or connected card, and when I raise on the turn, people are going to put me on some kind of draw. Even if the card isn't connected to my door card, I'm still going to raise. I don't want someone hitting his door card without me ever putting in a raise.

Big rolled-up trips are easier to slow-play. You don't mind letting someone catch their door card in that case, because if they do, you are likely to take a very big pot off of them. But there is also an advantage to playing rolled-up big cards fast. If there is a raise and a call to me on third street and I have a king showing, I might just raise it there. My opponents will likely put me on a pair and give me action appropriate for that hand, especially if I've played a big pair like that before.

It's true that by playing fast you may just win a very small pot. But you can't worry about that too much. If no one started with a hand, then you wouldn't have won much anyway. By playing fast you give yourself the opportunity to win a big pot.

When to slow down with rolled-up trips—There are only a couple of situations where you might slow down and not play your trips too aggressively. The most common occurs when an opponent hits his door card. Say that a player with a jack raised on third and you called with rolled-up threes. Then he bets on the turn, and you raise. He calls, then makes open jacks on fifth street and bets. There is really no good reason to raise there. First off, there is a pretty good chance you're behind, and you will be looking at a reraise. Also, if you do raise, you are telling him exactly what you have. He will be certain that you can beat J-J, and he may decide to get rid of his hand.

When you get to sixth street, if the player with open jacks checks, you have to bet. You don't want to give a free card, and there is a very good chance the player has a lesser hand that he will call you with. Note that a savvy player will look to check-raise you in that spot. He will realize that you have a strong hand—one that you need to bet if it is checked to you. But that will happen sometimes, and you really can't worry about it too much.

You should definitely look for these sorts of check-raising opportunities yourself. If you bet something like X-X-J-9-J and are called by a player who doesn't seem to be on a draw, then you know he must have a pretty strong hand—certainly better than one pair of jacks. That's a great spot to get in a check-raise.

The other time when I might slow down is if an opponent appears to have hit a straight or flush draw. If an opponent has X-X-8–9-T-Q showing on sixth street and raises when I bet, I'm just going to call and hope to fill up on the river. If I've got the high hand, I'll probably check again on seventh street and call his bet. There is essentially no way I'm going to fold rolled-up trips on the river, for the reasons I gave earlier.

Three Big Cards

Something like A-K-Q or K-Q-J is a pretty good hand, but obviously it is a hand that needs help. If and how I play this sort of hand depends on the previous action and what cards are exposed around me. When an ace raises, I will throw away three big cards. Very little good can happen in that spot. I might hit a pair of kings on the turn, and lose a lot of money calling down A-A. Plus, it's pretty tough for me to hit a straight with K-Q-J when my opponent holds A-A.

If I am in middle position and a queen raises in front of me, I will likely call the raise with a hand like A-K-J and see what develops. But I will call only if my cards are live. If two or more of my cards are out, I'm going to just fold right there.

Getting aggressive with big cards—When I'm in late position and it is folded to me, I will raise every time. This creates some good opportunities to steal antes or to put pressure on a player who calls with a marginal hand, like split 6-6. In that sort of situation, I stay aggressive and apply pressure on fourth and fifth streets. Of course, you need to pay attention to the cards that he catches. But as I discussed earlier, playing small and middle pairs makes for some tough decisions. With a king or a queen as your door card, if you play it aggressively through fifth street, you will force a lot of folds, especially in tournaments.

I sometimes reraise with three big cards on third street. For example, if a player raises with a jack and I have a king showing and all the other up cards are low, I will often reraise. There are a couple of good reasons to reraise. First, some good things can happen on later streets. I could make a high pair or pick up a straight draw. But it's also important to show people that you are capable of reraising with hands other than a high pocket pair. If you only throw in a reraise when you have a pair of aces, kings, or queens, you can be sure that people are going to take note of that and they are not going to give you any action when you get aggressive. You can't be a winning player in a tough game if you get no action.

This applies more in cash games than tournaments. Don't completely discount it, but consider the reasons against doing it in a tournament. First off, with chips being so precious, I'm not going to want to put chips in the pot with king high. And often in tournaments, you don't need to craft an image that will get you action—you just want to pick up small pots where you can get them. If the structure of the tournament allows for a lot of play and you think you can benefit from an "action" image early without costing very many chips, you can think about it.

Later streets with three big cards—Say that I reraised on third street with (A♦Q♠)K♥ after a player with a jack showing completed. At this point, my opponent is probably putting me on kings, and I'm going to play it like I have kings for a street or two. My exact action will be dictated by what cards we catch on the later streets.

When I get something like the two of spades, a terrible card that doesn't help me at all, and he also picks up a card that looks like a blank, like an off-suit four, I will usually check on fourth street. Often, a weak opponent will be scared to bet there; he's afraid that I'm looking to check-raise and will give a free card. The problem with betting in this spot is that the card I caught isn't going to scare him at all. There is almost no chance that a bet will win you the pot.

Fifth street with high cards—If I catch another blank, I will check again. If he bets, I will concede the pot. At that point the table will know for sure that I was reraising with a king and not much else, and that should get me some action down the line.

I will play it quite differently when I hit something that appears to help my hand. On fourth street, if I catch any big card or any card that matches my suit, I'll bet out. Most likely, the other player will call. If fifth street brings no help to me, I will usually check. In a cash game, there is just very little chance that a player who called with jacks is going to surrender at that point. In a tournament, there might be more of a chance to force a fold, especially if a player was getting short on chips. (Even then, if the player is short enough, he has already decided he is taking his jacks to the showdown.) But generally, I think it is best to check on fifth street if you haven't gotten any help. You would be surprised how many people will be scared of the check-raise and will give the free card in that situation.

On those occasions when I do hit a card that helps on fourth or fifth street—any pair, or even a high card that gives me a straight draw— I am going to play the hand as I would a big pair. Aggressively.

Three Flushes

There are two important things to look at when deciding whether to play a three flush on third street—the number of your suit that are out and the size of your cards. I won't call a raise on third street with three medium and low cards if I look around and see that more than one card of my suit is out. However, if I have (A♥K♥)4♥ and two hearts are exposed, I usually will call a raise if my ace and king are bigger than any up card on the board.

When my three flush seems playable, I'm looking to get in as cheaply as possible. I will limp and call a raise. Or if there is a raise in front of me, I'll call and see what comes on fourth street. I will not call two raises with a three flush.

When you miss on the turn—It is a huge mistake to chase flushes if you don't make a pair or a four flush on fourth street. Your odds of making the flush are no longer very good, and if you do happen to pick up a four flush on fifth street, you can lose a lot of chips trying to hit.

When you hit your four flush on the turn—When you have a four flush on the turn and your cards are live, you are almost always going to see the hand through to the river. You definitely want to call bets on every street as you try to make your hand. The only time you might fold on fourth street is if there's a bet and a raise before the action gets to you. It's not only an extra bet there, but the threat of being caught between raises on every street that you don't make your draw. (Ted Forrest has a great expression for this in chapter 17 on stud-eight-or-better: taking the gas pipe.)

Four flush in a multiway pot—There are many situations where it's best to play the four flush very aggressively. For example, say that a king raised on third street and was called by a ten, and I called with (Q♥9♥)4♥. On the turn I pick up the seven of hearts. The king bets and the ten calls. It would be criminal to just call in this spot. If my opponents have what I suspect—a pair of kings and a pair of tens—I will win that pot over 50 percent of the time, so I've got great equity in the pot. The guy with the tens is in a whole lot of trouble and I want to make him pay for being there. This is called "punishing the hitchhiker." If the kings reraise and the tens come along, I will raise again. In fact, I will reraise even if the tens fold. I'm a slight favorite against a higher pair at this point, so I might as well get as much money in the pot as I can.

When you are in a multiway pot and out of position on the turn, you need to decide how aggressive you want to be. Sometimes it's best to just call a bet and let the other players in the hand so they can build a nice pot. But often I like to raise, even if there are players behind. More frequently than you would think, players will call the two bets cold. You have to look at the cards around you and ask yourself, "How do I play this so I can get the most money possible in this pot?" Don't be scared to be aggressive in this spot. The other players are probably going to put you on a four flush anyway, so it is usually best to raise.

Fifth and sixth street plays—How you play on the later streets depends on what cards you catch. If you miss completely and are facing a bet, then you are going to call and try to hit your hand. But if you make a pair to go with the flush draw, you should usually lead at the pot or raise if someone bets into you. A pair and a draw is a favorite against an overpair on fifth street, so go ahead and put in a raise.

Conclusion

In seven-card stud tournaments, solid play is usually going to work out pretty well. Every time you play a hand, you have to start with a plan, based on your hand, your opponents' perception of your hand, and their hands. Even more than in cash games, you have to avoid losing a big hand, even if it occasionally costs you a chance to win more with your good hands. But if you play aggressively, get away from the riskiest situations on fifth street, misdirect some opponents into folding, and press your advantage on the later streets, you can build your stack.

CHAPTER 16

Seven-Card Stud: Tournament Strategy

by David Grey

I have made my living gambling since I moved to Las Vegas in 1985. I have played poker the whole time, starting in $15-$30 stud games at Caesars Palace, moving up, and then playing bigger games when the Mirage, and then the Bellagio, opened. I've played in the biggest games in the world for most of that time, and though the games are almost always mixed games, I started as a stud player and I still think it's the best form of poker for skillful players to make money from less skilled players.

Having played high-stakes cash games for so long, I originally played tournaments, like many cash-game players, because big tournaments had the biggest side action. It wasn't unusual for the guys to bust out of an event at the World Series or the Hall of Fame and start a cash game where the big winner made more than the winner of that event. I had some success in tournaments, winning a Hall of Fame watch (in limit hold 'em) and a World Series bracelet (in seven-card stud). I was proud to win those events, but that wasn't how I made my living. I was working at winning regularly against very good professionals and amateurs in high-stakes cash games and, back then, sports betting.

Poker has changed so much in the last few years that I, like all the other players in my game, had to reevaluate. Tournaments are so big that winning one is a huge windfall. In addition, the publicity and recognition—once something professional gamblers *avoided*—are now worth endorsements and other opportunities.

So I'm playing more tournaments now. I finished eighth in the Main Event in 2003 and won my second World Series bracelet (in no-limit deuce-to-seven) in 2005. Every time I place a bet, I do it to win, so I take tournaments very seriously. Because I still think of myself sometimes as a stud player, and I have had some success in stud tournaments, I have some idea of how to do well and give myself a chance to win.

This is not meant to be a comprehensive guide to how to play stud, or even how to play stud tournaments. It is my approach to seven-card stud tournaments. Understanding how tournaments differ from cash games and how tournament stud differs from tournament hold 'em leads to how I make a lot of my decisions in stud tournaments. That style of play is not significantly different from my general approach to cash games, so I know how to make it work. Maybe it can help you develop a winning style for seven-card stud tournaments.

How Tournaments—Especially in Stud—Differ from Cash Games

In the early rounds of a tournament, you should generally play similar to the way you would play in a cash game, because the limits are low compared to the size of your stack. At the World Series in 2006, there were two seven-card stud events. In the $5,000 buy-in event, players started with 5,000 in chips and limits were 50-100. In the $1,500 buy-in event, the limits at the first level were 10-20. At these early limits, playing a good, normal, solid strategy is correct.

In the later stages of a tournament, however, there are fewer players and the size of the bets is big compared with the size of the stacks. In cash games, basic strategy dictates that you get the correct price from the pot for the strength of your hand. You can continue with a hand that is likely to lose if you are getting the right price.

That is *not* the way to approach the later levels of a seven-card stud tournament. If you have an average stack, you don't necessarily want to play a pot with a guy who raises with a king showing when you have a six up and T-T in the hole. In a cash game, you may call and decide to fold on fifth street if you don't get help and you think by then that the other player probably has another king in the hole. After the first few levels, you can't afford to lose a full pot in a tournament and still have relative chip strength. You are definitely looking to play a top hand and move on people you think have nothing.

Say there are fifteen players left in the tournament. A player in early position with an ace or king showing raises. You probably don't want to play T-T unless you have some exceptional circumstances in your favor—he's almost all-in, you have a huge stack, you are pretty sure he is stealing, etcetera. Every position is worth money and so is every chip here.

In a tournament, unlike a cash game, you can make money by folding. In a cash game, you never make money by folding. In a tournament, however, folding and letting somebody else go broke makes you money. By doing nothing, you benefit from other players' failures.

Depending on the type of tournament you are playing and the payout scale, it may make sense to just get out of the way and let other people go broke. In a particular tournament, twelfth through fifteenth could pay one amount and ninth through eleventh could pay more, but just a little more. In that situation, you don't worry about jostling for position. But if you get to a spot where the payout jumps substantially, you may turn down a playable hand (especially one that the pot odds might suggest you pursue but where you could be an underdog) to let someone else bust.

It also depends on your goals. If you regularly play tournaments, you need to make final tables and finish in the top three spots every so often to show a profit. It may be worth giving up a few thousand dollars for finishing one spot higher to take a shot at picking up enough chips to put yourself in position to finish much higher. But if you don't play regularly and you won a satellite to get in, the difference between, say, $6,000 if you finish twelfth and $7,900 if you finish eleventh is meaningful when you got in for $150.

You have to divert from solid cash-game strategies involving the value of drawing hands and hands where you are probably an underdog. Even if the pot is laying you the right odds, your chip position and your survival have a value greater than one particular pot. In a cash game, every pot is a separate transaction; that's not so in a tournament.

In a tournament, you are not really trying to catch hidden trips to win a big pot. You want to win pots, and keep from losing pots.

The size of the pots you win isn't as important as simply winning and avoiding losing. In a cash game, you can play 2♥3♥6♥. I might even call two raises with that hand (even though I'm going to tell you how tight I generally play). You can catch a big draw by fifth street or get out. And you can win a huge pot if you hit your draw, especially if you can bring a couple other players all the way to seventh street.

In a tournament, it is too dangerous to catch a four flush and not make it. You can't even call on the river because you can't beat anything. Late in a tournament, you don't want to lose 20,000 of your 40,000 chip stack on a six-high flush draw. In a cash game, you take the loss and play another pot. It has no value outside the parameters of that one pot. In tournaments, everything is related . . . to your survival.

In cash games, when you are playing just for the value of one pot in a session of eight to ten hours, it is almost always right to keep going. Especially on the later streets, the pot is sufficiently big where you are getting the odds to call the last couple bets. But it's not like that in tournaments, where you can seriously impair your chances of winning for the entire "session" (i.e., getting eliminated from the tournament). Your biggest decision toward the end of a seven-card stud tournament is whether to play the hand on third street.

The next most important decision is on fifth street, because (a) that is when the betting limit doubles, and (b) calling that bet makes the pot big enough to where you are almost always making a mistake folding before the end. Therefore, calling on fifth usually commits you to three big bets. (There are exceptions, but pretty rare ones, like if you have 9-9 and your opponent has been leading the whole way and makes open kings on sixth street. You are already beat and probably drawing to two outs—or you are drawing dead.) Whenever possible, you want to make a third street decision that reduces the chances you have to make a difficult decision on fifth street.

In a cash game, every hand stands on its own. In a tournament, it isn't about making the most on every single hand. Sometimes it is about losing the least, especially because losing hurts you more than winning helps—when you're out, you're out.

Early in a tournament, you play it more like a cash game. Winning a big multiway pot with your three low flush cards is huge early on, and you have the starting chips to play that hand to fifth street a couple times and fold, or play it to the end and lose. Even in the early levels, you can't do that a lot without hitting, but you have the chips to make plays like that because you are getting the right price and the right implied odds.

When does it change?

Everything is relative to the number of people in the tournament. Let's say there are a couple hundred people in a tournament and the last three tables make the money. Until you are very close to the money, you should play your normal strategy. You can't worry about getting one person closer to the money when there are fifty players left. Play good, solid strategy. Try to steal when there is a chance to steal the antes. Call in good-value situations.

I have some specific ideas about short-stack play, but until you get close to the money, you are going to usually play your regular game even if it means you go broke. Weighing proper strategy (i.e., playing when the pot offers you the right price) against your survival is difficult, and though I recommend you place a very high value on your survival, you sometimes have to risk going broke. If you play too tight, you can become so low on chips that even winning with your last chips doesn't improve your position.

Assuming you are not in a situation where folding is worthwhile because you move up to a higher payout, it costs you chips every hand you wait. Even if you get that great hand and double up, you could still be too short-stacked to make a difference.

Here is an example from no-limit hold 'em. You are short-stacked with 20,000 chips. Blinds are 2,000-4,000 with a 500 ante. Nine-handed, there is 10,500 in the pot before the flop. You are looking for a chance to make your stand, but you get lousy cards in the big blind and fold to a raise. You still have 15,500 and eight more hands until it's your big blind again. What if just five hands go by before you pick up your double-up hand? You are down to 11,000 and winning brings you up to just 27,000. You have to wait for a double-up hand again, and if you wait just five more hands, you are down to 19,000.

If you went with whatever lousy hand you had in the big blind—which, by the way, was probably good enough to take the 3-to-1 the pot was offering—you would be in much better shape. If you lose, you're out. But if you don't lose, you have 44,500. Now you have enough chips to raise someone out of a hand, and if you get that same double-up hand five hands later, you could have 90,000 and be back in contention.

Realistically speaking, when you get to the later levels of a seven-card stud tournament and you are anteing 500 or 1,000 per hand, you might not pick up anything close to a premium starting hand for twenty hands. Or you could pick up great cards two hands in a row. You just have to play your hands until your chip position is dire.

Stay out of trouble when you can after the first level. If you have average chips and a pair of nines, what do you do when someone with a king or queen raises in a nonsteal position? If you are several levels into the tournament, you may want to pass. Do the math. In the $5,000 buy-in stud event at the World Series, if this happened at the 300-600 level, it will cost you 1,200 to see fifth street. Will this player stop betting if he doesn't improve? Can you afford to drop 1,200 chips to try to pick up another nine or pair your kicker? Can you afford to call the other player down, a total of 2,400 chips from third street to seventh?

There are more bad situations than good situations in poker tournaments. Winning the pot doesn't put you in a much better situation, but losing is devastating. To win the tournament, you have to beat everybody. But you can't beat everybody if you are eliminated. Survival is very important.

That's the fine line you have to walk: giving away some value to survive versus anteing yourself into a position where even if you get your great starting hand, you can't win enough chips to benefit.

How Stud Tournaments Differ from No-Limit Hold 'Em Tournaments

How you succeed in stud tournaments is almost the opposite of how you should play no-limit hold 'em tournaments. In no-limit hold 'em, a lot of successful players play very marginal hands to get lucky flops so they can bust somebody and double up. If they blow their chips that way, they finished 562 out of 800—no big deal when they pay just

80–100 and the big money is in the top three spots. But if they succeed, this is how they get a massive chip stack. With this strategy it's right to play 9♦7♦ for a raise, which you would never do in a cash game. But if you get lucky and catch 8♦6♣2♦, even if the other player has A-A and calls your all-in raise after the flop, you have a lot of cards you can win with. The players who get big stacks this way then take advantage of people trying to hang on for the money.

Except for taking a couple shots early in a tournament, this usually doesn't work at all in stud tournaments. This is limit poker. You can't double up on the guy who has aces or kings. If he sees a bunch of suited or connecting cards—or even if you are camouflaged and your board isn't showing anything—he is going to be suspicious if you try to get in more than one bet on any street. He'll put on the brakes. It's similar to what Howard Lederer explained in chapter 12 about limit hold 'em: you succeed in limit poker by making extra bets with your good hands, and getting away cheaper with your losing hands.

This makes starting-hand selection much more important in limit poker than in no-limit. You tend to go further with a hand in limit games and the big bluff factor isn't there. In no-limit hold 'em, if I raise and the big blind calls, it really doesn't matter what I have or what he has. I am usually going to win the pot because the dealer is going to put down Q-9-4, he'll check, I'll bet, and he'll fold. Of course, if he doesn't fold, everything changes. But most flops miss most players and the bettor who took the lead in that situation usually wins.

In limit poker, and especially in seven-card stud, people are not as dependent on what they catch as on what they already have. Yes, sometimes players have three suited or connecting cards and they either pick up a draw or fold by fifth street. Sometimes they can call a bet with a low pair and see if they catch something. But if an opponent starts with J-J-6, there is a good chance unless you catch some kind of scary board that they are going all the way with that hand. It doesn't matter if you have an ace or king showing. If you have a king showing and catch T-7 and they have a jack showing and catch 6-3, they probably aren't folding on fifth, because you might not have a pair of kings. You could have started the hand with 9-9 in the hole, or three clubs. At the end of a hand, it is hard to bluff someone when there are ten bets in the pot and they have to call just one more.

In no-limit hold 'em you see guys who can win with any two cards. It's different in stud. You can raise with any three cards and you will win some percentage of the time, depending on how tight other players are. But you have to give other players credit for having a hand. They may already have something they are playing through the end, and if they don't, they can always pick up something. That means you have to start with solid cards, especially as the tournament progresses.

Playing Tight—Why It Works in Stud Cash Games and Tournaments

The style I am going to describe to you is a tight one. It works for me in stud cash games and it adapts well to tournaments.

Most people can't play tight. There are very few really solid, tight players who have been successful. A lot of the successful players who have stayed successful for a long time in the cash games are guys who are a little more liberal than I think they should be. I'm not sure if they are getting lucky or they are so much smarter than me that they have figured out how to beat K-K with 4-4 consistently. But I don't know why you would want to set out to *try* that, when you can be the guy who usually has the K-K.

Everyone knows the tight style is the way to win, but most people don't have the temperament to stick with it. It works for me because I can stay with it no matter how I am doing in the game. I can lose the first five pots I play, all with good hands, and fold every hand for forty-five minutes if necessary, even if some of those hands look exactly like the hands my opponents used to beat my good hands.

I think most people show up to play poker (if they take the money seriously) thinking, "I'm going to play tight today. I am going to play so solid. I'm going to have the best hand when I'm in there."

That all goes out the window when they lose a few pots (or sometimes, depending on the player, after they win a few pots). People unravel. I don't, and you have to work not to unravel.

I hear this kind of thing from some blackjack counters. They can bet $50, $50, $50, $50, $50, waiting for the deck to get favorable so they can bet $500. For some of them, if they keep waiting and lose some of those first few $500 bets, all of a sudden they are $3,000 or $4,000 losers and they forget about counting and start betting $500 every hand. It's the same thing in poker. Most players start out disciplined, and then find a reason to go crazy.

In the cash games I play, no matter who is in the game, the play won't be ragged at the beginning. Everyone in those games has talent and ability—maybe not the same level or the same starting requirements, but no one is going berserk from jump street. After six hours, though, some people have had very bad things happen to them, and some have had very good things happen. It is rare after six hours of playing seven- or eight-handed that everyone is relatively even. After six hours in a $2,000–$4,000 game, you could have a few players near even, a $130,000 winner, a $100,000 winner, a $150,000 loser, and an $80,000 loser.

The biggest difference between the winners and losers in those games is the people who unravel. It's the same thing in tournaments, especially limit tournaments. If you play tight poker after the first few levels, you will get paid by the people who aren't playing solid and by those who started solid (when it's less important to play solid) and are unraveling.

Starting Hands—Separating the Winners from the Losers in Stud

It is an accepted part of seven-card stud strategy that you play speculative hands on third street that you can release when the betting limit goes up on fifth if they don't improve or you think you are too far behind. That certainly applies to calling with a pair when someone with a higher door card bets. In a tournament, I'm not big on calling with (5-4)-4, knowing someone raised with a king and if I don't pick up a draw or two pair by fifth street that I have to fold.

By fifth street, there is always a chance your small pair is the best hand, assuming your opponent doesn't have an open pair. Even if he isn't bluffing, he could have had some hand other than a pair of kings. He could have been on a steal or betting (Q♣T♣)K♣. Or you could be against him with (9-9)-6 and he has (8-8)-K. He might not even be bluffing and you could have him beat because he put you on sixes.

Unless you have some kind of never-fail intuition, you could get sucked into calling down with the worst hand. I am thinking that I have to throw my hand away unless it improves. Even if by some miracle my small or medium pair is still good, it is very penetrable.

It is frequently right to call on fifth street, for all the times the other player has a smaller pocket pair or a draw that hasn't panned out. Once you do that, however, now you've made the pot big enough where you have to call to the end. You almost always have the odds to call sixth and seventh street. (The exceptions are pretty obvious: when you were drawing and completely miss, and when your opponent is showing something like open tens and all you have is a pair of nines.)

So if it's a bad idea to fold in five, and you then have the odds to call on the last two streets, what do you do? What I do is try not to play hands that are beat from the start. The key time to make a good laydown isn't on fifth street. It's on third street, before you put a single chip in the pot.

Just because it looks nice doesn't mean you can't lay it down. It's ridiculous to call with (K-4)-K when a jack raises, a queen re-raises, and an ace three-bets. You have nothing in the pot to defend. Would you call with K-6-2? Of course not. So why would you call with K-K-4 if you know you're beat? What's the difference how bad your hand is if it's bad? You might not even have the second-best hand. The jack could have J♥T♥9♥ and the queen could have Q-Q-Q. You have to be able to throw a big hand away on third street when that many people show strength.

You have some latitude in cash games and you have some in the early part of a tournament too. Play your normal, basic, good, solid game. Where you really have to divert from cash-game strategy is later, when the limits go up.

In stud tournaments, the limits generally increase disproportionate to the ability to acquire chips in normal play. They start doubling and they go up fast. Soon, almost everyone but the chip leaders is short-stacked. My strategy changes in that I don't ever want to enter a pot where I don't think I'm a favorite.

Forget about pot odds in that situation. If a guy raises with a queen and I have T-T in the hole, I would probably fold unless I think there's a very significant chance that he has nothing and is stealing. If I have an ace in the hole, maybe I would call. Even then I am going to lay it down on fifth street if I don't pick up a ten or an ace. Sometimes people give up. They take their (J♥8♥)Q♥ and bet and catch an off-suit six on fourth street. If you catch a deuce, they might bet again in case you broke off. On fifth, if you catch an eight and they catch an off-suit four, maybe they just check to you. You bet; they fold.

That happens quite often. They weren't bluffing at the start but their hand didn't materialize. But if I'm playing (A-T)-T, I'm giving it up in five if it doesn't play out like that. Without an ace or king in the hole, I'll throw it away on third (though I wouldn't do that in a cash game).

You have to almost always be throwing away that hand to start, and never playing it beyond fifth. The limits go up too fast to call someone down. No matter how many chips you have, if you ever have an hour sequence where you lose 15 percent of your chips, you are now in a bad chip position.

This changes the hand values. Big unpaired cards go down in value, as do three flushes. Not only can you not afford to draw and lose, but you are unlikely to get multiway action later in a tournament, and you want a lot of people to pay you off when you hit that kind of a starting hand.

If you ever have an hour sequence late in a tournament where you break even, which isn't even a bad sequence, your good chip position becomes average. Your average chip position becomes short-stacked. The blinds moved up 50 percent plus other players got the chips of the players who got eliminated.

Playing the way I suggest, big pairs and rolled-up trips are obviously the main hands to play as the tournament advances and more people get eliminated. The first thing to remember when you play big pairs is that your hand does not exist in a vacuum. J-J is nice, but if a queen raised, a king reraised, and an ace made it four bets, you don't have anything; it's like you have 2-2. On the other hand, (K-8)-8 can look like a monster if four people have folded and you have just a three, a five, and a six behind you. If one of those players calls, it looks like your pair is probably good.

Everything is relative to what cards are out, your position, the positions of the other high cards, and anything that could help you decide whether the player with a higher card showing than your pair is stealing or betting strength. Naturally, you think that stealers tend to be late-position raisers. But look around. If the board is mostly made up of low and medium cards, the player in early position with the king could have (Q-6)-K. A smart player will keep track of how tight everyone is playing. He could even see a couple aces behind him and raise because (a) it is less likely either of them has another ace, and/or (b) he knows how they play and is stealing through them. You should be doing that, and you should figure out which other players are doing that.

Just as you should be more skeptical of a high-card raiser with a weak board, you can give more credit to someone raising into a strong board behind them. If there is a queen, a jack, a king, and an ace to act, the guy with the nine of hearts showing who raises is pretty unlikely to have 8-4 in the hole. He could have a very big hand like (K♥K♠)9♥, or a powerful drawing hand like (J♥T♥)9♥.

(There are varying schools of thought on how to play the big drawing hand, but most players won't raise with that hand. The drawing hands play well against multiple players because no matter what anyone has, if you pick up a queen and a heart, you have a huge number of outs against three aces. You want a lot of action on those hands, so you don't necessarily want to isolate by raising. Besides, if you raise with that kind of hand and get reraised by the player with the king, everyone else will probably fold and your draw isn't worth nearly as much.)

In general, if you are playing a big pair, you should play it fast. Narrow the field. Make the draws pay or give them the worst odds possible. The best situation unless everyone folds is to get someone with a lower pair.

It is no secret that big pairs play better against one opponent. You win the most chips with A-A or K-K against someone with a smaller pair. A-A in a five-way pot is a dangerous commodity.

In seven-card stud, if you start with a pair, you improve your hand about 60 percent of the time. That means if you had the biggest pair on third street, you automatically win the 40 percent of the time that the other player did not improve. That is a big percentage, especially considering that you win all the times when you bet and your opponent folds, and a lot of the times when you improve. Forty percent of the time, you could bet all the way, get called to the end, and win, whether or not you improve. The other 60 percent of the time is more random. You will lose 24 percent of the time, because that is when your opponent improves and you don't. The other 36 percent of the time, you both improve. Sometimes the other player improves more, like you make aces up but he makes three kings. But you will probably win a majority of the hands where you both improve.

When you have a big pair, the best hand you can be against is a smaller pair. Your big pair, heads-up, is still a favorite over a hand like 5-6-7 suited (and, obviously, a bigger favorite against drawing hands that aren't as strong, where there is a gap and/or only two of the cards are suited). But you can't expect to get much action on your aces and win when you are facing 5-6-7 suited. If the 5-6-7 hand catches a couple random cards, that player will fold, losing only a couple small bets. Two kings is rarely going to get many raises in against that hand unless the board is just perfect: that player catches another card of that suit on fourth street, and then another card for a straight on fifth. Then he makes a pair on sixth. Or the player has all those draws and makes two pair and the kings improve to kings up. Much more often, however, the player with the drawing hand either loses a few small bets and folds or hits his draw and wins a lot of bets.

Therefore, you have to play your big pairs fast. You are a pretty good favorite against one opponent. You want to collect all the bets you can against another pair, and keep out the drawing hands. You can lose a lot more to them than you can win, so you want to make it expensive for them to draw, or chase other players out of the pot to force them to play heads-up.

Antes

I don't think players consider the ante very much, to tell you the truth. I am saying this from twenty years' experience in cash games.

Players are usually much more focused on whether they have a hand when they play. That can create opportunities when the ante is seriously out of proportion to the limit. In 2006, the World Series of Poker imposed, in all the $1,000 or $1,500 buy-in stud, stud eight-or-better, and razz events, an ante of 5 in the initial level where the betting limits were 10-20.

With that kind of ante, you are going to have a hard time stealing any pots. And other players will have a hard time stealing from you, because you have to really loosen up your start requirements. You could definitely play (7-7)-3 because there is already 40 from the antes. If you had the low card and it's raised, there is a minimum of 55 in the pot and it costs you just 5 more to play. It is an insane structure.

Playing a Big Stack

Based on the style I recommend, you will generally not get your tournament successes by building a big stack early and bossing around the table. When you get a lot of chips, though, how you take advantage of them depends on the nature of your table and how late it is in the tournament. If you are still far from the money, don't play much different. Other than the kinds of stealing situations you would take advantage of with just an average stack, you are not going to be able to bluff people out of pots. That's just the nature of limit poker.

If you are near the money with a big stack, however, you should be more aggressive. Even being more aggressive, though, you won't be as aggressive as you would be in hold 'em. A short-stacked player on the bubble is just as likely to use your aggressiveness against you to pull himself back into contention as he is to fold into the money. (It helps to understand the kinds of players at your table.) Once the bubble bursts, it hurts to play aggressive. The shorter stacks are now in the money and don't have anything to lose by trying to double up on you.

The kind of aggressiveness that pays with a big stack is isolating shorter stacks when you have a hand. You are not going get them to fold. If they play with you at 1,000-2,000 limits with 9,000 left, there is a good chance they are raising or calling your raise with a hand they want to play to the end. Raise or reraise with a good hand to get against that player. Pretty quickly, he is in too deep to get out and he has to get lucky to win.

I can't overstate this: you won't run over this guy by stealing, because he obviously has a hand. If you have an ace showing and he has a ten, he isn't playing with you unless he has at least another ten. He has made a decision that you don't have another ace and nothing is going to change his mind (other than if you *catch* another ace). Based on his chip position, he has already decided that this is where he has his best chance to make a stand. That means when you play like you have an ace in the hole, *have an ace in the hole.* You will get paid all the way to the end and bust that player.

When you raise and a short stack calls, it is very unlikely they are folding. The medium stacks have some important decisions to make and can maybe be pushed around, but the short stack isn't in the hand unless he decided he has the best hand—he likely has at least a pair and maybe a pretty high pair—or is willing to gamble on hitting something. If a short-stacked player had the low-card bring-in, you might be able to bully them out of the hand. But once you get called, it's a suicide mission to continue unless you have the hand you are representing. If you have a few other small stacks behind you, I think you are better off just getting out of the way. It is unlikely they are all going to fold just because you raised with a jack showing. They are fighting for their lives. If they have 7-7, they aren't folding. It's not that unlikely that one of them has a playable hand.

You can still be aggressive and try to steal, but against a short-stacked player, shut down fast. If they call and you don't improve on fourth street, don't even bet. That's the proper way to play. You will pick up some antes, but you can't expect guys to fold on fifth street when they have so few chips left that their third street decision committed them to play the pot to the end.

Playing a Short Stack

Once you have 25 percent of the average stack in a stud tournament, you don't have enough chips to throw away anything that would be considered a reasonably good hand in a normal game. I'm not saying you should play a (7-5)-4 after a bet and a raise. Even if you don't have many chips, you can wait for something better than that. But it's hard to throw away a medium-sized pair when you are that short. If you have (K-2)-2, you still have more than 40 percent to win against (Q-7)-Q. If you continue anteing away for a sure thing, even when you double up, it will be insignificant. If your chips get below a certain level, they lose their value because even if you double up, you are still in a bad situation.

Just because you should be willing to take your shot with a hand that's possibly second best, make sure it's not worse than second best. If you have (T-6)-6 and a queen raises, you may decide the combination of the chance you have the best hand or could draw to a winner is enough to make this the hand. If you are acting last or can reraise and shut everyone else out, this might be your chance. But if a jack limps, a king raises, and a queen calls, forget it. Wait for a heads-up situation for your do-or-die hand.

These ideas for playing a short stack apply only later in the tournament. If you get short-stacked early, you can keep anteing and wait for a decent hand.

But say there are just twenty players left. The limit is 3,000-6,000 with a 500 ante. You have 11,000. If a bunch of players fold, play any hand you can find a reason to get excited about. If you make two pair out of anything, your stack goes up to 30,000. If you have any kind of hand—three high cards, a three flush, three connecting cards with two suits, a pair—you have to play. You are getting anted to death. If your stack diminishes much more, there will be no way to return.

The exception would be when you are near the money, or in the money where the payouts start increasing substantially. As I said before, you can make money folding in a tournament, and that's where you do it.

Conclusion

Solid play wins in cash games, it wins in limit poker, and it wins in stud. Therefore, you can adapt the principles of solid, conservative play to succeed in seven-card stud tournaments. So many players are entering World Series stud events that, even without much experience yourself, you can take advantage of all those no-limit hold 'em players who try to win at stud. If you understand how cash games differ from tournaments, how stud differs from hold 'em, and how the tournament changes when the betting limits increase, you can survive and maybe profit off the mistakes of the players who don't adapt. You might even pick up a good table and some cards and build a big stack. If you survive in a stud tournament, you always have a chance.

CHAPTER 17

Stud Eight-or-Better

by Ted Forrest

> *Whatever chapter Ted Forrest writes will be the*
> *first chapter I read.*
> —ERIK SEIDEL

Stud Eight-or-Better and Me

When I started playing poker in Las Vegas in 1987, you could find low-stakes stud eight-or-better games. With the explosion of Texas hold 'em—and I'm talking about the explosion in the late eighties and early nineties after California cardrooms could start spreading it—and the introduction of Omaha eight-or-better, the stud eight-or-better games dried up.

Ironically, the game has remained extremely popular at the highest and lowest levels of poker, but seldom in between. It is a regular part of the mixed games in L.A. and Las Vegas, at limits of $400-$800 and above. And it is a staple of split-pot kitchen-table games.

Even though I like to say my favorite game is whatever is being dealt, more often than not, stud eight-or-better is *truly* my favorite game. The game gives new players a chance. It can accommodate a lot of action and many different styles of play. A player could make almost every conceivable mistake on a hand and still end up with half the pot. But it also rewards good play—paying attention, taking advantage of certain situations.

I am pleased that it has remained part of the World Series and would like to see it become an even bigger part of tournament poker. I have a soft spot in my heart for stud eight-or-better tournaments.

In early 2004, when I was about a decade past playing much tournament poker, I went through a slump in cash games. It seemed every time I sat in a really big game, I couldn't win. I would have to spend a week beating up a smaller game to get the bankroll back to take another shot . . . then I'd lose again. It was almost like I thought I wasn't allowed to win.

I started working some things out as tournament season started. In 2004, the Bellagio Five-Star went for three weeks, ending in the World Poker Tour Championship. The day after that ended, the World Series of Poker started. I played just two events at the Five-Star, stud eight-or-better and the Main Event. I won the stud eight-or-better event, finished in the money at the WPT Championship, then went on to win my fourth and fifth bracelets at the 2004 World Series. That whole experience cemented in my mind the decision that I should devote myself increasingly to tournament poker. That win in the Bellagio stud eight-or-better event obviously helped a lot with all the great things I have gotten out of tournament poker since: two bracelets, two WPT final tables, a PPT win, and the 2006 NBC Heads-Up Championship.

Structure for a Stud Eight-or-Better Tournament

With so few stud eight-or-better tournaments these days, I will use the structure that the World Series of Poker has used for the past few years for its $1,000 buy-in event. This information came from the 2005 World Series $1,000 buy-in event, which drew 595 players. (I would bet that at least 5 percent of the field entered thinking they were playing seven-card stud.)

Notes on the Structure of the Tournament

1. This was reconstructed from accounts of the 2005 event on CardPlayer.com. There may be minor errors, but it is good

TABLE 17.1

Players	Ante	Bring-in	Stakes	Average
595	5	10	15-30	1,000
595	5	10	30-60	1,000
595	10	15	50-100	1,000
400	15	25	75-150	1,500
312	20	30	100-200	1,900
236	25	50	150-300	2,500
158	50	50	200-400	3,750
120	50	100	300-600	5,000
98	75	150	400-800	6,000
49	100	200	600-1,200	12,000
45	150	300	800-1,600	13,000
38	200	300	1,000-2,000	15,500
27	300	500	1,500-3,000	22,000
18	400	600	2,000-4,000	33,000
15	500	1,000	2,500-5,000	40,000
11	1,000	1,000	3,000-6,000	54,000
8	1,000	1,500	4,000-8,000	75,000
7	1,000	3,000	5,000-10,000	85,000
5	2,000	2,000	6,000-12,000	119,000
3	3,000	3,000	8,000-16,000	198,000
2	4,000	4,000	10,000-20,000	297,500
2	4,000	6,000	15,000-30,000	297,500

enough for the general information about how a stud eight-or-better tournament progresses.

2. The 595 players in this event started with 1,000 in chips. Until the final table, levels lasted sixty minutes. (In the 2006 event, players started with 1,500 in chips.)

3. I was eliminated from this particular event with over two hundred players remaining, so I can't tell you firsthand about what happened after that.

4. Some of the averages are rounded and the number of players at the particular levels are based on reports from CardPlayer.com.

They could be from the beginning, middle, or end of those levels. They are fine for our purposes, but they are approximations.

5. Day 1 ended with forty-nine players left. The tournament paid forty-five places.
6. Day 2 ended with eight players left. They played the final table on day 3.
7. Levels at the final table were increased to ninety minutes.
8. Calibrating tournament levels is a developing art. For 2006, this event's structure was changed to allow a lot more play at the beginning. The 2006 structure had two rounds with 5 antes and bring-ins, at limits of 10-20 and 20-40. This meant more play, but it also imposed relatively large antes compared with the betting limits, which translates into trying to steal more, gambling more, and playing more starting hands.

Framework for Tournament Play—Early

Stud eight-or-better tournaments generally move very slowly at the beginning, allowing you a chance to take your time accumulating chips. Because it is a split-pot game, you could potentially play a lot of hands early without your stack moving much.

In addition, the competition you run into in these tournaments, a lot of the time, tends to be players for whom stud eight-or-better is either their favorite game or their only form of poker. Other times, you may find an older crowd that grew up on split-pot games. Some players are new to the game and are just learning stud eight-or-better. You will find some opponents who thought this was a seven-card stud event. As a result, I think the overall field, on average, is a little bit weaker—at least in terms of tournament experience—than in other forms of tournament poker.

A third reason for traditionally conservative starting play is that the antes are small relative to the stacks. Obviously, if you become short-stacked, you can't wait around for a great hand, but you have to be pretty low in chips for the antes to force you to play. In the cash games I play that include stud eight-or-better, the ante will usually be

one-sixth or one-eighth of the upper betting limit. That kind of structure forces the action. If you wait for a great hand, those antes will
eat you up. Tournaments typically have an ante of approximately 10
percent of the upper betting limit. A 10 percent ante does not particularly encourage stealing or gambling.

This was the case with the World Series structure before 2006.
Other than the first round, where the antes and limits were small compared to everyone's stack size, the antes were one-tenth or less of the
upper betting limit. You got rewarded by leaning toward the conservative. Anytime you have an ante that is one-twelfth or less of the upper
limit, you don't really have to feel an urgency to play a lot of hands.

This was not the situation with the 2006 World Series structure.
At the lowest limits, the size of the ante altered the nature of the
game dramatically. In 2006, by putting in two levels before the 30-60
limit/5-ante level (instead of one as was the case in 2005), the upper
betting limit in the first level was just *four times* the ante. You have
to gamble more and steal more in that structure. That's not a license
to go insane, but you need to loosen up your starting hands—there
are 45 chips in the pot between the antes and the bring-in, so even if
someone completes the bet and there are 55 chips, it costs you just
10 (if no one behind you raises) to see fourth street—and look for
opportunities to steal.

But don't forget, whatever the structure, you have to adjust to
what your table is giving you. The first thing I thought when I saw this
structure was, "You really have to try to steal with those big antes."
David Grey, in chapter 16 on stud tournament strategy, looked at this
structure and said, "With that kind of ante, you are going to have a
hard time stealing any pots."

We are both getting at the same point: some people will try to
steal, some people will try to keep them from succeeding, and some
people will be oblivious. Who's at your table?

If everyone at your table is playing a basic neutral-ante strategy,
the antes are there for the taking. But if everyone is going the other
way, defending their bring-in, trying to steal, and trying to pick off
other steal attempts, you need to adjust. Likely, you will find both
types at your table, and you need to pick the players you need to steal
from (or through) and those you can pick up extra bets from because

you caught them stealing or they thought you were stealing when you brought a good hand against them.

If you can rob more than your share of antes, you will do fine. (Later on, when the betting limits, rather than the antes, dictate how you play, stealing antes becomes more important.) I know from experience that you can reach a final table without having any major confrontations. You have to get lucky and find yourself at a table where they just give you the antes, but it is the perfect way to win a tournament.

If the World Series keeps that structure (starting with antes of 5, a bring-in of 5, and limits of 10-20), you have to mix it up early on. After that (or if you are playing in a tournament with a more standard ante structure), I think that a conservative approach is warranted because you do have ample opportunity to slowly build up your chip stack. You really don't have to take crazy chances and gamble and build the pots up early. Even with the higher-than-normal first-level ante, you shouldn't go crazy, and you have to settle down if you have anyone in the hand with you beyond third street.

The limits are low enough to where you have time to wait for good starting hands and build up your chip stack at the expense of less experienced players. (Even if *you* are one of these less experienced players, just understanding the difference between tournament play and cash-game play can give you an advantage over an opponent who has played the game for a long time but has not adapted to the tournament format.)

I tend to press small edges less in a stud eight-or-better tournament than I would in a cash game. If I have a small edge in a cash game, I will generally push it. But in a tournament, I may not put in that last raise. I may choose to call when calling and raising are close, thus being able to get away from a hand cheaply if it doesn't materialize on fourth or fifth street.

What will force you to change strategy later is the size of the betting limits. If the limits are 15-30 or 30-60 for the first two rounds (or, for the 2006 World Series, 10-20 and 20-40) and you start with 1,000 to 1,500 in chips, you can get away from hands. Even at 100-200 betting limits with 2,000 in chips, it is certainly no time to panic. At ten big bets, you're okay. At less than seven big bets, that might be the time to sweat a bit. Compared with stud, however, you can more easily manage a short stack; you'll frequently get half the pot and there are more hands where it will be easy to get away on fourth or fifth street.

But you have to look out for potentially expensive traps. You can't play marginal hands for a few streets to see what develops. You can't afford to get in the middle of a raising war between two other hands. But other players, similarly, are at risk, so how you adjust will determine how you do as the tournament progresses. At the beginning, however, you have to understand the principles behind the conservative play necessary to accumulate chips during the early levels. And if the tournament has a big ante at the beginning, you need to be able to shift gears.

Starting Hands on Third Street

Scooping—In a split-pot cash game, the highest priority is on going after hands that allow you to win both halves of the pot. This is true in tournament stud eight-or-better, but with a twist. In some hands, there is no low. With opponents trying to conserve bets in a tournament, a mediocre high hand could prove stronger than a great low draw. That low hand on third street still needs to catch two more cards. The player holding that hand has to keep calling bets as you watch whether their low draw materializes. If you chase everyone else out of the pot, your opponent may be hoping to catch cards just to retrieve the chips he has to pay to catch those cards.

A high hand "scoops" the pot when there is no low, or the low draw folds and concedes the pot. Therefore, if you can pick your opponents, you can scoop a pot with a one-way hand. When you have a high hand or a hand with a lot of high potential, this is a good reason to thin the field because it then becomes less likely that someone will make a low.

The "push" and "pull" factor—Try to think of your playable hands as those with which you want to *push players out* of the pot, as well as those with which you want to *pull players in* the pot. You want to push players out with hands where you have a pair or could improve to a pair and possibly win the hand with the single pair heads-up. You want to pull players in with hands that are strong drawing hands: straight and flush draws with very low cards that are unlikely to win if you simply pair one of those cards. For example, with 5-6-7, you could possibly win with a single pair heads-up and would want to push players out. With 2-3-4, you want to pull players in.

Hands to play short-handed—Certain types of holdings play better heads-up or short-handed. Take a hand like (7-6)-7. This is the type of hand that plays best against just one opponent, even better if the other player is drawing at a low. If my one opponent has (7-4)-2 and I have 7-7-6, it will be tough for that player to beat me for high, and oftentimes he will fail to make his low.

Remember that (7-6)-7 is much better than (7-2)-2. If an opponent with a low draw pairs up, they can beat a pair of deuces or threes. They can't beat your pair so easily if you have sevens or eights.

A hand like (7♣6♦)7♠ is one with which you want to push people out. If you can't, it may not be playable. If someone showing a king raised coming in and two low hands called, you probably don't want to mess around with (7♣6♦)7♠. But if you are heads-up against the player with the king, you really aren't much of an underdog, even against a pair of kings. Your hand actually plays a lot easier than the pair of kings.

The spot you have to stay out of is where one opponent has you beat high and the other has you beat low. You don't want (7♣6♦)7♠ against two opponents where one has a low card showing, with a hand like (5♥2♥)3♦, and the other has (Q♣T♦)Q♠. Heads-up against the queens, you are okay. Against that low draw heads-up, you are in pretty good shape. You have three of that low-drawing player's cards blocked off. The low draw actually has to catch *two* good cards to pull ahead of your sevens. But against the two of them, especially if they pick up on the fact that you need to catch just right to beat either of them, you will be facing multiple raises on every street.

High pairs—Players often overlook this, but (K-X)-K is much better than (J-X)-J. You will frequently be up against an opponent who is drawing at a low who catches a brick and continues playing the hand. If you have a pair of jacks and your opponent catches a queen or king, you can get outdrawn for half if their low comes in, or for the whole pot if they pair their high card. If you are playing kings and your opponent catches a brick, it will still take two more cards to outdraw your kings to beat you high, or to get the low end because that brick did not help their three-card low draw. And if you put the pressure on, that low draw won't seem so attractive to keep chasing.

Forget (9-X)-9 and (T-T)-X. With those hands, any card your opponent catches—high or low—is a threat. Even jacks are very dangerous.

Rolled up—In general, with any type of rolled-up hand in stud eight-or-better I'm thinking about making the pot bigger. I am not going to slow-play rolled-ups. I don't care if I get a few callers or a lot of callers. The hand plays extremely well either way. I'm going to play them fast and hard and make a big pot. I don't worry if I push out opponents because that makes it more likely that I can scoop the pot. Remember, if you scoop a heads-up pot, you have made as much as winning half of a four-way pot.

High-only draws—In general, forget about high straight draws. Flush draws are very overrated. Flush draws that contain two big cards like (K♦J♦)4♦ should in most cases be folded. On the other hand, flush draws that contain two low cards can be played when your flush cards are live. A hand like (5♦4♦)K♦ is not a bad hand. While a hand like (K♦J♦)4♦ doesn't seem that different, it represents a huge difference. You can look to play a hand like (5♦4♦)K♦ 50 percent of the time or more, whereas you should rarely play (K♦J♦)4♦. Hands like (A♦5♦)K♦ have the potential to develop into very strong hands. And when you have the king showing you often can represent a big pair, which can become very valuable later in the hand.

Two-way draws—Two-way drawing hands, like (4-3)-2, either suited or unsuited, play better with a lot of players in the pot. The obvious hands you are going to play almost every time are aces with a low card (like [A-A]-3), three low cards, like (3-2)-4, (5-3)-4, and (6-4)-5, and three low suited cards, like (A♥5♥)6♥.

I want to make the pot big with two-way drawing hands because I would want to justify seeing fifth street with such a powerful holding. With less attractive drawing hands, like (4-2)-6, where I really need to catch a good card on fourth street, I may call and hope to get a number of other players into the pot. If I catch a nice card on fourth street, I can start thinking about making the pot big. And if I brick off on fourth, especially if I see an opponent picking up a low draw, I can get out cheaply.

When you have a hand like (5♠3♠)4♠, you have such a powerful two-way draw, you want to give yourself two chances to pick up a nice draw—a chance on fourth street and a chance on fifth street. Making the pot big actually serves two purposes. It is already correct with a medium-sized pot to continue with such a powerful draw. With a big pot, it is not even a difficult decision. The big pot also tends to tie other players with mediocre holdings to their hands if you pick up that big draw or big hand by fifth street.

Marginal hands—I want to play as wide a variety of hands as my opponents will allow. Naturally, I want to play (A♣3♣)2♣, but I am much more often looking at a hand like (6♣3♦)5♠. To play the lower-valued hands on the spectrum, you basically want to play these things cheaply. (7♥2♣)4♦ really is not much of a hand. It is playable only if you can limp in for the minimum and look to catch a good card on fourth street. But it is really not the type of hand you want to get involved in a big pot with because it is just too weak both ways. You have no high potential and you may not even have the best low draw. With these kinds of hands, you have to evaluate factors like position, door cards, live and dead cards, and the tendencies of your opponents.

If you have a low draw but it is not the best low draw, you should usually throw it away. The nightmare of stud eight-or-better is getting trapped between a high hand and a better low draw. If you have what looks like a second-best low draw, you need something else to play the hand, like straight or flush potential (including a two-card flush draw), or your cards need to be extremely live. For example, if you had (7♠3♣)5♣ and felt you were not leading in the low direction, the hand might still be playable because of the two clubs, assuming the other clubs were still live, and all the fours and sixes were still live. Even then, play the hand knowing you have to improve substantially or see the better low hand catch a brick on fourth street. If your low hand has an ace, you could take a card to see what develops. If you had (A♣8♥)5♠ and felt one opponent had a better low draw and the other had two kings, you could look at fourth street. An ace or a better card than your opponent with the low draw could change your position in the hand significantly.

You also have to be honest with yourself about your ability to play later in the hand. If you think you can outplay your opponents on later streets, or are less likely to make a mistake, you can call in marginal situations. If your opponents are capable of outplaying you, fold when the decision is close.

The role of aggression—On third street in stud eight-or-better, aggression plays a different role than in limit or no-limit hold 'em tournaments. I am not looking to be aggressive for the sake of aggression. I will be aggressive in two main situations: when I can push out opponents when my hand plays best heads-up, or when I have a hand for which I want to create a big pot and several other players have already put in a bet.

I will get aggressive to thin the field with big pairs, medium pairs (like [8-8]-6 or [7-5]-5), and medium connecting cards (like [7-6]-8 or [7-6]-5). With a hand like (7-6)-8, you want to try to eliminate hands like (7-2)-2 by raising or reraising, because that hand is pretty marginal, but it can pass you in either direction. Against a single opponent going low, (7-6)-8 has a good chance of taking the high side with just a single pair.

Medium pairs with a high card—like (7-7)-J—are essentially not playable. The only time such hands are playable are as an ante steal. If you are against just the low card and no one behind you looks interested in playing, you may want to raise and hope everyone folds. If you end up heads-up with the low card, you are okay with this hand. But if anyone has entered the pot voluntarily, it isn't really a playable hand.

With a hand like (8♦5♦)A♦, I will raise to thin the field, compared with a hand like (6♦2♦)A♦. The raise will promote my somewhat weak low draw and also has a better chance (than something like [6♦2♦]A♦) to pair up and win on the high side. Also, with (6♦2♦)A♦ suited, you don't mind if weaker low draws hang around.

But with lower connecting cards, like (3-2)-4, I will not get too aggressive on third street. I want to get in cheaply with these hands and allow other players to do the same. (The exception, of course, is if there are *already* a lot of players in the hand.) I like to play these hands multiway.

A second reason to get aggressive on third street is to build a pot with an extremely nice holding, such as three low suited connectors (e.g., [3♠2♠]4♠). In early position or without many players in the pot, I will call to get multiway action. But in late position, with several players already having put in a bet, I will raise to build a bigger pot. No one is going to fold at that point.

Late position on third street—The later you are to act on third street, the more information you will have about who is already in the hand and the likelihood of players coming in after you. If you have a hand like (8-5)-6 and a lot of babies behind you, you may just want to get rid of that hand. But if you are in late position and you see some mediocre door cards behind you (e.g., a jack where there is already another jack showing, a low card higher than six), you may want to get aggressive.

As I said before, you may raise with a hand in late position to build a pot when you would call with that same hand in early position. Take (4-3)-5 with live cards. If I am the first to act, I will just call, hope to get a few more players, and see what develops. In late position, though, I may be more likely to raise to build a pot after several players have limped in.

To play high pairs, you almost always need position. If you have (Q-Q)-J and you have the whole field behind you including an ace, this is a hand that you may just want to get rid of. But if you're in late position and you get a chance to see what the ace does, you may want to play if the ace folds or the ace just limps in. If the ace limps in behind another limper, you can be pretty confident that that player does not have another ace in the hole. Some players may try to make a goofy trapping play like this, but not usually. If you have two aces and someone has limped in, you should raise; you'll invariably get action.

You should throw away hands like (5-4)-4 with a field of low cards behind you. But in late position if no one has raised it you may want to take an inexpensive card off with these hands. A hand like (8-4)-2 is another hand that you might want to fold in early position with a lot of babies behind you. But if there hasn't been much interest in the pot or much aggression you might want to call and limp in with these hands in late position.

The "benefit" of early position—Of course, the advantage of late position is knowing how many opponents you will have in the hand. There is a corresponding benefit to early position, though. Even though you have to throw away more hands and guess at the action behind you, there are several situations in which you can take control of the hand. The starting point is the nature of your holding: do you want to push players out or pull them in?

Combining your early position with the door cards behind you, you can maximize the value of a lot of marginal hands. If I have (4-4)-5 and there are a lot of low cards behind me, especially deuces, threes, fours, and sixes, it is an easy hand to drop.

But if a deuce brings it in and I have (4-4)-5 in early position with all paints behind me, I'll go ahead and raise it. If someone does wake up with a big pair behind me, I am not even much of an underdog heads-up, especially given that there are a lot of babies left in the deck. And make no mistake, when I do raise it in this position with (4-4)-5, I *want* someone with a bigger pair to reraise it and possibly make a player with (7-2)-7 or (7-2)-8 fold.

You compensate for starting out of position by making good decisions based on your opponents' up cards. To take advantage, however, you have to decide: do you have a pushing hand, or a pulling hand? Position plays an important role in determining whether your best choice would be to call, raise, or fold, given the likely possibilities of people playing behind you.

This can get very complicated. You may notice a player behind you, who you think has two kings. That player will raise if you call, or reraise if you raise. You have to think, "Do I have the kind of hand that I want to play heads-up against two kings or do I want a lot of callers in this pot?" If you want a lot of callers in this pot and you are facing someone itching to raise with two kings, you certainly should not raise with (3♠2♠)4♠. Limp in and let the kings raise. Maybe you can still get some more customers.

If there are already several players in the pot, I will play my hand in a very straightforward manner. Once it is likely that there will be action in this pot, my decisions on raising and calling will be based on the strength of my hand and whether I want to make a big pot or whether I want to see a cheap fourth street.

Stealing antes—Stealing antes is out of the question if someone other than the low card has entered the pot. A steal situation is typically when you are in late position, no one has entered the pot, and you have an ace in the door. If you get called, you can catch good, your opponent can catch bad, and you can still take the pot after fourth street. But be very aware when your opponent has picked up a draw he's going to see the river with. So be willing to put on the brakes.

You don't necessarily have to be in late position to steal, if the table is letting you steal and the players after you with low cards (if any) don't look too interested in playing the pot. The ace is such a powerful card in stud eight-or-better that raising with it might not even count as stealing.

Another steal situation is when you are the last or second-to-last low card. I will often choose to steal if no one has limped in and the bring-in is a tight player who often folds his low or is easily controlled.

Acting after a raise—Again, your decision comes back to whether you have a pulling hand or a pushing hand. With a pushing hand, you can make it two full bets and probably play heads-up. With a pulling hand, you have to decide between calling (if your hand benefits from multi-way action) and hoping other players will put in the full bet, or folding. If your hand works only one way, you at least want to be leading in that direction. Yes, you want to push players out if you have (Q-Q)-T, but if a king raised, you would be smart to fold. You should get rid of marginal low draws like (4-2)-8 that don't figure to be leading. If some low cards have limped in and someone raises, somebody will probably have a better low draw, so you don't want to get involved.

Playing the bring-in—You should rarely bring in the low card for a full bet. An exception might be at a fairly tight table where you had something like (T-T)-2 in the hole and the board isn't very threatening. But except for that unusual situation, bring in for the minimum bet and then decide how to play the hand after everyone else acts. Don't forget, when you bring it in for a full bet, you are in first position with the whole field behind you. But if you make just that minimum bet, you are effectively in last position because you get to benefit from everyone else acting before you have to make another decision.

With a strong hand like (5♠4♦)3♦—by the way, I like (5♠4♦)3♦ better than (4♠2♦)3♦ because you can catch eight cards instead of four to give yourself an open-ended straight draw—just bet the minimum. This is not only a hand where you want to pull people in, but you can still build the pot by reraising if someone in early position makes it a full bet and several players call. If several players limp for the minimum and the raise to a full bet came from late position, you should probably just call. You want those limpers to call. They are much more likely to call the raise to a full bet than they are your reraise.

Concluding Thoughts on Third Street

If you make a tiny mistake on third street, this can lead to compounded errors throughout the rest of the hand. It is easy to make that small mistake and catch just enough to keep you in to make another mistake on fourth and fifth streets. One of the most important decisions is whether to play the hand at all. Be honest about your abilities. You can do well in a stud eight-or-better tournament, maybe even win it, admitting all the while that you are capable of getting outplayed.

For opponents to outplay you, you have to become an accomplice by taking hands into situations where that can happen. You also need to understand your opponents. Are they the kinds of players who seem able to extract the maximum when they have an opponent trapped in the middle? Do you have the type of holding that could potentially get you trapped?

You really want to avoid situations where you are just literally taking the "gas pipe" between two opponents who have better hands in both directions. On the other hand, if you are playing with extremely passive opponents—it is usually just the bring-in to see fourth street and they rarely engage in raising wars—then you can play more hands.

Play on Fourth, Fifth, and Sixth Streets

Learn to get away cheap—Remember that powerful two-way draws like (5♦3♦)4♦ and (3♦2♥)A♦ are going to be hard to come by. More typically you're going to get hands like (6-4)-8 and (6-5)-3—hands that could catch a very nice-looking card on fourth street, in which case you'd certainly want to continue. But they are also hands that if you do brick off, you really want to be conscious of avoiding situations where you can get trapped for a bet and a raise. Even though it is just a half a bet, oftentimes when you brick off on fourth street, you need to fold these mediocre holdings because you don't want to get caught in the middle.

If you are going to play marginal hands that need to catch right on fourth street—and I think you should—you must learn to release them quickly. Otherwise, play tighter on third street and avoid marginal hands altogether because you can make expensive mistakes, even early in a tournament.

One common mistake of players in stud eight-or-better is that they value their hands in a vacuum. Second-best cards can be very expensive. You have to play your hand in relation to the other hands, the other exposed cards, your position, and the abilities of yourself and your opponents.

You may have straight and flush draws on sixth street. This, in itself, is not necessarily enough to put your head down and call a capped bet. You have to anticipate whether the bet is going to get capped between a made low and a high hand. The pot might not even be big enough to warrant taking the gas pipe for the full cap, even with a straight draw, a flush draw, and a low draw.

Representing a hand—if you have a big card showing, you want to be pretty conservative about representing a big pair unless you actually have it. Opponents will find a lot of reasons to call you if that's all they think you have. In general, if you are playing for just half the pot and you have a big card up, you should actually have that big pair most of the time.

Dead cards—Stud eight-or-better, like seven-card stud, is very dependent on the up cards and your hand being live. When you put your opponent on a low draw, remembering the exposed low cards is very important. Say that you are pretty sure your opponent has started with three unpaired low cards. If that player catches a low card, did that make a four-card low or pair one of the cards in the hole? You can make a pretty good determination of this with a combination of mathematics (e.g., if two sixes are dead and your opponent catches a six, it is very likely that the six did not pair your opponent's hole cards) and reading players to decide the answer.

In general, you will often be in hands where it is pretty clear your opponents are not playing the large cards. Therefore, it becomes a little more important to focus on the cards eight and below. (It is probably worthwhile to make note of dead nines because the nine can complete a lot of straights.) Bricks or paints are less important to remember if it is clear your opponents are not playing for high.

Knowing the odds—Stud eight-or-better can be a very mathematical game combined with a hand-reading game. Your decision will frequently come down to the math: are you getting the right pot odds and the right implied odds based on what you anticipate your opponents will do?

Sometimes, the math is straightforward. You may have nothing but a low draw and your opponent will break into open kings on sixth street. How many cards to you need to complete your low? There are potentially sixteen cards to make your low, out of forty-six cards, subtracting just the six you have seen. But you also have to deduct for your opponent's four open cards. If, for example, you have

and your opponent has

your chances are actually 15 out of 42. What about the exposed cards for the other hands? If two players who threw their hands away had low cards (other than 2-3-4-8) showing, your chances are now 13 out of 36, or 2.77-to-1. If you played this hand during the second round of the 2005 World Series of Poker (or the third round of the 2006 Series event), heads-up except for the bring-in (which folded), and your opponent made it a full bet on third street and bet on each succeeding street, the pot would contain 350 and you would have to call 60. And remember, you can win only 175, not the whole 350. You would be getting the right odds to call, barely.

What if, in that example, you had both checked on fifth street? The pot would be 120 chips lighter, so you would have to call 60 for a chance to win 115. So the payout for hitting your draw is just under 2-to-1, much less than the 2.77-to-1 you would need to call.

But I don't usually advocate checking the best high hand heads-up on fifth or sixth street. If your opponent is showing (X-X)-2-3-5-J on sixth street, I don't think checking a pair of queens is a good idea at all. You might check the best high hand accidentally. If your opponent is showing (X-X)-2-3-5, it would be natural to check two queens. Your opponent could have many hands that are a favorite and you don't want to risk getting raised. But if your opponent's hole cards are A-K, he may check behind you. Against a mathematically inclined opponent, that check may enable you to bet and win the pot if he bricks off on sixth street.

This situation comes up quite often and it is frequently profitable to fold a low draw on sixth street when you are heads-up and the pot is not large. Of course, you can see the importance of remembering what cards have been exposed.

Players will frequently ignore that they are drawing to only half the pot, especially with a great draw. For example, you might think you have some great draws with a 7-5 low draw and an ace-high flush draw. But if one opponent has two pair and the other has a made six low, you have nothing but a flush draw to win half the pot. And, against good opponents, you will have to call a capped bet for that draw. The pot is rarely large enough to justify that call.

Check or bet?—As I explained about pot odds, I don't think you should give your opponent a chance to draw for free for low. Heads-up with a high hand like a big pair, you should be betting, unless your opponent's board is very threatening. If your opponent checks behind you, it probably means he has nothing more than a low draw. Your opponent got a free card from you, but you gained information.

A very conservative opponent might have four to a low plus a pair or straight draw on fifth street and check, but I definitely don't recommend that kind of play. If the high hand checks and you've got high and low draws, especially with a threatening board, you should bet, both because you have so many ways to improve and win a bigger pot, and because you can induce a fold, which would be better than making your low and having to split the pot. If you are on the low side, you shouldn't check if you have something to go with your four-card low, even if it's just a gutshot straight draw.

But know your opponent. A majority of players, even if they check while you are drawing, won't fold a high pair to a bet on fifth street. If you are sure your opponent will call—and your high draw is a gutshot draw—take the free card.

Call or raise?—I see players raise too little in stud eight-or-better. Don't miss a raise because you are afraid of getting drawn out in one direction if you have the lead in that direction. First, if you raise your opponent might fold, so you won't get drawn out this time. Second, raising sets up an image that makes people more likely to fold hands against you that you want them to fold, because they are afraid you're going to punish them. You get drawn out on more if you don't get in bets and raises in these situations.

For example, if you have made an 8-6 low on fifth street and you know one opponent is drawing at a wheel and the other has open kings, you raise it once and your wheel-drawing opponent calls the two bets. The guy with the kings makes it three bets. It is a mistake not to make it four bets here. You want to send the message, "If you're going to play with me, I'm going to punish you."

Smart opponents are going to avoid playing hands with you, just as you should avoid playing hands with them if they punish you for drawing when caught between made high and low hands. If you put in those raises, opponents know they will have to pay the maximum price to draw out.

Granted, you may increase your chances of getting knocked out of a tournament playing this way. Some players will insist on drawing even if it means calling capped bets on several streets, and they will occasionally hit their draws. But you also increase your chances of winning the tournament. If your goal is just to make it into the money, you can't play this style. But if this is your goal, you are unlikely to win, and the big payouts are concentrated among the top few finishers.

My advice about raising brings up a situation I like to call "the gas pipe."

"The gas pipe"—avoiding it and inducing opponents to take it—
The gas pipe is my term for getting stuck between two opponents
who could beat you high and low. Smart, aggressive players will keep
reraising until the betting is capped. Those capped bets from fifth
street on—and occasionally earlier—are, literally and figuratively,
suicide for the tournament player who is drawing against a pair of
made hands, or ignorant that he has the second-best hand. Exploiting
and avoiding gas pipe situations is an important skill, especially in
tournaments, because you can't rebound from this kind of mistake
by reaching into your pocket and buying more chips.

Gas pipe situations usually develop on fifth street, when one
player has made their low and another player is confident they have
the best high hand. Sometimes, especially when some players are on
short chips, you may see capped bets in multiway pots on third and
fourth streets. The more likely situation, however, is on fifth street,
where one player has made a seven or eight low and another player
is drawing to a better low. A third player has made trips. If the player
with the made low and the player with trips are smart, they are going
to give the third player the gas pipe, betting and raising until it is
capped, forcing the player on the draw to call or fold.

To risk the gas pipe, you need a very powerful draw, like a flush
or straight draw combined with a low draw, to go against a made low
or a hand like two pair or three of a kind. You need some potential to
win the pot in both directions, or for the pot to be very large initially.

When you have a high hand, you generally want to avoid capping the bets on multiple streets unless you have a straight, a flush, or
a full house. Otherwise, you could find yourself on the wrong end of
the gas pipe! With one of those premium high hands and a low hand
raising, you can cap the betting without many worries. You have the
field drawing dead or nearly dead on the high side. It is scarier to cap
the betting with a hand like two pair, which is likely the best high
hand, but is vulnerable to straights and flushes.

Avoiding the gas pipe is another reason why you can't look at
your hand in a vacuum. For instance, on fifth street, if you have (A-4)-
5-8-5, that *seems* like a playable hand. But if you read one opponent as
having four low cards to a flush and the other as having four to a low
straight, you may have to fold that hand. If you are facing a bet and a

call, you would clearly call on fourth street with (A-4)-5-8 or on fifth street with (A-4)-5-8-5. But I would not be willing to take the gas pipe by calling capped raises with this kind of hand. If your opponents start a raising war, you know you are up against powerful hands in both directions, almost certainly better than what you are drawing to.

You have to get out of these situations early. It's possible you could jump in the lead in one direction with the next card, but what happens if you and your opponents all catch good? In cash games, players can lose a lot of money chasing like this. It's even worse in tournaments, though, because all it takes is one hand with a couple streets of capped bets to break you. Your whole tournament can easily ride on avoiding this kind of hand.

In my opinion, trips are generally the weakest hand you want to have when trying to force someone to take the gas pipe. Even then, don't try to get in a battle of raises with the low hand if there are flush or straight possibilities among your opponents. I might even be willing to cap the betting with aces up.

If you are drawing low after fifth street or think you need to improve your made low, it's not worth taking the gas pipe unless you have something else going for your hand. You need more than the potential to win half the pot. You need some scoop potential to take this kind of risk in a tournament.

Taking the gas pipe is excruciatingly expensive. If you start a hand with ten big bets, you can call off 40 percent of your stack just to see sixth street. Realistically, if you are going to be calling four bets on fifth street, which would represent, say, 25 percent of your stack, you need to have the lead in one direction. The only exception would be if you had a hand like (4♠3♠)2♠5♠T♥ and you are up against trips and an eight low. This kind of hand is potentially strong enough in both directions to warrant calling the cap and taking the gas pipe. But you could be potentially risking 50–80 percent of your stack, so it is a significant amount of your tournament life. One of the awful things about the gas pipe is that you can call off nearly all your chips and you have to finish yourself off knowing you are drawing almost dead, because the pot is so big, and you have so badly crippled yourself, that you have to have to finish the hand and your stack with some Hail-Mary calls.

When you are on the low side, facing two high hands, don't get too anxious to induce capped betting. I have seen players on fourth street capping raises with just their low draws. A sharp opponent could easily seize that opportunity to make it three bets, hoping to knock the other high hand out, which is exactly what you *don't* want. Just go ahead and take 2-to-1 on your money and try to play the pot inexpensively, but three-way, until you make your low. Once you make your low, then you should raise at every opportunity.

While you are drawing for low or with a made low without high potential, don't rush to raise. Raising on fourth street or even fifth street could scare off an opponent trying for low but drawing nearly dead. If I had little or no high potential, I would just call and let that other low in, because I want to earn half the money he is putting into the pot. But if I pick up a pair along the way and think the high hand has only one pair, it might be time for a raise.

Remember the consideration you have to weigh: will the player drawing dead call? If you raise too early in the hand, that player can get away cheap. The longer you wait to give an opponent a reason to take the gas pipe, the more likely it is that you will achieve that result.

In a potential gas pipe situation, your moves depend on the nature of your opponents. If your opponents are not especially aggressive, it may cost you just a bet or two to see the final few streets and let your hand develop. But if they are aggressive—especially if you are in a hand with two aggressive opponents—you should be more inclined to fold a marginal holding.

The River

You get a lot of situations on the river where the pot is big enough that the losing player has to call at least one bet. You can win (and save) a lot of chips in stud eight-or-better by maneuvering to make those extra bets when you win, and save them when you lose.

Call or raise with a one-way lock?—In a multiway pot with players to act behind you, do you call or raise with a one-way lock? You need to take several things into consideration. If you raise here, what is the likelihood these players will be suspicious and call anyway? And can you get one or more players in the middle to call a cap? Some players with one side of the pot overvalue the importance of getting that last call out of the losing player. If you raise and the losing player folds, all you lose is half a bet. When you raise, however, and that player calls and you end up capping it, you gain one and a half bets in a three-way pot. So you are risking only half a bet to win one and a half bets with a cap.

When not to bluff—One situation in which you should almost never bluff is when your board shows you were going for low. Opponents will call you with almost anything when you have that low board because they will believe any pair could take half the pot. (A benefit of this tendency is that a low board that conceals a high hand will help you get paid off by players with very weak high hands who put you on a low.) When the situation is reversed, you usually have to call down an opponent with a low board who may have just a low or who might be silly enough to bluff while showing low. On the other hand, when your opponent is going for high and bets the river, you can sometimes make a cautious fold.

Getting a better high hand to fold—Most of your success in stud eight-or-better should come from maximizing the return on your winning hands and minimizing your losses on your losing hands. But sometimes you can get a better high hand to fold in a multiway pot and steal the high half. You need the following for this to work: (1) one opponent with a made low who has bet or you know will bet; (2) a hand that has shown strength, based on your betting and the board cards; and (3) an opponent with a high hand that may be better than yours but which he can fold—ideally one pair, though possibly two little pair. (You also need to know that your opponent is experienced enough to not just call down with anything. Against opponents who will take any hand to the end, you make money off them in stud eight-or-better the way you make money off them in every form of poker: make them pay off your good hands. You can't get tricky against that kind of player.)

If you and the made low are betting and raising, your opponent is looking potentially at four bets on the river. He's going to be under a lot of pressure to call four bets with a single pair. But this really works only if the other player with a high hand has nothing more than a pair. If he has two pair and a rough low, you may not be able to get him off the hand. You have to be careful you aren't the one putting in four bets and losing, but if you can put him on a hand that's better than yours but not good enough to take the gas pipe, you may be able to steal half the pot.

A corollary to this is that if you have a hand where you have a reasonable expectation of winning half the pot and you would call on the river anyway, it may be worth a raise to steal half the pot. It's not costing you a full two bets if you raise and are wrong, because you were already going to call one bet. You are risking just one bet. Remember that if you have the image of the kind of player who will raise often on the river, your opponents are just going to put their heads down and call. If you think that is the case—or is going to happen because of the way you are playing—it may be better to save that bet and not raise.

Part of this is based on your feeling about the opponent with whom you are competing for the high half of the pot. Is this player going to put his head down and risk taking the gas pipe, or is he the kind of player who will get away from his hand (and does he have the kind of hand he can get away from)?

Let's say you are showing three low cards and a pair of eights. You may be able to raise out the player with a bigger pair. Someone with two jacks or two queens is going to be under a lot of pressure to fold. That player has to worry not just about calling the two bets—yours and the player with the low hand—but two more if you and the other player each reraise.

If you are at a table long enough to develop an image, make it the image of a player who raises every time on the river with a winner in one direction. Not only will you win more against the second-best hands in that direction, but this will help you steal half the pot on the occasions when you have the better beat in that direction.

Heads-Up on Later Streets and the River

You also have to be aware of situations where you are heads-up at the end of a hand and you can make or save a bet. Here is an example.

An opponent shows

You are almost positive he started with a low draw. Here, you could bet a pair of aces or better almost with impunity, because he could not catch a card to beat you. You should bet and hope he paired kings or jacks and gets suspicious and will call you.

Another situation you will get is where it looks like you both are drawing for low. You miss and maybe your opponent did too. If you have something like a pair of sevens and your opponent is showing (X-X)-2-7-J-K-(X) with no flush possibility, you should bet the sevens on the end. If your opponent paired jacks or kings, he'll probably bet if you check and you'll call. If he paired something lower than sevens, he'll check if you check, but he might call if you bet. He could put you on a low draw and think his pair of deuces is good.

This is a defensive play and it works best against good opponents. Against a more timid opponent, you may not want to bet your sevens. That kind of opponent might fold a smaller pair and, if you don't bet, check a bigger pair.

When deciding how to play the later streets heads-up, take into consideration your opponent's likely hand and what your opponent thinks you have. (Some of this, I admit, is a feel thing.) As you develop your sense of what your opponent has, you can sometimes nail down the exact number of cards he could call you with, as opposed to the number he could raise or fold with. Betting then becomes a mathematical decision if you can narrow down both his draw and what he believes you have.

There are situations where you are almost sure your opponent is drawing to a low. The easiest situation is where you have a high hand that he can't beat if he is drawing to a low. By sixth street, even if he has a gutshot straight draw for high (which he would raise you with if he hits), you can mathematically determine whether it is best to check or bet. How many payoff cards does he have, based on what he is drawing at combined with what he believes you have? How many payoff cards does he have where he makes, say, a pair and pays you off versus totally missing (in which case he would fold if you bet)? And how many cards can he hit where he makes his low and you split the pot, making the further betting a wash?

Here is an easy example. Your opponent shows

on fourth street and you are fairly confident from how the hand plays that he is drawing to a low. He catches K♥Q♠ on fifth and sixth streets. Your board was (X-X)5♦8♥ and you've caught bricks on fifth and sixth too, but you actually have

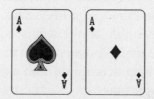

in the hole. Here, you have a very strong hand. In fact, he can't beat it. So you should always bet, if you are correct that he had the low draw.

Here is a second, closer example. You have a pair of eights. Your opponent is showing (X-X)-2-7 and you believe he has two nonpaired low cards in the hole. He catches K-J. You should bet the eights. You can write down the outs: there are six cards he can catch to beat you for high (three kings and three jacks). There are up to twelve cards he can catch to make his low (fewer if he doesn't have an eight and/or you are holding some low cards that don't pair with his), which would be a wash. And if you have a potential low draw showing, there are up to twelve cards he could hit to make a lower pair on the end and potentially call a bet on the end.

Remember to think about whether your opponent believes you have what you are representing. If you have been betting all along with a king door card, ask yourself whether this player believes you have a pair of kings. If you think he believes you and won't call if he can't beat kings, you should check on the end, especially if his hand has some straight or flush potential. You will probably call, hoping he made just a low.

If my opponent is suspicious and I have a big pair, I might be more inclined to bet, especially if I think the other player is on a low draw and has little chance to beat my pair for high. If I had two aces and my opponent turned up (3-2)-4-5-K-Q on sixth street, I would certainly bet the aces, especially if he was suspicious that I actually had them. He can catch six cards to make kings or queens, where he would certainly call on the end. Altogether, he has eighteen pair cards he could hit and call on the end if he believes I have only a low. He can catch only six cards that he would raise with: two aces and four sixes. He might raise if he catches one of the four sevens, but we will split the pot if that happens. There are only twelve cards he can catch at the end where he would fold: the nines, tens, and jacks.

Therefore, if he is suspicious about whether I have a high hand, I would bet the aces because he has eighteen payoff cards that lose, twelve folding cards, eight cards to make his low and split the pot, and only six raising cards with which he will scoop the pot. (If we change this situation and he is not suspicious about my hand, then he won't call me with a low pair on the end. I would be inclined to check on the end because he won't call with twelve of those eighteen payoff cards.)

Strategy for Late Tournament Play

The changing character of the tournament—Later in the tournament, you will see less multiway action. For one thing, the inexperienced players who play a lot of hands have been weeded out. Also, in most tournament structures, the betting limits are structured to make it too expensive to play a lot of hands with an average-sized stack later in the tournament, or at least expensive to play them on fifth street and beyond.

You will see more pots played heads-up to the end, so you want to avoid speculative hands or big pairs like kings or queens when you are potentially against aces or hands with straight and flush draws. That doesn't mean you always fold them on third street, but you want to avoid taking them to the expensive streets when you have little chance of improving and each bet is expensive in relation to the size of your stack.

If you have two kings and the low card gets aggressive with you heads-up and catches an ace, it is probably time to get rid of the hand. It is too expensive for you to be wrong.

You also may find more stealing opportunities as the tournament goes on. There are circumstances in which you can become more aggressive at the beginning of a hand with marginal cards. I would normally consider (J-7)-7 unplayable, but it could be a stealing hand based on the types of players at the table (their stack sizes, their door cards, how much they have been respecting your and other players' raises). If you have (X-X)-A, you don't want to pass up many chances to steal.

When you try to steal and get called, put on the brakes. If you don't catch a great card on fourth street (unless your opponent catches a worse card), give up the hand. The ability to steal is important, but without the ability to put on the brakes, you will probably be a net loser in your steal attempts.

You should handle steal attempts differently in stud eight-or-better than you would in hold 'em. In hold 'em, if you raise before the flop, you will probably bet the flop 80 percent of the time. If you complete the bet in stud-eight-or-better and get called, you should continue with the bluff much less frequently. When you catch good and your opponent catches bad, continue with the bluff. If you both catch good, you may want to take a couple extra seconds and check, hoping they check and you outcatch them on fifth street. But if they bet into you and you haven't developed much of a hand, it's time to give it up. The more times you can limit the cost of failure to the initial completion bet on third street, the better chance you have of building your stack without ever playing a pot.

The bubble—When you are near the bubble, there are more stealing opportunities, once you identify opponents to whom it is extremely important to make it into the money. You should be inclined to steal more against that type of opponent. You also need to identify the opposite kind of player, the kind who is playing the way you are playing. Against players taking advantage of the situation to become more aggressive, you have the opportunity to take a strong hand against them and win a big pot. Likewise, you need to avoid running into them on your stealing excursions. If they peg you as one of the thieves, they are looking to cash in on their big hands from *your* aggression.

Short-stacked—Situations can come up in tournaments where your stack size justifies going all-in with a hand you would otherwise fold. A big pair is probably better than a marginal three-card low if your stack is low enough.

Maybe you don't have much of a hand, like (9-9)-T, but you have a pretty short stack. By going all-in on third or fourth street you ensure that you will get to see all seven cards and you can't get raised out of the pot. This has certain advantages. (9-9)-T isn't much of a hand, but you're probably actually a favorite against (4-3)-5, which is a much more playable hand if you had enough chips to see the hand all the way through. So if your chips are so short that you can commit them all early in a hand, you're going to see the whole hand through, and this has certain mathematical advantages. But you need to be pretty low in chips to do this. If I had a big stack, I wouldn't want to jeopardize my chips with a hand like (9-9)-T.

What is "short-stacked" in these tournaments? At the 100-200 level, if you have 1,400, you can still play hands that you could potentially fold on fourth and fifth streets. But with that stack, if you get involved in an expensive pot, it could cost you nearly all your chips. To stick with the hand beyond fourth street, you need to either start with a hand that figures to have a good chance to win half or all of the pot, or catch just right on fourth street. When your stack is low enough to get all-in (by raising) by fifth street, then you have to regard any hand you play as your chance to double up or bust. You can't call any bets and get away from the hand, and you can, by raising, get yourself all-in (or close) and guarantee that you will see all seven cards.

There is no formula, but I think in the range of three to five big bets, you have to regard any hand you play as a chance to get all your chips in the pot. It almost doesn't make sense to put in a full bet on third street with so few chips if you aren't going all the way with the hand. At seven big bets, you are short-stacked and have to be quick to get rid of hands that don't improve on fourth street, or avoid even playing if you can't see fourth street cheap, but you have the option of looking at a card a few times. You are short-stacked at seven big bets, but not desperate.

Short-stacked, I would take a big pair over a marginal low hand. Maybe throw away marginal low starting hands when you are short-stacked, like (7-2)-5, especially if there is a chance you will have to compete with another player drawing low. You should still play quality low starting hands if you are on short chips. Hands like (5-4)-3, (6-4)-5, and (A-4)-5 are great hands and you should generally be willing to put your tournament on the line with them. (Obviously, if your low drawing hand is extremely dead—like you have [5-4]-3 and you see three deuces and three sixes on the board—you don't want to play that hand, regardless of your stack size.)

Once you get to seven big bets or less, these are the kinds of questions you have to ask before playing a hand: (a) Are you "short-stacked" or "desperate"? (b) With a marginal low hand, do you have enough chips to see fourth street for the minimum (and will the table let you do that)? (c) What kind of hand are you likely to be up against? (d) If you are short enough to get all your chips in by the first couple streets, is there likely to be a hand behind you on third street that you don't want to face? (e) If you are making your stand (or potentially making your stand) with a low hand, is your hand sufficiently live?

When facing short-stacked opponents, you have to sort out this paradox: short-stacked opponents are easy to steal from because they aren't going to play unless they are prepared to make a stand, but once they play, you can't get them off their hand and they are likely to have something better than you are stealing with. Be aware of the short stacks acting behind you. It is easier to steal from people who have chips when it seems like they are protecting their stack. If you are setting yourself up to play a hand against a short stack, you better have something.

The Final Table

The final table in a stud eight-or-better tournament starts eight-handed. The real money is in the top three positions. Your goal, of course, is to win the tournament, but you aren't going to win the tournament when the game is eight-handed. Don't become preoccupied with knocking out other players, especially when you have a big stack. When you sit down at the final table, you should be thinking in terms of increasing your stack to the point where you can make it to the top three.

Don't gamble to knock players out. The money doesn't really increase enough from place to place outside the top three to be worth sacrificing chips. Make the right decisions to increase your stack, whether that is stealing or value-betting your strong hands.

This is true in any form of tournament poker, but especially in stud eight-or-better, where you are playing a very mathematical game. Don't go against the math because you have an opportunity to knock out a shorter-stacked opponent. Let your opponents make that mistake.

Heads-Up

There is a big difference playing heads-up compared to facing one opponent in a full-table game. Heads-up, you don't get to see the six other exposed cards.

Your success in heads-up play—and this applies in every form of poker in tournaments as well as cash games—depends on what your opponent is doing. You need to understand your opponent's style and develop a style that works against that style.

Say your opponent raises to a full bet every time you have the low card. If he has (X-X)-Q, (K-6)-8 is a playable hand. There are no rules about what is playable heads-up, but you would obviously prefer to have bigger cards than your opponent if he has a high door card. There is also a benefit in having two low cards with a high card that is higher than your opponent's door card.

To a lot of players, playing heads-up means they should play as aggressively as possible. To me, playing heads-up means finding the style that works best against an opponent's style. And if that opponent is playing very aggressively, playing aggressively myself isn't necessarily the answer.

Against the super-aggressive player, I play as if they have a door card and two random hole cards. The trick is figuring out which hands are a favorite against two random cards. I haven't run numbers on this, but I think the answers would surprise some people. In the example above, I believe (K-6)-8 is a favorite against (X-X)-Q.

Adapting to an aggressive player, you next have to ask yourself whether they are capable of putting on the brakes. If they are, you can turn the tables and convince them to drop their hand—or know they have a real hand when they continue. If they are the kind of player who just pounds all the way through, you will have to give up some hands and let them continue being the aggressor when you make a hand. You don't have to win half the hands if you let your opponent hang himself when you pick up a hand.

If your opponent folds too much, then you should raise more. Maybe you beat this opponent by winning more than 50 percent of the hands, but you have adapt to the situations where they don't give up. You need to put on the brakes or have a hand. It can really demoralize an opponent who keeps folding, then looks you up to find you have a strong hand. But you can undo the benefits of your aggressiveness (and their passiveness) if you lose those stolen chips by taking a marginal hand against them.

It's great if it is as easy as that. Some players, especially if they don't have much experience heads-up, settle into a style and don't change it. Good opponents, if they are experienced playing heads-up, know how to adapt. Once you put them on a style and adapt, they will try to take advantage of how you adapt. That means, of course, that you have to detect those changes and make some of your own.

CHAPTER 18

Razz

by Ted Forrest and Huckleberry Seed
Narrated by Michael Craig

Razz, a thoroughly frustrating form of poker, is currently exacting its cruelest revenge in history: despite all reasonable efforts to assure its extinction, it refuses to die.

Long gone are the days of the early and mid-nineties when the Horseshoe or the Mirage offered daily $300–$600 to $500–$1,000 razz games, or where Ted Forrest could drive to the Bicycle Club in L.A. and play $400–$800 razz. "The problem is," as Forrest explained, "the old razz players have died off."

ESPN gave the game a shot in its 2004 World Series of Poker broadcast schedule, airing an episode that should have ended razz for good. Despite a final table featuring Howard Lederer, John Juanda, T. J. Cloutier, and Russ "Dutch" Boyd, the episode was marred by the pros constantly grumbling, "I hate this game," and having Lederer and Juanda commit to great hands only to keep pairing up. Lederer's perfect four-card hand ended in three pair. Juanda ended one hand saying, "I was going for a full house."

Still, the ending could have been great, featuring grizzled pro T. J. Cloutier versus Dutch Boyd. But it was anticlimactic, with Boyd badly misplaying several hands and T.J. winning almost by default.

Suffice to say, ESPN will not be televising razz again anytime soon.

The untelevised 2005 razz event at the World Series nearly convinced Harrah's to drop the game altogether. The tournament went a day longer than scheduled and the final table didn't finish until 7 a.m. The oldest player at the table, O'Neil Longson, dozed off and looked like he might not survive the experience, until he rose, vampire-like, building strength through the night and winning his third bracelet.

But razz, like O'Neil Longson at that final table, refused to succumb. A record 291 entered the 2005 tournament, and 409 played in 2006. The return of H.O.R.S.E. to the World Series deserves some credit for sparking interest in razz, as does Full Tilt Poker. Full Tilt was one of the first sites offering regular razz cash games and, occasionally, tournaments. It was also one of the first sites offering H.O.R.S.E. sit-n-gos and multitable tournaments, which included razz in the rotation.

During the 2006 World Series, I used the event as an excuse to get a razz lesson from Ted Forrest and Huckleberry Seed. Forrest won a razz bracelet in 1993 and finished third in 2003. Seed had two razz bracelets, in 2000 and 2003.

The interview, taking place the night before the 2006 razz event, was a unique experience. It was, first and foremost, a playing lesson, the fruits of which will be shared in the remainder of this chapter. But it was also a history lesson, and a nuanced one at that, like hearing two old vaudeville comedians arguing who was on the bill at the Keefe in Pittsburgh in 1917. (Though Ted is barely forty and Huck is still in his thirties, each used the expression "back in the day" at least once that night.)

One example of their banter:

HUCK: You ever do the third-person-in-the-pot bluff, where you come in with a junky hand?

TED: After it's raised and called?

HUCK: Yeah.

TED: How junky?

HUCK: Like a 9-8 in the hole and a baby up?

TED: I don't really like the Oldsmobile hand.

HUCK: I saw you do it once with 9-8, or maybe T-9. You three-raised it.

TED: I don't like that in my repertoire, unless it's a queen and a jack raising it.

HUCK: That's the ultimate tricky play. You'd never expect someone to three-raise it on a bluff.

TED: I think the trick if you try that play is that it makes your chips disappear. I wouldn't recommend being in that spot without a three-card eight or better. To be honest, I don't remember the hand happening that way.

HUCK: Don't worry, it happened. Table 3. Mirage. $500–$1,000 razz.

TED: Who were the opponents?

HUCK: I forget. I know Mark Spirit was in the game but I don't think he was in the pot . . .

They also had a detailed discussion of the first hand they ever played against each other back in 1991. Seed remembered all their hole cards and up cards from the hand. With perfect recall of a hand from fifteen years earlier, it's no wonder he is a master at a game where one of the keys to success is remembering the exposed cards.

I was able to divide the ranging discussion into fourteen categories. It is not a comprehensive guide to the game—"razz in a nutshell," as Ted Forrest termed it. I have employed the convention in this chapter of attributing the comments to Forrest and Seed at the beginning of a section. If there is no attribution at the beginning of the section, the words are mine.

Starting Hands

Ted Forrest: A general rule of thumb with razz is that you would like to have a three-card eight. The lower, the better, and the more duplicate cards of your hand that you can see on the board, the better.

Several factors allow you to expand or contract the definition of a playable starting hand:

- Whether other players have limped
- Whether the bet has already been completed (and, perhaps, reraised)
- The antes
- The opponents still to act—their cards and how they play
- Your chip stack relative to the limits

Ted on the antes: In the first level (based on the 2006 World Series structure, with 10-20 limits and a 5 ante), you would loosen these up somewhat because the antes are so big in comparison to the bets. With that kind of ante, you just have to get in there and mix it up. Play your three-card nines and hope for the best. Not that you can't fold them, but you have to get into the hunt by fourth or fifth street.

Ted on the up cards: The cards that are exposed are so important that they can actually make some three-card eights and three-card sevens unplayable, depending on the cards you need to make your hand.

Defending the Bring-In

It is a big mistake to indiscriminately defend the high-card bring-in.

Ted Forrest: If you find people at your table defending the high card, just that little bit of an advantage can be enough for you to win at razz. In general, I wouldn't recommend defending the high card unless the circumstances are unusual: the raiser is all-in, you have a strong reason to suspect a steal, and you have the perfect hole cards—and by "perfect hole cards," I don't mean A-2 in the hole. You could have 3-5 in the hole with 3-5s and 2-3s showing. (In fact, with that same board, I would much rather have 3-5-paint heads-up against A-2-8. It will be hard for the A-2-8 to make an eight low with all the threes and fives out.)

But it is a mistake players are frequently seduced into making.

Ted: A common mistake people make is they will have a king showing and A-2 in the hole. A deuce will raise and a three will call and a five will call and an ace will call. The bring-in will think, "I'm getting 10-to-1 on my money," and call. Maybe they have a chance against one of those players, but they have the worst hand out of the five. You need the other four to brick off on fourth street—just to be even!

Even against a raise and one call, it's usually a mistake to defend the high card. Remember: the raise doesn't necessarily mean that player has a hand, but if someone calls a raise, they usually have a real hand.

Huckleberry Seed: One exception would definitely be with that high ante at the first level of the World Series event. There are 40 chips in the pot with the antes. The bring-in makes it 45 chips. If someone raises, it's 55. If you are the bring-in with a king showing and have A-6 in the hole, you have to put in 5 more.

Ante Structure

The World Series structure in 2006 began with an enormously high ante, 5 chips, compared with a bring-in of 5 and limits of 10-20.

TABLE 18.1

Level	Ante	Bring-in	Limits
1	5	5	10-20
2	5	5	20-40
3	5	10	30-60
4	10	15	50-100
5	15	25	75-150
6	20	30	100-200
7	25	50	150-300
8	50	50	200-400
9	50	100	300-600
10	75	150	400-800
11	100	200	600-1,200
12	200	300	1,000-2,000
13	300	500	1,500-3,000
14	400	600	2,000-4,000
15	500	1,000	2,500-5,000
16	1,000	1,000	3,000-6,000
17	1,000	1,500	4,000-8,000
18	1,500	2,000	5,000-10,000
19	2,000	2,000	6,000-12,000
20	3,000	3,000	8,000-16,000
21	4,000	4,000	10,000-20,000
22	4,000	6,000	15,000-30,000

The ante was still high at 5 chips after the bring-ins and limits increased to 5/20-40 at the second level. After staying at approximately 10 percent—a standard-conservative level—antes again jump at level 16 and beyond to 20 percent of the upper-limit bet.

Both Forrest and Seed consider the antes an important playing consideration, and in the World Series structure they are a defining strategic characteristic of the tournament.

Ted Forrest: In general, in the first level, you should try to steal the antes. Hands that wouldn't normally be playable if the ante was 1 or 2, which is normal for 10-20, become playable and sometimes re-raising hands. A hand like A-5-9 against a raising seven—normally, I wouldn't mess with a hand like that in a 2 ante/10-20 game. But with a 5-chip ante, if your opponents are aware of the structure and may be trying to steal the antes more often, A-5-9 is playable.

Just to put it in perspective, the ante for the 50-100 level is 10, the normal ante. That's twice the ante of 10-20 but the limits are five times as high. As the tournament progresses, it goes down to a fairly low ante structure. The 300-600 level has a 50 ante, which is fairly low. The 400-800 level has a 75 ante, which is lower than the 100 you might expect. At 600-1,200, the ante is 100, which is at the low end of the 100-200 range of antes for that size limit.

Huckleberry Seed: It's nice to have different ante structures because some players can't adjust from high to low antes and then back to high. The tournament will start raise-raise-raise. All the people who aren't used to playing a lot of razz—which is just about everybody—will think they can just jam like they do in hold 'em. Then, when the antes get small, the good players will be able to trap and work different plays and those new razz players who play all these hold 'em tournaments won't know what's going on.

The Importance of the Exposed Cards

Everyone knows in stud games that the exposed cards are important. In razz, they are more important than in any other game.

Ted Forrest: The up cards in razz are so important that in some cases, a three-card seven is a favorite over A-2-3, depending on the board. This is an extreme example, but let's say one player has a three showing with A-2 in the hole. The other seven up cards are 4-4-4-5-5-5-7. Someone starting with 4-5-7 would be a huge favorite over A-2-3. In razz, you are only thinking about aces through eights. That's eight-thirteenths of the deck, so every exposed card is extremely important.

When the good players get aggressive, you can put them on duplicated cards in the hole. When a beginning player gets aggressive, it's more likely he has A-2 in the hole.

Huckleberry Seed: When an opponent catches a low card, you have to ask yourself whether it improved their hand or paired them up. If you are just starting in razz, you have to use the cards that are already out to decide if they paired. An experienced player who already knows the math can add that to their observations. Sometimes you can just tell from a player's initial reaction whether the low card helped or paired up.

Stealing

Ted Forrest: Razz is an interesting form of tournament poker in that you can build up your chips without getting too involved in major confrontations. The way you do this is to, at opportune times, raise when you have the low card and hope to steal the antes. The best thing is to have everyone fold and end the hand right there. The next best thing is to get called by the high card. A lot of the time, you are going to have the high card beat, and even if you don't, if you outflop him, the high card has to worry about being two cards behind. The other thing that could happen is that you get called by one opponent (or more) and hope fourth street goes your way. If you don't improve on fourth street, you just give up and wait for the next opportunity.

This is what you are doing based on your table without much regard for your hole cards. You will play some of your playable hands the same way, but not always. You need a seven or lower showing to steal. It is better to steal with 7-Q or 7-7 in the hole with a three showing than to have two paints. Just those couple extra low cards out of the deck make it less likely your opponents have a hand.

Huckleberry Seed: If I think no one else at the table can play the stealing game with me, I'm going to build my chips by stealing and sometimes throw away legitimate hands where I might be a favorite. I don't have to deal with the variance of being a small favorite when I can accumulate chips by getting people to fold. One year, I had good tables and, starting with 1,500 in chips, I built it up to 10,000 while almost never playing a big confrontation.

Ted: Once people have limped in after the bring-in, I would not suggest stealing. If I have a legitimately good hand, I would tend to raise. But that is not a stealing raise. Once a low card limps, it is pretty unlikely you will take the antes before fourth street. And if you raise to represent a strong hand for the purpose of stealing on fourth street, you have the danger of catching worse than your opponent—and you may have more than one opponent coming in after you—and having to give up in a situation you were unlikely to succeed with to start.

Sometimes you can play your better hands by limping, which will make it look like you aren't stealing too much. If you raise every time you have a low card in the door, your opponents eventually aren't going to give your raises much respect. With your good three-card hands, the limp shows them that you don't try to take the antes every time.

Huck: I steal a lot of pots by limping in. A lot of times, I will limp because there are some low cards behind me. If they fold, I may be able to take the pot by betting on the next street.

Ted: Sometimes your steal has more credibility with a higher baby showing. If you raise with a seven showing, people generally give you credit for a three-card seven. If you raise with a five or lower showing, they may think you have a three-card eight or nine.

Here is a bit of an advanced play that is easier at the earlier limits, especially that first level at the World Series, with 10-20 limits and a 5-chip ante. Say someone raises in. You aren't sure he has a real hand. You have 5-6-T (with the ten, of course, in the hole) and no babies behind you. You might want to call. At the first level, it costs you just 10 and there are already 55 chips in the pot. By calling, you are representing a three-card eight or better and hope to outflop him. Plus, once in a while, your 5-6-T might be the best hand. The time to do this is when the antes are high.

Don't forget, when someone raises in, they might be stealing. But when you call a raise, it looks like you have a three-card eight. This makes this play work best against good opponents, who were themselves in on a steal. Now you have two ways to win this hand: you could already be in the lead, or you could flop something good and take the lead.

I would like to be at a table of mainly tight players and one or two players who like to defend the high card. When the loose players at the table have low cards, I will rarely try to steal. I am going to steal when the tight players have low cards. A lot of my stealing hands will be better than the hands the high card will defend with.

Know Your Table

The emphasis on stealing in razz makes it essential that you understand the dynamics of your table and how your opponents are playing. Naturally, some of this requires the intuition and experience of a Ted Forrest or a Huckleberry Seed, and that can't be taught. When I asked about raising with a playable hand with other low cards behind, Forrest said, "It depends on who has them. Are they reraising-type players? Do they look like they're folding? Do they look like they're calling? *A lot of times, they are telling you, without knowing they are telling you.*"

Fortunately, assuming you aren't at a three-handed table with Forrest and Seed, you don't need off-the-charts ability to improve your observational skills at the poker table. And a lot of it is about observing betting and playing styles simply by paying attention to the bets and shown-down hands.

Ted Forrest: It will be very apparent very quickly how most players play, and they aren't going to change much. There are those who play only three-card babies and they are probably going to do that from wire to wire. There will be those players who steal in or call in with rougher hands and you will recognize that fairly early in a tournament.

A lot of luck in these tournaments depends on what kind of table draw you get. The table helps me decide my game plan.

Huckleberry Seed: If you have just one or two good players at your table, try to avoid them and just take turns working on the other players.

Ted: There are variations of good players. Sometimes, a good player is someone who sits there and waits for a hand, which is probably a good enough strategy to build your chips in these razz tournaments. Just steal through those players. Some good players like to play a lot of pots. Wait until you have a good hand to mess with those guys.

A series of steal plays becomes possible with the right kind of table.

Ted: Another possible steal is to limp with a low card, especially if you have tight players with low cards behind you. If they raise and you limped without a very good hand, you can just fold. But often, those players are just waiting for three babies and folding when they don't get them. If you are lucky to get this kind of table, just call the bring-in with any low card showing. In general, you are going to win most of the pots where you are heads-up with the high card.

Playable Hands—Call or Raise

How you interpret and respond to the action at your table when you have a playable hand depends on a number of factors: the action before you, the exposed cards of the players behind you, the playing styles of the players behind you and those already in the pot, how "live" your hand is, your table image, the size of the antes, and numerous other factors. How do you balance those things?

Ted Forrest: Here is an example of a rough hand. You have 5-6-7, which is normally a playable hand, but the board is A-A-A-2-4-X-X.

I certainly wouldn't fall in love with this hand. It is hard to make a seven low with three aces, a deuce, and four exposed. And the types of hands you will make will be very rough—a rough eight, a rough nine. If there is any action to speak of, your hand is worth no more than a steal attempt. You might as well have 6-6-7. If you get any competition, you have to outflop them, or just get rid of the hand. If one of the aces raised in front of me, I suspected he had a real hand, and there were any babies behind me, I wouldn't consider playing it.

If you have a three-card eight or better and the high card has already called a full bet, even if you know the raiser has a better hand than yours, you should go ahead and cap the bets because your hand is definitely worth more than a third of the pot with a high-card hand trailing along for capped bets. That high card will often catch a card where he has to fold and you will continue with that dead money in the pot.

Don't hesitate to throw away, immediately or on fourth street, otherwise playable hands when multiple opponents make it clear they have better hands and your cards aren't reasonably live. On the other hand, if you think someone has a better hand and you have something like A-4-8 but you look around and see aces, fours, and eights on the board, you should play the hand.

If no one has come in and you have a three-card seven, you should generally raise with it. If the antes are high, there is no use slow-playing. If the antes are such that it's worth it to limp in early position with a strong hand—I'm talking about your cards being duplicated on the board—then limp sometimes with strong hands and rough hands. What is your table image? If you know they have you marked down as someone who raises with any playable hand, they won't be deterred by your raising with a strong hand. But if they are timid and the antes aren't especially large, give them a chance to come in. Someone may raise you, either with a second-best hand or because they think your limping is a sign of weakness.

I think you should generally raise, though, even if there are some babies behind you. The danger with raising with a three-card seven is getting reraised by someone who has that beat. But it's not that often someone has a three-card seven beat. And that reraise gets rid of other playable hands that could outflop you. It is pretty rare that you want multiway action in razz.

Huckleberry Seed: If you have a three-card eight, you raise and a three-card lower reraises, and a three-card nine (or better) throws their hand away, you are happy the third player is out. In a low ante structure, you might limp and hope to trap a third player with a worse hand into coming in. You want to save the trapping plays for the levels where the antes are low.

Ted: One of the things I like about limping with an extremely strong hand is that you can reraise if someone behind you puts in a full bet. You should consider doing this if your cards are very good (meaning that you see them on other people's door cards), ensuring that you see fifth street. For example, if you have A-3-4 and there is an ace, a three, and a four showing, you have a hand you are going to see fifth street with no matter what. Your opponent may not have a hand that strong, so you may as well make the pot big.

Controlling the size of the pot when you have a perfect hand serves two purposes. First, if you do catch a bad card on fourth street, it is definitely worthwhile to see fifth street. Your hand is good enough to do that anyway, but now you are really getting the odds to take another card. But the bigger pot also serves a second purpose: it encourages your opponent to make a bad decision. If he raised with a marginal hand, catches bad, and folds, his fold is correct (but you got one more bet out of him). That extra bet, though, might tie him to the hand and encourage him to call in a bad spot.

Huck: There is also a benefit of controlling the size of the pot *smaller* sometimes. If I am playing at a table where I can steal a lot, I will usually just limp in. I am not looking to play any big pots. With a good hand, how big a favorite could I be? If my hand starts going bad, that big pot could make it harder for me to get away, even though it was correct for me to raise or reraise to begin with.

Huckleberry Seed and the Agony of Razz

This matter of playing a big hand defensively was a point of disagreement between Forrest and Seed. Forrest prefers to play the odds: get more money in the pot when you are the favorite. Seed, however, is risk-averse (though he might say "variance-averse") when he has the ability to steal.

HUCK: In one razz tournament I was in a groove. I never had to play a pot. If I had A-2-3, I'd just throw it away. No need to gamble in a big pot.

TED: I never thought I played that good. If I had A-2-3 and my cards were good, I'd usually be in there.

HUCK: I don't want to gamble with a certain percentage of my stack. Say I have 6,000 and we are playing 200-400. It has been raised and reraised—

TED: Then it costs you just 400 and you have the best hand.

HUCK: But I know the other player will probably raise it again. If they are both players who like to jam, I might be gambling a third of my stack on this hand, half if this happened at the 300-600 level.

TED: If Huck is at such a good table where he can just steal them blind and these two players come in jamming the pot, maybe he might not be able to steal them blind.

HUCK: These are the kind of players—[Note: it was clear by this point in the discussion that this actually happened to Seed a couple years ago. He wanted to throw away the hand, didn't, and regretted it.]—who don't play many hands but when they do, they like to jam because they think they are going to make up for all the hands they threw away.

TED: The time I would throw away A-2-3 would be when the fours, fives, and sixes were exposed and my hand wasn't live.

HUCK: What if it was raise-call-reraise-call?

TED: Unless my cards weren't live, I'd call.

HUCK: In a five-way pot?

TED: You are a money favorite if your cards are live.

HUCK: Look at the variance you are exposing yourself to in a five-way pot.

TED: Sometimes you win those five-way pots.

HUCK: In a tournament, you want to build your stack and cut down on your variance.

TED: Unless I'm risking a huge percentage of my stack and the table is really juicy and they are letting me get away with murder, I am probably going to play the hand.

HUCK: If I was a marginal favorite with a hand, I would throw it away. If I'm calling 400 and earning 450, I don't need that 50. I can use the 400 better on another hand where I can get someone in bad shape on fifth street.

TED: I think I could make money playing Huck's discards.

Fourth Street and Beyond: Putting Opponents on Hands

Ted Forrest: When you and your opponent both have legitimate hands—one of you raised it and the other called—you have to start putting the other player on a hand. You really want to be aware of the cards that have been exposed and people's actions with their hands. If a smart player has a seven showing and there are two threes and a four gone and this smart player will not stop raising with a seven, I would not assume he has A-2-7. I would think he has 3-4-7. You want to combine mathematics with physical tells when players catch babies to determine whether that baby has paired them or made them a draw. Sometimes, you know. If there are three deuces out and your opponent catches a deuce on fourth street, you can be pretty sure he has a four-card hand.

Getting Away from Hands (or Not)

Ted Forrest: Generally, if you can pass your opponent on the next street if you catch good and he catches bad, there is enough money in the pot to call. Most players, if they are drawing live on fifth street, will stay to the end. I think, if you are a big underdog by fifth street, it is a mistake to keep drawing. Another thing to keep in mind is that whoever has the best *draw* on fifth street is usually the favorite. A six draw with a king is a favorite over a made 9-8.

Huckleberry Seed: There is nothing wrong in a tournament with folding in a marginal situation where it may be slightly right to call. In a cash game, you might call because you are getting the right price. But in a tournament, preserving your chips for situations where you can use them more profitably is better than taking a risk in a marginal situation.

Defending Against Stealers

Ted Forrest: If you are at a table where someone is getting greedy, reraising with a legitimate three-card eight might be a way of getting that player to slow down. You want him to leave some of those antes for you.

   If it is my game plan to wait for a good hand where I am a favorite and gamble, I would wait and trap a stealer by just calling. But if a large part of my plan is to steal the antes myself, I am going to reraise that player and let him know he can't barge in every time without worrying about getting reraised.

Huckleberry Seed: If you have position on the stealer, it's good to reraise him a couple times.

Ted: If the stealer has position on you, that can be even better. You can get your bet in first. The stealer now needs a decent hand to reraise you. When the stealer acts after you, limp in with your good hands.

The Bubble

Ted Forrest: Identify the people who want to sneak into the money and steal through them. It is easier in razz than in other forms of poker to identify what strategy they are using: they are playing only three-card eights or better. That is an easy strategy to beat if you know that is what they are doing.

Short-Stacked

Ted Forrest: When you get short-chipped, you should play your hands in a straightforward manner unless you have a very easy stealing situation—you are the last low card and no one has followed the bring-in. The shorter your stack is, however, the more honest you have to play. You are probably going to get action, so you should have a good hand when you put your chips in.

Huckleberry Seed: What do you consider short-chipped? I would consider 2,000 at the 200-400 level as short.

Ted: That's borderline. If I had 1,400–1,500 in chips, I almost have to wait for a good hand. With 1,400, you could afford to risk 200. If you get caught, you can put the brakes on. But if you have just 600, you can't afford to steal. You better have a hand.

Huck: You should have enough for one more bullet, or to see fifth street. Twelve hundred or more, or at least three times the upper betting limit.

Ted: That is about right: 200 on fourth, 400 on fifth. Plus about 400 more. On fifth street, if you go all-in, they will definitely call you, even as a huge underdog. You want to have enough chips for that.

The Beginner's Chance

After discussing all these strategies and feeling comfortable understanding them, I couldn't help ask the ultimate questions: What should I focus on in my first razz tournament? What chance would I have?

Huckleberry Seed: When you put your chips in the pot, experienced players will know what you have. Mix up your strategy. Try different things. Mix people up as much as you can. Worry about all the cards that are out. Keep track of those cards.

Ted Forrest: Play your three-card eights, unless there is a lot of action and your cards are dead. Try to steal once in a while.

Huck: Occasionally, limp with a low card up as a steal, hope nobody raises, and maybe you can catch a good one and they all go out on fourth street. And sometimes steal by raising. With the limp-steal, you are getting so much greater odds for it to work. (But not at the first level with the World Series structure—don't limp in that structure.) You might want to limp a few times with good hands to get opponents to think that's how you play. That sets up the limp-steal. One mistake beginning players make is think they are going to reraise or limp and reraise on third street to represent a big hand. All that really accomplishes is building the pot to where they are going to want to chase you more.

Ted: If you are a fundamentally sound player, you will be at a disadvantage to players who really understand razz, but you can make it to the money with nothing more than solid play—if you get somewhat more than your share of starting hands. It is an added advantage to be able to dance around a little bit and mix it up in the right spots. Anybody playing basic strategy is going to get crushed by a good poker player.

Here is one thing you should remember: the average player in these razz tournaments is pretty weak. So playing by the book should be good enough to build up your chips. But when you match up against good readers, good razz players who have a little speed to their game, you will be at the mercy of getting good starting cards.

Razz is one of the purest forms of poker, because the good players will make the money and the bad players will lose the money. It's a beautiful, beautiful form of poker.

All three of us played in the razz event the next day—I was, frankly, surprised that they ended the evening citing a need for sleep, since both had amazing constitutions—and made it late into the evening. Huck Seed, one table from me, went out at the end of level 7. My own chips were dwindling and I probably threw away some opportunities because I irrationally wanted to outlast him. I succeeded and, as near as I can tell, Ted Forrest (who was across the room) and I got eliminated at the same time, during level 8.

None of this proved anything, though I can say for sure I was the only one who had any reason to be happy about the outcome.

PART V

CONCLUDING MATERIAL

CHAPTER 19

Roshambo and the Mental Game of Poker

by Rafe Furst

Editor's Note

Undoubtedly, the mental game of poker is something every player would like to understand better. It is, however, the most difficult part of the game to teach. Nearly every chapter of this book has some disclaimer about how hard it is to read opponents. You need experience, innate ability, etcetera etcetera etcetera. I insisted that each collaborator also specify some player-reading or hand-reading skills that amateur players could acquire and improve upon.

To the uninitiated, roshambo (a.k.a rock-paper-scissors) is a children's game. To those with a passing knowledge of the contemporary tournament poker scene, it is an adult game where the competitors *behave* like children. To the participants, however, it is serious business masked by humor and silliness.

If you can't see the relationship between roshambo and the mental game of poker, you need to open your mind. Or play at a table with Rafe Furst, an extraordinary mental warrior who could buy a car (or several) with all the money he has made playing roshambo, not to mention the training it has provided him.

Just before turning in this manuscript, I was seated to Rafe's right at a Full Tilt H.O.R.S.E. tournament. During a round of seven-card stud late in the tournament, I was second to last to act with A-Q-Q, one of the queens showing. Everyone folded after the bring-in, so I raised. Furst, with a ten showing, reraised. I thought for a moment that he might have another ten in the hole and considered the reraise a declaration: "I have pocket tens so don't try drawing." I also thought that he might have put me on a steal and was merely representing strength. I just called, letting him think he caught me and I was sticking around for the flop. (The possibility I never considered was rolled-up tens, which is what he had.)

What I was *mostly* debating, though, was whether Rafe would play a strong hand strong against me. He had to know I would expect him to raise with nothing if he thought I was stealing. Was he actually behaving in the stereotypical way, trying to resteal? Or would he think I would assume that he was "camouflaging" a strong hand by playing it strong?

The waters became clearer when I picked up an ace on fourth street. Forget this mental stuff, I have aces up! But he picked up a ten on fifth street.

In the end, I lost a lot of chips to his quads. At a certain point in the hand, I outguessed myself and made an extra bet to "expose his weakness." But I also thought about his signature roshambo move, which is to offer to play you, then say, "I always start out with rock," just before the throw. Therefore—and I was aided by that ten on fifth street, which would have put him ahead if he had just one ten in the hole—I concluded he was trying to deceive me by playing straightforward.

Against Rafe Furst and other great mental warriors, the question *Does he have it?* is far too simple. You have to ask, *Would he play like he had it if he had it?*

Sure, it's easier being smart when you have quads, but every poker hand involves a series of close decisions where you have to evaluate whether your opponent is playing consistent or contrary to the cards, and your opponent is doing the same. Even though we are conditioned by watching the closing hands of no-limit hold 'em tournaments to think poker comes down to one big decision, that is usually not the case. Whoever wins the war of attrition, constantly fighting mental skirmishes and coming out with the best of it a little more than average, is going to win.

I personally think the best role models for roshambo are Vizzini and Westley in *The Princess Bride*. Rafe Furst obviously prefers Miyagi and

Daniel from *The Karate Kid*. I could argue the point with him, but why should I? He has a World Series bracelet and is one of the best roshambo players in the world. I can't top that, so I let him have all his *Karate Kid* references; I just stuck his chapter here at the end of the book.

Wax On, Wax Off

In poker, often the player who wins is the one who is able to think just a little deeper than their opponent. For instance, let's say I have bluffed and been called the last three showdowns that you have seen. Now you are facing an all-in bet from me on the river and are wondering whether I am bluffing again. Logic would dictate that the past is a good indicator of the future and you should call. Or would it? Maybe I want you to think that I am bluffing, realizing that you have observed my previous behavior. Maybe I really have the goods this time and want you to call. Then again, maybe I figured you'd think about that and decide that *this* time I'm not bluffing and you'll fold to what actually is another bluff. Or wait, could I be twisted enough to think that you'd fall for *that* old trick, and really be holding the nuts?

Not only do you find this type of multilevel thinking between different hands in a session, but also within the play of a single hand. As you probably know from *Mike Caro's Book of Tells*, a player who acts weak probably has a strong hand, and vice versa. But since so many people understand this, often you will find an experienced opponent acting weak, hoping you will put him on being strong, when in fact he really is weak.

Of course, this thinking can regress indefinitely. If you think one level too deep or not deep enough, you've lost the battle of wits and fallen into the trap your opponent has set for you. At the same time, you are trying to confound your opponent with similar logic bombs and misdirection. What can you do to calibrate your internal depth gauge?

I recommend you find a worthy opponent and roshambo for money. Whether it's ten cents a throw or $100 a throw, you will quickly find yourself descending to deeper and deeper levels of thinking. Like Daniel-san in *The Karate Kid*, you may not realize that your poker skills are being honed until faced with a *rock-rock-rock-is-he-going-to-switch-to-scissors*-like situation at the final table of the WSOP.

FURST: Against expert roshambo players, you have to go many levels deep in your thinking.

CRAIG: How many levels do you usually have to go to win?

FURST: The amount never varies: one level deeper than your opponent.

Beware My Tiger Style!

Dan Harrington points out in his excellent treatise, *Harrington on Hold 'Em*, that there is more than one "correct" playing style for no-limit hold 'em tournaments. Look at the contrasting styles described for the game in chapters 3 through 6 of this book. Although Howard Lederer, Chris Ferguson, and Andy Bloch do not play an identical style, you don't have to read those chapters very closely to see the similarities. Now look at Ted Forrest's "rebuttal" in chapter 5. Different winning players, different styles.

Each style matches up with other styles differently, and the way you make the most money is by convincing your opponents you are playing one style when you really are playing another. This is analogous to roshambo where you might favor a move or pattern for a while (e.g., paper, scissors, rock, paper, scissors, rock . . .), and then once you think your opponent has caught on, you switch it up, throwing the sequence that beats what your opponent would do to counter your pattern. The key in your roshambo training is to experiment and get comfortable with as many different styles as possible so that at any point you can adjust instantly. This is what poker players mean by "shifting gears."

In Your Head

Roshambo, like poker, is a game that is very technical at the beginning and intermediate levels, but at the advanced and professional levels it becomes more about psychology. Part of the psychology of course involves tells—unintended or involuntary actions that give away information. Even though the tells you find in roshambo won't translate well to the poker tables, the *practice* of observing your opponents at all times will. One of the biggest areas that most novice poker players can improve on is to always be looking for tells in their opponents, even when not involved directly in the hand. To be sure, it's not easy to concentrate in this way for hours at a stretch, but you can improve your tell-reading stamina dramatically through roshambo.

In addition to picking up information on your opponents, you will need to camouflage your own play and feed your opponents as much misinformation as possible. Although talking about the current hand during a tournament is a no-no, there are times when it is appropriate to use your Jedi mind tricks to convince your opponents to act in a certain way.

In roshambo, my power move against new opponents is to say, "I'm going to throw rock," and nothing else. I am doing this to induce in you a belief that I'm *not* going to throw rock, at which point I will throw rock. Or if I think you are the type to believe that I will do as I say, then I'll do so with the intention of throwing scissors (or paper, depending on whether I think you will be aggressive or not). In poker, if I were to bluff you out of a pot I might tell you that you made a good laydown ("I had the flush"). I do this only partly because I'm a compulsive liar. Mostly I do it because I think you will believe me and thus (a) you will have misinformation about how I play, and (b) I will know and be able to exploit it later. But don't get cute and try to use this against me at the tables; if I think you've read this and are trying to get me to lie to you about my hand, I might just switch it up on you and tell the truth!

Children's Game, Huh?

If you are disillusioned by the fact that I might lie to you even after the hand is over, I've got news for you. *Poker is a brutal game, and you'd better get tough psychologically if you want to win.* Pros will sometimes recount situations where they were playing against weaker opponents and they can see it in the eyes: the amateur has had enough and is psychologically beaten, even if they still have chips left. "He was ready to go home" the pro will say, or "She was just looking for an opportunity to give me all of her chips." It is in this battle of wills that roshambo has the most to teach us about poker.

I recommend finding an evenly matched roshambo training partner and building your way up to a thousand throws a day (always play for money). You will notice that there are times when you are so in your opponent's head that it seems like they have an LED readout on their forehead telegraphing their next move. At other times you will feel like the neon sign. What's important to keep in mind is that however you feel—whether the hunter or the hunted—your opponent feels exactly the opposite. When you are in control, this is the time to hone your killer instincts and try to break your opponent. No mercy! Cobra Kai! And when you are on the ropes and feeling like there is no hope, you must channel your inner Daniel-san and fight back—don't make me break out my Crane Style!

There will be those who dismiss the importance of roshambo as a training tool for poker, but then there were those who thought online poker could never produce a world champion either. There's a new breed of poker player ready to take the throne, and their battle cry is, "Nothing beats rock!" The question is, will you throw paper?

A Few Words About Your Teachers

by Michael Craig

Full Tilt and Me—The Early Days

On April 3, 2004, I wandered around the Bellagio poker room, hoping to meet some of the best poker players in the world. They were all strangers to me, though I had some notion they would tell me about a giant poker game they periodically played with a publicity-shy billionaire. It was the first day of the Bellagio Five-Star World Poker Classic, a series of poker tournaments that concluded with the World Poker Tour Championship.

The closest I came was a promise from Barry Greenstein to talk at some future date, and a few seconds eavesdropping on Howard Lederer and Erik Seidel. All I caught was Howard's tail end of a hand description: ". . . that was a real pigsty." Howard was wearing a long-sleeved white T-shirt with a small red triangular logo. I caught the name on the logo, but didn't understand the meaning: Full Tilt Poker.

It turned out that I was one of the first people to ever notice that logo. It was the first day of the first tournament after Full Tilt had begun operating as a play-money online poker site. Even during the summer, after I met Howard and conducted a series of interviews for *The Professor, the Banker, and the Suicide King,* Full Tilt was largely unknown. They gave out T-shirts at the World Series. They didn't start offering real-money games until later that summer. From my meetings with Lederer, I could see that he was pouring himself into getting the site as much exposure as possible, but outside our discussions on his back patio, I rarely heard about the site.

A lot has happened in the three years between the opening of the Full Tilt Poker sites and the publication of this book. I have to believe falling in step behind Howard was an omen. He won the tournament that day, and Full Tilt has gone on to become one of the best places to play poker online. I was lucky to watch it every step of the way, and to eventually work with several of Full Tilt's pros to produce this book.

Meet the pros!

Andy Bloch

Andy Bloch began applying his analytical mind and programming skills to gambling at an early age. While still a teenager, after a couple trips to a Connecticut jai alai fronton, he wrote a program to profitably bet the outcome of jai alai matches.

Several years later, after obtaining a pair of engineering degrees from the Massachusetts Institute of Technology (MIT), he wandered into the recently opened Foxwoods Casino while between engineering jobs. He discovered a game the casino was experimenting with in the blackjack pit, Wild Bill Hickock's Aces & Eights Poker. Like blackjack, the players drew cards and competed with the house. Because it had a variety of wild cards and bonus payouts, the optimal strategy for the game was not obvious, nor was it clear whether the house even had an edge.

Bloch wrote a program for beating the game and formed a team to press the player's edge for as many hours as possible. Within six months, Foxwoods discontinued the Hickock game, but it put Andy on the circuitous path that resulted in his becoming, fifteen years later, one of the most respected and well-known poker players in the world.

He began playing poker at Foxwoods, winning a no-limit hold 'em tournament in December 1993. Forming the Hickock team also brought him in contact with members of the infamous (and still secret) MIT Blackjack Team. (He had not, in five years at the school, known any of the rotating cast of traveling blackjack card-counters.)

By 1995, he had quit engineering, moved to Las Vegas, and was managing the MIT team and developing his poker skills. Writing programs to simulate games sped up the learning process dramatically.

In months, he found strategies that other pros took decades working out. For example, after being introduced to Chinese poker, he finished in the money in five Chinese poker events in Las Vegas between September and December 1995. (After winning an event at the Hall of Fame in December 1995, he met another computer programmer who had made the final table and found they took a similar approach to poker. That started Andy's friendship with Chris Ferguson.) Although Bloch had to cut back on poker after starting at Harvard Law School in 1996, he continued as a player-manager of the blackjack team.

At loose ends after getting his law degree, he played some poker, considered a career in public-interest law jobs, and moved to D.C. to help his sister raise her young daughter. He decided to commit himself to tournament poker in 2002, positioning himself perfectly to catch the boom times to follow.

In 2002, he made the final table of the Jack Binion World Poker Open in Tunica, then wrapped up the year at the place that launched his career in gambling, and then in poker, Foxwoods. He won the seven-card stud event and made the final table of the sixth event of the World Poker Tour's inaugural season. Just three months later, he made a second WPT final table in Los Angeles.

Andy Bloch has enjoyed tournament success at events around the world and in every form of poker. He has finished in the money in England, Ireland, France, and Monte Carlo. He has made final tables in no-limit hold 'em, seven-card stud, limit hold 'em, Chinese poker, stud eight-or-better, razz, Omaha eight-or-better, and pot-limit Omaha.

For some reason, however, until 2006, he had little success at the World Series of Poker. Between law school and a self-banishment during part of the Nick and Becky Binion Behnen years, Bloch did not typically play a full schedule of events at the Series, and missed some years entirely. But in 2004 and 2005, he played most of the events and cashed just once, finishing ninety-fifth in a 2005 $1,500 pot-limit hold 'em event, earning $1,625.

In 2006, however, Andy Bloch ended the drought in grand fashion. After striking out in the first six events, he cashed in consecutive Omaha eight-or-better events and made his first World Series final table in five years, finishing eighth in no-limit hold 'em. (When he made the final table, he said, "I owe it all to this book, because working on the

pre-flop chapter has really made that part of my game more solid.")
That payday made it easier to plunk down the $50,000 buy-in for the
H.O.R.S.E. event.

In three marathon sessions in the H.O.R.S.E., Andy finished second to the legendary Chip Reese, dominating a final table that included winners of twenty-nine bracelets and five players who had
won at least three. The finish confirmed Bloch's position as a cunning
and solid all-round pro, capable of playing his best poker against the
world's best under the biggest spotlight. (Reese and Bloch became
the first players to make over a million dollars outside the Main
Event at the Series.)

Richard Brodie

Richard "Quiet Lion" Brodie categorizes himself as an "advanced-
intermediate" poker player. He can afford to be modest. His poker
achievements since 2003—he only started playing Texas hold 'em at
that time—may not have matched the rest of his résumé (yet), but he
has set the bar impossibly high.

Brodie, who has been retired since the mid-nineties, has worked
as a software engineer for two of the most famous organizations of
the computer age: Xerox PARC and Microsoft. He was employee
No. 77 at Microsoft and is the original author of Microsoft Word, one
of the world's most popular computer programs. Although the program has been rewritten on a continuous basis since Richard wrote
his last line of code, he was the original author and has been credited
with some of its most important current features, like automatically
underlining misspelled words.

Since he left Microsoft, he has authored two books, *Getting Past
O.K.* (about why your life isn't necessarily perfect after you get everything you think you wanted, and how to improve it) and *Virus of the
Mind* (about the new science of memes, the mental programming
that can create mental viruses that operate among people the same
way software viruses operate among computers).

Although Richard played some kitchen-table poker with Bill
Gates, he had never played Texas hold 'em until his friend Andy

Bloch told him about making a pair of final tables during the first season of the World Poker Tour. Richard, a novice to tournaments, began playing online sit-n-gos and multitable tournaments, learning and winning, and played in his first live tournament in July 2003. It was a $1,000 no-limit hold 'em event at the Bellagio and he finished second. Since then, he has continued to play frequently and successfully online (until Washington made it illegal to *play* online poker in 2006). He has finished in the money four times on the World Poker Tour, two times at the World Series of Poker, and made a total of seven final tables in other tournaments.

Chris Ferguson

Chris Ferguson is a living paradox, a study in the contrast between appearance and reality, and a demonstration of how appearance can *become* reality.

Chris's physical appearance at poker tournaments—the long hair, the beard, the cowboy hat, the mirrored shades, the utter unflappability—is both mysterious and intimidating. Yet he manufactured this image to dissuade opponents from regarding his moves as the product of years of studying game theory and working out the percentages for optimal play.

Somehow, the brainy former college student *became* that cool guy. Of course, it took a lot more than long hair and a cowboy hat. It took achievements unmatched in tournament poker, and it took delivering them on a consistent basis.

Ferguson's first recorded tournament successes, occurring during the first half of his thirteen-year doctoral odyssey, were inauspicious but eclectic: fourth place in a pai gow tournament in March 1993, and another fourth in an Asian stud event that May.

His 1994 résumé is the poker player's equivalent of a war correspondent's passport: L.A. Poker Classic, Masters of Poker Championship (four cashes), L.A. Poker Open (three cashes), Big Poker Oktober (two cashes), and the Hall of Fame. The list of events is likewise varied: stud, limit hold 'em, lowball, razz, Omaha eight-or-better, no-limit hold 'em, stud eight-or-better.

Chris did the same thing for the next five years, though always a little better. Between 1995 and 1999, he finished in the money at the World Series of Poker twelve times, making seven final tables. In California tournaments, he was routinely cashing and occasionally winning: limit hold 'em in 1995, pot-limit Omaha and a pair of no-limit hold 'em wins in 1996, limit hold 'em in 1998, pot-limit hold 'em in 1999.

During this period, Chris was living at home, inching toward his PhD, and working "odd jobs" for the likes of the Department of Defense and the California Lottery. At UCLA, his specialties were search algorithms and artificial intelligence. For Ferguson, it was playing games, something his parents (both math PhDs) and his older brother Marc (a computer programmer) did all the time while he was growing up. He was also learning quantitative analysis in securities trading.

In late 1999, his advisor gently told him, "Chris, it's time to graduate." With his research grant running out of funding, he got his PhD in computer science, moved his office across the street, and began day-trading securities. He became friends with the manager of the office, Ray Bitar.

Less than six months later, everything he had worked toward in poker came together at once. In early May 2000, he won his first World Series of Poker bracelet, in seven-card stud. After finishing in the money two more times as the Series wound down, Ferguson won the World Championship and $1.5 million, a story famously chronicled in James McManus's *Positively Fifth Street*.

Even as the Jesus-cowboy-rock-star persona edged closer to reality, success in poker really didn't change Chris Ferguson. He continued trading stocks and playing online poker and other games with Ray Bitar, and continued haunting medium buy-in events along the West Coast. Bitar and Ferguson started a business to develop online poker software. The software business, later named TiltWare LLC, dominated their activities by 2003 and they withdrew from securities trading.

Since 2000, Ferguson has run roughshod over the World Series of Poker. In 2001, he cashed six times and won his third bracelet, in Omaha eight-or-better. In 2003, he did even better, cashing a record eight times (subsequently tied), making a record five final tables, and winning two more bracelets, his second in Omaha eight-or-better and one in half-stud/half–hold 'em. He cashed four times in 2004, three final tables and twenty-sixth in the Main Event. He cashed six times in 2005, making a pair of pot-limit Omaha final tables, and three more times in 2006. When Harrah's inaugurated its World Series of Poker Circuit in early 2005, Ferguson made his claim on those events, making three final tables and winning twice in 2005. He also won ten of twelve televised heads-up matches, finishing runner-up in both the 2005 and 2006 NBC Heads-Up Championships.

Ask Chris his favorite times in poker, however, and he is likely to tell you about sixty-hour weeks competing for play money on IRC Poker in the early nineties. "I really don't like to play poker for money," he has said, "but I'm glad other people want to."

Ted Forrest

Ted Forrest has made a living by confounding opponents more than any poker player on earth. He has done it for almost twenty years, at all stakes, in cash games and tournaments, in all forms of poker, and all over the world. There will never be an agreement over the best poker player in the world, but Forrest has excelled in so many different situations for so long a period that his name has to be on the short list.

Some of Ted's unpredictability as a poker player stems from the unpredictability of his life. The son of a pair of English professors, he has always followed his own course, freely accepting the risks, uncertainties, and setbacks that have popped up along the way. He left college just before graduation to work as a maid at a motel on the rim of the Grand Canyon. When he moved to Las Vegas to play poker, he was so broke that he initially survived on a bottle of milk and ketchup packets, and then on a single meal per day at a local shelter.

He loved those experiences—the freedom and the risk. Ted Forrest possessed the perfect temperament to play high-stakes poker. He also had two other characteristics that were essential tools for a professional gambler: a willingness to gamble and an iron constitution. Over the years, Ted has wagered large amounts of money on his physical prowess—performing a standing backflip, drinking ten beers in an hour, running a marathon on the hottest day of the year. (They haven't all worked out. He suffered a permanent injury to a pectoral muscle during a tennis/weightlifting bet in 2003.) He has also played poker for as long as 105 hours at a time. Ted has a gambler's sense of knowing the right price, but even then, he has been willing to take a leap of faith when he thought the situation called for it. He has been unafraid to rely on himself, unafraid to take a chance, and unafraid of losing.

Before 2003, Ted focused on high-stakes cash games, playing tournaments only occasionally. Nevertheless, his results were astounding. At the L.A. Poker Classic at the Commerce in 1992, he won two events and made ten final tables. In 1993, at the World Series of Poker, he became just the second player to win three bracelets in a single year; he played only six events in that Series.

Periodic tournament appearances resulted in other flurries of top finishes. Four final tables at Foxwoods, 1993. Three final tables at the Diamond Jim Brady, 1994. Three runner-up finishes at the U.S. Poker Championships, 1996.

In 2001, *Card Player* surveyed sixty top players for their opinions of their peers. In cash games, Ted Forrest ranked as the best overall player, the best mixed-game player, the best stud player, the second-best stud eight-or-better player, the second-best short-handed player. Even though he was not a regular tournament player, the other players voted him the best razz tournament player and the fifth-best tournament player in stud and stud eight-or-better.

That was even before Forrest concluded that he should vie for a share of the growing prizes and collateral opportunities that came with high-profile televised tournament poker success. He finished fifth in the first World Poker Tour Championship in 2003, and began playing in all the big tournaments in 2004. At the Bellagio Five-Star World Poker Classic in April 2004, he played just two events, winning in stud eight-or-better and finishing in the money at the second WPT Championship. At the World Series immediately following, he won his fourth and fifth bracelets, in seven-card stud and no-limit hold 'em. In the week after the Series, he finished third in a televised no-limit hold 'em event at the Plaza.

In 2005, he made regular successful appearances on Poker Superstars. He also finished second in a televised Full Tilt tournament. His best performances were in May at the Mirage, when he finished, on back-to-back final-table days, second in the World Poker Tour event (his second WPT final table of the year) and first in the Professional Poker Tour event.

In 2006, he grabbed the biggest piece of spotlight of his professional career. At the second NBC Heads-Up Championship, he careened from the brink of defeat to an amateur in a preliminary round to defeat Chris Ferguson (the 2005 runner-up) in a masterful three-game performance in the final.

Rafe Furst

Until 2006, Rafe Furst was known in poker for everything *except* his skill. He had maintained, possibly intentionally, an image as a happy-go-lucky guy with a lot of gamble. Like Chris Ferguson, the image obscured a formidable competitor with tremendous skill. Furst is, in fact, a happy-go-lucky guy and he does like to gamble. Always concealed, however, were his impressive credentials for figuring out games and his drive to succeed.

Rafe first became known as "The Guy Who Busted from the Main Event in 11 Minutes." In 2003, the first year ESPN featured pre-final-table action from the World Series of Poker, it focused on Rafe, who was the first player eliminated, out of 839. Furst's public persona was further set by his connection with the increasingly infamous Tiltboys, a group of silly, obsessed gamblers who had apparently shed their past successes in academics and business. They were the Stanford poker game (originally organized by Furst) that never grew up. They played roshambo for big money.

But the other Tiltboys garnering publicity also became known for feats of tournament poker skill. Phil Gordon finished fourth in the championship two years before. Perry Friedman, who bore the ridicule of the other Tiltboys as a badge of honor, won a bracelet in 2001. Rafe Furst, in contrast, was the guy who busted in eleven minutes. His most notable poker success was making the final table, dressed in drag, of a ladies-only event at the Bay 101 Casino.

The real story was revealed slowly, piecemeal. Rafe attended Stanford University, where he earned a BS in symbolic systems and an MS in computer science. He worked as a computer science researcher specializing in artificial intelligence at the Kestrel Institute. He left his Silicon Valley success behind in 1996 to start Pickem Sports, a company bringing promotional sports events to the then mostly unknown Internet. He and Perry Friedman sold Pickem for $7 million in cash and stock in 1999.

Since he left that company in 2001, he has built up an even more unconventional résumé: traveling through Europe, Africa, and Asia; with Phil Gordon, joining the Cancer Research and Prevention Foundation (PreventCancer.org) and raising money with the Ultimate Sports Adventure (a yearlong fund-raising odyssey in which they traveled to over 100 sporting events in an RV) and Bad Beat on Cancer (through which they have enlisted hundreds of tournament poker players to donate 1 percent of their tournament money to CRPF); founding ExpertInsight.com with Gordon; and winning a fortune at roshambo, a game still considered silly and childish by the public at large but a game-theory laboratory by its practitioners.

In 2005, Rafe cashed three times in the World Series. He followed that up with a victory in the Ultimate Poker Challenge.

In 2006, Furst's skill and ingenuity in games blossomed for a large audience. At the second event of the 2006 World Series of Poker, he outlasted over eleven hundred players, triumphing at a televised final table to win his first bracelet, in pot-limit hold 'em. He then returned home to Los Angeles and didn't play again in the Series until just prior to the Main Event.

Rafe Furst now has a bracelet and four other cashes in the last two years at the World Series of Poker. He has finished in the money in four different forms of poker: Omaha eight-or-better, stud eight-or-better, no-limit hold 'em (twice), and pot-limit hold 'em. It would appear Rafe is now only beginning to reach his stride.

Phil Gordon

Phil Gordon has taken a path to poker success and fame that has been both calculated and serendipitous. In addition to his success on the World Poker Tour and at the World Series of Poker, he has become one of the world's best-known and highly respected poker personalities, hosting *Celebrity Poker Showdown* on Bravo, writing three best-selling instructional poker books, and responding to the unprecedented demand for his services on network and cable TV broadcasts, motivational speeches, instructional DVDs, and even podcasts.

Phil had planned on becoming a professional poker player. How he succeeded on such a grand scale, however, is a testament to the meeting of talent and serendipity, not planning.

In 1993, Gordon was a young computer programmer working for Lockheed in the Bay Area. Five nights a week, he supplemented his income by winning regularly at $6–$12 hold 'em in the local cardrooms.

With a bankroll of $10,000, he finally decided to quit his day job and concentrate on poker. He would grind out a living at poker, building his bankroll, expanding his skills, and gradually moving to bigger games. Nowhere did the plan involving writing books, winning (or even playing) tournaments, or becoming a commentator-analyst-teacher.

The same day he quit Lockheed, however, some former colleagues talked him into joining their start-up company. He liked them and they needed his skills, so he agreed to put poker on hold for six months. He made them include a small starting bonus in their offer, so he could at least add to his bankroll during this brief time away from poker.

For three and a half years, Phil Gordon worked eighty-hour weeks without a break, rarely spending a day without writing program code. When the company, Netsys Technologies, sold out to Cisco Systems in late 1996, Phil was finally liberated to pursue his dream.

But what was that dream? He was twenty-seven, single, and he had enough money from his Netsys stock to be freed from the responsibility of work, for at least a little while. He was bitten by the travel bug, spending a year living out of a backpack in Africa. He spent another two years in Australia, South America, Europe, and Southeast Asia.

Gordon had ridden the upturn in the stock market in the late nineties and was enjoying his extended leave of absence from the working world. When the bottom dropped out of the high-tech market in early 2001, Phil was at a loss. After working so hard, then not working at all, he suddenly had to contemplate another change in strategy. His friends—similarly brilliant programmers and businessmen, a sick group of gamblers who called themselves the Tiltboys—talked him into playing the 2001 World Series Main Event, if only to get out of the house.

After qualifying in the last multitable satellite for the 2001 championship, Phil Gordon made the final table and finished fourth out of 613 players, earning almost $400,000. It was just Phil's first World Series final table, but it started him on the path of all that followed: a pair of World Series final tables in 2002 and another pair in 2005, a World Poker Tour win (at one of his old haunts, Bay 101, no less), three books, and all the podcasts, television appearances, speeches, and DVDs. Shortly after finishing his chapter for this book, Gordon took down the elite, small-field FullTiltPoker.net Championship, winning $600,000 in front of a live national TV audience.

With Rafe Furst, he developed innovative ways to raise money for cancer research and prevention, including the Ultimate Sports Adventure and Bad Beat on Cancer. In 2005, he and Furst also started ExpertInsight.com, an educational media company that connects experts with people who want to expand their knowledge and skills.

David Grey

David Grey is a survivor. When people look at the increasingly famous poker players populating the highest-stakes games in Bobby's Room at the Bellagio, they see a number of new faces, some people who have been there several years, and "the old-timers": Doyle Brunson and Chip Reese.

And David Grey.

Only Brunson, Reese, and Grey were playing in the corner of the Mirage when it opened in 1989, upstairs at the Bellagio when it opened in 1998, in Bobby's Room when it opened in 2005, and are still there. He has seen dozens of players become regulars in that game, win six- and seven-figure sums, and eventually go broke.

David moved to Las Vegas in 1985. He had become a skillful horse-player back East, but usually blew his winnings on trips to Atlantic City. He came to Vegas to take a more businesslike approach to gambling. He has become one of the world's most consistently successful professional gamblers, moving from horses to sports and, of course, poker.

Despite his reputation as a solid, conservative poker player, David has a lot of gamble in him. He has become part of gambling legend for paying his vegetarian friend Howard Lederer $10,000 to eat a cheeseburger, teaming up with Lederer in what was then probably the highest-stakes golf match ever against Doyle Brunson and Mike Sexton, and making a golf bet with Huckleberry Seed that led to Seed accomplishing an historic feat in proposition betting. (See Seed's biography for that one.)

Because Grey adhered to the now outmoded code that professional gamblers should keep a low profile, he was not, until 2004, a regular on the tournament poker circuit. In occasional appearances at Binion's for the World Series and the Hall of Fame, however, he established himself as a dangerous tournament player, winning at limit hold 'em at the Hall of Fame in 1991 and seven-card stud at the World Series in 1999. In 2003, he finished eighth in the World Series Main Event.

Since 2004, he has joined his cash-game colleagues by playing more tournaments, with impressive results. In addition to regular appearances on Poker Superstars, he has finished in the money at five World Poker Tour events. He also won the World Series's prestigious deuce-to-seven championship in 2005.

Howard Lederer

Howard Lederer is one of the world's most accomplished tournament poker players. His appearances as a commentator for televised poker events are a reminder of his brilliance in analyzing tournament poker. His actual credits, coming in the days when the World Series Main Event drew hundreds, rather than thousands, are often overlooked.

The collective memory of tournament poker is short enough that Howard, in his early forties, is one of the greybeards.

Back in 1987, when Lederer was enjoying some of his initial success as a working poker player in New York, he came to Las Vegas for his first World Series. He finished fifth in the championship, becoming the youngest player to make the final table.

The regulars in Howard's game at the Mayfair Club comprised a Murderers' Row of tournament poker: Dan Harrington, Jay Heimowitz, Mickey Appleman, Steve Zolotow, and Noli Francisco. During 1988, he became friends with an unemployed stock trader named Erik Seidel who had joined the game and encouraged Seidel to give the Series a try. Erik finished second in the championship to Johnny Chan and went on to win seven World Series bracelets. Howard himself made two final tables in 1988.

He won events at the Diamond Jim Brady in Los Angeles in 1991 and the Queens Poker Classic in 1992. He moved to Las Vegas in 1993 and made a pair of final tables at the World Series in 1993 and 1994.

Lederer won the no-limit deuce-to-seven event at the Hall of Fame in 1994 and 1995. His success in this event says a lot about his genius for games. No-limit deuce-to-seven is a nearly extinct form of poker. Howard told me that Jack McClelland described the average age of a deuce-to-seven player as "dead."

The game is all about having the proper theoretical framework and reading opponents. And deuce-to-seven tournaments tend to draw only the best high-stakes players.

In 1995, in addition to winning the event a second time at the Hall of Fame, he also finished second in the tournament's Main Event. (He was also runner-up in the final Hall of Fame Championship in 2002.) Phil Hellmuth, the winner in 1995, still uses the victory over Howard as evidence of his heads-up prowess.

In 2001, Howard Lederer won his first World Series bracelet, in the Omaha eight-or-better championship. He prevailed over a final table that included several of his future Full Tilt colleagues: Chris Ferguson (seventh), Layne Flack (third), and Allen Cunningham (second).

The next year, 2002, Howard won his second bracelet, this time in deuce-to-seven. Later that year, he was runner-up in the last Hall of Fame Championship. The tournament success, while it brought some recognition, was not how he made his living. He did that in high-stakes cash games, first in New York and then at the Mirage and Bellagio. He was also a professional sports bettor, until his arrest in the late nineties by heavy-handed authorities. Furthermore, his tournament poker success was spread across all the games: final tables in limit and no-limit hold 'em, different forms of lowball, Omaha eight-or-better, stud, stud eight-or-better, and even Chinese poker. He was also competing in chess and backgammon tournaments during much of this time.

But Howard made a decision after the 2002 World Series: he was going to devote himself to becoming a great no-limit hold 'em tournament player. His reasoning and results are characteristic of the man, in several ways. First, there was the foresight. The World Poker Tour Enterprises, a production company filming poker tournaments, had just formed. It had no broadcast contract and cobbled its season out of the then occasional tournament schedule, a few online sites willing to run live tournaments, the Bellagio, and some friends of the Bellagio. But Howard saw that tournament poker could become big and he wanted to be in the middle of the action when it happened.

Second, there was his pride. After making the final table in the World Championship fifteen years before, he had yet to cash a second time in that event.

Third, there was his drive. Everybody who knows Howard Lederer recognizes that his will is unshakable. The results speak for themselves: two wins during the first season of the World Poker Tour, three wins and three additional final tables at Bellagio tournaments between April 2003 and April 2004, seven cashes and four final tables at the 2004 World Series. And he went deep in the Main Event in 2003 and 2005.

Ironically, Howard has leveraged that success to a point where his legacy has receded into the past: a series of best-selling instructional DVDs, poker fantasy camps, tournament commentary, and endorsements, including of course his association with Full Tilt Poker.

Mike Matusow

Mike "the Mouth" Matusow has turned his charismatic, controversial presence into fame on a worldwide scale. He has become so well-known from his televised battles with Phil Hellmuth, Sean Sheikhan, Daniel Negreanu, and Greg Raymer that his skill and ingenuity at the poker table have often been overlooked.

His rise to notoriety and success had humble beginnings. When he was twenty-one and working in his parents' furniture store, he scraped together money to blow at the local casinos. While he was cursing out a slot machine at the Palace Station after losing all his money, a man named Phil walked by and asked him why he was wasting his time on video poker.

"I could teach you something so that you'd never have to work another day in your life."

Remarkably, the stranger spent the next several weeks mentoring Matusow, teaching him poker strategy and having the young man stand behind him while he played. (After a few minutes, Mike wanted to buy into the game, but Phil insisted that he only watch at first.) He picked up the game quickly, winning in low-stakes games around Las Vegas. He also worked as a dealer.

In the mid- and late nineties, he played mostly in limit hold 'em cash games, graduating to the higher limit games at the Mirage and, when it opened in 1999, the Bellagio. He proved to be a natural at tournament poker, however. In 1997, in one of his first tournament appearances at first-ever games of Omaha eight-or-better, he finished second in the World Series $2,000 buy-in event. The $81,700 encouraged him to play more tournaments and for higher stakes, and led to a friendship with event winner Scotty Nguyen. (Ted Forrest finished third in the event.) He took a quarter stake in Nguyen the next year when Scotty's backer pulled out before the Main Event. Scotty, of course, won, and the cash further encouraged Mike's dreams.

Matusow's own breakthrough at the World Series took place in 1999, when he won his first bracelet, in no-limit hold 'em. This began a string of eight consecutive years (still running through 2006) of making at least one World Series final table. In 2001, he finished sixth in the Main Event. In 2002, he won his second bracelet, this time in Omaha eight-or-better. In 2003 and 2004, he made no-limit hold 'em final tables, and famously tangled with Greg Raymer deep in the Main Event.

What people didn't know was that Mike Matusow's antics were fueled by a threat to his freedom caused by his own prior bad choices.

He had been a recreational drug user for several years but had quit in 2003. Acting on a false tip, an undercover policeman befriended Mike and, unable to find any leads to Las Vegas's drug scene—Matusow had already quit—he convinced him to round up some drugs for his "friend." Accused of dealing drugs, he poured himself into winning the Main Event, losing all sense of perspective. Mike later pled guilty of a lesser offense and was sentenced to six months in jail. (The sentence began in October 2006, less than a week after he finished third in the WPT Aruba event.)

Mike's historic 2005 tournament year started with the final three months of his jail sentence. At the end of a horrendous World Series, a pair of friends had to convince him to play the Main Event. Out of over 5,600 players, he made his second Main Event final table in five years and finished ninth, earning $1 million. In November, he won the Tournament of Champions, following an epic battle with Hoyt Corkins and Phil Hellmuth, and cashed a second million-dollar check.

Since then, Mike has turned in several impressive TV tournament performances, and undoubtedly won and lost several fortunes. He remains one of poker's most captivating personalities and, more important, one of its most talented.

Huckleberry Seed

Huckleberry Seed is an enigma. He is one of the world's most successful tournament poker players, and has been since the early 1990s. Despite the increasingly high profile of professional poker players, Seed almost never speaks in public and has revealed little about his background or methods.

In 1989, Seed left behind his engineering studies at CalTech to play poker. He won his first tournament in Reno in January 1990 and hasn't looked back. In his first World Series, in 1990, he made a pair of final tables. He also made a pair of final tables at the Hall of Fame and a pair at the Diamond Jim Brady.

Those early successes demonstrated Huck's acuity in all the games, winning at no-limit hold 'em and making final tables in stud eight-or-better (twice), stud (twice), limit Omaha, and deuce-to-seven.

He followed up by finishing second in the Main Event of the Queens Poker Classic in 1991, and making three final tables in the World Series in 1992. In 1994, he won his first World Series bracelet, in pot-limit Omaha.

In 1996, he entered the Main Event of the World Series just moments before it started, the last of 295 competitors. He went on to win the championship and $1 million. Seed made the final table a second time in 1999.

In the absence of a public persona to accompany his success, he has become a legendary character for his exploits away from the table. A phenomenal athlete, he has supposedly made a fortune in proposition bets. He defeated an NBA pro one-on-one, and won what has been considered the greatest prop bet of all time. He won $35,000 by shooting four rounds of golf under 100 in one day. Making the feat brutally difficult were the following obstacles: he had to complete every round, even if he was over 100 (and he shot exactly 100 in the first round, so he had to play five rounds that day); he was limited to three clubs; he couldn't use a cart; and he had to play on the hottest day of the year in Las Vegas. Amazingly, his scores improved every round.

Huckleberry Seed has also established himself as one of the most successful players in the history of the World Series of Poker. In addition to his championship win and PLO bracelet, he won bracelets in razz in 2000 and 2003. Since his World Series debut in 1990 through 2006, he has finished in the money thirty-three times and made nineteen final tables.

Keith Sexton

Keith Sexton was raised in Dayton, Ohio. His mother and stepfather, both professional gamblers, ran a poker game in Dayton, which gave Keith his first exposure to the game. His first jobs were dealing poker in Dayton. At the age of seventeen he began playing professionally, and has gambled for his livelihood ever since.

After ten years of full-time play in Ohio, he moved to Las Vegas with his wife and three sons. For another decade, he was a regular in the $100–$200 and $200–$400 stud games at Caesars Palace and the Mirage. Between 1991 and 1994, he cashed in four stud events at the World Series, including a runner-up finish in the 1992 seven-card stud championship.

He followed the surge in interest in tournaments and, in particular, no-limit hold 'em, making televised final tables in 2005 on the World Series of Poker Circuit and at the Tournament of Champions. He also added another runner-up finish in the stud championship at the 2005 World Series, his fifth World Series of Poker final table.

The next generation of Sextons are also avid poker players. Their fierce kitchen-table game has been profiled by ESPN, and Paul, who has a degree in electrical engineering, won $30,000 from a $12 investment in an online tournament and finished fifth in one of his first World Series of Poker events, in 2005. (Paul also finished in the money in the 2006 Main Event.)

Gavin Smith

A native of Canada, Gavin Smith earned a degree in economics and discovered poker at charity casino events in Ontario in the mid-nineties. Within a few years, he was dealing poker and starting his own poker club. He began competing in U.S. tournaments and won a pair of events at Foxwoods in 1999 and 2000. He made his first TV final table at the Plaza Poker Championship in 2004.

Starting in mid-2005, Gavin began one of the great runs in tournament no-limit hold 'em in recent years. On May 16, 2005, he won a $2,000 buy-in event at the Mirage Poker Showdown. Just eight days later, he won the WPT Main Event at the Mirage. He cashed four times at the 2005 World Series, and in October made a second WPT final table at the Doyle Brunson. In January 2006, he made his third WPT final table in eight months in Tunica, and was named the World Poker Tour's player of the year for season four.

Smith's outstanding play continued well into 2006. At the World Series of Poker Circuit Main Event in New Orleans, he finished second. He then cashed another four times in the 2006 World Series, including eleventh place in the $50,000 H.O.R.S.E. The day after the H.O.R.S.E., he won the Poker Dome World Pro-Am Challenge.

Editor's Acknowledgments

This book was the result of a year of intensive work, and it would have been impossible for me to conceive, organize, and complete it without the efforts of the following people.

The collaborators, of course: Andy Bloch, Richard Brodie, Chris Ferguson, Ted Forrest, Rafe Furst, Phil Gordon, David Grey, Howard Lederer, Mike Matusow, Huckleberry Seed, Keith Sexton, and Gavin Smith. I am lucky for the friendships I developed (and, in many instances, exploited) during the past year.

Family and friends: the biggest sacrifices in producing this book were made by my wife, Jo Anne, and my kids, Barry, Ellie, and Valerie. Thanks also to Myrna and David Messenger, Robert Craig, Barton Craig, and Elaine Weiser Mendelsohn. I also benefited from the understanding and counsel of Peter Alson, Amy Calistri, Ted Corse, Kay Creighton, Nolan Dalla, Linda Geenen, Anthony Holden, Ken Kurson, Robert Kurson, Mike Miller, Steve Popuch, Harold and Hillary Schmulenson, Joanne Schlesinger, and Des Wilson.

TiltWare and affiliates: Raymond Bitar, Richard Bitar, Raymonda Bitar, Jason Newitt, Ian Imrich, Bob Wolf, the L.A. office staff of TiltWare, and Michelle Clayborne and the entire Full Tilt team at the 2006 World Series of Poker.

Other professional poker players who offered advice, friendship, or just the enjoyment of their presence and skills: John D'Agostino, Steve Brecher, Annie Duke, Perry Friedman, Clonie Gowen, Sam Grizzle, Jennifer Harman, Melissa Hayden, Phil Hellmuth, Phil Ivey, John Juanda, Phil Laak, Erick Lindgren, Erik Seidel, David Singer, Jennifer Tilly, and Robert Williamson III.

Other friends I have made through poker: Deborah Giardina and her assistants at Wynn Las Vegas, Denisha Campbell and Catherine Pitts; Andy Beal and Craig Singer; Matthew Parvis, Eric Morris, and Eddy Kleid at *Bluff;* Jennifer Creason; Roxanna Kaveh; Susan Lederer; Fabiola Lopez; Joe Reitman; Howard Schwartz and his staff at the Gambler's Book Shop; and Richard Lederer.

The people responsible for creating and making available the resources I used from TwoDimes.net, PokerStove.com, CardPlayer .com, WorldSeriesofPoker.com, and the Hendon Mob Database.

People who worked with me directly on completing the book: Amy Calistri, for her work in transcribing interviews and discussing all aspects of the book during the early part of the project; April Kyle for transcribing interviews and reviewing portions of the manuscript as the deadline approached; and Jay Greenspan for his help in the interviewing and writing of chapter 15.

Warner Books: my editor, Dan Ambrosio; my friend and original editor, Colin Fox, who acquired the project for Warner but left before the completion of the book; and the numerous people at Warner whose skills in editing, design, and marketing made this book possible.

That said, all errors are mine, and it's even money that someone in these acknowledgments pointed them out (or would have) and I ignored or overruled them.

About the Editor

From 1986 to 1999, Michael Craig was a securities lawyer. He has also been a law school instructor, stand-up comic, and screenwriter. His breakthrough in escaping a lucrative law practice came in 1997 when *Cigar Aficionado* hired him to write the story of how two cigars were worth over $2 million in one of his cases. After leaving the practice of law in 2000, he wrote two books about business and finance.

Some table chatter from the Mirage poker room in October 2003 led Craig to uncover the story of the richest poker game of all time, which was the subject of *The Professor, the Banker, and the Suicide King.* Since its publication in June 2005, he has spoken about poker in front of TV and radio audiences, Texas securities traders, and Yale students. He has produced two of the longest articles ever written about poker, an 8,000-word three-part profile of Ted Forrest for *Card Player* in late 2005 and, for *Bluff*, a 19,000-word two-part narrative of Andy Beal's epic high-stakes games against the pros at Wynn Las Vegas in early 2006. He has also written a column for *Card Player* and currently writes columns and features for *Bluff*, including profiles of several contributors to this book. He is also responsible for The Full Tilt Poker Blog by Michael Craig (www.fulltiltpoker .com/poker-blog). While working on this book, he attempted to apply its lessons to online poker tournaments and won prizes totaling over $100,000.

This is his fourth book. He can be contacted at suicideking@ fulltiltpoker.com.